THE NEW HISTORY
OF LITERATURE

THE
ENGLISH
LANGUAGE

THE NEW HISTORY OF LITERATURE

Volumes 5 and 7 will be published in 1988.

THE
ENGLISH
LANGUAGE

·

EDITED BY

W. F. BOLTON

and

DAVID CRYSTAL

Peter Bedrick Books
New York

First American edition published in 1987 by
Peter Bedrick Books
125 East 23rd Street
New York, NY 10010

Library of Congress Cataloging-in-Publication Data

The English language.
  (The New history of literature)
  Bibliography: p.
  Includes index.
  1. English language.   I Bolton, W. F. (Whitney French), 1930–
  II. Crystal, David, 1941–   .   III. Series.
PE1072.E55   1987   420   87–47749
ISBN 0–87226–134–4

Printed in Great Britain

10 9 8 7 6 5 4 3 2 1

CONTENTS

INTRODUCTION

'The common tie of society', Locke called language; 'that composite and multiform speech – fitted, like a mirror, to reflect the thoughts of the myriad-minded Shakespeare', De Quincey wrote of English. For the language of the greatest poets is only a particular employment of the faculty which at once distinguishes human beings from all other creatures and provides a common human bond. In this volume, writers contribute introductory essays on the general nature of language; the sounds, grammar, and stylistic varieties of present-day English; the history of the language; and the role of English in the modern world.

As long ago as 1876, the leading historian of English, Henry Sweet (whom George Bernard Shaw took as the model for Henry Higgins in his play *Pygmalion*, later made even more famous in the musical *My Fair Lady*) remarked that 'the growth of a language like English can be observed in a series of literary documents extending from the ninth century to the present day. . . . But before history must come a knowledge of what now exists. We must learn to observe things as they are without regard to their origin'. Sweet here suggested a division of language study into the historical (or DIACHRONIC) and descriptive (or SYNCHRONIC), the former tracing the development of the language from age to age and the latter studying it at a single moment in time, usually the present – the only state of the language that the vast majority of its users, including its writers, ever know. But Sweet went further in the passage just quoted: he gave priority to the descriptive approach. Here his words went unheeded for over seventy years, and have only recently gained acceptance in university courses in English. The present book has adopted them as a basic principle, arranging the material so that the present-day language is fully surveyed before the retrospect of the past is begun.

The scheme has more than theoretical advantages. The student is given in the first instance a firm understanding of his own language, and can compare the former stages of English with this. Moreover, the terminology of language description is best introduced as it relates to modern speech, but it then becomes available as well for characterizing the English of centuries past. The arrangement of the book consequently assumes that the reader will go through it continuously from beginning to end, but the chapters have been planned with a great deal of autonomy and can be read as independent studies in their various fields. To achieve this independence, some material has had to be repeated from chapter to chapter. Readers are in any case urged to read the first chapter, in which the broad outlines of the modern view of language are sketched with reference both to what follows and to what have for long been the most common – and the most erroneous – ideas about language.

From chapter two onwards, the subject is specifically English. It is convenient to talk about the structure of a language in terms of its sounds, its forms, and its sentences, and of what the structure operates on as its vocabulary. The distinctions that the language makes at the level of sounds receive attention first because the contrasts they embody are basic to the rest of the system. The system extends from individual sounds to formal patterns, like *chose* from *choose*, *houses* from *house*, *ungentlemanlinesses* from *un* + *gentle* + *man* + *li* + *ness* + *es*. Obviously if the sound system did not make regular contrasts, the complicated correct sequence could not be distinguished from the equally complicated but impossible **man* + *gentle* + *un* + *li* + *es* + *ness*[1] (although it contains the quite acceptable *man* + *li* + *ness*, etc.), but equally obviously the selection of the correct sequence is not a matter of sound but of another level of structure entirely: form. And the organization of elementary or complicated words into the strings we call phrases, clauses and sentences is, by the same token, yet another level of structure ('syntax') as well, although it partakes of the distinctions of form so that we accept *The dog bites the man* but not **The man the dog bites* as a sentence (but *The man the dog bites is my brother*); *A house is red, Houses are red*, but not **A house are red* (except, for example, in *The guardians of a house are red setters*).

Priority is given to these considerations of organization because many students of a language begin with the assumption that the language is the words in its vocabulary: *Schwester* 'means' *sister* in German, or is the German word 'for' *sister*. Far more important is the fact that English has no sound like the *r* in German, no sequence of sounds like the *Schw-* in German, forms no plurals by adding only *-n* as German does in *Schwestern*, and if the sentence *I*

---

[1] Here and throughout this book, the asterisk signifies an unrecorded linguistic form; in synchronic description, an impossible one; in diachronic, a hypothetically reconstructed one.

wish you could have seen my sister were 'translated' into German word-for-word, no German speakers would recognize it as their own language. Yet for all the misleading prominence that vocabulary has had, it is still the aspect of language that is the focus of all the other categories: the three levels of organization must organize something in addition to each other, and what they organize or structure are the items in the vocabulary of the language, its words. These, moreover, have long been and will probably to some perhaps reduced extent remain the chief concern of writers looking for 'the right word', and of critics analysing their success or failure in finding it.

This consideration brings us to chapter six, the first of two reviews of the problems and potentialities of language study in the analysis of utterances, including those we call 'literature'. Stylistics proceeds by mapping the specialization in each of the categories of language, that is sound, form, syntax and vocabulary, that distinguish a given utterance from the more general linguistic practice of which it is a part. It is a form of synchronic linguistics applied to literature, among other things, much as physiology can be applied to identify a single member of a species as well as to generalize about the structure and function of the species as a whole.

The second section of the book likewise offers several chapters of description followed by one of application, this time in the historical or diachronic dimension. The two which describe the growth of the language over the centuries begin with its derivation from the parent language and trace it down to the present day; their dividing-line is the death date of the greatest poet of the English Middle Ages, Chaucer, in 1400. The final two chapters deal with the social context of English language studies, and the identity of English in the modern world.

The volume is intended as an introduction to linguistic study that will serve to outline the essentials and at the same time point the way to further investigation. The bibliographies for each chapter are similarly inceptive. The field of English linguistics is so vast that they can be only selective. What is more, it is so active that they rapidly fall out of date. The reader is urged to consult them both as a guide to the sources of the views and information that each chapter puts forward, and as a suggestion for the next stage of further reading.

1

LANGUAGE AND LANGUAGES

Frank Palmer

The language we speak is one of, perhaps, 4,000 or more throughout the world. We cannot be sure of the precise number; estimates have varied between 2,000 and 4,000, but it seems probable that even the higher figure is an underestimate. A recent survey of the languages of Africa lists over 700, yet this excludes from its list all the Bantu languages which form the largest single language group, including almost all the languages spoken in the southern half of that continent; and Africa is only a small part of the entire world.

One of the reasons why we cannot give a precise figure to the number of languages in the world is simply lack of information about the languages themselves. Probably less than 10 per cent of them have ever been seriously investigated and perhaps as many as a half are still virtually unknown. Attention has naturally been focused upon the languages of greatest political or commercial interest, such as Hausa, Arabic, Hindi, Chinese. The national languages of most countries have been described, though not always in a satisfactory way, but in many countries the national language is only one of many. In Ethiopia, for instance, the official language, Amharic, has been described in a number of grammars dating back to the seventeenth century, but only one of them is really adequate and the phonology (the sound system) of Amharic has hardly been considered at all. There are, moreover, between 30 and 50 other languages in Ethiopia, but only about 10 of these have been investigated, and the only complete grammars of most of this small number were written by a single scholar as long ago as the end of the nineteenth century.

It is difficult in principle to decide how many languages there are in the world, because it is often not clear whether we are dealing with different languages or different dialects of the same language. We must be careful, however, to use the terms LANGUAGE and

DIALECT in a systematic way. In ordinary conversation people often make the distinction between dialect and language in terms of spoken and written languages, so that in this sense English, Arabic and Chinese are 'languages', but most of the speech-forms of Africa are 'dialects', perhaps even 'mere dialects'. This would, of course, reduce the numbers of languages to a few hundred and largely solve the problem of deciding how many languages there are, but it is a quite unsatisfactory viewpoint. Many of these 'dialects' are by any reasonable standard languages in their own right (the notion that they are in some way inferior, primitive or exotic is, as we shall see shortly, untenable), and in any case, they always *can* be written down, and in some cases *will* probably be written down, either in the Roman alphabet that we ourselves use or in the national script of the country in which they are spoken (Ethiopia, for instance, has its own writing system).

There is a further problem. The Chinese system of writing carries little or no indication of the way in which the language is spoken – there is almost no systematic correspondence between the written symbols and the sounds of the language. As a result, a speaker of Mandarin Chinese and a speaker of Cantonese can both read the written form though their speech is quite different. Neither can understand the other, and if they read a text aloud, they will read it quite differently. It is rather as if there were in Europe a system of writing such that the same symbols could be read as 'I see a dog' or 'Je vois un chien'. In fact we find something like this in our numerals; 1, 2, 3 can be read as 'One, two, three', 'Un, deux, trois', 'Ein, zwei, drei', etc. Chinese is an extreme case, but English spelling too does not provide a very clear indication of the pronunciation. It turns out moreover that, precisely because of the much maligned vagaries of English spelling, the same written text can be used by people with very different kinds of English. Natives of London, Edinburgh, New York or Sydney will read the same texts with complete ease, but if they read them aloud, they will read them quite differently, and this is in part possible simply because we do not expect the English spelling to be a faithful representation of the way we speak. Paradoxically perhaps, one of the greatest assets of the English language is that there is no one-to-one relation between sound and symbol.

It is obvious, moreover, that in these days of mass communication we all succeed in understanding the speech of people whose words would have been quite unintelligible to our grandparents. We have learnt familiarity with the speech of Liverpool, of Glasgow, of Texas (often perhaps in an inaccurate or caricatured form) and it could be argued that some of these 'dialects' are so different that they ought really to be thought of as different languages and that with the help of radio, films and television we have, in effect, learnt new languages. It is an open question, then, whether English really is just one language – whether the English of Bombay is the same language as that of Manchester. But this is an academic point – it depends on the definition of language.

Let us assume that we know what is meant by *the* English language and turn to another question – whether this language is in any sense better or more important than other languages in the world. From the purely linguistic point of view the answer to this question is a simple 'No'.

This is not to say that English is not a very important language, but only from two other points of view. First, it is probably the language with the largest number of native speakers (people for whom it is the first language) – though this estimate depends on whether or not we regard Chinese as one language; if we do, English comes second. But it is quite certain that English is the language that is spoken or understood by the largest number of people in the world, either as a second or as a foreign language; it is certainly *the* modern international language.

Secondly, English is important, as this collection clearly shows, for its literature. Yet there seems to be no clear evidence that the quality of English literature (or its quantity) is in any way dependent upon the nature of the language itself. This is not to deny the close links between literature and language, but it is to say that they are, perhaps, incidental. Of course, the language is the vehicle for the literature and, as translators know well, English literature is and will always remain essentially English. In other arts there is no such restriction. Painting and music are obviously more international because they can more easily cross national boundaries; the instruments of the symphony orchestra produce the same basic sounds in Germany as in England, but Shakespeare can never sound like Goethe. (Literature does, in one sense, cross these national and 'linguistic' boundaries – the literature of one country may profoundly influence that of another – but this observation even further weakens any belief that the literature derives from any intrinsic excellence of the language itself.) More importantly, there are 'literary' languages, languages which have a long tradition of literature and which have thereby acquired not only the 'producers' – the authors whose very existence obviously depends upon the tradition (even when they try to be non-traditional), but also the 'tools' – the linguistic forms and their meanings; we need only consider the number of words in the English language as evidenced by the *Oxford English Dictionary* – and sheer quantity of words is a relatively unimportant characteristic of a language. But, however possible it may be to link literature with the social, political, or economic features of the society in which it is produced we cannot be at all sure that it is in any way linked with any characteristic of the language. In other words, we cannot disprove the thesis that if the inhabitants of Britain had been the same in all other respects but had spoken a Bantu language, they would not have produced an equally fine body of literature.

We are, of course, all inclined to feel that our own language is in some ways better or more natural than that of other people. The grammarian Jespersen tells of the little girl who made the wonderful discovery that pigs are called pigs 'because they are such swine'. A similar story appears also in Aldous Huxley's *Crome Yellow* where, looking at pigs wallowing in the mud, a character remarks, 'Rightly is they called pigs'. A little sophistication, indeed the mere recognition of the fact that there are other languages, teaches us to expect that languages other than ours will have different words for the same things, but it takes much more sophistication to realize that many of the other characteristics of the language may be different too. Many learners of a foreign language never accept, in their practice at least, the idea that the sound system of the language is different; they are willing to change the words, but still pronounce them in their own familiar way. Even those who are more sophisticated find great difficulty in accommodating themselves to the intonation of the new language; deep down perhaps they feel that the patterns they use must be the correct ones – the ones that most naturally carry the intended meaning. But there are more subtle points than this. Few speakers of English realize that the order of words in English is arbitrary and conventional – there is no 'natural', 'logical' or other reason why the subject should come before the verb and the object after it (though, admittedly, the exact reverse of the English order does not seem to occur in many other languages). In Welsh the verb (or at least part of it) comes first, before the subject; my own son at the age of 10 had to learn Welsh and complained that it was a stupid language because 'every time they want to say something, they ask a question'! Even at that age he had come to accept a purely English device – the use of word order for questions – as a necessary characteristic of language.

Professionals, too, sometimes fail to see that what is strange about another language is on closer inspection no stranger than what happens in their own. M. Bréal, who at the very end of the nineteenth century wrote a book entitled (in its translated form) *Semantics* and thereby invented this term, commented on the superiority of the Indo-European languages over the other languages of the world. His chief evidence is the ambiguity found in other languages; in Chinese, for instance, the same sentence may mean 'The saint aspires to Heaven', 'He is a saint to aspire to Heaven' and 'He is a saint who aspires to Heaven'. But we can easily match this in English with a sentence that is now a notorious example in linguistics classes: *It's too hot to eat*. This has three obvious different interpretations – and others are possible with sentences of the same structure; sentences of this grammatical type are 'multiply ambiguous'. More recently a writer suggested that one characteristic of the Bantu languages is 'syncretism of the grammatical elements', i.e. that one grammatical form may have a number of different functions, and he quotes Swahili *na*: 1. to have; 2. with; 3. and; etc. A moment's reflection will reveal that these three functions have much in common ('to be with' is 'to have' especially in a society where private property is unknown), and again we may look for a parallel in English – the verb 'to be' is used, for being in a place, for existing (*There are people who . . .*), for class membership (*He is a teacher*), for identity (*This is John*), to mark duration (*He is reading*) or intention (*They are to be married*), and for the passive. It has at least seven functions.

In spite of this it is still thought sometimes that English and the other European languages are civilized languages whereas many of the languages of the world remain primitive. From a linguistic point of view this is a fallacy. Of course a language reflects in some respects the society in which it is spoken, but this is almost entirely confined to the vocabulary – the vocabulary required for the artefacts, institutions, etc. peculiar to that society. English has the words to talk about art and about science – words for 'sonnet', 'surrealism', 'hydrogen', 'nuclear reactor', 'industrial dispute' – for which a language of Africa might have no parallel. But that language would almost certainly have many words that have no translation in English. Well-known examples are the three words that Eskimo has for snow – depending on whether it is falling, on the ground, or the hard-packed material for making igloos, and the vast number of words that the Bedouin has for his camel, depending on size, age, sex, colour and use. This does not imply that these are primitive languages, except solely in this one fact that they have a vocabulary adapted to primitive societies. It does not even seem to be true that such languages have a smaller vocabulary; there have been tales of languages with only a few hundred words (and the same has been said of the language of the Wiltshire ploughman), but on investigation these tales have proved to be false. Moreover, all the other characteristics of a language – its sound system, its grammar, even the structure of its semantics – seem to be utterly unrelated to the society in which it is spoken. Surely this must be so; otherwise the language of Shakespeare could not have been used as it has been used, with only slight modifications, for the purposes of modern science. If we go even further back, it is probable that the language of our remote ancestors was much more like the English we speak today, than, say, a North American Indian language, though the societies of these ancestors and of Indians may have been equally primitive and equally distant culturally from our own.

If there are no primitive languages, are there exotic languages and difficult languages? Perhaps there are, provided it is understood that these are relative terms – exotic and difficult for the speaker of English or of a European language. In absolute terms there are certainly no difficult languages – the reply to a complaint that a certain language is difficult is simply 'Why, even the little children can speak it'. Judgements about languages are often made on purely superficial grounds. A language is often thought to be strange or difficult simply because it does not use the Roman script. This is, no doubt, why many people are scared by Russian. Yet a new script, provided it is alphabetic and not like Chinese which has virtually a different symbol for thousands of different words or parts of words, can be learnt in a few days, a tiny fraction of the time it takes to learn a useful portion of the vocabulary. A slightly more justifiable complaint can be made against the sounds of the language, but here too the exotic nature or difficulty of the sounds can easily be overrated by the non-specialist. Most English people would have difficulty with the Swahili word for 'cow', *ngombe*, but the difficulty lies only in the fact that the sound indicated by the *ng*, which is exactly the same as in English *sing* (a 'velar nasal') comes at the beginning of the word in Swahili, but in English can occur only in the middle or at the end; a familiar sound in an unusual position causes difficulty. A slightly more complex example is the initial consonant of the name of the language Twi spoken in Ghana (phonetically [ʧʸ]). This consonant does not appear as such in any European language and therefore sounds very strange to

European ears, but its component parts do occur – it involves no more, in effect, than a combination of the first consonants of the English word *church* and of the French word *huit*, produced simultaneously. It is true, nevertheless, that some languages have sounds that are quite unfamiliar to European ears. English makes no systematic use of the back part of the mouth, the 'uvular' and 'pharyngeal' areas, yet Arabic has no less than four different consonants in that area (and even French has one!). But, on the other hand, English makes a distinction between vowel sounds that would sound alike to speakers of many other languages. In an area of articulation in which many languages have only one vowel, English distinguishes between the vowels of *cat, cut, cot, caught, cart,* and *curt*.

Moreover, we are inclined to fail to realize how limited is the use made by European languages of the total capabilities of the vocal mechanism. Almost without exception the whole of the articulation of sounds in European languages is powered by air expelled from the lungs (it is 'pulmonic egressive'). Yet there is no natural or physical reason for this. In some languages air for articulation is drawn in, instead of being expelled – this produces the implosive consonants of West Africa (and even in one form of American English). In other languages sounds are produced by suction – the clicks of South Africa (we use clicks in English but only, it has been said, for addressing horses, babies and attractive young ladies!). Pressure can be created by moving the larynx (the 'voice-box') itself and this produces the ejective or glottalized consonants that are to be found in such widely separated places as North America, Korea and Ethiopia. Perhaps if we must talk about exotic languages it is English that is exotic in its restriction upon the use it makes of its phonetic potential.

The way in which languages use the phonetic 'tools' they have varies, and a language that uses them in an apparently non-European way will be thought difficult and exotic. Many of the languages of Africa have two or three tones; the tones distinguish different words, different entries in the dictionary. In Agau, for instance, a 'Cushitic' language of Ethiopia, *sǝr* on a low tone means 'boy', but on a high tone it means 'vein'. But these are simple compared with the languages of South-East Asia. Chinese has no less than five tones, though not all of them are level tones – that is to say, it does not just distinguish between five different pitches, but has, in addition to level tones, falling and rising ones. Yet it is by no means certain that this is in absolute terms any more difficult than what happens in English. It is usually said that English is not a tone language but that it makes a great deal of use of intonation. That is to say, it makes use of the pitch of the voice, but not to distinguish words as such. This is not strictly true. The difference between *export* the verb and *export* the noun is largely carried by pitch features. Although the usual explanation is that the verb has stress on the second syllable and the noun stress on the first, experiments have shown that what the speaker of English actually listens to is almost entirely a matter of pitch. In any case, is this use of intonation any easier or more natural? If we say *She's very pretty* with one intonation tone (a fall or a low rise) it is a compliment; if we say it with another (a rise–fall) it is far from complimentary – it means something like 'She's very pretty but . . .'. This is, of course, a wholly English feature – a linguistic convention of the English language that is, surely, quite as strange as the use of tone by the tone language.

It would be easy to give countless further examples of 'exotic' features in languages, but they usually turn out on reflection not to be very strange. The Celtic languages, for instance, are characterized by 'initial mutation' – by, in naive terms, the practice of changing the first 'letter' of words as in Welsh *pen* 'head', but *ei ben* 'his head', *eu phen* 'her head', *fy mhen* 'my head'. But why should it be any more strange to change the beginning of a word rather than the end (cf. English *wife* but *wives*) or the middle (English *foot* but *feet*)? Moreover, to talk about changing 'letters' distorts the facts. In speech (and speech must be regarded as primary – see below, p 16) the difference between the forms is simply one of the phonetic features of voice, friction and nasality. It is not a matter of replacing one consonant by another but simply of voicing (vibrating the vocal cords), of friction (partially instead of completely obstructing the passage of air) or of nasalization (lowering the soft palate to allow the air to escape through the nose); b = p + voice, ph = p + friction, mh = p + nasality. The change from one consonant to another in mutation involves the minimum of effort. An even stranger feature is to be found in the report that in some North American Indian languages the words for 'river' and 'mountain' are verbs. At least this sounds a strange feature until we think of English *It is raining*. There does not seem to be any more compulsive reason why we are permitted to say this instead of 'There is rain', or 'It is rivering' instead of 'There is a river'. Of course, the two are different – rain is temporary and rivers permanent, but that is not what would usually be thought to be the essential distinction between noun and verb.

There is one clear moral to be drawn. Linguists must never be surprised at anything they find in language. We have no means of judging what limits there are upon the patterns of phonology, grammar or semantics in languages. A new language will always bring surprises, though on reflection we often find that the novelty is basically no stranger than what we find in more familiar languages.

If there are no primitive, difficult or exotic languages in any strict sense of these terms, can the languages of the world be characterized or classified in any other way? One classification was that suggested by the early-nineteenth-century scholar W. von Humboldt – into ISOLATING, AGGLUTINATIVE and INFLECTIONAL languages. In the isolating languages each word is a single grammatical form that is unchanged in all its occurrences – in technical linguistic terms it is a morpheme with but only one allomorph; Chinese and some other languages of South-East Asia are examples of this type. In the agglutinative languages words are made up of a string of grammatical forms (morphemes) in a fixed order, but again the forms are unchanged in their various occurrences. Examples are Turkish and, to a large extent, Swahili. In Swahili, for instance, *nilikuona* consists of *ni* 'I', *li* past tense, *ku* 'you' and *ona* 'see'. Each of these elements is separable and re-placeable by another so that we can have *alikuona* 'he saw you', *aliniona* 'he saw me', *nitakuona* 'I will see you', etc. The inflectional languages are represented by Latin and Greek and many of the modern European languages. In these the various grammatical elements cannot be separately identified. It has been pointed out for instance that in Greek the *o*: of *luo*: 'I loose' identifies number, person, tense, mood and voice and it is rarely in this language that we can separate the elements (though this is possible perhaps with *lusontai* 'they will loose for themselves' – *s* future, *o* indicative, *n* plural, *t* third person, *ai* middle or passive). It has been thought by some that languages have progressed through these stages – first of all being isolating, then by grouping the elements into clusters and becoming agglutinative, and finally by 'fusing' the elements and becoming inflectional. The last stage is then thought of as the classical ideal, followed in more recent times by a breakdown into isolating types – for not only did Chinese once have inflection, but English is surely very largely an 'isolating language', since it has lost most of its 'endings'. But this view is not supported by any real evidence, and, in fact, most languages have characteristics of all three types. In English there are many words of the isolating type (all the prepositions, for example), the formation *take/taken/taking* is agglutinative, while *take/took* is an example of inflection. But a more important criticism of this classification is that it is in terms of one feature only of a language – the morphology of the word. Studies of this kind, 'typological' studies as they are called, are valuable, but they are essentially studies of parts of a language rather than of a language as a whole, and ought not therefore to be used for classification of languages.

The best-known type of classification of languages is into language families; and the language family that has been most thoroughly investigated is Indo-European, which includes almost all the languages from India to Ireland (Turkish, Hungarian and Basque are the notable exceptions). The Indo-European family can be sub-divided into groups; in Europe the four most important are *Romance*: Spanish, Portuguese, French, Italian and Rumanian; *Germanic*: English, German, Danish, Norwegian, Swedish; *Celtic*: Welsh, Breton, Gaelic; *Slavic*: Serbo-Croat, Czech, Slovak, Bulgarian, Russian, Polish. But this classification into families and. into groups is very largely a purely linguistic exercise and does not provide much information beyond the classification itself. Indeed there are two conclusions that must *not* be drawn, though they often are. First, it must not be assumed that the linguistic divisions represent racial or ethnic divisions. There is no such thing as the Indo-European race. The notion of the 'Aryans', which formed such a basic part of Nazi policy, was largely a result of this mistaken view – the term 'Aryan' having been used by philologists for 'Indo-European'. A moment's reflection shows clearly the fallacy of this assumption. Black Americans now speak, as their native tongue, an Indo-European language, but are clearly not the same race, if 'race' means anything at all, as their white fellow countrymen. Equally we may reflect whether it is sensible to consider the millions of Hindi and Bengali speakers in India (these are Indo-European languages) as racially closer to Europeans than the Hungarians or the Basque-speaking peoples of Bilbao. Secondly, and perhaps a little more surprisingly, linguistic relationship is no clear guide to the history of the people who speak or spoke the languages. Some measure of what is called 'linguistic palaeontology' is possible – it can be argued that, because the relevant words are to be found throughout many of the Indo-European languages, the ancient 'Indo-Europeans' had domesticated cattle and used wagons and that they lived in a European-type country where there were pigs, wolves, bears and many other familiar animals. But it is by no means certain that the spread of a language always meant the migration of a population or conquest by an invading master-race. Certainly we know how the Romance languages came into being – a result of the spread of Latin by the Roman Empire. Often, however, there seem to be no cultural changes accompanying the arrival of a new language form. Archaeologists have searched in vain for evidence of the coming of the Celts. It seems fairly certain that Celtic languages were spoken in much of Western Europe at the time of the Roman conquests but there is no break in the cultural features evidenced by archaeology for us to speak of a Celtic invasion at any time.

It does not make much sense, therefore, to talk about a Welshman as being a 'pure Celt' (though I have seen this as a description of a Welsh actor). It is true that the language he speaks is Celtic and true that there is a distinctive culture that is associated with that language, but that does not imply that he himself is Celtic. Indeed the popular misconception about a Celtic race is belied by the equally popular image of the short, dark Welsh, the tall, fair Scots, not to mention the dark-haired, blue-eyed Irish. Equally it makes no sense to talk about the Rumanians as 'of Latin stock', because Rumanian is a Romance language. Not only is it doubtful whether they differ physically from their 'Slavonic' neighbours (not to mention the 'non Indo-European' Hungarians), but it is doubtful whether even their ancestors were 'Latin' – the Romans brought their language but did not replace the original inhabitants of their Empire with their own people.

The language family is often illustrated by a family tree as in Figure 1.1. But it is a mistake to take this idea of a linguistic family tree at all seriously: there is no direct descent, and this genealogical model can be most misleading. For every language is a complete hybrid deriving from a variety of sources – even more perhaps than are the nations of the world. If we look at modern dialects rather than languages we find that any one dialect at one time may have derived from several dialects of a previous age – it may have a multiplicity of 'parents', some of whom it may share with other dialects, and this is almost certainly true of the 'Indo-European dialects' from which the language groups are purported to have descended.

Indo-European is not, of course, the only language family, though it is the one that has been most studied – studied continuously since a famous address in 1786 by Sir William Jones in which he argued for a common source for Latin, Greek and Sanskrit. Other well-known families are Semitic (chief members: Arabic,

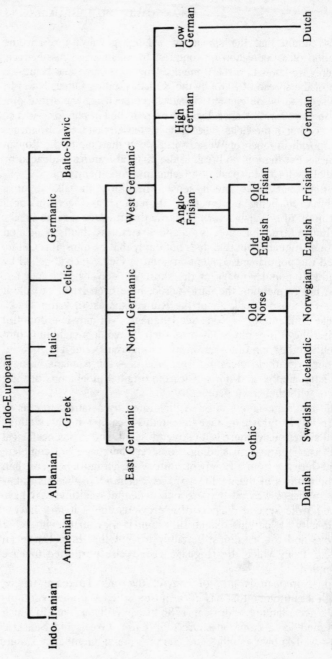

Fig. 1.1. The Indo-European Family Tree (with Germanic only set out in detail)

Hebrew and some languages of Ethiopia), Bantu and Malayo-Polynesian. The languages of the North American Indians are to be placed in a large number of different families, and there are, perhaps, a dozen or more families in Africa. Territorially, and in numbers of speakers, Indo-European is the largest, but this is not evidence of any special quality of the speakers of the Indo-European languages or of their ancestors, except in one respect – that they had writing. For our ability to establish this huge Indo-European family as compared with the numerous much smaller families of Africa or North America depends largely upon the existence of the classical languages. For all we know, languages in other areas may be as closely related as the languages of the Indo-European family, but without the 'key' – written records of much older languages – the relationships cannot be established. This point is quite clearly shown by just a few examples. We know that English words *cow* and *beef* are the same words if viewed historically, both derived from a single Indo-European 'root', the former having come through Germanic, the latter through Latin (and even then not directly, but probably first through a non-Latin dialect of the early languages of Italy). If we had no written records we could never have guessed the relationship. An equally striking example is provided by English *wheel* and Hindi *cakka*, again with a common origin; the Greek word *kuklos* (from which we have English *cycle*) and the Latin word *circus* are also from the same root as these. Further examples can be found in the numerals, which in spite of being derived from common roots now look and sound so different in the various languages, especially those for '4' and '5' – English *four*, French *quatre*, Welsh *pedwar*; English *five*, French *cinq*, Welsh *pump*.

Looking for language families tells us nothing more, then, than that linguists have succeeded in certain areas in establishing certain kinds of linguistic relationships between languages. These relationships are essentially of a formulaic kind, for they are expressed by setting up formulae for IE (Indo-European) – formulae which sometimes look (as they are perhaps intended to look) like an ancient language but which at other times can hardly be thought to have existed as linguistic forms. We find initial consonant clusters of the type *^{w}ðh and *k^{w}Φh; we obviously cannot read much 'reality' into these.

It is easy to be fascinated by some of the discoveries of comparative philology – to realize, for instance, that the same root appears in *feather, pin, pen* and the *-pter-* part of *pterodactyl*, and *helicopter*, or to resurrect the Latin of the Roman soldiers from the Romance languages – a Latin in which the word for a horse was *caballus* and not *equus* (French *cheval*, Italian *caballo*, etc.) and the word for head was *testa*, literally a 'tile', not *caput* (French *tête*, etc.) Most dictionaries are, for this reason, 'on historical principles'. Yet it is a mistake to be so fascinated by the history of a language or languages, to fail to see that languages, as they now are, can and indeed should be studied in their own right. The Swiss linguist Ferdinand de Saussure was the first scholar to state in a clear directive the need to distinguish between the SYNCHRONIC and the DIACHRONIC aspects of language – between the study of a language at a particular point in time (perhaps, but not necessarily, the present), and the study of a language through time. A moment's reflection will show that synchronic studies are logically prior to diachronic ones – we cannot trace linguistic change from period A to period B unless we know the facts about the language at each period. Yet many scholars have failed to see the need to keep these two aspects of language apart and often have heaped confusion upon confusion in that they not only have tried to describe present-day language in terms of its history, but have also combined this with the natural human propensity to think that what has gone before is always better than what we have now and have, therefore, made statements that give preference to the older form. When for instance, people say of a word that it 'really means . . .' (that, for instance, *nice* really means 'precise'), they are not merely tracing the history of the word, but also claiming that the older meaning is the correct one. But why? Surely *nice* today means 'nice'!

The confusion of synchronic and diachronic studies of language takes at least four forms. First, there is, as we have seen, the belief that the older forms are the 'correct' ones. An extreme form of this point of view sees languages as in a state of decay – the Romance languages as being a degenerate form of Latin – having lost, for instance, all the case inflections of the noun and even many of the endings of the verbs. By such a standard, English is in an advanced stage of decomposition. This kind of approach to a language is nonsense: There is no way by which we can judge one state of a language to be better than another, and the judgements that have been made have simply assumed that highly inflectional languages are somehow in the most perfect condition, presumably because the classical languages Latin and Greek were of this kind. The real difficulty in looking backward for a 'better' or 'more correct form of a language' is that we cannot, in principle, decide how far back to go. Should English just go back to Anglo-Saxon or to Proto-Germanic or to Indo-European? The example quoted in the previous paragraph, the meaning of *nice*, provides a good illustration of this point. The modern meaning ('agreeable' etc.) appears only at the end of the eighteenth century. The other meanings are all of the kind 'delicate', 'precise' etc. and we may be led to think that this is the 'real' meaning of the word. The earliest meaning is usually given as 'foolish' – closely connected with the Latin from which it is derived, *nescius*, 'ignorant'. Is not this then *really* its real meaning? Perhaps not, for *nescius* is derived from a negative root plus a root meaning 'to cut' (found also in *schism*, *scissors*). The 'real' meaning of *nice* might then be 'blunt' since we cannot go back any further.

Secondly, it is easy to confuse historical and non-historical explanations. We are often asked, especially by foreigners, why English has a particular form. Why, for instance, do we say *feet* and not **foots*? The most likely answer that a question of this kind will elicit (though naturally, this will mean consulting books or an English scholar) is that English once had a plural ending in -*i* and that there was in 'pre-English' a plural form of the word *fōt* which was *fōti* and that the final *i* influenced the preceding vowel and was then lost: the process known as MUTATION. Now this may be very interesting and foreign students may well remember the form simply because they have heard the explanation. But an explanation can be non-historical – an explanation, that is to say, in the sense of placing a form in its regular pattern. If, for instance, we are asked why we say *He ought to go* instead of **He oughts to go* (cf. *He wants to go*) a historical explanation is that *ought* is the past tense of *owe* and that past tense forms do not have -*s* endings. But a non-historical explanation is much more illuminating: *ought* is one of a group of a special class of verbs in English which have a particular place in English syntax and of which none has an -*s* ending in the 'third person form' – *will, shall, can, may, must, ought* and (in the negative and question forms at least) *dare* and *need*.

Ought leads on to our third point – the confusion of synchronic and diachronic features in the grammatical description of the language. '*Ought* is the past tense of *owe*' is a false statement. It may be true that '*Ought* WAS the past tense of *owe*' but the past tense of *owe* IS *owed*. Similarly, some school texts still ask for the singular of *dice* and the answer expected is *die*. But *die* is NOT the singular of *dice* – it has its own plural *dies*. I am not sure whether *dice* has a singular at all, though for many people the singular is the same as the plural, *dice* (What do we say – 'There is a . . . on the floor'?)

Perhaps we prefer to avoid the problem altogether and talk about 'one of the dice'.

Fourthly – and this is a rather more subtle point – it is all too easy to use words in describing a language that carry with them by implication, if we are not careful, the notion of a historical process. Words of this type are 'assimilation', 'palatalization' and the word 'change' itself which appear in many descriptions of languages without any clear indication whether or not a historical process is being implied. Let us consider 'palatalization' in Italian. We have in Latin *centum* and Italian *cento* an example of the change of an initial velar [k] to a palatal [tʃ] consonant. In Italian *amico* 'friend' and *amici* 'friends' we also find a change from a velar to a palatal (indicated, in the writing, by the letter *c* which is 'hard' before *o* and 'soft' before *i*). But there are obviously two different kinds of change, two different types of palatalization: the one is the development of Italian from Latin, the other is Italian as it is today – one diachronic, the other synchronic. Of course, it can be pointed out that Italian *amici* with a palatal has come from Latin *amici* with a velar and that the synchronic palatalization results from the diachronic palatalization; but this important observation can be made ONLY IF we keep the two aspects distinct. Some linguists have been so afraid of this confusion that they have banned all 'process' words from the vocabulary of linguistic description. They have argued that in a language no one form ever actually changes into another – *foot* does not literally change into *feet* on paper or in our brains, and that therefore 'change' can only imply historical change and should be avoided. But if it turns out to be convenient to talk about one form changing into another or at least to write one's description of a language in symbols that imply such change, there seems to be no valid reason for not using such language or such symbols – provided that we are sufficiently sophisticated never to confuse diachronic and synchronic.

It is important also to realize that language is to a very large extent spoken language. There are very few people who write more than they speak and the sum total of written texts in the English language would be insignificant in volume if compared with the amount of spoken language produced at the same time. Moreover, our initial training in language is the spoken rather than the written word. Children have mastered all the essential parts of their language – almost the whole of its sound system and its grammar as well as most of the basic vocabulary – before they begin to write.

However much, therefore, we may be impressed by the literature of our language, we ought not to forget the importance of speech. It is a mistake to attempt to establish norms for speech that are based upon the writing. Because English spelling is so notoriously non-representative of the sounds of the language (but this defect can be exaggerated – see below) we are used to the idea that English may not be pronounced as it is spelled. Nevertheless many people feel that the written language somehow indicates the 'correct' form. As with comments in terms of history we sometimes hear 'We pronounce it that way but it's *really* . . .' and a spelling pronunciation follows – that, for instance, we say [bɑ:skit] but it is 'really' [bɑ:sket]. If two words are spelled differently but pronounced the same, a statement that they are pronounced in the same way will often meet with incredulity or contradiction. Many people would insist that *mince* and *mints*, for instance, are pronounced differently because the second 'has a t' in it; but this is an inference drawn from the spelling that seems to have no validity at all for the spoken form.

The written form has in fact sometimes influenced the pronunciation – though not of really odd words like the notorious-*ough* set. The days in which *waistcoat* was pronounced [weskɪt] have gone and the pro-nunciation favoured by the spelling has prevailed, and the days of the pronunciation [fɒrɪd] for *forehead* seem to be numbered. Yet this completely spoils the nursery rhyme about 'the little girl who had a little curl right in the middle of her forehead' who 'when she was good was very, very good, but when she was bad she was . . .'! There has not been a similar general change for *breakfast* or *cupboard*, though in certain types of 'polite society' 'spelling' forms of even these have been heard.

Nevertheless, it would be foolish to ignore the fact that we are a literate society and that spelling pronunciations can be used to clear up ambiguities: 'I said compl*i*ment, not compl*e*ment' or 'v*o*cation not v*a*cation' are perfectly possible utterances in English. The danger is in assuming that these special pronunciations are 'normal' or 'more correct'.

There is an opposite way of looking at the relation of speech and writing. Instead of requiring speech to conform to writing we may demand that our writing conforms to speech. English, we are sometimes told, is 'not a phonetic language' though Spanish is – and presumably is superior for that reason. But to talk about 'phonetic languages' is to talk nonsense. All languages are phonetic – except perhaps the 'dead' ones, since 'phonetic' means, according to the *O.E.D.*, consisting of vocal sounds. What is usually meant is that the writing, the orthography, is PHONEMIC, that there is a one-to-one relation between distinctive sound and symbol.

Most proposals for spelling reform aim at producing such a writing system for English (though not all of them: some aim at a 'narrow' phonetic orthography showing all varieties of sound, not a phonemic one showing only those that are distinctive in the language). But few stop to ask if it is necessarily a virtue of a language that its orthography should faithfully represent speech. We have already noted the nature of the Chinese script which allows people speaking quite different languages to communicate, and that it is perhaps to our advantage that English spelling is in a small way similar, since this easily permits people with different kinds of spoken English to use the same writing system (or almost the same, since there are a few differences across the Atlantic).

In fact, for the native speaker at least, there seems to be very little advantage in having a script that faithfully represents the writing. All that is needed is that the written form can be identified and then read aloud. For this purpose much less than a complete phonemic transcription is needed – as is made clear by the use of shorthand by secretaries. This quite deliberately implements the fact that for the purpose of identification as speech much of our writing is redundant, and can be left out. Indeed, some alternative forms of writing quickly, or of writing in a condensed form for advertising, have shown we can leave out most or all of the vowels and still produce something that is intelligible, e.g. *Dtd mdn hse 3 brms.* . . . Arabic has been described as a natural shorthand script for this very reason. The vowels are all indicated by marks above or below the actual writing itself and though they are always to be found in print, they are usually left out in handwriting. This is particularly remarkable when it is remembered that almost the whole of the morphology (the inflection) of Arabic is carried by vowel change – as in English *take/took* or *goose/geese*. Thus we have *kataba* 'he wrote' but *kutiba* 'it was written'. Even so, with all the vowels omitted the writing can be read with ease by a native speaker. It is true that it will be difficult for a foreigner. But orthographies are surely not to be designed for the foreign language learner; if they require a written form, phonetic transcriptions can always be provided.

There is a much more important reason why the spelling should not faithfully represent the sound. If we had a phonemic spelling for English we should no longer form the plural of *cat, dog* and *horse* by merely adding *s*. Phonemically the added endings are /s/, /z/ and /ız/ respectively. These three are distinct in terms of the sounds of the language but grammatically ('morphemically') they are identical. Surely a spelling which uses one symbol here, and so ignores the fact that differences between the endings of *cats* and *dogs* are phonetically similar to those between *loose* and *lose* [luːs] and [luːz], is to be preferred to one that distinguishes them. Worse, if we had a phonemic spelling we should have to provide quite different representations for *photograph, photography* and *photographic* since these are [fəʊtəgrɑːf], [fətɒgrəfiː] and [fəʊtəgræfɪk]; the first two of these have no vowels at all in common. Yet the pattern found in these three is shared by all words of a similar type e.g. *telegraph, telegraphy* and *telegraphic* and even if someone invented say, a 'domograph' no English speaker, would have difficulty in pronouncing its name or the related words *domography and *domographic*. Spelling then is not, or should not be, phonemic; it might perhaps be argued that it should be 'morphophonemic' (halfway between phonemic and morphological), but that is another question.

Finally in this section, let us glance at the main differences between spoken and written language. Some of the differences are obvious. Clearly they are in different media. Also, as we have seen, English spelling does not correspond to the speech sounds so that (to take obvious points) *x* represents two sounds /ks/ but *th* only one (though it may be either /ð/ or /θ/). The writing has only five vowels, but however we analyse the English spoken vowel system we cannot reduce it to less than six (and some scholars would argue that there are over twenty). The need for at least six is shown by the contrast of the six 'short' vowels, a contrast that appears totally in only two sets of words in English: *pit, pet, pat pot, putt* and *put*; *rick, wreck, rack, rock, ruck* and *rook* (note the devices used to account for the 'extra' vowel). But there are more serious problems. It is by no means clear that there ARE words or sentences in speech as there are in writing. Both words and sentences belong to the conventions of writing and they are not marked in speech as they are in the written form. That is to say, there are no spaces between words in the spoken language – not even 'slight' pauses as one grammarian thought, though there are some devices (known as JUNCTURE FEATURES) that SOMETIMES mark some word divisions. This can be proved by showing that we can distinguish in quite normal speech between *keeps ticking* and *keep sticking*, between a *nice cake* and *an ice cake*. Yet we do not distinguish in normal speech between *a pier* and *appear*. The device is not always available. Sentences too are not always marked by intonation, though one might have expected this. Two sentences such as *I'm not going, I'm tired*, can be said with a single intonation (a single TONE GROUP) whereas *That one's mine* can be uttered with a double intonation tune. Further, of course, as we have already seen, intonation can do a great deal that cannot be done in the writing. In this respect the written form is a vehicle far inferior to speech.

On close inspection we find that even the grammar of the spoken language is different from that of the written. In the written form, for example, there are three main kinds of plural formation of the noun as exemplified by *cat/cats, sheep/sheep* and *foot/feet*. There are three similar types in speech, but the members of each class are not the same. For in writing, *postman/postmen* is like *foot/feet*, but in speech it is like *sheep/sheep* – the single and plural forms are identical. If someone says 'the [pəʊstmən] came up the street' we cannot tell if there was one or more than one of them. Moreover, the plural *houses* is perfectly regular in writing but utterly irregular in speech, for the plural of [haʊs] is not *[haʊsɪz] but [haʊzɪz]. There are plenty of other examples – the reader need only consider *does* which is as regular as *goes* in the written language, but quite idiosyncratic in speech. One may expect irregularity with verbs like *do* since they are auxiliaries and perform a semi-grammatical function, but English has just one 'full' verb with an irregular -*s* ('third person') form. I have for some years asked audiences of students and others to tell me which one it is, usually without a reply – so unaware are we of the characteristics of our speech. The answer is *say* with the form [sez] not *[seɪz]. Oddly enough, and without justification, the written form *sez* is sometimes used in humorous writing as an indication of sub-standard speech – but it is in fact a faithful indication of the speech of most of us.

Just as we ought not to confuse synchronic and diachronic aspects of a language, or speech and writing, so we must keep clear the distinction between FORM and MEANING. Some linguists, especially 'structural linguists', have been accused of neglecting meaning. This is probably fair, but it happened only because they succeeded in some degree in making useful observations about the form or structure (if we use 'structure' in that sense) of a language, but found meaning too difficult to handle. But the simple point is that the two can and must be kept distinct wherever possible and one lesson that has been learnt is that grammatical categories cannot, without confusion, be defined in NOTIONAL terms. It is valueless, for instance, to define NOUN as 'the name of a person or thing'. For is fire a 'thing'? Is peace? Is suffering? If the answer to these questions is 'Yes', since they are not physical objects, the only reason is presumably that they are indicated by nouns – and so the definition is circular. The point can be made by trying to prove that *suffering* is a noun in *His sufferings were intense* but *suffered* is not in *He suffered intensely*. But why not? Are we taking about 'things' in the first sentence but not in the second? Similarly, singular and plural cannot be defined in terms of 'one' and 'more than one' since this does not account for the difference between *wheat* which is singular and *oats* which is plural. (Do we really think of wheat as a single object and oats as a collection of objects?) More striking examples are provided by gender in French and German. If masculine, feminine and neuter are defined in terms of male, female and sexless creatures we have no explanation at all for the use of the feminine *la sentinelle* in French to refer to the very male guardsman, while a young lady in German is referred to by the most inappropriate neuter nouns *Fräulein* and *Mädchen*. Clearly, then, the categories of number and gender are formal categories – based upon the form and in particular, the syntax of the language – *The oats are, The wheat is; la table, le livre; der Kopf, die Stadt, das Haus* (in French and German the choice of the article is one of the relevant formal features).

There are more subtle points than this. Tense has, or should have, no direct connection with time. Indeed it is related that in one North American Indian language the tense distinctions do not refer to temporal features at all, but to spatial relations. This ought not to be surprising. There is no 'logical' or 'natural' reason why a language should always refer to time relations on each occurrence of a verb. It would seem that the division into past, present and future, however natural it may appear in terms of chronological time, is, in so far as it relates to the meaning of forms of the verb, largely a feature of certain western Indo-European languages. The Latin trio *amo, amabo*, and *amabam* is by no means typical of languages in general. Indeed it is very doubtful whether even English has this three-term category of tense. Basically the English system distinguishes only two tenses as exemplified by *take* and *took*. Of course, English has ways of referring to future time, but this is in itself of no more relevance than that it has ways of referring to greater and lesser distances. The only question of relevance is whether it has SPECIAL forms for future time and the answer to this question is in all honesty 'No'. The traditional grammars refer to *will* and *shall* as the auxiliaries used to provide the future tense. (This is usually accompanied by the wholly fictitious paradigm *I shall, you will* etc. with the alternation of *shall* and *will*.) But these two verbs pattern exactly as do *can* and *may*, and there is no reason therefore to isolate them as tense markers, unless we treat all the 'basic' forms of the verb as tenses and so end up with about 200 tenses for English. Moreover, if we insist on looking for a future tense why should we select *will* and *shall*? In colloquial English at least, *going to* is equally common or perhaps even more common, and it has the added advantage that unlike *will* it always refers simply to future time. *Will*, unfortunately, can be used to express willingness or habit (*He'll not be there for hours*) or even probability (*That'll be John*), so that we have either to distinguish two verbs, one used as the future auxiliary, the other not, or else say that the English future tense is often used not to refer to future time!

There are even stronger paradoxes if we turn to past tense. For though there is every reason for distinguishing a present and a past tense as exemplified by *takes* and *took*, it turns out that the past tense is often used where there is no reference at all to past time as in *I wish I knew* or *If I knew.* ... The past tense is used simply for 'unreality', for non-existent or improbable contingencies. A way out of this is to treat these as the English subjunctive or one of the forms of the subjunctive; but it is a strange subjunctive that in almost every case is identical with the past tense. There is really no problem. Just as French gender does not refer directly to sex (though there is indirect reference – hence *l'homme* is masculine and *la femme* is feminine), so tense does not always refer to time relations.

The formal categories of the language must be defined not only without direct reference to notions of non-linguistic features such as time or sex, but must as far as possible be defined in terms of the characteristics of the language itself and not in terms of any other language. It is because we are inclined to think in terms of our own language that we find it difficult sometimes to learn new languages. I have already commented on our natural 'ethnocentric' attitude towards language – we never REALLY believe in the patterns of another language. But there is another influence perhaps even more dangerous – that of the classical language, and in the case of Europe, of Latin. We may smile when we hear of the missionary who reported that Japanese was 'defective in the gerund' but Latin grammar is, perhaps, still with us. When teachers have maintained, as some have, that the teaching of Latin was essential for the teaching of English grammar, they have been right, for the English grammar they taught was essentially Latin grammar clothed in English words and it is not surprising that the pupils failed to understand it until they were introduced to the original model. No longer, perhaps, do our children learn the paradigm 'Table, O table, table, of a table, to or for a table, from or by a table,' but some English grammars will have a place for the genitive and the dative in English and I strongly suspect that the chief motivation for the insistence on the retention of a future tense is the feeling that Latin had one, that Latin. is grammatically the best model, and that English must have one too.

We have not yet asked 'What is language?' It is easy enough to provide a definition that merely identifies – something like 'The communication system based upon the vocal organs used by human beings'. It is also possible to characterize languages in terms of the kinds of statement that can be made about it. Such a characterization is to be found in the later chapters of this book where various aspects of language are discussed – sound systems, morphology, syntax, semantics, varieties, history, and social use.

There are, of course, communication systems other than human language, but are these to be regarded as language, and, if not, why not? Many animals communicate by the use of sound; some of the apes make use of a system of a considerable number of different calls. Not all animal communication is by sound; one of the most remarkable systems is that of the dances of the bees, by which one bee can inform the others of the direction and distance of nectar-producing flowers. Human communication, as we have already seen, is fundamentally based upon the noises we make. Writing is derived from this, and other systems such as semaphore and Morse are, in turn, derived from the writing system. But there are communication systems used by human beings that are not based primarily upon the language system – though they can always be 'verbalized', since we can always talk about anything that we understand. An example is the system used by traffic lights. This is not derived from any one language though the Red, Green and Amber can be interpreted as 'Stop', 'Go' and 'Get Ready'. There are other natural systems too, such as those of facial expression and gestures; strangely enough, these are not always easily translated into speech.

Clearly language is much more complex than any of these and there is no difficulty in practice in distinguishing between language and non-language systems, no greater difficulty perhaps than in distinguishing between men and apes. But it is not at all clear where we should, in principle, draw the border-line. It is difficult if not impossible, that is to say, to establish what are the theoretical restrictions and limitations on language. We find it almost impossible to establish what features a language must have in order to be a language. In recent years there has been interest in attempts to discover the universal features of the language – those features that all languages have and must have if they are languages. There is some attraction in the idea that there are such universals since this would explain why children are able to learn their language in such a remarkably short time. For closely related to the idea of such universals is the idea that the human brain is genetically 'programmed' for language, and that they are, therefore, already present in children when they begin to learn to speak. But there are problems with the attempts to establish such universals. First, the investigators themselves are always, so to speak, engaged in language. They are quite incapable of standing aside, as perhaps a visitor from Mars might, and looking completely objectively at language. Their observations are necessarily influenced largely by their own preconceptions. Let us take a rather trivial but obvious example. Is the distinction between nouns and verbs a necessary distinction in language? Must all languages make this distinction? Investigation shows that MOST languages, in fact, have two distinct word classes that can without any hesitation be labelled 'noun' and 'verb' respectively. But this is not true of ALL languages. There are some which have instead word stems which by the addition of suffixes 'become' nouns or verbs; in these languages the distinction is not between different words in the sense of different lexical stems in the way in which *cat* is different from *penetrate*, but between different forms of the same lexical stem – there are examples in English, e.g. the noun with the forms *man* and *men* and the verb with *man*, *mans*, *manning* and *manned*. Could we have a language without any distinction of this kind? Almost certainly if there were such a language we should be quite unable to understand it and equally unable to describe it. Secondly, we cannot establish what are the universal features of language, in the sense of NECESSARILY universal features, by examining all the languages of the world. For even if we find a given feature to be universally present, this is no proof that it is a necessary universal – it is possible that for some languages this is a result of a common origin and for others that it has been borrowed. We simply cannot tell whether its universality is merely accidental. Thirdly, no kind of serious experimentation is possible. We cannot for obvious moral reasons take a large number of infants and use them as 'guinea pigs' to establish what is, and what is not, possible in human language. There is a famous story of the Egyptian King Psammetichus II who attempted an experiment with two new-born infants. He wished to decide whether the Egyptian race was older than the Phrygian, and for this purpose arranged for two new-born babies to be reared apart from all contact with human speech. After two years the children were heard to cry 'Bekos' when asking for food; since this was the Phrygian word for bread, Psammetichus reluctantly concluded that Phrygian was the older race. Modern experiments would, no doubt, be more sophisticated, but are unthinkable.

The American linguist C. F. Hockett suggested that there are seven characteristics that are not all shared by other communication systems. The first feature is that of DUALITY – that a language has a phonological system and a grammatical system – that it is, as some linguists have said, 'double-structured'. This is not now accepted by many linguists; one modern theory sees no clear distinction between such levels, while another recognizes not two 'strata', but six. But basically the point Hockett is making is that there is no direct correlation between the element of sound in language and what it 'stands for'. With traffic lights the sign 'Red' means 'Stop', but the sounds of a language do not mean anything at all – the smallest units of language that can be correlated with meaning are far more complex than single sounds. Secondly, language is PRODUCTIVE – all speakers can understand and produce sentences that they have never heard before. This point was not always fully appreciated by some linguists, but today it is considered to be of fundamental importance. It is quite clear that the number of potentially possible sentences in any language is, like the system of numbers in mathematics, infinite. This can be proved in mathematics by pointing out that however large a number is mentioned we can always add one to it; similarly, in language, however long a sentence may be, another word can always be added. The structure of language involves 'recursion' of the kind illustrated by 'This is the house that Jack built', 'This is the mouse that lived in the house that Jack built' and so on – if necessary *ad infinitum*. It is clear from this that we do not learn sentences by mere repetition (as the parrot does) – we create and understand new ones all the time. Thirdly, language is ARBITRARY; there is no necessary connection between a sound and what it means – *chien* is as good as *dog* for the name of the animal. Some communication systems use symbols that are iconic, that in some way directly represent their meaning: the hieroglyphs were drawings of objects, the bees' dance shows in a direct form the direction of the nectar. There are, of course, some words of this kind in all languages – the onomatopoeic words like *cuckoo*, but these form only a tiny section of the vocabulary.

A fourth feature is INTERCHANGEABILITY. Speakers can become hearers and vice versa, but traffic lights do not relay information to other traffic lights. Fifthly, language is HIGHLY SPECIALIZED – there is a close relationship between linguistic behaviour and the results it achieves. I am not sure that this is true. It probably derives from a behaviourist approach to linguistics (stemming from the great American linguist Bloomfield) in which meaning is thought of in terms of stimulus and response. Unfortunately the same words will produce quite different reactions, and a physical stimulus quite different linguistic responses. It has been pointed out that in accordance with a behaviourist theory, the response to a painting might be 'Dutch' but in actual fact someone might well react with 'Clashes with the wall-paper' or 'Hanging too low'. There is not much specialization here. Sixthly, language can be, and often is, DISPLACED, dealing with events removed in time and space. One linguist once commented that language was invented for the purpose of telling lies. As long as primitive man merely made noises in response to his immediate sensations – for instance to indicate to his fellows that he could see food – he had not acquired language; but as soon as he made the same noises when the food was not there he had learnt to speak. Finally, CULTURAL TRANSMISSION is an important characteristic – a language is handed down from generation to generation. The forms of language (though not, perhaps, the ability to speak) are not known instinctively, but have to be learnt. This, of course, is the reason why languages differ in the different parts of the world and even within small areas where there is little cultural contact.

These characteristics of human language may largely, perhaps, be summarized by saying that it is far more complex than other communication systems. The complexity of language is, of course, related to the greater intelligence of human beings, though equally their greater intelligence must have developed as a result of their acquisition of language. It might well be argued that the definition of human should be in terms of 'the speaking animal' rather than 'the tool maker', especially now that it is known that the apes use primitive tools.

We do not know when human beings began to use language (even if we knew exactly how to define language). At some time in their evolutionary history they developed the organs of speech, for these organs are in origin the organs for eating and breathing and have become highly specialized for the purpose of speech. These organs are, however, entirely made of flesh and do not affect the bone structure. They do not, therefore, survive in fossils, the best that can be done is to estimate from the bone structure of skulls and jaws the extent to which language as we know it, with its great variety of sounds, would have been physically possible. There can be little doubt that the origin of speech must be traced to noises similar to those made by apes and gibbons, but precisely how and when humans significantly advanced beyond them we shall never know. There have been many theories of the origin of language. Most of them are fanciful, and in any case, seem to ask only how the particular sounds of language were selected. The naivest theory, perhaps, is that primitive humans had a natural feeling for the right name for objects; this is surely belied by the arbitrary nature and variety of sound-meaning relations in language throughout the world. Another view is that they imitated the natural sounds – that language, therefore, originated with onomatopoeia, with words like *cuckoo*; but this would not have taken language far – the number of onomatopoeic words in language is very small. Others have suggested that language developed from the natural noises we ourselves make – our sighs, our groans, etc; there may, perhaps, be a little truth in this – danger signs may well have developed from cries of fear, but this does not take us even as far as the present ape 'language', and tells us nothing at all about human language. A further theory sees the origin of language in the imitation by the tongue of natural gestures. None of these theories can ever be proved, or disproved, and they are all largely uninformative.

Language is essentially a human characteristic – this is well known. Though it is related to greater human intelligence, however, there is reason to believe that it is not dependent solely upon greater intelligence, or at least not solely upon the fact that human beings have a much larger brain than all other creatures. There is evidence that the human brain is in some way specialized and that speech is, therefore, restricted to humans for neurophysiological reasons. This is proved by the fact that there are some sub-normal humans with brain sizes smaller than those of the apes. These humans can nevertheless be taught to speak. In contrast, although there have been a number of experiments in teaching apes to use human language in some form (usually without the use of speech sounds), the level of success has been far from convincing. Undoubtedly these apes have shown a high degree of intelligence, but the 'language' they have learnt can hardly be identified with human language. Another possibility, as we saw earlier, is that the human brain is genetically 'programmed' for language. A further idea, which has been backed by investigation, is that in other creatures there is no direct link between the various regions of the brain that deal with sensation, but that these are independently linked to the areas that are concerned with the emotions, appetites, etc. In humans, by contrast, there are direct connections and, in particular, links between the regions of sight and hearing. In human language, it is argued, the naming of objects, the association of sound with 'things', is a necessary first step and this is possible only with a brain that can directly link sight and hearing. Since human beings alone have a brain that can do this, they alone can speak.

These last few paragraphs demonstrate once again what was said in the opening sections of this chapter – how little we know about language and languages. All too much of our knowledge, moreover, is distorted by prejudice and misconception. In the twentieth century we are becoming more curious about ourselves and our behaviour, and even more determined to make only precise and objective statements about it. But the field of scientific investigation of language is still vast and largely unexplored.

2

PHONOLOGY: THE SOUNDS OF ENGLISH

Peter Barnes

This chapter deals with the sound-system of English. It does not however attempt a detailed survey of the whole subject, because authoritative studies of this kind are already available (see Bibliography – though even the works cited there cannot hope to have said all there is to say on such a vast topic); and also because of limitations on space – this is not a book on English pronunciation alone but on various different aspects of the language. In what follows, therefore, the aim has simply been, first, to explain something of the ideas we need to handle 'the sounds of English', then to show, by selected examples, how these ideas might work out in practice.

The subject-matter of Chapter 1 was language in general and illustrations were taken from a number of different languages. It is now being presumed, however, as can be seen from the titles of this and succeeding chapters, that each of a number of aspects of English can be examined more or less separately, without doing undue violence to the facts. For instance, we can take an utterance – say 'Where's that big atlas got to, Mary?' – out of a conversation, and while of course we are quite ready to admit that such an utterance represents a great deal more than two seconds or so of sound, nevertheless we can consider it as if it were little more than that. We can ignore (which in an ordinary situation we would not) the fact that the sentence is a question, that the word *atlas* is a noun, that *big* means 'large', and so on. By ignoring all this, we are not falsifying the data, we are merely doing one job of description at a time; describing a language, or even a relatively small part of one, is such a herculean task that we may easily be forgiven if we attempt to take it bit by bit. Furthermore, as has been pointed out in the preceding chapter, since there is no necessary correspondence between sounds and what they 'stand for', there are strong grounds for claiming that the sound-system of a language can be studied separately, because that separation reflects a basic fact about language in general.

To talk clearly, at any length, about the 'sounds of English' (or of any other language) unfortunately involves terms of an unfamiliar kind, and we must spend a fair amount of time, first of all, clarifying what we mean by 'sounds' (and indeed, in a later paragraph, by 'English'). We will have to adopt a minimum of theory, with its accompanying technical terms, to describe, classify and label these sounds; such terms are lacking in the everyday vocabulary. These labels will first of all refer to the human vocal mechanism, and not particularly to any one language; for there is no sense in which a sound is 'English' by nature – only the use to which it is put is unique to one language. And there is of course no sense either in which particular sounds are characteristic of a particular racial group – human beings find it difficult or easy to make this or that vocal noise because of their linguistic environment since birth, and not for genetic reasons. The children of West Indian immigrants in London, for example (frequently in spite of their parents' West Indian accents), find no difficulty in speaking perfect Cockney; the American English of fully assimilated Africans, Chinese or Puerto Ricans is potentially the same as that of their Mayflower-descended neighbours, and any differences are ascribable rather to social class or regional factors than to 'race'. In view of this then, we can begin our discussion of the English sound-system by asking how human beings produce the vocal noises they do.

Basically, a noise is a disturbance in the medium which separates the source of the noise from the hearer. This medium is of course usually air. The disturbance originates in changes of air-pressure (generally known as SOUND WAVES) emanating from the nose and/or the mouth. The air in the VOCAL TRACT (the wind-pipe, pharynx or throat, mouth and nose – see Fig. 2.1) can be made to move either outwards or inwards by various kinds of AIR-STREAM MECHANISM. For our purposes, this will almost always be of the type known as PULMONIC EGRESSIVE – lung air being pushed upwards and outwards by the contraction of the space available for it in the lungs. Other air-stream mechanisms rarely occur in English, or occur only on the fringe of the linguistic system, as in the 'clicks' (often spelt 'tut tut', 'tsk tsk', etc.) used by English speakers to express sympathy or disapproval, for instance, or to encourage beasts of burden. As the air moves through the vocal tract, up into the cavities of the pharynx, mouth and nose, we can interfere with its passage in a variety of ways; this interference, as we shall see, may merely involve altering the size and shape of the cavities (by moving the tongue or the lower jaw, for example) or it may involve blocking off the air-stream altogether. The shape and position of the speech-organs is called ARTICULATION; and as the articulation changes, so of course does the sound-wave it gives rise to. Since that sound-wave is perceived by the listener as a 'sound' (or 'sounds'), there seems to be justification for describing sounds in articulatory terms. The study of how our speech-organs can be moved and positioned to produce one sound-type or another is the subject-matter of ARTICULATORY PHONETICS, and its categories are by far the most common way of describing speech-sounds. Perhaps, however, we ought to remind ourselves here that the title ARTICULATORY/AUDITORY PHONETICS would be more appropriate; for it must be remembered that our hearing-sense 'monitors' the sounds we ourselves are articulating. There is a feedback to the brain via the ear, whereby we can check, as it were, that the instructions sent to the muscles of the

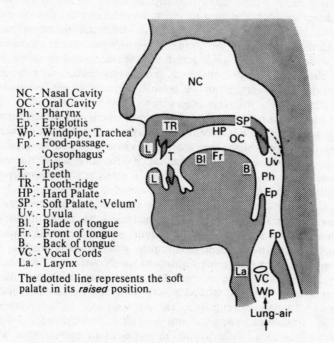

NC.- Nasal Cavity
OC.- Oral Cavity
Ph. - Pharynx
Ep. - Epiglottis
Wp.- Windpipe,'Trachea'
Fp. - Food-passage,
         'Oesophagus'
L.   - Lips
T.   - Teeth
TR. - Tooth-ridge
HP.- Hard Palate
SP. - Soft Palate, 'Velum'
Uv.- Uvula
Bl. - Blade of tongue
Fr. - Front of tongue
B.   - Back of tongue
VC.- Vocal Cords
La. - Larynx

The dotted line represents the soft palate in its *raised* position.

Fig. 2.1. The Organs of Speech

articulating organs have produced, in auditory terms, the intended result. There is thus a close, built-in link between what we hear and what noises we speak.

It is possible, then, to describe sounds by detailing the salient characteristics of the speech-apparatus at the time of production; but there are at least two good reasons why our description can never be more than approximate. The first is that no two human beings have identical versions of that apparatus. Individual differences will inevitably mean that our description is a generalization; that is, we will have to take 'sound' as meaning 'type of sound', however precise the descriptive labels may appear. The second reason lies in the complexity of the speech-organs and of their simultaneous activity in the act of speaking; the difficulty of measuring this activity is such that an exact statement of ALL the articulatory variables involved in the production of one sound by one set of speech-organs is probably impossible (if only because the measuring devices themselves would tend to interfere with articulation to such an extent that it would no longer resemble natural speech). We must therefore be prepared to accept that our phonetic description will appear, in absolute terms, rather rough and ready; but it will be a great deal more precise than the vague and impressionistic labels and the loose metaphors we often find applied to the sounds of speech. The approximateness of the description, however, should be seen in the light of our purpose in carrying it out – which is to be able to identify all those differences of sound which are capable of being perceived, consistently, by the human ear. Any differences below this threshold, after all, could not be used in anything other than a subconscious, non-meaningful, and therefore non-linguistic way. Such differences are thus not the concern of the linguistic analyst, and our phonetic description will be OVER-precise if it takes note of them.

Up to now we have used the word 'sound', in both its singular and its plural form, rather indiscriminately – we have for instance allowed it to suggest (one of) a number of separate, or at least separable, units put together in sequence to form an utterance. Yet when we examine graphic displays of speech (which are produced by instruments giving us in effect partial pictures of the sound-wave), then we see immediately that what we think of as a series of units, of separate events, is in fact not a series at all but, from the physical point of view, one continuous noise. On this purely acoustic level, sound is not treated as representing an utterance of a language but as a complex sound-wave, defined in the physicist's terms of frequency, time and amplitude, and varying more or less continuously from any one fraction of a second to the next. Must we then abandon, on evidence of this kind, the idea of segmenting the utterance, of cutting it up into its component 'sounds', the better to examine it? The answer to this has almost always been 'no': it is still open to us to segment speech in this way provided we accept that each unit, each 'sound', in the sequence merges into its neighbours (or into silence if at the beginning or end of the utterance), and that therefore there will be no point of time at which sound A 'becomes' sound B. An analogy sometimes used in cases like this is that of two hills with a valley between them – although we cannot point to two lines on the ground where the valley stops and the hills begin, nevertheless it is still meaningful to talk of two hills and a valley (perhaps because the notions of 'hill' and 'valley' do not depend on boundary-features so much as on the characteristics of their central parts). No doubt it is a gross oversimplification of the physical facts to conceive of the phonetics of an utterance as a series of units, even if we add the idea of TRANSITION-FEATURES joining them together; but there is also no doubt that there will always be oversimplification in talking of phenomena as complex as articulation. In fact, we will see below that once we look at either the sound-wave or the articulatory continuum from the point of view of the LINGUISTIC units it represents, there will be stronger reasons for accepting the imposition of a 'segmental' framework of analysis. (Indeed, the examination of the physical properties of the sound-wave from this point of view has led to much new thinking in phonetics. The question has been asked, 'What acoustic features in this mass of noise are crucial for the perception of this or that linguistic unit?' and answers to it have proved most revealing. We shall not, however, have much further to say on this topic, since it requires specialized knowledge which is here rather outside our scope.)

We have decided, then, to consider a 'sound' as an articulation, that is as a typical set of movements and/or positions of the speech-organs. 'Typical' means typical of the infinite number of possibilities which would produce the same auditory effect; and 'same' in this last phrase means for any practical linguistic purpose the same. Having arrived at this definition, if such it can be called, the next task is to set up articulatory categories for describing the various sounds, and this we must now proceed to do.

The first line is traditionally drawn between VOWELS and CONSONANTS, terms which (in spite of their long pedigree) are notoriously difficult to define. For our purposes at the moment, the distinction can be made by specifying that if the air-passage is constricted (either partially or wholly blocked) from the larynx upward, then this 'stricture' marks the articulation as that of a consonant. Vowels will simply be sounds produced without this stricture. Thus a sound-sequence like (that which represents) the word *sat* in English has a consonant-vowel-consonant type of arrangement. Now, this definition appears to be fairly arbitrary, and so indeed it is. The reason for this arbitrariness is that there are no classes into which sounds NATURALLY fall. We may think we see such classes in the way our own native language arranges its phonetic material, but this would be a mistake (and a mistake of a type to which generalizations about language are rather prone), because it takes for granted that our language is 'natural' to all human beings, rather than merely seeming natural to those who happen to speak it. If there are thus no natural classes on the articulatory phonetic level, then our classification system will have to invent its own. As far as our knowledge of actual languages goes (which is probably not very far), our classification will tend to reflect the kinds of phonetic differences which languages have been found to make use of; but the arbitrary factor must remain, turning up throughout our categories at this level of analysis and certainly not only in the case of the first two, vowel and consonant. (However, our categorization will also reflect the fact that our concern here is to describe a variety of contemporary English.)

To take consonants first, we have so far specified the presence of a stricture in the air-passage. If we can now state WHERE, in the cavities above the larynx, the passage is constricted, and then HOW (i.e. by what organs and to what extent) this constriction occurs, then we will have provided ourselves with at least two methods of description. For example, if we ask where a stricture is located, we can label a fair number of positions without difficulty (see Fig. 2.1): between the two lips (sounds so produced are said to be BILABIAL), e.g. the *p*-sound of *pan*; between the lower lip and the upper teeth (LABIO-DENTAL), e.g. the *f*-sound of *fix*; between the tongue and the back of the upper teeth (DENTAL), e.g. the *th*-sound of *thick*; between the tongue and the tooth-ridge (ALVEOLAR), e.g. the *s*-sound of *some*; and so on. The roof of the mouth, from tooth-ridge to uvula, we can divide up (again more or less arbitrarily, our main guide being the kinds of distinction we have found languages making in this area) into hard palate and soft palate (or velum); the hard palate in turn can then be sub-divided into as many parts as are thought necessary. In PARTICULAR cases, whether we need to catalogue certain finer distinctions and ignore others can depend on what use the language concerned makes of the total phonetic possibilities. And since this chapter deals with the phonetics of one variety of English, the distinctions to be drawn will in general be based on what seems most convenient for our examples of the ways in which the English sound-system operates; we will be able to adjust our general classes of sound in the foreknowledge of the ways in which English uses the resources of the human speech-mechanism.

A so-called 'consonant-chart' (see Fig 2.4, p 54) is one widely used type of general classification. As we have seen, the terms on the horizontal axis, from bilabial onwards, form a set of labels for positions in the vocal tract where consonantal stricture may occur, i.e. for PLACE OF ARTICULATION. On the other, vertical axis, the labels refer to the MANNER OF ARTICULATION – HOW the passage is constricted – and we shall now look at this second set of terms.

First, the STOP (or PLOSIVE) consonants. These involve the pressurization of air pushed up from the lungs into the vocal tract; if this pressurization is to take place there, the outlets (nose and mouth) must be closed against it. The nasal cavity is shut off by raising the soft palate against the back wall of the pharynx, thus sealing the passage. The mouth, however, may be sealed in a variety of ways, as we have seen – bilabial as in *bee*, alveolar as in *tea*, velar as in *key* – and when this CLOSURE in the mouth is released, the resultant explosion of pressurized air will sound different according to the position of the speech-organs at that moment. According to the place of articulation, in other words, the shape of the oral cavities will differ, as between for example a dental and a velar stop; so the air which is contained there and which resonates there on its release, will produce a different impact on the air outside, i.e. a different sound-wave (and hence, in auditory terms, a different sound). And this will of course be true also of articulations other than stops.

Second, the NASAL consonants. These are like the stops in that there is a complete closure at some point in the mouth, but different from them in that the soft palate is lowered, allowing air to escape freely, and only, through the nose. Examples are the sounds at the end of the words *ram* (bilabial nasal), *ran* (alveolar) and *rang* (velar).

Third, the LATERAL consonants. These are formed by a closure between the middle (i.e. not the side) part of the tongue, and a point along the front or top of the mouth. The closure is not complete, however, since the sides of the tongue are kept lowered (sometimes one more than the other, exceptionally only one side) and air is allowed to escape over them. The *l*-sounds in the words *fly*, *lily* and *fool* are examples.

Fourth, the FRICATIVES. Here the air is forced out, with a 'hissing' noise, through a narrowed passage formed between, for example, the tongue-tip and the tooth-ridge, as in the *s*-sound of *see*, or between the tongue-tip and the upper teeth, as in the *th*-sound of *these*. The noise so produced is often referred to as AUDIBLE FRICTION.

The remaining categories needed for the English consonants are less easy to handle within the set of terms we have outlined so far. For instance, the *r*-sound of *red* or *very* usually has no audible friction and will therefore not fit into the fricative category. Indeed, one is scarcely aware of any stricture at all. However, the label FRICTIONLESS CONTINUANT has been used elsewhere, and we will accept it here rather than be forced either to treat such sounds as 'non-consonants' – i.e. as vowels – or to redefine 'consonants'. That is, we will take the *r*-sound as having a stricture of a very weak kind.

Another difficulty is caused by the nature of the 'aitch', the sound which begins words like *hit* and *hot*. This is produced simply by breathing out, the vocal organs being in the position of the following vowel-sound. There is no stricture as for the other consonants; this sound is therefore a sort of 'breathed vowel'. But we will probably wish to treat it like a consonant, for reasons which, as in the similar case of *r*, will be more concerned with how the language uses the sound than with how it is articulated; such reasons should become clearer later on. And if we do wish to treat it along with the other consonants, we can refer to it as a fricative, since we can claim that most of the noise is made by the air passing over the irregular surfaces of the pharyngeal and oral cavities, and there is thus audible friction.

A further difficulty is found with the so-called SEMI-VOWELS, the initial sounds in words like *yet* and *wet*. Here we plainly have a vowel-like articulation: no stricture at all, and the vocal organs in very much the same sort of positions as for the vowels in e.g. *pit* and *put*. However, we have not yet gone far enough with our analysis to see why such sounds have so often been treated as consonants, and further discussion of the semi-vowels must therefore be left till later in this chapter (see p 47).

We have now established, or rather borrowed, a rough framework within which the place and manner of the articulations involved in English consonants can be described. There is however a further dimension to be considered – that of the modification which the larynx may impose on the stream of egressive lung-air. The larynx is the so-called 'voice-box' or 'Adam's apple' at the top of the windpipe (see Fig. 2.1, p 31), and within it are two lips, or folds, running from front to back. These are the VOCAL CORDS. They may open and close (VIBRATE) very rapidly as the air passes upwards between them, and if they do then the articulation is said to be VOICED – i.e. it is accompanied by VOICE (or VOICING), the name given to this vibration. If on the contrary the vocal cords are not vibrated but held open for the air to pass freely through the space between them, then the sound will be referred to as VOICELESS. Thus the consonant-articulations can be voiced or voiceless; that is, each type of articulation will produce not one but two sounds. For example, compare the middle consonant-sounds in *fuzzy* and *fussy* (voiced and voiceless alveolar fricatives), *stable* and *staple* (bilabial stops), *saver* and *safer* (labio-dental fricatives), etc. Most of the consonant-articulations we have detailed above occur in English in both voiced and voiceless forms; this is not the case, however, with the nasal consonants or with the *h*-sound – for practical purposes, the former are always voiced, and the latter always voiceless.

Traditionally, consonant-sounds are labelled in the order (i) voiced/voiceless, (ii) place of articulation, and (iii) manner of articulation. Thus for instance the *g*-sound in *foggy* is usually called a 'voiced velar stop'; and so on. Labels of this kind are, as we have seen earlier, no more than rough and ready; each of the three terms in 'voiced velar stop' could be expanded further – in the case of 'voiced', does the vocal cord vibration continue throughout the different phases of the stop-articulation, and at the same intensity? Exactly where on the velum is the 'velar' closure made? For how long is the closure of the 'stop' held, and how much pressure is built up before the explosion? In addition, we could ask what the lip-position is, to what extent the jaw is opened, what the front part of the tongue is doing, and so on. However, our three-term consonantal labels will probably be adequate for our present purpose; we can refine them later if we find the language using sound-differences with which our terminology cannot cope.

Let us now turn to the vowel-sounds, and attempt to set up a general classification-system which we can use to describe, economically, the vowels of English. We have already defined vowels negatively, by saying that their articulation is NOT like what is held to be typically consonantal. To this we can now add the assertion that vowel-sounds are voiced – for us, therefore a 'voiceless vowel' is a contradiction in terms. Vowel-sounds, unlike consonants, cannot be described according to the location and type of stricture, since the negative definition specifically excluded stricture. The principal factor to be described here is the size and shape of the oral cavity; and this can be done in terms of where the highest point of the tongue is, relative to four extreme positions. The notion of 'extreme' is the following (see Fig. 2.2): when (the highest point of) the tongue is in position (a), any further movement upwards or forwards, all else being equal, would produce a stricture, hence by definition a consonantal type of sound; in position (b), any movement upwards or backwards would similarly produce a consonant; in position (c), the jaw is at its maximum degree of opening, and the body of the tongue is pushed forward as far as possible; and in position (d), the jaw is again wide open, with the tongue this time pulled back as far as possible without, once again, causing a stricture. If we connect up these four points in a drawing we shall have a rough picture of the so-called 'vowel-area', within which the highest point of the tongue must be if a vowel-sound is being articulated. This shape can be formalized into the 'Cardinal Vowel' diagram first proposed many years ago by Daniel Jones, and now in widespread use (see Fig. 2.3, p 40). In this diagram, the area is divided up into, on the vertical axis, CLOSE, HALF-CLOSE, HALF-OPEN and OPEN; and on the horizontal axis, into FRONT, CENTRAL and BACK. For our purposes, we may assume that the eight numbered reference-points represent vowel-sounds that are more or less fixed from the auditory point of view – i.e. that any speaker of any language will produce the same sound as any other speaker if they both put their tongue in the position described above for e.g. 'Cardinal Vowel no. 1'. Therefore any other vowel may be plotted on the diagram relative to these Cardinal points. For instance, the vowel in the English word *kit* may be described as a very centralized version of C.V. no. 1; that in *cot* as half-way between nos. 5 and 6; and so on.

However, our descriptive apparatus for vowel-sounds will need to take account of (at least) two additional factors. The first of these is lip position; if the lips are ROUNDED (and protruded), as for instance in the word *caught*, then the overall shape of the oral cavity is changed, and so therefore is the sound produced. Lip-rounding, more or less noticeable according to individual speakers, their regional accent, etc., is characteristic of several of the English vowels, and this additional modification will thus be necessary to our description.

Secondly, we will need to take account of those vowels which are not PURE, i.e. in which there is a clearly distinguishable movement of the tongue from one vowel-position to another, rather than a relatively steady state. Vowel-sounds of this type are known as DIPHTHONGS; examples are to be found in words like *boy, bay, bough*, etc. (The answer to the question 'why are these not to be treated as TWO vowel-sounds in sequence, merging into one another as

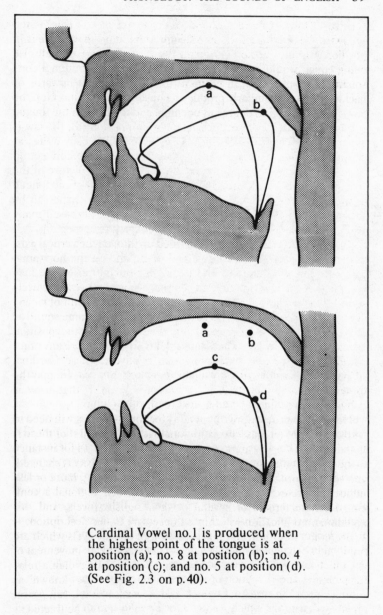

Cardinal Vowel no.1 is produced when
the highest point of the tongue is at
position (a); no. 8 at position (b); no. 4
at position (c); and no. 5 at position (d).
(See Fig. 2.3 on p. 40).

Fig. 2.2. Tongue-positions at Extreme Points of the 'Vowel-area'

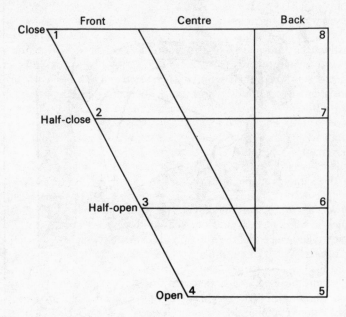

Fig. 2.3. The Cardinal Vowel Diagram

adjacent sounds in any case will always tend to do?' should emerge from the discussion below.)

So far we have been largely concerned with setting up categories within which we can describe and classify speech-sounds (and in particular those of English) from an articulatory point of view. To some extent, however, we have found our choice of descriptive categories dictated, or conditioned, by NON-articulatory criteria, by considerations of 'how English uses' the various resources of the sound-producing mechanism. We ought now to move on to this more abstract, more linguistic level; to move from the phonetic to the specifically PHONOLOGICAL. The questions to be asked at this point are no longer of the type 'how is this noise produced, and how can its production be concisely described?', but rather of the type 'what part does such and such a phonetic feature, or set of features, play in the transmission and reception of various kinds of meaning?'. We shall confine our examples to English, just as we outlined only those phonetic categories which we need for English sounds, but most of the ideas and methods to be used may of course be equally applicable to any other language. That is, there are theories and techniques of GENERAL PHONOLOGY just as there are of GENERAL PHONETICS.

Let us begin looking at the sound-differences which can be used 'distinctively' in English – i.e. to distinguish meanings – by taking a MINIMAL PAIR of words (so-called because the two words differ as regards only one of their sounds), such as *bit* and *bet*. These two are consistently recognized by an English speaker as 'different words', with different meanings. The phonetic difference between the two vowel-sounds is therefore distinctive – a change in tongue-position from one sound to the other will produce a change of meaning. If we then go on to make other changes at the same place – the vowel in the middle – we will find e.g. *beat, boot, bat, Bert,* and so on. If we change, on the same principle, the consonant at the beginning, we will produce examples like *bit, pit, sit, mitt, kit, lit,* etc.; and similarly, *bit, biff, bin, big,* etc. by altering the final consonant. So there is a sense in which a word of this kind consists of three UNITS or PLACES IN STRUCTURE, since there are three, and ONLY three, places at which changes in vowels or consonants can be made. And clearly, to see a word like *big* as a structure of three abstract units is very different from considering it as a sequence of three sounds, in terms of vocal cord vibration, tongue-height, lip-position, and so on. We can to some extent combine these two approaches by seeing the sound as representing, or REALIZING, the phonological unit. The unit itself we may call a PHONEME; and when we view the sounds as realizations of phonemes, we can refer to them as ALLOPHONES of the phonemes. So the word *big* consists phonologically of three phonemes, realized by their appropriate allophones.

This notion of a phoneme and its allophones is a crucial one for much of what follows in this chapter. At first blush, it undoubtedly sounds rather abstruse and technical, but it is a tool which, in this or another similar form, can help to elucidate a great deal of confused thinking on the subject of 'sounds' in language. The reader is thus urged to assimilate the idea before proceeding further.

Now so far our examples have been written in ordinary English spelling, but such are the vagaries of this orthography that it would be more precise to allot symbols to our phonemes, so that we make it explicit that e.g. *pit* and *mitt* differ only as regards the beginning, and not at the end. The tradition has grown up (and not just for English) of using the Roman alphabet for many of these symbols, with additions and modifications where necessary, and of enclosing them in slant lines to indicate that they represent phonemes and not ordinary letters. Thus *pit* and *mitt* will be transcribed phonemically as

/pɪt/ and /mɪt/.[1] The following is a list of the phonemes of English, with a symbolization and a 'key-word' for each.

VOWEL-PHONEMES				CONSONANT PHONEMES	
Symbol	Key-words			Symbol	Key-words
/iː/	bead	peat	bee	/p/	pie
/ɪ/	bid	pit	—	/b/	by
/e/	bed	pet	—	/t/	tie
/æ/	bad	pat	—	/d/	die
/ɑː/	barred	part	bar	/k/	{ core
/ʌ/	bud	putt	—	/g/	guy { gore
/ɔː/	board	port	bore	/f/	{ fear
/ɒ/	'bod'	pot	—	/v/	vie { veer
/uː/	booed	—	boo	/θ/	thigh
/ʊ/	—	put	—	/ð/	thy
/ɜː/	bird	pert	burr	/s/	sigh { sink
/ə/	—	—	—	/z/	— { zinc { ruse
/eɪ/	bade	pate	bay	/ʃ/	shy { ruche
/aɪ/	bide	—	buy	/ʒ/	— { rouge
/ɔɪ/	buoyed	—	boy	/h/	high
/aʊ/	bowed	pout	bough	/m/	my { ram
/əʊ/	bode	—	bow	/n/	nigh { ran
			(and arrow)		
/ɪə/	beard	—	beer	/ŋ/	— { rang
/ɛə/	bared	—	bare	/l/	lie
/ʊə/	—	—	boor	/r/	rye
				/j/	— { year
				/w/	Wye { weir

(One vowel, /ə/, is not exemplified in this list, because monosyllables like those used above as key-words are always stressed when quoted in isolation, and /ə/ does not occur except in UNSTRESSED syllables. Minimal pairs can be found, however: compare unstressed *but*, as in 'But *really* I didn't!', with unstressed *butt* – an opposition between /ə/ and /ʌ/; or 'An *orange*' with 'In *orange*' – /ə/ and /ɪ/. In fact /ə/ occurs a good deal more often than any other vowel in conversational English; and furthermore its use currently seems to be spreading to many words hitherto pronounced with /ɪ/).

Notice first of all that there are gaps in the lists of key-words; there are no words to fit in these places for one of two reasons: either (a)

---

[1] The transcription used here is that devised by A. C. Gimson and exemplified in his *Introduction to the Pronunciation of English* – see Bibliography, p 344.

because the words are possible English ones which the language does not happen to use – examples are */bʊd/ or */paɪt/; or (b) because the phoneme concerned is not allowed to (= does not in practice) occur in that position in a word – for instance, */ŋeɪ/ or */be/ are not possible English words. We shall be mentioning below at greater length (pp 46–7) the idea that a language allows the speaker to combine its phonemes together only in specific ways.

Secondly, we should notice that the symbols themselves are chosen with their traditional values very much in mind. For example, the letter *t* is chosen to symbolize a phoneme which is usually realized as a voiceless alveolar stop, and phonemes with similar allophones in other (European) languages are very often written with the same *t*-letter. This practice has the advantage of reminding us, by our experience of ordinary writing in these languages, how the symbol should be realized; but it also has the disadvantage of inviting confusion between orthography and phonemic transcription – hence the importance of the slant lines enclosing phoneme-symbols.

Thirdly, we could reduce the total number of phonemes from 42 to 34 at a stroke, by treating the eight diphthongs as sequences of two vowels we have already catered for. For example, /eɪ/ as in *pate* would be the /e/ of *pet* plus the /ɪ/ of *pit*. This we shall not in fact do, for reasons discussed later, but it is an example of the ways in which other analyses of the same material might treat the phonemic contrasts differently. However, these relatively minor differences of approach to the phonology need not concern us here.

Fourthly, and perhaps most importantly, we should now make it clear that the variety of English we are describing is only one among many; many, indeed most, speakers of English would find that our list of phonemes did not correspond exactly to their own speech. For instance, a Scots would be unlikely to distinguish between /u:/ and /ʊ/ (e.g. between *fool* and *full*); nor would a speaker of 'general' American have a contrast between /ʌ/ and /ə/; and a Cockney would not have an /h/ at all.

Up to now we have been using the term 'English' in rather a loose fashion, and it would be as well if we were to explain the limitations to be placed upon it. The accent of English which we are (have been and will be) talking about is that known as RECEIVED PRONUNCIATION or RP for short. It is the accent regarded (at least up to quite recently) as 'standard' in the United Kingdom, though the number of speakers who use it is relatively small. Other labels applied to it are 'Queen's English', 'the Oxford accent', 'correct', 'educated', 'upper-class', 'BBC', 'high-falutin'', 'affected', 'high-class', and a large number of others, all equally misleading in that they do not identify or describe the accent, so much as approve of or condemn it, for reasons which are usually socio-cultural rather than linguistic. RP is the accent generally used in nationally or internationally broadcast news-bulletins by the BBC, and it is the norm in the 'straight' theatre – i.e. departures from it are normally motivated by the playwright or the director (one would not be altogether surprised to hear a Macbeth with a Scottish accent, but Lear will speak RP). Furthermore, it is spoken all over the United Kingdom, and to that extent is non-regional; it is not the local accent of Londoners, for instance, as is often assumed. The subject of RP is bedevilled with prejudice and mis-information, no less among the highly educated than among those with very little formal education. Current attitudes to RP and to the other accents of the English are part of our 'culture', in the anthropologist's sense, and we will find it difficult if not impossible to react to these accents in a totally rational way; but this does not of course prevent us from recognizing our own linguistic prejudices as such, rather than attempting to rationalize and justify them. Be that as it may, for our purposes here the most important point to bear in mind is that the linguist's own view of English accents is largely irrelevant to the description of one of them, whether he or she speaks it or not. We may regard RP, for instance, as a bastion of traditional moral and social values; or (perhaps more sensibly) as the mark of a large social group, defined in other ways by the socio-economic status and the educational background of its members. In whatever way we look at it, we should not allow such non-linguistic judgements to intrude on our description of linguistic features. We may strongly disapprove, for instance, of the habit which RP speakers (among many others) have of 'dropping the *r*' before consonants, e.g. of pronouncing *hard* as /hɑːd/ rather than /hɑːrd/, but our feelings on the matter are or should be entirely divorced from our descriptive statement, that 'in RP, /r/ does not occur before consonants'.

The choice of RP to represent 'the sounds of English' in this chapter is dictated by a variety of factors: its wide intelligibility among speakers from other parts of the English-speaking world, and the thoroughness of the descriptions of it available in print, are two of the principal ones. 'English' as applied to a form of pro-nunciation, therefore, means here 'a type of accent coming under the general heading of RP', unless otherwise stated.

We now have before us, then, a list of the 42 English phonemes, consisting of 20 vowels and 22 consonants. We have referred to them as abstract 'phonological units'; from the point of view of describing the articulatory, physical facts of utterances, we talk about each phoneme being 'realized' by a sound – the 'allophone'. We must now take account of the fact that recognizably DIFFERENT sounds represent the SAME phoneme, depending on the context in which it occurs. That is, a given phoneme (say the English /t/) will have MORE THAN ONE allophone: /t/ is realized as a DENTAL stop (tongue-tip against the upper teeth rather than against the tooth-ridge) before /θ/ or /ð/, the dental fricatives, as in *eighth* or *write this*; before a vowel in a stressed syllable, it will be ASPIRATED (i.e. the explosion will be followed by a breathy release of air, often involving audible friction, before the vocal cords start vibrating for the vowel-sound) – compare the aspirated sound in *tore* with the unaspirated /d/-allophone in *door*; before a pause, it will very often be UNEXPLODED (i.e. the oral air-pressure is not released, as elsewhere, by pulling the tongue sharply back from the tooth-ridge, but reduced to normal by drawing air back down into the lungs), as in *There's a cat*; and so on. The phonetic detail need not detain us for the moment; the important point is that the /t/-phoneme is realized by several quite different sounds, depending on its position. One sometimes hears it said that 'there are 42 sounds in English'; but statements like this seem to confuse phonemes with allophones, to ignore what we have seen as a crucial distinction between the level of phonetics and that of phonology.

Sometimes the rules for the selection of an allophone in a given context appear rather arbitrary – why aspirate the /t/-allophone before a stressed vowel, after all? – and the answer to the question 'why?', as so often in language-analysis, is simply 'because the language is like that' or 'because that is what speakers of the language say'. Sometimes the rules appear to result from a pressure towards economy of articulatory movements, as when /t/ is a dental stop before a dental fricative. And sometimes, as in the case of the unexploded final stop before a pause, it is not clear whether its occurrence in that position is governed by arbitrary linguistic pressures, by phonetic economy, or by both.

To take a few further examples of allophonic variation: /r/ in a word like *try* has a voiceless allophone, but in *dry* a voiced one; the sound representing /iː/ in *sea* is slightly shorter (all things being equal) than that in *seed*, but slightly longer than that in *seat*; the /l/ at the beginning of *lull* sounds different from that at the end; and so on. Thus, in a phonological description of English, we have not only an inventory of phonemes, but also a list of allophones for each, with an accompanying statement of the contexts in which the different sounds occur. And we have not yet finished, for there is still another facet of how the phonemic side of a language works.

This next stage concerns the question of which sequences, or combinations, of phonemes are permitted, and which are not: in what ways can we combine the phonemes to make up English words and syllables? As we saw earlier, for instance, /ŋ/ cannot occur at the beginning of a word, and neither can /ʒ/, whereas /h, j, w/ cannot occur at the end. The group /str/ is allowed at the beginning, but not /stl/ or /ʃtr/. We can end a word with a vowel, provided it is one of /iː, ɑː, ɔː, ɜː, uː/ or the diphthongs; but none of these vowels occurs before /ŋ/. /r/, as we have mentioned, is found only before vowels; and so on. Prohibitions of this kind are known as PHONOTACTIC RULES; they are 'rules', of course, only in the sense that they reflect what invariably happens in the language, or what never does. These were the considerations which led us earlier to claim that */bʊd/ and */peɪt/ were 'possible English words', which the language did not happen to make use of; i.e. they are permitted by the phonotactic rules. On the other hand, */ŋeɪ/ and */be/ are not so permitted, and are therefore not 'unused' so much as IM-POSSIBLE words for the English speaker. Non-occurring words of the first type need a moment's reflection (and often a look in a dictionary) before they are ruled out; words of the second type sound un-English to a degree, and are frequently quite difficult for us to pronounce. Commercial concerns (or their advertising agencies) very often make use of the first type of word to provide a name for a new product; but they would usually avoid un-English phoneme-combinations. We would be likely to believe an English-speaking engineer who told us that *pite* (/paɪt/) was the technical name for a special component of a jet-engine; but we would be more sceptical about a /ŋeɪ/.

If we now go on to examine further the phonotactic rules of English, we ought to find that, as predicted earlier, the notions of 'vowel' and 'consonant' become clearer. The rules will produce a vast number of possible English words, and we will notice that the possibilities in one position in one type of word will tend to resemble those in another position elsewhere. For instance, if we look at what phonemes can occur between /b/ and /t/ in monosyllables, or between /sw/ and /m/, or after /fl/ and before a pause, we will find only phonemes drawn from our list of vowels. If we ask what can replace the /b/, the /t/, etc., the answer will be a consonant. In other words, we divide the phonemes into these two groups because broadly speaking they seem to 'pattern' in either one way or the other. Further support for this is provided by a case we have already mentioned – the non-use of /r/ before consonants; that is, the statement of where /r/ occurs corroborates our finding that vowels and consonants pattern differently. Going outside the phonotactic rules, we may notice that before vowels the definite article *the* is pronounced /ði:/ or /ðɪ/ and the indefinite article /ən/; before consonants, on the other hand, the former is /ðə/ and the latter /ə/. In short, the language seems to force us to recognize these two large groups of phonemes.[1]

We can now see that our vowel/consonant division on the phonetic level, the apparent arbitrariness of which we noted at the time, is one which derives in fact from the phonological level. We divided the articulation-types into two groups, using the convenient criterion of 'stricture', because we knew in advance that this would more or less reflect the distinction we would be forced to make in the phonology. We would then have been able to claim that consonant-phonemes have consonantal allophones, and vowel-phonemes vowel-allophones. We can see that this apparent symmetry is in fact an artifice, and rather a misleading one at that, since it obscures the important difference between (a) sounds and (b) the way they function.

This is also perhaps the place to tie up another loose end. On p 37, mention was briefly made of the 'semi-vowels' /j/ and /w/. We can now explain the term more fully by noting that these two phonemes, belonging structurally to the CONSONANT group, have some VOWEL-SOUND allophones. That is, the two levels do not 'match' at this point, hence the use (now traditional) of the catch-all term 'semi-vowel'.

Thus the terms 'vowel' and 'consonant', in most discussions of English pronunciation, are used in two very different ways. Up to now we have not consistently observed the distinction, but from now on we will use VOWEL-SOUND and CONSONANT-SOUND for the phonetic articulation-types, reserving VOWEL and CONSONANT for the structural categories into which phonemes seem to fit in English. The first phoneme in *yet* or *wet*, therefore, will be a consonant realized by a vowel-sound allophone; and we can thus dispense with the vague 'semi-vowel' label.

We may now at last feel that we have equipped ourselves with

---

[1] Diachronic observations further support the division: in the history of English, there is no sound-change that involves both what we have called vowels and what we have called consonants.

enough theoretical and terminological apparatus to handle a partial, outline description of the 'sounds of English'. Unfortunately there appears to have been little alternative to such a long preamble, for phonetics and phonology comprise a highly technical subject. Attempts to understand something of the workings of a sound-system, enormously complex as it will inevitably turn out to be, involve us in technicalities which we cannot very well do without.

Let us look first, then, at the consonant-phonemes of R.P., at where and how they are realized in the current of speech. The consonants are often divided into two large groups, the 'voiced' and the 'voiceless', and, as we have found with other terminology, these two labels occur in descriptions of both the phonetics and the phonology of English. We have seen earlier what they mean in articulatory terms – vocal cords vibrating, or held open; but they have also been commonly used to identify the two classes of consonant-PHONEMES. That is, we risk once again a confusion of the phonetic with the phonological. We should perhaps ask ourselves what exactly are the main criteria on which we would divide the consonants into these two large groups: for instance, when one phoneme from the group /p, t, k, f, θ, s, ʃ, h/ occurs at the end of a word, then the vowel preceding it is relatively SHORT; but when that final consonant is other than one of these – i.e. drawn from the group /b, d, g, v, ð, z, ʒ, m, n, ŋ, l, r, j, w/ – then the vowel is relatively LONG (particularly in stressed syllables); all this provided the vowel concerned is one of the group (/iː, aː, ɔː, ɜː, uː/ or one of the eight diphthongs. Compare *moot-mood, leak-league, mouth-mouthe, race-raze,* etc. (see pp 53–4 for a further look at this pattern). So in the way in which they seem to affect the choice of allophone in the preceding vowel, these two groups of consonants indeed appear to differ one from the other. (Note that we have included /h, j, w/ in the pattern, although as we have said earlier they do not occur at the ends of words; for other reasons [see below] we will wish to include them here.)

A second criterion for this grouping of the consonants is that all the phonemes in the first group are invariably realized by VOICELESS allophones; while those in the second group are in some contexts (e.g. between vowels) realized by VOICED sounds, and in others (e.g. immediately before or after a pause) by sounds which are partially or wholly VOICELESS. And a third criterion is that allophones of the first group are very often, all things being equal, articulated with greater energy, more breath-force, than their counterparts from the second group.

From this we see that though there certainly is evidence for dividing the consonants in this way,. the division does not always 'match' the phonetic division of the allophones into voiced and voiceless articulation types.

Let us now look at another pattern, or set of patterns, within the consonants, this time a less general one – the group of six 'stop-consonants' (so-called, though really of course it is their allophones which are stops, not the phonemic units themselves). These six are /p, t, k, b, d, g/, and they form a sub-group within the consonants, not only because their allophones share a common phonetic feature of stop-articulation, but also and perhaps more important, because they function in similar places in structure. Where one of them can occur, the others are at least likely to be permitted also. Consider

PLACE OF ARTICULATION

MANNER OF ARTICULATION	BI-LABIAL	LABIO-DENTAL	DENTAL	ALV-EOLAR	POST ALV.	PALATAL	VELAR	GLOTTAL
STOP	p,b			t,d			k,g	
NASAL	m		n				ŋ	
LATERAL			l					
FRICATIVE		f,v	θ,ð	s,z	ʃ,ʒ	(ç)		h
FRICTIONLESS CONTINUANT				r				
SEMI-VOWEL	w					j		

Fig. 2.4. Chart of English Consonants

Each of the symbols in Fig. 2.4 represents a sound which commonly, but by no means always, realizes one of the English consonant phonemes. Where there are two symbols in a box, the first represents a voiceless sound, the second a voiced. The symbol (ç) stands for one realization of the initial cluster /hj/ – see pp 50–51. The 'semi-vowels' /j/ and /w/ are included here by the virtue of their occasional consonant-sound allophones – see below. The allophones of /w/ are always accompanied by lip-rounding; those of /ʃ, ʒ/ and /r/ often so.

the following formula (really an extract from our phonotactic rules): (/s/+) stop-consonant (+/r, l, j, w/). This is a quick way of writing down what appears to be a major pattern among those groups (or CLUSTERS), of either two or three consonants, which can begin English words. The pattern will produce two-consonant clusters of /s/ + stop-consonant, as in *spy, sty, sky*; or of stop-consonant + /r, l, j, w/ as in *cry, play, dune, twice*; or it will produce three-consonant clusters like those in *spray, street, scream*. There are other initial two-consonant clusters, such as /sm, sn, θr, fj, tʃ/ etc., but none of these may be preceded by /s/ or followed by /r, l, j, w/ to form three-consonant clusters. There are gaps and restrictions[1] in the pattern, though one notices that these irregularities themselves seem to show a degree of 'sub-patterning', e.g. the non-occurrence of /pw, bw, dw, gw/ or of /tl, dl/; or the fact that if /j/ is the last of the consonants in the cluster, then only /uː/, or sometimes /ʊə/ or /ʊ/, can follow.

We might note several other sub-patterns which have emerged from the discussion above. For instance, /p, t, k/ versus /b, d, g/; /p, b/ versus /t, d/ versus /k, g/; /r, l, j, w/ 'going together' in much the same way as the stop-consonants went together.

The above brief look at one small area of the phonemic structure of English has already served to illustrate the complexity we referred to earlier, a characteristic we must expect to find, indeed, whenever we look closely at any aspect of a language. At all events, it seems indisputable that there is more than a simply phonetic, articulatory connection between these six stop-consonant phonemes; and further consideration of other patterns into which they enter (e.g. clusters at the ends of words) would certainly tend to support the contention.

If we now go on to look at the phonetics – i.e. at the allophones – of some of the oppositions derived from our pattern-formula, then we may find sub-systems operating here, too. For instance, in the pairs /pl-bl/ as in *plead-bleed*, /tr-dr/ as in *try-dry*, /kl-gl/ as in *clue-glue*, or /tj-dj/ as in *tune-dune*, in these oppositions the allophones of /r, l, j, w/ are VOICELESS after /p, t, k/, but VOICED after /b, d, g/. So we can say that part of the opposition at least is carried by the allophone of the neighbouring phoneme, rather than only by the allophone of the phoneme we have changed; and experiments have shown, for instance, that the perception of the

---

[1] There will be fewer of these if we allow borrowing from other languages, such as *Gwen* from Welsh; or non-R.P. forms like /tl,dl/ (instead of /kl,gl/) found in, e.g. Ulster; or rare examples of a pattern like *gule* for /gj/ or *dwarf, dwindle* for /dw/.

voiceless allophone of the SECOND phoneme is crucial for the identification of the first. Thus in /pli:d-bli:d/, we seem to 'hear' one word rather than the other more on the basis of the /l/ than on that of the /p/ or /b/.

If we accept this, then we can no longer view an English word as, on the phonological level, simply a row of phonemes in a permitted order, each with its allophone on the phonetic level; for we are obliged to recognize that the relationship between the phoneme-sequence and the corresponding sound-sequence may be, from the perception point of view, much more subtle than simply a case of phoneme no. 3 being represented and identified by allophone no. 3c, and so on. So we must be prepared to complicate our phoneme-idea, in practice, still further (another case where we need to do this is mentioned below).

Let us now continue our examples with a less general one – the phoneme /h/. This is rather different as regards the phonetics of its allophones, as we saw, from the other consonants, since there is not normally a stricture. Secondly, whereas the other fricatives seem to be 'paired' – /f-v, θ-ð, s-z, ʃ-ʒ/ – /h/ is not. Thirdly, it can occur only before a vowel (though note that /ʒ/ is also restricted, this time by non-occurrence at the beginning of a word). Fourthly, there is the question of the initial clusters /hj, hw/, and we will now go on to examine these two briefly.

The first of them, /hj/, patterns like the other clusters which end in /j/ in that it too must be followed by /u:/ (as in *Hugh*, *huge*, *humour*, etc.). But in many people's speech, what we actually hear for the cluster is a single sound, similar to the so-called '*ich*-Laut' in (some) German (e.g. in *mich*, *dich*, *sich*, etc.); this is the voiceless palatal fricative. Thus we have a situation in which TWO phonemes are realized by ONE sound; so again we must allow a further complication into our picture of the relationship between phonemes and sound-sequence. (We could conceivably claim, in fact, that English has another phoneme – let us write it '/ç/' – which is realized by this voiceless palatal fricative. This would allow us to retain the one-to-one relationship of phoneme and sound, but we would have to set up another phoneme for the sake of a very few words, all with /u:/. It seems preferable by comparison to treat it as /hj/, because the cluster fits relatively neatly into the pattern of consonant + /j/ + /u:/ that we have already discerned. Furthermore, some speakers do consistently say /hj/ as a sequence of two sounds – the first sound of *who* plus the first of *you*, more or less; other speakers, more significantly, sometimes say it as one sound, sometimes as two – for these people, therefore, we could not allow a phonemic opposition between '/ç/' and /hj/.)

The second cluster we are considering, /hw/, is similar to the first, in that there is often a single sound – this time a voiceless fricative, made with the rounded lips as the point of stricture, and also with tongue-raising at the back – functioning as the allophone simultaneously of the two phonemes. However, only a very restricted number of RP speakers use /hw/ consistently; most do not have it in their phonotactic rules, except occasionally in very studied or carefully 'correct' speech. Where it does occur in RP, we would probably want to regard it as a 'spelling-pronunciation' – i.e. a pronunciation which supposedly follows the orthography rather than the other way round. Compare *whales* with *Wales*, *which* with *witch*, *whiled* with *wild*, etc. The reduction of /hw/ to /w/, incidentally, does not appear to be a modern tendency – an example of the 'lazy', 'corrupt' speech of to-day – but to have a long pedigree in the history of the language. Note also that speakers of e.g. Irish and Scottish English do consistently maintain the /hw-w/difference reflected in the *wh-w* spellings, and this is one of the ways in which those accents are definably different from most forms of RP.

Let us now turn to the /r/, noticing first that in many other accents of English – e.g. 'West Country', Scottish, Irish and most forms of American – the occurrence of (their) /r/ is much less restricted than /r/ is in RP. In these accents, /r/ occurs before both pauses and consonants, as well as before vowels, whereas RP (as we have seen) permits it only when a vowel follows immediately. The device which many English pop-singers adopt, of using an American type of r-sound in all these positions, succeeds in giving their pronunciation a characteristically 'mid-Atlantic' flavour – envied and copied by some, deplored as almost unpatriotic by others.

In RP, we cannot say that /r/ 'does not occur at the end of a word', as we can in the case of /h/, for if a word (e.g. when said on its own) ends in one of the vowels /ə, ɜː, ɪə, ɛə, ʊə, ɔː, ɑː/, then we find an /r/ added when another word beginning in a vowel follows immediately. For example, the words *porter, fur, beer, care, tour, core, star* are pronounced /pɔːtər, fɜːr/ etc. in phrases like *the porter isn't here, fur on the back, beer all the time, care about it, tour England, core an apple, Star and Garter*. Notice that in these examples there is an r-letter in the spelling; but in addition there are a fair number of words which end with one of these vowels, but do NOT have an r-letter to represent the/r/-phoneme; e.g. *China* /tʃaɪnə/ (and many other names of countries), *idea* /aɪdɪə/, *Shah* /ʃɑː/, *draw* /drɔː/, etc. It should not surprise us that there are commonly-heard pronunciations like 'China-r and America', 'the very idea-r of it', 'Shah-r of Persia', 'draw-r a picture', and so on. These are often condemned by purists as containing an 'intrusive *r*', which the word 'does not really have'. Apart from the confusion here about the nature of written letters (which are after all a representation of the spoken form, not the other way about), we should remember that the vast majority of RP speakers use this 'linking *r*' both when the spelling includes the letter and when it does not – a fact publicly deplored in many a 'letter to the Editor', but nonetheless probably widespread in the speech of the writers of such letters. There is clearly a rule in RP (a phonological rule, of course, not a spelling one) of the kind formulated at the beginning of this paragraph. Young children learning RP, along with the rest of the language, do not of course have the process complicated by the orthography, and their speech consistently reflects the rule in words new to them, e.g. proper names like *Anna* ('Anna-r isn't coming'), *Shaw* ('Johnny Shaw-r and his brother'), and so on. However, children later learn that some of these forms are disapproved of by the adult world, in particular by parents and schoolteachers; they learn furthermore that some instances of 'intrusive *r*' are regarded as more objectionable than others – e.g. in our examples above, 'China-r and America' is much more often to be heard than 'draw-r a picture' among those who are careful that their pronunciation in public should sound 'correct'.

The result of all this is that many speakers of RP are inconsistent in their use of this /r/-feature; and the work of describing their usage is made more difficult by the operation of this type of non-linguistic factor.

We have seen something of the descriptive problems that arise in attempting statements about various parts of the English consonant-system. We shall now go on to consider some examples from the vowels, and perhaps we should bear in mind that there is some disagreement among linguists here (more at any rate than with the consonants). It is not so much a disagreement on the facts, of course, as on the analytical framework which should be used to describe them. A digression on the merits and salient features of various descriptions would be out of place in this context, and we shall therefore not attempt to argue the case for the schema adopted in the following paragraphs. However, it should be recognized that there is no one 'correct' or agreed way of handling the data.

The broadest division we can draw in the vowel-system is between 'long' and 'short' vowel-phonemes, that is between /iː, ɑː, ɔː, uː, ɜː, eɪ, aɪ, ɔɪ, ɑʊ, əʊ, ɪə, ɛə, ʊə/ on the one hand, and /ɪ, e, æ, ʌ, ɒ, ʊ, ə/ on the other (see list on p 42). This division is made on the basis, once again, of both the phonetics and the phonology. To take the latter first, we have already seen that the 'long' vowels may occur at the ends of words – *do, die, dare*, for example – whereas the 'short' vowels normally do not (with the exception of /ə/, which is a special case in other ways, too). We have also seen that only the 'short' vowels can occur before /ŋ/; here the exception is /ʊ/ (which is again exceptional in that it cannot begin a word). Secondly, as regards the phonetics (i.e. the ALLOPHONES) of the vowels, the main descriptive point to be made is that the 'long' vowels are pronounced relatively LONG in syllables (particularly accented syllables) which have a 'voiced' consonant at the end; and relatively SHORT in those with a 'voiceless' consonant at the end – compare *feed* with *feet, maze* with *mace*, for instance. Length variation is much less marked among the allophones of a 'short' vowel, for the nature of the following consonant does not appear to affect it to any very noticeable extent – compare *bid-bit, as-ass*, where the vowel-sounds may well be of equal length. (The list of 'key-words' on p 42 gives further examples.) Earlier, we used vowel-length as one of the criteria for separating out 'voiced' and 'voiceless' consonant-phonemes; and, conversely, we have now used this division of the consonants to help us separate out 'long' and 'short' vowel-phonemes. The systems thus interlock and, in part, define each other.

We are again faced with a terminological difficulty here, in that we are using a pair of adjectives on two levels: (a) the phonological, where 'long' and 'short' refer to different classes of vowel-phonemes; and (b) the phonetic, where allophones are long or short in the everyday sense of 'relative time'. English has no other suitable pair of adjectives, and we have therefore had to make do with the typographical device of enclosing the words in inverted commas where they refer to the phonology. Thus the 'long' vowels have both long and short allophones, the 'short' vowels only short; again the two levels do not 'match'. Similarly, 'voiced' and 'voiceless' consonant-phonemes, as we saw earlier, do not always fit with the phonetic classes of voiced and voiceless sounds; nor indeed did vowels and consonants fit with vowel-sounds and consonantsounds, though there at least we could use two sets of terms.

Looking again at the length-differences in the vowel-sounds, we can see another case in which a change from one phoneme to another is perceived mainly through the allophone of the

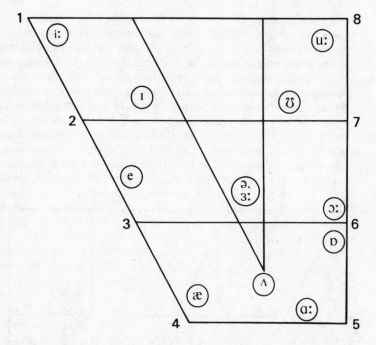

Fig. 2.5. Cardinal Vowel Diagram, with English Vowels ('short' and 'long' simple only)

Each of the circles on the diagram represents the articulation of a typical allophone of the phoneme symbolized. The allophones of /ɔ:/ and /u:/ are almost always accompanied by lip-rounding; those of /ɒ/ and /ʊ/ usually by only slight rounding, and sometimes by none at all. (A similar diagram for the 'long' compound vowel-phonemes is given in Fig. 2.6)

neighbouring phoneme. In minimal pairs like *leaf-leave* (/li:f-li:v/), where the vowel-sound may be twice as long in the second word as in the first, this length-difference seems to be very important to the perception of the /f/, rather than the /v/, and thus the difference between the two words may well be carried rather by the length of the /i:/-allophone than by the /f/- or /v/-allophone. Again, our theory of phonemes will need to take account of the (frequent) cases of this kind.

The 'long' vowels divide up further, as we have already indicated, into two sub-groups: the SIMPLE VOWELS /i:, ɑ:, ɔ:, u:, ɜ:/, and the COMPOUND VOWELS /eɪ, aɪ, ɔɪ, aʊ, əʊ, ɪə, ɛə, ʊə/. By using these two new terms, we can reserve 'diphthong' for vowel-sounds which have an audible glide from one tongue-position (and/or lip-position) to another, and 'pure' for those vowel-sounds where the articulation is relatively stable. There is a tendency among some R.P. speakers, particularly perhaps those with a London background, to diphthongize /iː/- and /uː/-allophones (especially those used at the ends of words, e.g. *tea, two*). These diphthongal glides are very short, from a centralized Cardinal Vowel no. 1 (in the case of /iː/) or no. 8 (in that of /uː/) to a less centralized position – i.e. towards the Cardinal point (see Fig. 2.5). These variants can be described as DIPHTHONGS which are allophones of SIMPLE vowels. Conversely, we also find pure vowel-sounds

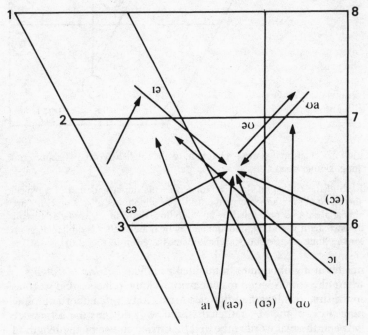

Fig. 2.6. Cardinal Vowel Diagram, with English Vowels ('long' compound only).

Each arrow represents the 'gliding' articulation of a typical allophone of the phoneme symbolized. The allophones of /ɔɪ/ and /ʊə/ (and /ɔə/) usually have slight lip-rounding at the start, those of /aʊ/ and /əʊ/ towards the end of the glide.

realizing the compound vowel-phonemes (again in some people's speech only): e.g. /ɪə, ʊə, ɛə/, as in *bearded, cure anything* (with 'linking *r*'), *daring*, etc.; in these cases we often hear a PURE vowel-sound realizing a COMPOUND vowel-phoneme.

The compound vowels can be sub-divided into three kinds (see Fig 2.6): those gliding towards an /ɪ/-type (/eɪ, aɪ, ɔɪ/), towards an /ʊ/-type (/aʊ, əʊ/), and towards an /ə/-type (/ɪə, ɛ ə, ʊə/). The last kind, along with /ɑː, ɔː, ɜː/ of the simple 'long' vowels, are of course subject to the rule concerning 'linking *r*' which was mentioned above.

Another pattern which has sometimes been discerned in the English vowels is the pairing of 'long' and 'short' phonemes, so that /iː/ goes with /ɪ/, /ɑː/ with /æ/, /ɔː/ with /ɒ/, /uː/ with /ʊ/ and /ɜː/ with /ə/ (the other two 'short' vowels, /e/ and /ʌ/, are left without a 'partner'). The reasons for doing this are partly phonetic resemblances – e.g. the articulatory differences between /iː/ and /ɪ/ are similar to those between /uː/ and /ʊ/ (see Fig. 2.5). Partly they involve the different phonemic forms a word may take when unstressed – e.g. *sir* when stressed is /sɜː/ but its 'weak' form is usually /sə/; stressed *been* /biːn/ may similarly become unstressed /bɪn/; etc. And partly the reasons are MORPHOPHONEMIC – i.e. concerned with those phoneme-differences which are correlatable with grammatical (or specifically 'morphological') changes: for instance, to produce the negative form of *can* /kæn/ and *shall* /ʃæl/, one of the phoneme-changes in R.P. is that from /æ/ to /ɑː/ – thus *can't* /kɑːnt/ and *shan't* /ʃɑːnt/. In spite of all this, we might hesitate before going on to say that for instance /iː/ and /ɪ/ belonged to the same phonological unit – the same 'super-phoneme' – since the link between them is by no means CONSISTENTLY evident. There are relatively few examples in English (though probably they occur with some frequency) of these linked forms, whether the link is a matter of accentuation or of morphological change. However, there certainly are patterns to be discerned of this type, even if they are only partial ones.

We have so far ignored the question of the relation of vowel and consonant, on the one hand, with SYLLABLES on the other. The subject is a complex one, and we shall only note here, and accept, the generally-held assumption that each vowel-phoneme belongs to a separate syllable, i.e. that a monosyllabic word will only have one vowel in it. Now, many if not most RP speakers usually pronounce words like *flier* and *flower* as MONOSYLLABLES. They could not, therefore, be analysed as two-vowel sequences, /aɪ-ə/ and /aʊ-ə/; it appears we must set up two more vowel-phonemes where we find that these two are not only different from each other, but different from all the other vowels. Let us transcribe them as /aə/ and /ɑə/, since their allophones would begin roughly where those of /aɪ/ and /aʊ/ begin, gliding in the direction of a central vowel-sound – an ⸢[ə]-type. The opposition between /aə/ and /ɑə/ would therefore be carried by the position of the highest point of the tongue at the start of the diphthong – with /aə/, this would be between Cardinal Vowel no. 4 and the central open position; with /ɑə/, between that position and Vowel no. 5 (see Fig. 2.6). It is worth noting that a system of this kind fits into the analysis of the vowels we proposed above – we would simply have added two more 'long' vowels (of the sub-class 'compound' and the sub-sub-class 'gliding towards an [ə]-type'), without therefore being forced to elaborate new categories; in a sense, these two new phonemes would fill 'gaps' in the system we have already outlined.

Two-syllable pronunciations of /aɪ-ə/ and /aʊ-ə/ do exist, but they are characteristic of a very careful, deliberate style which is recognized as a departure from that of ordinary conversation. Usage also varies here, in that not all speakers will reduce the two syllables to one in the same situations; and the grammar may be a factor in which words a speaker reduces first – *higher* is perhaps less likely to be reduced to a monosyllable (/haə/) than is *hire*, because it has two grammatical 'bits' – *high* and the comparative suffix-*er*. However, there are certainly many people who distinguish reduced /aɪ-ə/from reduced /aʊ-ə/, and both of these from /ɑː/; these speakers have sets of three (minimally different) monosyllabic words, such as the triplet *tire*, *tower* and *tar*. Other speakers use a different pattern: they have another 'long, simple vowel – we could write it as /aː/ for /aɪ-ə/ in words like *flier* and *tire*, and use /ɑː/ for /aʊ-ə/ in words like *flower* and *tower* (thus no longer distinguishing between e.g. *tower* and *tar*, *cowered* and *card*, etc.). Others again use /ɑː/ for all these words, and *tire*, *tower* and *tar* become homophones.

The language appears to be particularly fluid in this area; and there are other cases too where a reduction in the number of syllables, in ordinary, rapid, colloquial speech, produces forms which it is difficult to fit into a 'static' descriptive framework.

The syllable-reduced forms we have been discussing are also examples of another descriptive problem: how to account for changes taking place at the moment in the system being described. We saw in chapter one of this book that the linguist is usually concerned with 'synchronic' description – that is, with the language as it is (or was) at one point in time. However, the truism that 'spoken languages are permanently in a state of change' applies to the sound-system as much as to the grammar or the vocabulary. In most of our discussion so far, we have assumed relative stability in the systems we have chosen to exemplify, but this cannot always be done, as we saw with the /aɪ-ə/ and /aʊ-ə/ reductions. Before leaving the subject of the vowel-phonemes, we shall look at two further cases where the phonology seems to be changing.

First, the vowel /æ/. This has a LONG allophone (most often heard in monosyllables with /b, d, g, ʒ, m, n/ at the end), whereas the regular 'short' vowel pattern is for very little length variation to take place; examples are *cab, stand, rag, badge, Sam, pan*. The allophones of other 'short' vowels differ very little in this respect – the similarity in the length of the vowel-sounds in *pot-pod* or *sit-Sid* contrasts with the short-long difference in those of *sat-sad* or *pat-pad*. One speaker's habits may differ from another's, and differ again from one situation to the next, so that any single comprehensive statement about the pattern of long and short /æ/-allophones in RP would almost certainly be over-generalized. The most we can say here is that there clearly exists a tendency to lengthen the vowel-sound of /æ/ before some 'voiced' consonants, particularly in monosyllables. (One explanation that has been proposed for this contemporary tendency is that since the distinction between /æ/ and /e/ (in e.g. *sad* and *said*), is carried simply by a small difference in tongue-height, it is being 'reinforced' by the addition of a further phonetic feature – length, already used elsewhere in the vowel-system and thus 'ready to hand', as it were.)

Another change taking place within present-day RP is the loss of the compound vowel /ɔə/. This phoneme has not been included in our earlier discussion because its disappearance seems already well under way: most speakers of RP (particularly younger people) probably do not use it at all, at least in ordinary colloquial speech. Words hitherto pronounced with /ɔə/ now have /ɔː/; thus the distinction between e.g. *pour* and *paw* (/ɔə/ and /ɔː/), *bored* and *board, lore* and *law*, etc. has been lost, and these are now pairs of homophones. There is a related tendency, though perhaps less far advanced as yet, for /ʊə/ also to be replaced by /ɔː/. Thus many speakers of RP nowadays say e.g. *sure* and *poor* as /ʃɔː/ and /pɔː/ (i.e. the same as *Shaw* and *paw*), though the number who have no /ʊə/ left at all is probably still quite small – pronunciations of e.g. *cure* and *tour* as /kjɔː/ and /tɔː/ (rather than with /ʊə/) tend still to be regarded as 'affected'. We might feel less wary about making a firm statement here than in the cases of the syllable-reduced forms or of the long /æ/-allophone; in a fairly general variety of colloquial RP, there is no /ɔə/ phoneme, and occurrences of /ʊə/ are relatively infrequent.

We shall now leave the subject of phonemics, and move on to a different but related area of English phonology. This is the area of so-called NON-SEGMENTAL features – i.e. features which extend over one OR MORE THAN ONE phoneme, over phoneme-structures like syllables, words, and longer stretches of the utterance.

The first of these features is STRESS. This is roughly defined here as relatively greater energy of articulation expended on a syllable (said to be STRESSED) as compared with other, less-energetically articulated syllables (said to be UNSTRESSED) in the immediate environment. This stressed syllable will be HEARD as louder and more sonorous. This is a rough and ready categorization of syllables (e.g. how much greater is 'greater', and how is it to be measured in ordinary speech-situations?); but we can sometimes supplement it, or help to confirm a decision as to whether a syllable is stressed or not, in at least two ways. First, we can examine the allophones of the phonemes in that syllable – e.g. if a 'long' vowel allophone is not as long as it might be in this phonemic context, or if the initial /p, t, k/-allophone is unaspirated, then the syllable is probably to be judged 'unstressed', since the features of (maximum) vowel-sound lengthening and of aspiration are particularly associated with stress. Secondly, in many cases we can also check on the choice of the phonemes themselves. A number of common words in English have more than one phonemic 'shape', a STRONG FORM and one or more WEAK FORMS: for instance, *can* in 'You *can* tell' is the strong form /kæn/, but in '*You* can tell' it is weak – /kən/; *does* is strong, /dʌz/, in '*Does* he like it?' but a weak /dəz/ in 'Does *he* like it?'; similarly *will* is strong /wɪl/ or weak /(ə)l/, *been* is /biːn/ or /bɪn/, *an* is /æn/ or /(ə)n/, and so on. In most cases, the use of a strong form, where there is a choice, correlates with the syllable concerned being stressed.

However, it is comparatively rare to find stress being used on its own to carry a major contrast in meaning, without the help of other non-segmental features. When syllables make use of stress alone, its function is usually no more than to impart a rhythmic 'beat' to the utterance. Stress is significant much more often when working together with a second non-segmental feature, PITCH. Pitch is the name given to the auditory effect of changes in the rate at which the vocal cords vibrate. That is, during a VOICED sound (for practical purposes the voiceless sounds do not have pitch at all) the vocal cords allow air through in short bursts between the closures, and this gives to the sound-wave a FUNDAMENTAL FREQUENCY (to use the physical term), measured in cycles per second, or Hertz (Hz).

We do not perceive a sound-wave as a series of vibrations with a certain frequency, however, but as a musical note – a pitch – which we perceive as (a) 'high' or 'low' relative to what we know, or expect, of the speaker's pitch-range; women and children will have 'higher voices' than men, and some individuals differ from the average within these groups, e.g. 'he's got a very deep voice, for a child'. We also perceive pitch relatively in another sense, as (b) 'higher than', 'lower than', or 'the same level as' neighbouring pitches.

The pitch of a syllable may be LEVEL; or it may glide up or down from one level to another (a RISE or a FALL), or quite often up and then down (a RISE-FALL), or the reverse (a FALL-RISE); and occasionally it may even go in three directions – up, then down, then up again, though this 'rise-fall-rise' seems to be sufficiently rare in English for us to disregard it here. An utterance may contain anything from one to many syllables, and each syllable will have either a level pitch or one of the above gliding pitches. These pitches are not of course random, but organized into a systematic sequence, PATTERNED, and it is these patterns which are known in phonology as INTONATION.

The difference in intonation between (rising) '*Really*, Mr Jones?'[1] and (falling) '*Really*, Mr Jones!' is a matter of a choice which the language offers the speaker, a choice from among several permitted possibilities, each with a different meaning in the particular context. Such a contrast in meaning is brought out by a more specific example, such as the following: a wife's request for an opinion – 'Do you like my new dress?' – might be answered by her husband with the monosyllabic 'Yes'. If he said this with a rise-fall, it would imply 'It's *very* nice'; if with a fall-rise, it would imply 'Yes . . ., but . . .'; and there would of course be a number of other possibilities. The wife's reaction to the first *yes* will be considerably more favourable than to the second, yet the vocabulary, the grammar, the stress and of course the phonemes are the same in each case. In this example, pitch alone (working within the intonation-system) has distinguished sharply between two very different types of meaning; and the wife is quite justified in reacting with pleasure (or annoyance) to the response, for the husband has deliberately (if unconsciously) chosen an intonation-pattern from the range of possibilities which English allows him, to fit the meaning he wishes to convey.

Though the non-segmental features of stress and intonation can,

---

[1] From this point, the PROMINENT WORD(S) in these examples will be *italicized*.

as we have seen above, be considered separately, they seem to work very much together in English. Once we know what the intonation-pattern is, and how it is distributed over the syllables, then we can to a large extent predict which of them will be stressed. For instance, in the sentence 'But you said *John* did it!' the information that there is a fall in pitch on *John* means automatically that that syllable is stressed; but the reverse is not true – knowing a syllable is stressed does not tell us anything about its pitch.

Now within an intonation-pattern, it will be noticed that changes – jumps or glides – in pitch occur, on at least one of the syllables. (If the utterance contains only one syllable, as in the husband's *Yes* above, a pitch-change will necessarily occur on that syllable, since one such change is obligatory in every utterance.) It will also be noticed that such syllables are, obligatorily again, stressed. In our last example above, *John* was of course the syllable treated in this way. This concentration of pitch-features and stress is called ACCENT; its function appears to be to 'emphasize' a particular word (or the only word) in the utterance, to make it stand out as important. To put it another way, a word is made PROMINENT by accenting one of its syllables, or prominence is REALIZED by accent; and accent is a combination of phonetic features – (a) stress (with its associated vowel-sound length, aspiration, etc.), and (b) pitch. So not only can speakers choose which intonation-pattern to use, but also which words they are going to make prominent; not only which pitches will make up the pattern, but how they will be distributed over the words and syllables.

However, there is one area where a choice cannot normally be made at all, namely the way multi-syllabic (or POLYSYLLABIC) words are made prominent. Each English polysyllable is made prominent by accenting ONE of its syllables, and there is no choice as to which one; the ACCENTUAL PATTERN of such words is fixed, and learnt along with their phonemic structure, grammatical status, lexical meaning, etc., when they are first assimilated into the learner's vocabulary. Thus '*ac*cident' is made prominent by accenting the first syllable, 'e*norm*ous' by accenting the second, 'abso*lute*ly' by accenting the third, 'responsi*bil*ity' by accenting the fourth, etc. Often, the morphological structure of the word will determine, or help to determine, its accentual pattern; e.g. *responsibility* is like other words with that type of suffixation (*-ibility*, *-ability*) in being accented on the *-bil-*; and there are a large number of cases like this. However, most English speakers are familiar with the dilemma of knowing a word (in the sense of knowing its place in the grammar, its meaning, and its spelling), but of being uncertain how to pronounce it. This uncertainty is very often about where the accent should go in the word (hence the controversy over the pronunciation '*con*troversy' as opposed to 'con*trov*ersy'); and as a result, the uncertainty is also about the phonemes – compare those of /ˈkɒntrəvɜːsi/ and /kənˈtrɒvəsi/ (the mark ' being used here before an accented syllable). Apart from marginal cases like this, our statement above that the accentual pattern of English polysyllables is 'fixed' holds good; dictionaries can indicate it, by various typographical devices, and teachers of the language can prescribe it, without much fear of contradiction. So if we say, for instance, 'That's her *signature*', we have chosen to use (apart from the grammar and the vocabulary) a certain intonation-pattern, and also to make *signature*, rather than *that's* or *her*, the (only) prominent word; but the placement of the accent on the first syllable of *signature* is, as it were, done for us, in advance.

We can see from this that intonation in English, working together with stress, functions MEANINGFULLY in allowing the speaker to single out a particular word for emphasis; to prove the point with a minimal pair, contrast 'It's *his* book' (i.e. 'not *hers*') with 'It's his *book*' (i.e. 'not his *newspaper*'). But this is not the only way these non-segmental features can convey a difference of meaning. As we saw in our earlier husband-wife example, the two *Yes* responses differed substantially in meaning, yet their accentual pattern was of course identical (since there was only one syllable concerned, it was automatically accented). So the change was the result not of siting the accent on a different word, but of changing the pitch which helped to make up that accent, i.e. of changing the intonation-pattern. This type of meaning is often called ATTITUDINAL, because it is concerned with the attitude of the speakers towards the overall situation in which they are speaking. This 'situation' will include the nature of what has preceded in the conversation (or the fact that this utterance is the first), what grammar and vocabulary is being used, what words are made prominent, and so on, together with non-linguistic factors like the personal relationships between the participants in the conversation (whether as speakers or listeners), their age, sex, status, frame of mind, etc.; in addition, the utterance may be accompanied by non-verbal effects like gesture and facial expression, which seem to function on the fringes of the linguistic system, without actually taking part in it. All these factors – linguistic, non-linguistic, and 'fringe' – may play a part in the choice, and interpretation, of the speaker's intonation, and hence in the meaning of the utterance.

We assume that a change of intonation in a given situation will change the attitudinal meaning; we also assume, of course, that the same utterance in two different situations will imply different attitudes. For instance a *Good morning* may be interpreted between equals as merely friendly; the same greeting, with the same intonation, might very well seem over-familiar to a superior, or rather patronizing to a junior.

The conclusion we must come to is that here is an area of meaning that is almost impossible to cope with in its totality – there are too many variables, and too many of these are non-linguistic, and unamenable to systematization and labelling. The best we can do, probably, is to show that a change in intonation-pattern is capable, all other variables remaining constant, of differentiating between one general type of meaning and another; but we shall not be able to state at all clearly either the nature of each type or the degree of difference between them. Furthermore, it is only in a specific situation, real or imagined, that we can show even this to be true; the notion that a certain intonation is associated with a certain range of meanings in English, without reference to the situation in which it occurs, seems a doubtful one. For instance, if it is claimed that 'a fall tends to sound definite' we can easily find a counter-example in which the meaning seems to incline rather to a wondering, or questioning, or puzzled kind of attitude. Similarly, it seems likely that ANY English intonation may occur with ANY grammatical structure, provided only that the situation and the speaker's attitude to it make that particular combination of syntax and intonation appropriate. There is after all an infinite range of situations and attitudes; and we should not rule out any combination at all until we find a sentence which it is IMPOSSIBLE to imagine being said with a certain intonation-pattern.

We have so far seen that English intonation functions in two main ways: (a) in conveying attitudinal meaning ('Really!' vs. 'Really?', 'Yes!' vs. 'Ye-es . . .'), and (b) in emphasizing specific words in the utterance ('*That's* her signature' vs. 'That's *her* signature' vs. 'That's her *signature*'). We should also note that the latter effect in particular – prominence – may have ramifications of meaning far beyond the obvious points (that in saying, for instance, 'That's *her* signature', the speaker is also saying his concern is with WHOSE signature it is, and with the fact that it is *hers* rather than someone else's). In addition to this, he is implicitly claiming that the listener and himself already share an item of knowledge – they both know that what is in question is a signature, and which one it is they are talking about. The effect of this is to link what is now being said with what has been said (or in other ways experienced); it engages the listener in the speaker's perception of what they do or do not share; and thus the 'meaning' is very much more than that the speaker is particularly concerned (to continue the above example) with the identity of the signatory.

To take a further example: a telephone number, say 633733, is read out (in two groups of three figures each) as 'six double three, *seven* double three'. The prominence on *seven* indicates to the listener that this is the new information, and hence that what follows is already known, i.e. that it is *double three* again. Similarly, the well-known case of football results: 'Arsenal 2, *Chelsea* . . .', which pools enthusiasts will mark as a draw without waiting to hear that Chelsea also scored two goals – they have already been implicitly told that *Chelsea* is the new information, and thus that what follows will be simply a repeat.

Furthermore, intonation may often serve to help delimit grammatical units – phrases, clauses, sentences – to the extent that the beginnings and ends of intonation-patterns tend very frequently to coincide with the beginnings and ends of such units. And where there is potential ambiguity between two grammatical structures, the intonation – the choice of patterns, and where they begin and end – may well serve to disambiguate them. For instance, compare the intonation of *The police, who wear para-military uniforms, are all trained in riot control* with that of *The police who wear para-military uniforms are all trained in riot control*, in which the distinction between so-called NON-DEFINING and DEFINING relative clauses can be clearly signalled in speech by the intonation-patterns and their distribution over the utterance (just as it is in the conventional written form by the punctuation or its absence).

We shall now move on to consider, in summary fashion, the nature of the intonation-patterns which carry out the above functions; that is, how the patterns are structured internally, and how they are made up out of their component parts – syllables, each with a gliding or level pitch.

If we start with utterances consisting of a single monosyllable, as being the shortest and easiest to handle, we find of course, that the word concerned – e.g. *Yes, No, Now, Ten, Up, Thanks* – is prominent (by definition, since every utterance has at least one prominent word), and that its single syllable is therefore accented; and this means the syllable will display both stress and pitch-features. The gliding pitches we have mentioned are all allowed to occur here: fall, rise, rise-fall and fall-rise. There are probably sub-divisions to be made also, into e.g. a fall which starts about the middle of the pitch-range and falls to the bottom (LOW fall), as against another which starts towards the top and falls similarly to a low pitch (HIGH fall), as against a third which starts high but only falls as far as a middle pitch (MID fall); thus:

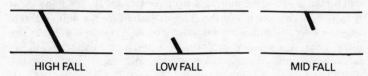

If we could show that the potential meaning-difference between any two of these three is of the same order of importance as that between e.g. a fall and a rise, then we should have to increase our number of basic possibilities. Of course, the kind of judgement we will have to make is more or less subjective and arbitrary; there is no easy way of measuring this 'importance'. We may feel confident in claiming that a rise is sufficiently different from a fall, in their potential effect on the attitudinal meaning, for us to place these two unequivocally in separate phonological units (here, inton-ation-patterns); but there will always be cases where our in-tuition does not provide a clear answer – for instance, if two rises both start at the same pitch, but the first finishes slightly higher than the second, do these belong to TWO patterns, or varieties of the same one? and how much difference must there be between the finishing pitches to make a 'significant' opposition? This is mark-edly different from the minimal pairs we found in phonemics, where we were able to ignore gradations of meaning – *bet* and *bat* were simply 'different words with different meanings'. If we wish to treat intonation also from this general point of view – in terms of 'phonological units' to which individual pitches or pitch-sequences 'belong', or which they 'realize' – then we shall have to accept a substantial degree of arbitrary simplification. With this in mind, and for the sake of brevity, we shall assume here that *Yes* and *No*, etc., generally occur with only four significantly different intonation-patterns: falling to a low pitch; rising from a low pitch; rising from a fairly low pitch, then falling back to low; and falling to low, then rising again. The following represent typical varieties:

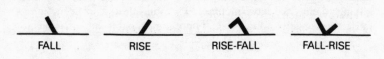

If we now increase the length of the utterance by adding un-accented syllables after the accented one, ('*Yes*, Mary', '*No*, thank you', etc.), we can show that the pitch of these is automatically dictated by the nature of the pattern chosen on the accented syllable. Thus in '*Yes*, Mary' the two (unaccented) syllables of *Mary* will be low and level if there is a FALL on *Yes*, or on ascending steps if there is a RISE starting there. If the pattern is a rise-fall or a fall-rise, the two unaccented syllables as it were 'carry' the shape of the pitch movement up or down:

FALL   RISE   RISE-FALL   FALL-RISE

(The accented syllables are represented by the mark O .) In utterances like these, the accented syllable is called the NUCLEAR SYLLABLE and any unaccented syllables following it comprise the TAIL. The nuclear syllable, together with any tail-syllables, com-prise the NUCLEUS of the intonation-pattern. So '*Really*, Mr Jones!', one of our earlier examples, can now be seen as having an in-tonation-pattern consisting of a nucleus, which itself consists of a nuclear (accented) syllable (*Real-*) followed by four (unaccented) syllables in the tail (*-ly Mister Jones*). Also, our monosyllabic ex-amples like *Yes* and *No* can be seen as having patterns consisting of a nucleus with only a nuclear syllable, and no tail.

If we go on to look at still longer utterances, we shall find that for practical purposes they ALL have a nucleus at the end. That is, they (or rather their intonation-patterns) will finish with an accented syllable, with or without unaccented syllables following it, which behaves just like the examples above. So in 'Was he *really* allowed that?' the nucleus begins on the accented *real-* and is continued by the tail syllables *-ly allowed that*; i.e. from *really* onwards the pattern is just the same as in '*Really*, Mr Jones?' If the accented syllable begins in the middle of a word, then the nucleus still starts there – English intonation seems to have very little respect for word-boundaries; thus in 'It's *enormous*' or 'That's *ridiculous*' the nuclear syllable is the second one in the prominent word. So an English intonation-pattern always ends in one of a limited number of sub-patterns – nucleus-types; we have assumed four such types here.

However, there may be syllables BEFORE the nucleus, as in several of the examples above; and one of these, or more than one, may also be accented. If the utterance does have more than one accented syllable (which implies of course more than one prominent word), then it is the LAST of these syllables which will begin the nucleus. For instance, in '*I* don't know *why* he's *coming*', where *I*, *why* and *com-* are all accented, *com-* is the nuclear syllable (and *-ing* therefore the tail). Now in cases like this, an important point is that we can vary the type of nucleus (e.g. from rise to rise-fall) WITHOUT altering what precedes it; and, vice-versa, this pre-nuclear sub-pattern, or HEAD, can be varied WITHOUT altering the nucleus-type. Furthermore, a change from one type of head to another will bring a different attitudinal meaning, just as in the case of a change of nucleus-type.

All the ways in which various sequences of accented and un-accented syllables may be disposed on the pitch-scale, in each type of head, are too complex to be displayed here. The following are no more than examples of four common types; the only variable is the pitch of the head-syllables, yet each of these utterances would carry a different attitudinal meaning in the same situation:

I don't know *why* he's *coming*

There remains a further sub-pattern to be discerned – the PRE-HEAD. This comprises any unaccented syllables before the first accented one. In 'It's a *terribly hard job*', for example, the head begins on the third syllable, and the first two – *It's a* – make up the pre-head; in 'That's *lovely*', the nucleus begins on the second syllable, and the first is the pre-head. It will be found that the pre-head too can vary independently (of both the head and the nucleus), and vary meaningfully. In the following two examples, only the pitch of *It's a* differs, hence can be responsible for a change in attitudinal meaning:

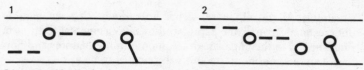

It's a *terribly hard job*

So our intonation-pattern may consist of a nucleus alone, e.g. '*No*-one'; or the nucleus may be preceded by a pre-head: 'There was *no*-one'; or by a head: '*Robert said* there was *no*-one'; or by both pre-head and head: 'But *Robert said* there was *no*-one'. Cases like these, and all the others discussed above, are comparatively simple ones – indeed, perhaps they give a misleading impression of a rather mechanical neatness; but there is no denying the subtlety and complexity of the way we use intonation and stress in English.

The choice of which words to make prominent, and of which intonation-pattern to use, is of CRUCIAL importance in our everyday use of the language, yet we are seldom explicitly aware of the role these choices play in our conversations. We say, 'It's not what he said, it's the way he said it that annoyed me', but this type of remark is the nearest we usually come to referring directly to the in-tonation-system – we lack a vocabulary for describing it. Our writing and printing, too, are largely inadequate for representing the non-segmental features – the use of italics, a question-mark, an exclamation-mark, a sequence of full stops, underlining and so on are rarely sufficient. The examples we have been quoting in this discussion of intonation were of course chosen to make maximum use of these typographical devices, but even so they are not un-ambiguous. Novelists find they need other means, in addition, of indicating stress and intonation, e.g. 'He said, coldly', 'She re-marked, in a wondering tone', 'His voice sounded oddly flat', and so on. Playwrights need to include directions to the actors, such as 'Mary (*enthusiastically*):' or 'Inspector (*sounding official and pompous*):'; indeed, one of the reasons for the wide range of inter-pretations which different actors bring to a part lies in the inability of the written medium – of the author's words – to specify in-tonation. Students of modern foreign languages need contact with native speakers of the language they are learning, since there is probably little to be found in textbooks on its intonation; and because the role of intonation is so little appreciated, foreign learners of, say, English will not often be judged by English speakers as having a foreign accent, if they use the wrong pattern, but rather as having the wrong attitude – a much more serious matter, in most situations. All in all, there seems little doubt that we tend to underestimate grossly the part played by non-segmental features in English; and in the linguistic description of those features and how they work an enormous amount still remains to be said.

We have now come to the end of this discussion of the 'sounds of English'. It has necessarily been brief, but little attempt has been made to gloss over the difficulty and complexity of the task which faces the descriptive linguist, in this area of language as indeed in any other. It should be clear that, to deal with even the limited examples we have chosen from the phonetics and phonology of English, we need to use our tools – the technical terminology – as precisely as possible. The everyday vocabulary for describing the sound-systems of a language tends far too often, as we have seen above, to vagueness and ambiguity. To do the job of even partial description properly, there seems little alternative to a painstaking, sometimes laborious regard for technicalities; otherwise we risk doing less than justice to an involved but fascinating subject.

3

MORPHOLOGY: THE FORMS OF ENGLISH

D. Allerton with M. French

I

INTRODUCTORY

1. WORDS AND MORPHS

In this chapter we shall present an outline sketch of English morphology and discuss some of the problems involved in our analysis. Morphology studies the forms of a language, in particular the forms its words take. By 'form' here we mean not simply the phonetic make-up of words but rather their structure in terms of grammatical or meaningful units.

The two-level nature or 'duality' of human language (as compared with, say, traffic signals) has already been discussed (in chapter 1): if we are to describe a language adequately, we need a set of basic units or building blocks for each level. This means we need a grammatical equivalent to the phoneme or phonetic distinctive feature.

Words themselves clearly have meaning and are used to build up sentences, but we cannot consider them as basic units because they are not always minimal – they are often susceptible to further analysis. Consideration of the words *clerk, tramp, worker, writer* reveals two words which are grammatically indivisible and two words, *worker* and *writer*, which can be analysed into meaningful parts *work, write* and *-er* 'person who undertakes the activity in question'. Since these parts are not themselves further analysable they are minimal meaningful elements or MORPHS.

Words like *clerk, soldier, work, write* which are not further analysable can be said to consist of a single morph and therefore to be SIMPLE words; further examples are *log, radio, delight, parliament, shine, one, for, red, exotic*. Words like *worker, writer* which consist of more than one morph can be called COMPOSITE; further examples are *boys, loved, lovable, inexpensive, football, dentist.* Since, as we indicated, morphology studies the way words are grammatically built up, it will have no direct interest in simple words: in fact the field of morphology can be defined as the structure of composite words.[1]

The first task of the morphologist, therefore, is to establish the morphs of the language: this is not without its problems. The principal characteristic of the morph is its meaningfulness, but how are we to decide whether elements are meaningful or not? It is not necessary that we should always be able to describe exactly the meaning of morphs – it is difficult enough to describe the meaning of some words, e.g. *the, than, to* (in *I want to*) – but we should insist that the contribution of each morph to the overall meaning remains constant in different environments. Thus while it is easy to recognize an element with recurrent semantic value in *re-establish, redevelop, recharge, re-cover* (= 'cover anew'), it is difficult to see any consistent meaning for the *re-* of *receive, relax, respect, recover* (= 'reacquire; resume normal state')[2] Similarly there is no semantic justification whatever for regarding *cartridge* as *cart* followed by *ridge* despite the virtual identity in phonetic form.

Our test of RECURRENT semantic value meets difficulties in face of the so-called UNIQUE MORPHS: these elements always occur with the same companion element, from which they are, therefore, strictly speaking, inseparable; the elements they accompany, however, demonstrate their morph status by occurring freely with the same meaning in other contexts. For example, although we recognize a recurrent element *-berry* /-bərɪ/ in *blackberry, strawberry, raspberry, cranberry,* etc. what are we to say of *rasp-* /rɑːz-/ and *cran-* /kræn-/,[3] which occur only with *-berry*? Similarly, do we accept an element *-ation* in *ovation* on the grounds that this is an abstract noun and parallel to *protestation, quotation, starvation,* etc.? If so, what do we do with *ov-*, which has no independent existence whatever? Certainly *rasp-, cran-, ov-,* etc., are not fully-fledged morphs – at best they are unique morphs or quasi-morphs; nor are these normal occurrences of *-berry* and *-ation*. On the other hand we seem to be

---

[1] It should be noted that we distinguish between composite, compound and complex words. See below pp 77–8.

[2] Note that whereas the first group (*re-establish*, etc.) normally has initial /riː-/ the second group (*receive*, etc.) usually has initial /rɪ-/ (or even /rə-/).

[3] Not to mention the question of whether this *black-* and this *straw-* are the same as the ordinary words *black* and *straw*, or, for that matter, whether *-berry* is the same as the independent word *berry*.

missing something, if we regard *cranberry, ovation* and their fellows as nothing more than simple morphs.

2. *MORPHS AND MORPHEMES*

We have defined morphs without explicit reference to their phonological form, but it is natural to expect that any linguistic sign should have a consistent form so that the language may function efficiently. We do find, however, that some functional elements vary in form from one context to the next: thus the terminal -(*e*)*s* of *cats, dogs, horses* has the regular meaning 'more than one' yet has three different phonological forms, /-s, -z, -ɪz/. The three forms never contrast, having identical semantic value, and they may be regarded as members of the same morph-class or MORPHEME. The different morphs of a single morpheme are said to be its ALLOMORPHS. The vast majority of English morphemes have a single allomorph, and for them there is no real necessity to make a difference between MORPH and MORPHEME.

The allomorphs /-s, -z, -ɪz/ are phonologically conditioned in their occurrence, but if we view the -*en* /-ən/ of *oxen* as a member of the same plural morpheme, then its occurrence is morphologically conditioned, i.e. it is determined by the presence of the neighbouring morph *ox*.

Sometimes we meet morphs which are free variant allomorphs of the same morpheme: the word *plaque*, for example, has the variant forms /plæk/ and /plɑːk/ which are completely interchangeable; similarly the morpheme -*ness* with its alternative pronunciations /-nɪs/ and /-nəs/, e.g. *kindness* /'kaɪndnɪs, 'kaɪndnəs/.

Where the difference in form between morphs is more marked, linguists are less inclined to class them as belonging to the same morpheme. And very often, in such cases, this decision can be justified by finding a context where the two morphs contrast. Thus, although *un-* and *dis-* appear to be identical in meaning and morphologically determined in *unethical* and *dishonest*, they nevertheless contrast (at least for some speakers) in the environment -*interested*. (It could be maintained that in such cases we are dealing with two different words *interest(ed)*, each of which selects a different prefix.)

A further problem in morphemic analysis is homonymy, or, to be more specific, HOMOPHONY. We shall, for instance, meet some occurrences of the phonological sequence /reɪs/ (*race*) with the meaning 'competition in speed'; other occurrences will have a quite different meaning, roughly 'ethnic group'. In this case we are clearly justified in analysing two separate morph(eme)s, both having the same phonological form. On the other hand, the two senses of (*a*) *paper*, '(an) academic lecture' and '(a) newspaper' would probably be regarded by most speakers of English as specializations of the same basic element, an example of POLYSEMY. But what of the many problematical intermediate cases, e.g. *dressing* 'sauce; manure; bandages; stiffening agent', *chair* 'professorial appointment; seat', *suit* 'set of garments; legal action; set of playing cards'? Similarly for purely grammatical morphs: how many different elements do we recognize in the *-ing*s of *walking, meeting, towelling*?

3. *FREE AND BOUND*

Having appreciated, if not solved, some of the problems of morphs and morphemes, let us return to the question of morphological structure. We are, as we said, mainly concerned with composite words, and occurring in these we find two kinds of morph: some morphs occur elsewhere independently as simple words, e.g. the first part of *boy-s, love-d*, the second part of *un-fit, re-let*, and both parts of *foot-ball*; other morphs occur only within composite words, e.g. the second part of *boy-s, love-d*, the first part of *un-fit, re-let*. The first class of morphs are generally referred to as FREE, the latter as BOUND.

This whole definition rests, of course, on an understanding of the term WORD, which is largely given to us by an orthographical tradition that is unsure in many crucial cases, particularly compound words, e.g. *matchbox, horse-box, telephone box*. This means that the concept WORD really needs to be redefined in a more satisfactory way, something we unfortunately have no space for here. But we should state that the essence of word-ness is not so much the ability to stand alone (this is more a requirement for SENTENCE status); rather it is a question of the 'separability' of a morpheme in context. This can be tested by the operations of (1) insertion between it and its neighbours, (2) freedom of re-ordering with its neighbours, (3) omission of its neighbours.[1]

Since it is individual morphs which are bound, it is quite possible for a morpheme with more than one member to have (a) all allomorphs free, e.g. /græf, grɑːf/ *graph*, (2) all allomorphs bound, e.g. /-s, -z, ɪz/, etc. 'plural', (3) one or more bound, one or more

[1] In this respect cf. the 'separability' of English *I work*, French *je travaille* with Latin *labor-o*.

free, e.g. the free morph /tʃaɪld/ *child* and the bound morph /tʃɪld-/ (or /tʃ ld-/) *child-* (as in *children*) are both members of the same morpheme.

4. *ROOTS, STEMS AND AFFIXES*

Morphemes in most languages fall into two classes, ROOTS and NON-ROOTS, depending on whether they are primarily lexical or grammatical in function. If their lexical value is paramount (in which case they normally belong to relatively open classes, and the range of possible substitutions for them is large), they are termed ROOTS and generally have a clearly definable meaning, e.g. *boy*, *work, foot, love, dent-* (in *dentist, dental*), *Franco-* (in *Franco-German*, etc.). NON-ROOTS, on the other hand, normally have a more abstract, less specific meaning and have a relatively important grammatical function; they belong to relatively closed classes, e.g. *un-, -er*, plural -(*e*)*s, the*, infinitival *to*. AFFIXES may be defined as bound non-roots.

English affixes are always morphs belonging to a morpheme with no free allomorphs, and at least one of the morphemes to which they are added (to form a word) will have a free allomorph. Thus the *un-* of *unkind*, the *-er* of *worker*, the *-s* of *boys* and also the *-ren*[1] of children will all be affixes. The *-ist* of *violinist* will also be an affix of course, and it remains an affix even when it is added to another bound element like *dent-* in *dentist*.

The elements to which affixes are added are termed STEMS (or BASES, with 'stems' as one kind of 'base'). Roots may be regarded as minimal stems. For instance, although we recognize *boy-, worker-, football-* all as stems in the plural forms *boys, workers, footballs*, of these stems only *boy* is a root, the other two being further divisible.

In English most roots are free, but we have already met some which are bound, viz. *child-*, and *dent-*. An overall picture of the three types of morph might be presented thus:

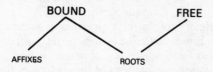

BOUND   FREE

AFFIXES   ROOTS

---

[1] This morph is an affix in accordance with the definition, since, although the /tʃɪld-/ *child-* to which it is attached is not free, the same morpheme does have a free allomorph /tʃaɪld/ *child*.

where each of the three lines corresponds to a class of morph. Strictly speaking, however, a fourth class would be necessary to account for the so-called 'structural words' like *the*, *of*, infinitival *to*, etc., which are free and yet have grammatical rather than lexical meaning. The following scheme might therefore be more appropriate:

	BOUND	FREE
GRAMMATICAL	AFFIXES	SIMPLE STRUCTURAL WORDS
LEXICAL	BOUND ROOTS	FREE ROOTS

5. *WORD COMPOSITION*

Amongst affixes there seem to be two fundamentally different kinds: DERIVATIONAL affixes, or simply DERIVERS; and INFLECTIONAL affixes, or simply INFLECTORS (also called INFLECTIONS[1]). DERIVED words (i.e. those formed with derivational affixes) may, in all contexts where they appear, be replaced by a simple word, to give a sentence of the same type, e.g. *untrue* may always have *strange, false, good, true* or some such word substituted for it; similarly *lovable (good, huge, dark), worker (clerk, man)*. INFLECTED words, on the other hand, at least in some contexts, can only have their place taken by a word of similar structure. This is because inflectional affixes normally play a part in expressing syntactic relations between words and phrases while derivational affixes do not. Thus inflectors play a prominent part in such sentential co-occurrence relations as *concord* and *government*. Examples of English inflections are -*s* 'noun plural', -*ing* 'gerund/participle'. We may observe that neither *boys* nor *playing* may be replaced by a simple word of the same grammatical class in such an utterance as:

The boys were playing outside.

In other words: *boys* may not be replaced by a simple noun; *playing* may not be replaced by a simple verb.

Since their primary role is the expression of meaning and relationships at the phrase, clause or sentence level, inflectors are not usually regarded as forming new lexical items. No one, for example, would expect separate explanations in the dictionary for *ride, rides,*

---

[1] This term has the disadvantage of also being used to name the process by which inflectional affixes are used.

rode and *ridden* or for *fox* and *foxes*,[1] but they might do for *hope* and *hopeful* or for *green, house* and *greenhouse*. The study of the production of new lexical items is usually referred to as WORD-FORMATION and involves two processes:

(i) DERIVATION: by which derivers are added to give derived words (strictly, stems), e.g. *hopeful, unkind, worker, gentlemanly*.
(ii) COMPOUNDING: by which stems are joined to other stems to give COMPOUND words (strictly, stems), e.g. *greenhouse, football, washing machine, football player*.

Composite words with more than two elements may include both processes, derivation and compounding, as in our examples *gentlemanly, washing machine, football player*. Why have we classed *gentlemanly* as derived but the other two as compound? A brief answer to this question would be: because of the respective syntactic relations between the parts of each word. To explain this we must refer briefly to two basic notions of syntactic analysis, IMMEDIATE CONSTITUENTS and TRANSFORMATIONS.

All languages have a hierarchically structured grammar, in the sense that each sentence can be said to consist of a sequence of elements, each of which in turn may consist of a sequence of elements, and so on. Morphemes are of course the ultimate constituents, but each element at each level (or rank) may be thought of as a construction, i.e. a set of immediate constituents. An example of the organized constituent structure of a whole sentence is:

EVEN FAIRLY NEW RECRUITS MAY SHOOT QUITE WELL

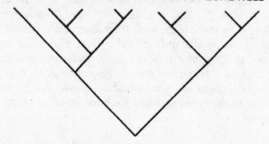

where, for instance, *fairly new recruits* has as immediate constituents *fairly new* and *recruits*.

---

[1] Such groups are often described as LEXEMES.

A transformation[1] is the explicit statement of a relationship holding between two structures which differ in their status and/or sequence of elements. For instance *The castle is attacked* or *Someone/ they attack(s) the castle* is clearly related to *the attack on the castle*, and they may be regarded as TRANSFORMS of each other.

The return to our examples: *gentlemanly* will be felt by most speakers to be related to *manly* or *friendly*, and there are no combinations of the type ⋆*gentle-brave*, ⋆*gentle-good* to compare it with; its immediate constituents are therefore *gentleman* and *-ly*, and it is a derived word with a compound stem. *Washing machine* already has a word division (at least an orthographical one), and certainly the relationship of *wash* to *-ing* must be closer than that of *-ing* to *machine*, as is evidenced by the transform *machine for washing*. Following similar procedures we must analyse *football bootmaking firm* (despite the orthography[2]) as:

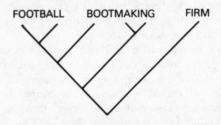

Thus the important point in studying word-formation is not so much to classify words of different structure as to describe the processes by which they are built up, and, when words are classified, it is in accordance with their immediate constituents. It goes without saying that inflectional affixes also build up words (though not to form new lexical items), and some linguists have used the term COMPLEX WORDS to refer jointly to derived and inflected words, i.e. to non-compound composite words. An overall classification of the types of word we have described may be presented thus:

---

[1] We here use the term in the narrower sense proposed by Z. S. Harris, *Language* 33, 283–340. We exclude mere realization or exponence relationships and do not necessarily presuppose a generative framework.

[2] We give the form used in *The Guardian* 23rd August, 1968 (back page). We personally would prefer *football-boot making firm*.

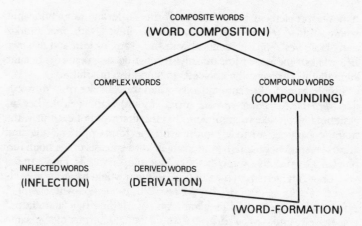

COMPOSITE WORDS
(WORD COMPOSITION)

COMPLEX WORDS

COMPOUND WORDS
(COMPOUNDING)

INFLECTED WORDS
(INFLECTION)

DERIVED WORDS
(DERIVATION)

(WORD-FORMATION)

6. *TYPES OF AFFIX*

Affixes may be further classified according to the serial order in which they occur relative to the stem. PREFIXES precede the stem, SUFFIXES follow the stem, and INFIXES interrupt the stem. English has both prefixes and suffices, but no infixes.[1] When infixes do occur, they have the effect of making discontinuous a stem (or root) which is normally an uninterrupted segment.[2] Some languages, e.g. Arabic, Hebrew, use infixation to such an extent that discontinuous roots are extremely common.

So far we have tended to assume that all our morphs will be concrete segments which are simply added together to produce words and sentences, as, for instance, *failure* /'feɪljə/ may be described as an addition of *fail* /feɪl/ and *-ure* /-jə/.[3] But how do we analyse such words as *closure* /'kləʊʒə/ and *departure* /dɪ'pɑːtʃə/, where the /-j/ of *-ure* has, so to speak, blended with the /-z/ of *close* and the /-t/ of *depart* to give /-ʒ-/ and /-tʃ-/ respectively? Where is the cut between the two morphs to be made? Apparently in the middle of this consonant in each case. We are faced with almost the

---

[1] At least no straightforward additive infixes. All cases of internal change might be said to manifest replacive infixation (e.g. *hang-hung*), and *stand-stood* might be described as a case of subtractive infixation (of the /n/). Cf. below.

[2] A language in which additive infixes occur is Tagalog (spoken in the Philippines). We may cite Bloomfield's examples (*Language*, p 218), viz. Tagalog /um/ and /in/ in the words /su'muːlat/ 'one who wrote' and /si'nuːlat/ 'that which was written' compared with the root /'suːlat/ 'writing'.

[3] Leaving out of account the question of stress.

opposite problem in a word like *children* /'tʃɪldrən/ (also/'tʃldrən/), where /tʃɪld-/ (or /tʃld-/) is clearly to be linked with *child* /tʃaɪld/ and where *-en* /-ən/ is identical with the /-ən/ of *oxen* and *brethren*. But what of the /-r-/? Presumably[1] it must be assigned to either the stem or the affix, but the choice is to some extent arbitrary.

Problems of a different type arise when we consider pairs of words like *shelf-shelve*, *sheath-sheathe*, *house* (noun)-*house* (verb). Let us assume, for the sake of argument, that the first word of each pair, the noun, constitutes a single morph, with the forms /ʃelf/, /ʃiːθ/ and /haʊs/ respectively, and that the second word consists of the noun form plus an affix meaning something like 'put into/on to a –'. How can the verb be segmented in each case? One solution would be *shelve* = /ʃel- + -v/, *sheathe* = /ʃiː- + -ð/, *house* = /haʊ- + -z/, where /ʃel-/, /ʃiː-/ and /haʊ-/ would be allomorphs of /ʃelf/, /ʃiːθ/ and /haʊs/ respectively, and /-v/, /-ð/, /-z/ would be allomorphs of the same morpheme 'put into/on to a –'. The drawback of this solution is that it ignores the fact that the verb is systematically formed from the noun by voicing the final (fricative) consonant. The question these data raise, then, is whether we should be prepared to assign morph status to phonetic features such as /VOICE/ rather than restrict ourselves to segments as we have done so far. Some linguists do accept morphs with such a form, calling this variety of affix SIMULFIXES.

Closely related to simulfixes are SUPERFIXES, which are said to occur when features or feature patterns extending beyond a single phoneme – over syllables and words – may be added or changed in a stem. English accentual patterns could be given this affixal status when they differentiate nouns from verbs, e.g. /'ɪnsʌlt/ (noun) from /ɪn'sʌlt/ (verb) *insult*; sometimes changes in the phonemic sequence are also involved, e.g. /'sʌbdʒɪkt/ (or /'sʌbdʒekt/) (noun) beside /səb'dʒekt/ (verb) *subject*. Depending which (if either) we take as the stem, /'--/ 'noun' or /-'-/ 'verb' could be regarded as a superfix.

7. *OTHER KINDS OF MORPH*

A further debatable practice in morphological analysis is the use of ZERO morphs and morphemes, which were first suggested by Sanskrit grammarians. A zero morph of the English noun plural morpheme has

---

[1] Hockett has proposed analysing an EMPTY MORPH /-r-/ in this case. But so long as we define a MORPH as a minimal meaningful unit, a meaningless morph like /-r-/ appears unacceptable. For cases where a single sound (or phoneme) seems to represent two morphemes, e.g. French *au* /o/ = 'à + le' Hockett has suggested the term PORTMANTEAU MORPH. *Departure, closure*, etc., could be said to involve OVERLAPPING realizations.

been assumed by some to occur in a word like *sheep* (PLURAL). It would be present in *The sheep are grazing* but absent in *The sheep is grazing*; it would be unclear whether or not it is present in *The sheep must graze*, since the sentence is ambiguous. Because of this difficulty some linguists prefer to say that the morpheme in question, e.g. 'plural', simply fails to occur with words of this type, e.g. *sheep*; for them this word would thus have neither a singular nor plural form but a 'numberless' one.

Zero morphs are at least normally members of morphemes with some positive manifestation. Zero morphemes, on the other hand, have a much more shadowy existence: they are by definition never realized. It is therefore with some apprehension that we view the possibility of a zero morpheme of singularity for English nouns. We would prefer to speak of the singular as being unmarked and the plural marked. English word-derivation offers some more plausible cases, viz. the identity in form of many nouns and verbs, e.g. *shame*, *fall*, considering the fact that many nouns are formed from verbs with an affix, e.g. *betray-al*, and vice versa, e.g. *fright-en*. But how is one to say in a purely synchronic account whether *shame*, for instance, is a verb and a zero-derived noun, or a noun and a zero-derived verb? Historical origins have no direct relevance in this matter.

Perhaps the most serious difficulties of description to confront us are those concerning such word-pairs as *foot-feet, dig-dug* and *heat-hot*. *Foot* /fʊt/ and *feet* /fiːt/ are clearly related, both semantically and grammatically, and to a certain degree they have a common phonetic form. At first sight, then, the best solution is to regard /f–t/ as a (discontinuous) root with two possible infixes, /-ʊ-/'singular' and /-iː-/ 'plural', but it obviously goes against the pattern of English nouns to have a singular morph – the singular is usually unmarked. It is, perhaps, preferable then to consider /fʊt/ as a single morph which is in conditioned variation with /f–t/ in the plural.

Both of the above treatments nevertheless depend on the acceptance of infixation and a discontinuous morph in the plural form *feet*. Some linguists argue that, since English does not have either of these phenomena except in this and other cases of vowel alternation, they are both unacceptable.[1] REPLACEMENT MORPHS or

---

[1] A solution which avoids these difficulties, but is unsatisfactory in other ways, is to posit a zero morph in the plural.

REPLACIVES have therefore been proposed. In the present case, for instance, *feet* could be said to consist of /fʊt/ plus /iː←ʊ/ (where ← is read as 'replaces'). It is clear, however, that replacement is an operation, not a segment, and thus cannot be added to other segments.[1]

8. *WHAT MODEL OF DESCRIPTION?*

Nevertheless we might instead regard replacement (also subtraction) as an alternative PROCESS to addition. This would presuppose a different model of grammatical description, in which, instead of describing formal items and the patterns they occur in, we rather list certain basic items and then give the operations or processes which they undergo. The former model of grammar has been termed ITEM AND ARRANGEMENT (I.A.) and the latter ITEM AND PROCESS (I.P.).

Whatever model of grammatical description we privately favour, however, we must constantly bear in mind that our aim is to present a picture that will render the complex phenomena of the English language intelligible. We shall endeavour therefore to give a straightforward account, our approach being uncommitted to any particular type of description and perhaps appearing ad hoc. In this way we hope to achieve a clear presentation of the material which leaves the choice of analysis to some extent to the reader.

II

INFLECTION

A. *GENERAL*

Some grammatical categories, e.g. noun plural, verb past tense, are obligatorily marked by the presence (or absence) of particular affixes; we have termed such affixes INFLECTORS. The inflectors of English are relatively few in number, so each has quite a high frequency of occurrence. It is therefore worthwhile giving an account of each individual affix.

From the functional point of view, the inflectors of English fall

---

[1] SUBTRACTIVE morphs have also been proposed, e.g. for French adjectives for which the masculine form may be extremely simply derived from the feminine – by the subtraction of the final consonant, e.g. /plat-pla/ *plate – plat*, /lɛd – lɛ/ *laide – laid*, /frɛʃ – frɛ/ *fraîche – frais*, etc.

naturally into two groups, NOMINAL and VERBAL; the only exceptions to this are the debatable cases of adjectival comparison (*-er*, *- est*) and adverbial *-ly*, both of which are partly derivational in character. The two groups are represented as follows:

NOMINAL
$\{-Z_1\}$ 'noun plural'
$\{-Z_2\}$ 'possessive'
$\{-Z_3\}$ 'noun substitute'
with possessive determiners
$\{-m\}$ 'oblique'
with pronouns
$\{-self\}$ 'reflexive; emphatic'

VERBAL
$\{-Z_4\}$ '3rd person singular present'
$\{-D_1\}$ 'past tense'
$\{-D_2\}$ 'past participle'
$\{-ıŋ\}$ *'participle/gerund'*

The braces { } mark a morpheme label. In the field of inflection we shall find it most convenient to refer to morphemes in this way, since some inflectors vary considerably in their phonetic (and orthographical) form. We have adopted as morpheme labels either the usual phonemic form e.g. $\{-ıŋ\}$ or (where there is phonologically conditioned variation) a morphophonemic formula e.g. $\{-Z_1\}$. In those cases where there is partial or complete homophony between affixes, we have used subscript numerals to distinguish the different morphemes. For instance all four morphemes $\{-Z_1\}$, $\{-Z_2\}$, $\{-Z_3\}$, $\{-Z_4\}$ include the allomorphs /-s/, /-z/ and /-ız/; $\{-Z_1\}$ and $\{-Z_3\}$ also include other allomorphs.

The morphophonemic formulae /-Z/ and /-D/ stand for sets of (allomorphic) variants whose occurrence within the set is automatically determined by the sound system of English. Each set contains three members with the following distributions:

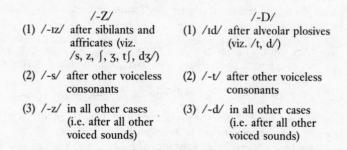

/-Z/
(1) /-ız/ after sibilants and affricates (viz. /s, z, ʃ, ʒ, tʃ, dʒ/)

(2) /-s/ after other voiceless consonants

(3) /-z/ in all other cases (i.e. after all other voiced sounds)

/-D/
(1) /ıd/ after alveolar plosives (viz. /t, d/)

(2) /-t/ after other voiceless consonants

(3) /-d/ in all other cases (i.e. after all other voiced sounds)

/-z/ is the variant selected when all three would give an English phonological sequence, e.g. the plural of /pen/ *pen* is /penz/ *pens*, not /pens/ or /'penɪz/, although these are perfectly acceptable English structures (the words *pence* and *pennies*); whereas /-s/ and /-ɪz/ only occur in environments where /-z/ would produce an impossible English sequence, e.g. /kæts/ not */kætz/ *cats*, /'hɔːsɪz/ not */hɔːsz/ *horses*. It is therefore reasonable to regard /-z/ as the morphophonemic base form, with /-s/ and /-ɪz/ replacing /-z/ when it is phonologically excluded; /-d/ may similarly be regarded as the morphophonemic base for /-t/ and /-ɪd/. We have therefore chosen /-Z/ and /-D/ as appropriate symbols for the whole morphophonemic alternance.

At this point we should note another important case of morphophonemic variation – this time one which affects the stems of inflected words:[1] each of the vowels /ɜː, ɑː, ɔː, ɪə, ɛə, ʊə, ə/ in stem-final position is automatically followed by an /r/ before {-ɪŋ}, {-ə}, {-ɪst} (the only inflectors with a vocalic onset which occur after vowels), e.g. /'pɜːrɪŋ/ *purring*, /'stɛərɪŋ/ *staring*, /'pjʊərə/ *purer*, /'sɔːrɪst/ *sorest*. This rule applies only when there is an *r* in the spelling, i.e. in words which originally had an /r/. Pronunciations like /'drɔːrɪŋ/ *drawing* are not generally accepted as standard. (All these remarks of course apply only to dialects which, like the so-called Received Pronunciation that we take as our norm, have no preconsonantal and word-final /r/.)

B. *NOMINAL INFLECTION*

1. {-Z₁} '*noun plural*'
The category of NUMBER is a feature of the noun phrase, being a potential characteristic of every one; it also appears in verbs but only when they are finite and when they are in concord with the subject noun phrase. In the noun phrase itself number seems to be marked in two ways:

(i) in the choice of determiners: singular *this, that, a(n), one, each*, etc., vs. plural *these, those, two, three*, etc. (some determiners being neutral).

(ii) in the use of the {-Z₁} suffix in its various forms.

The regular (in the sense of productive and most frequent) form of the noun plural morpheme is morphophonemic /-Z/.

Phonologically irregular forms of the plural morpheme may be placed in five groups:

[1] This applies equally to derived and compound words and to phrases.

(a) A couple of dozen words which end in a voiceless fricative but in the plural take /-Z/ with a voicing of the final fricative, e.g. with /f-v/ *shelf-shelves, knife-knives*; with /θ-ð/ *mouth-mouths; sheath-sheathes*; with /s-z/ only *house-houses*.

(b) The word *penny* has a plural with /-s/ viz. *pence* /pens/. (This has an abstract meaning beside the regular *pennies* which has a concrete meaning.)[1]

(c) Seven words are marked for plural purely by a change of vowel phoneme (in one case two changes): /æ-e/ *man-men*; /uː-iː/*goose-geese, tooth-teeth*; /ʊ-iː/ *foot-feet*; /aʊ-aɪ/ *louse-lice, mouse-mice*; /ʊ-ɪ/ + /ə-ɪ/ *woman-women*.

(d) Three words take /-ən/ or /-rən/ with vowel change: *ox-oxen; child-children; brother-brethren* (the latter in the restricted sense of 'members of a religious fraternity').

(e) Learned and foreign formations of various types. These are virtually all words which occur predominantly in the written language, and consequently pronunciation varies in a number of cases. Examples are *alga-algae, stimulus-stimuli, crisis-crises, stratum-strata, criterion-criteria, phenomenon-phenomena* (all Latin and Greek patterns).

Nouns are often divided into two classes, COUNT nouns and MASS nouns, according to whether they have a number distinction or not. Count nouns like *table* have a plural form (*tables*) and co-occur with determiners like *a, one* in the singular, and *two, three, many* in the plural, while mass nouns like *furniture* have no plural form and collocate not with *a, one* but with *some* (/səm/ 'a certain quantity of') in the singular. But the division is not without its complications.

For one thing some nouns like *sheep, aircraft* may be plural or singular without any change in form; others like *cattle, police* are always plural as is clear from the verb concord (*the cattle are eating, the police are coming*) but have no sign of plurality in their form. On the other hand, there are words which have an apparent plural form, i.e. end in /-s, -z, -ɪz/, but which have no equivalent singular form: some of these behave like singulars, e.g. *news, billiards*; others like plurals, e.g. *trousers, premises*. In other cases again, we are faced with apparent singular-plural pairs, e.g. *ash-ashes, content-contents* which do not exhibit the regular meaning relationship.

Further problems occur in the lack of concord of certain singular

---

[1] At one time *die-dice* followed a similar formal pattern, but now *dice* is usual for both singular and plural.

nouns with a collective meaning (*the Government believes—the Government believe*) and in the apparent irregularity of *sort, kind* in such locations as *these sort of books*. (In fact *sort of* and *kind of* might be best regarded as inserted word phrases with a meaning ' . . . and its/their like'). An overall classification of nouns with respect to the number morpheme might be represented as shown on p 88.

2. $\{-Z_2\}$ '*possessive*'

This morpheme is sometimes described as GENITIVE rather than POSSESSIVE. In fact almost all the principal meanings of *John's X* (where X is a noun) can be glossed, if not by 'the X possessed by John', then at least by 'the X belonging to or appertaining to John'.

In the case of nouns derived from transitive verbs which require a human object, *John* is normally construed as the object, e.g. *John's defeat, arrest, education*; but where the verb is intransitive, or transitive with the possibility of non-human objects, then *John* is taken as the subject, e.g. *John's arrival, death, discovery, attack*.[1] But if subject and object are unambiguously marked by prepositions, these rules may be relaxed, e.g. *John's defeat of the champion, John's discovery by the talent-spotter* (the latter type being less normal).

When the X element in a phrase *John's X* is a de-adjectival abstract noun, we can generally reconstruct an underlying proposition *John is/was/etc. A*, where *A* is the adjectival stem of X. For instance, *John's happiness* implies *John is/was/etc. happy*.

Certain uses of the $\{-Z_2\}$ extend beyond animate nouns. Time expressions are particularly amenable to 'possessivization'. Singular quantity time expressions appear in this form when the head word is a mass noun, e.g.

one/a day's travel, (in) one/a week's time;

when the quantity is plural, of course, the possessive form is not marked in the spoken language but is traditionally written, e.g. *two hours' sleep, four weeks' notice*. Expressions which name a specific time may also be possessivized, e.g. *today's Guardian, last week's match*.

Apart from these cases $\{-Z_2\}$ occurs in some fixed phrases like *for (John)'s sake* (which means little more than 'for (John)'), *out of harm's way*, etc.

$\{-Z_2\}$ is identical in form with the main varieties of the $\{-Z_1\}$ 'plural' morpheme, viz. /-s, -z, -ɪz/, but it differs from $\{-Z_1\}$ in

[1] Cf. also the triple ambiguity of *George's photograph is in the paper.* (1 = 'taken of George', 2 = 'taken by George', 3 = 'owned by George'.)

being perfectly regular with nouns, there being no other form possible than these three. This means of course that, at least in the spoken language, $\{-Z_1\}$ and $\{-Z_2\}$ will be homophonous for the large majority of nouns. The written language keeps them apart, e.g.:

	SINGULAR	PLURAL
PLAIN	boy /bɔɪ/	boys /bɔɪz/
POSSESSIVE	boy's /bɔɪz/	boys' /bɔɪz/

But wherever there is an irregular plural formation, the possessive singular and the plain plural are kept apart:

	SINGULAR	PLURAL
PLAIN	wife /waɪf/	wives /waɪvz/
POSSESSIVE	wife's /waɪfs/	wives' /waɪvz/

In this case the possessive plural has the same form as the plain plural, but in the case of nouns with uniform singular and plural like *sheep* the possessive plural is homophonous with the possessive singular (*sheep's*). Where the plural morph is not of the /-Z/ type at all, all four forms are distinct, e.g.

	SINGULAR	PLURAL
PLAIN	man /mæn/	men /men/
POSSESSIVE	man's /mænz/	men's /menz/

cf. *child, children, child's, children's.*

We hinted earlier that $\{-Z_2\}$ is not a normal inflector. Normal inflectors may be thought of as being added to a single word. $\{-Z_2\}$, however, applies to a noun phrase rather than to a noun. For example, in *the intelligent boy's marks* it is clear that *intelligent* modifies (*the*) *boy* not *marks* and that the *'s* therefore applies to the whole phrase not just to *boy*, as is evidenced by the related structure (*the*) *marks of the intelligent boy*. As a consequence it is perfectly possible for $\{-Z_2\}$ to be separated from its noun, whenever the noun is followed by a modifier. It may be instructive here to compare $\{-Z_2\}$ with $\{-Z_1\}$:

> The boys across the road
> The boy across the road's bicycle.

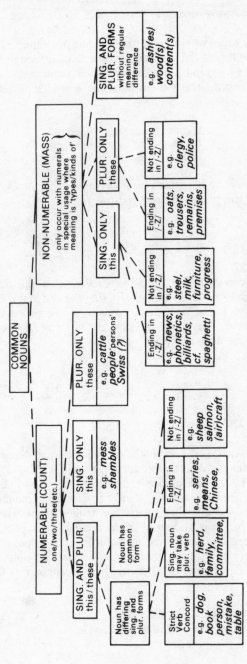

Fig. 3.1. Number in the English Noun

N.B. (1) Mass nouns occurring in a singular form normally collocate with *some/səm/* while count nouns in the singular do not.
(2) A whole group of nouns have dual membership of the mass and count groups e.g. *stone, crime virtue, paper, rubber* (the latter two with a specialized count meaning). As a result usage with the numerals (and indefinite article) is ambiguous, e.g. *two stones* = (1) 'two pieces of stone', (2) 'two types of stone'.
(3) Some count nouns are sometimes marked for number, but sometimes not – particularly with quantity expressions and verbs of sporting activity, e.g. *four million, two foot (six), (to hunt) duck.*

In certain cases (referred to by Zandvoort as the 'classifying genitive') {-Z$_2$} may function not with a noun phrase but with a simple count noun (even though this could not alone form a noun phrase). Thus *a doctor's degree* in the context *He's working for . . .* can be regarded as an expansion of *a degree*, so that *doctor's* is simply a modifier like *doctoral*.[1]

Although, as we have seen, possessive complexes do have functions parallel to those of determiners and adjectives, they also appear in nominal positions, particularly as predicates of the verb *to be*. Sometimes this use may seem elliptical, although often it would be unusual to use the 'omitted' noun, e.g. *in the butcher's (shop), at my uncle's (house)*. *He met her at St John's* could be expanded with *Church* or *College* but could also be meant and interpreted as the name of a town (in Canada), when it would not be expandable.

In such instances the noun to be supplied (if any) is inferred from the context of situation, but it may be clear from the linguistic context, either within or outside the sentence: *You may not like this hat, but have you seen my sister's? That book is Colin's.* Closely related to this use is the use after *of* in *this hat of my sister's* and *that book of Colin's.* The relatedness of all these structures is demonstrated by the fact that all of them select the *mine-yours* form of pronouns, e.g. *That book is mine*, whereas all other uses we have examined of the possessive have been replaceable by the *my-your* form, e.g. *my book, her generosity.*

{-Z$_2$} has various phonological values with the pronouns including /-Z/, /ə(r)/ and suppletion combining with them to give the following forms:

I/me-my	it-its
you-your	we/us-our
(thou/thee-thy)	they/them-their
he/him-his	who/whom-whose
she/her-her	one-one's

Of these, *its* is perfectly regular, *whose* and *his* regular apart from the fact that the vowel is fixed for the possessives /hu:z/, /hɪz/ but variable for the plain forms /hu:, hʊ/, /hi:, hɪ/ (the /h/s are obligatory only in stressed positions). In addition, regular pronoun

---

[1] Jespersen regards such cases – citing *ship's doctor* beside *statesman* – as a special type of compound noun, and they certainly do have a tendency to be limited in range and to favour stress on the first element – both features of compound nouns.

possessives exist for *one (one's)* and for compounds with *one* and *body*, e.g. *someone's, nobody's*.

3. {-Z₃} *'noun substitute'*

Only the personal pronouns distinguish in form between a determiner form and a nominal form of the possessive, the latter marked by {-Z₃} which has the variant form /-n/ in *mine, thine*. Thus, although *This is John's book* is reducible to *This is John's, This is my book* appears as *This is mine*. *His* is unmarked for nominalization and *its* lacks a nominal form for most English speakers.[1] Since the form with {-Z₃} appears as a complete noun phrase in such occurrences as *It's mine, better than mine, mine seem good*, it is best regarded as a pronoun.

4. {-m} *'oblique'*

{-m} is a second inflection limited in its use to pronouns. From the formal point of view it is difficult to carve out separate morph segments for the personal and case elements in *we* /wi:/ and *us* /ʌs/.[2] On the other hand, the two are perfectly parallel in function to the more clearly demarcated /hɪ- + -m/ *him*, /hu: + -m/ *whom*.

In order to avoid these difficulties of segmentation it might be more profitable simply to list the stressed forms in an ordered way, (see table of personal pronouns and determiners on p 91).

As regards the uses of the {-m} form of the pronoun, we may today go so far as to call it the normal, general form, although historically it represents the accusative case (chiefly used to mark verbal and prepositional objects). Now, the subjective case is the exception rather than the norm: in fact it only occurs regularly with all speakers as a simple subject preceding the finite verb. Cases where vacillation[3] is common include: *It's ME/I; We looked for a job, Tom and I/ME; It was I/ME who looked for a job; It was ME (that) they were looking for*, and the ambiguity of *You know John better than ME*, where *I* is possible but pedantic in the subjective meaning. It is interesting to note that because the prevalent pattern *Tom and ME were . . .* has been prescribed against, some speakers have by over-correction extended the use of *I* to non-subject cases of co-ordinate noun phrases, e.g. *You know Bill and I, between you and I*.

---

[1] Is the following acceptable English? *Both the boy and his dog have brown eyes but his are darker than its.*

[2] Usual reduced forms /wɪ/ and /əs/.

[3] The form appearing to be more common is given first.

PERSONAL PRONOUNS AND DETERMINERS

SUBJECTIVE PRONOUN	OBLIQUE PRONOUN	POSSESSIVE DETERMINER	POSSESSIVE PRONOUN	REFLEXIVE EMPHATIC
aɪ *I*	miː *me*	maɪ *my*	maɪn *mine*	maɪˈself *myself*
ðaʊ[1] *thou*	ðiː[1] *thee*	ðaɪ[1] *thy*	ðaɪn[1] *thine*	ðaɪˈself[1] *thyself*
hiː *he*	hɪm *him*	hɪz *his*	hɪz *his*	hɪmˈself *himself*
ʃiː *she*	hɜː *her*	hɜː *her*	hɜːz *hers*	hɜːˈself *herself*
ɪt *it*	ɪt *it*	ɪts *its*		ɪtˈself *itself*
wiː *we*	ʌs *us*	aʊə/aː *our*	aʊəz/aːz *ours*	aʊəˈselvz/ aːˈselvz *ourselves*
juː *you*	juː *you*	jɔː *your*	jɔːz *yours*	jɔːˈselvz *yourselves*
ðeɪ *they*	ðem *them*	ðɛə *their*	ðɛəz *theirs*	ðəmˈselvz *themselves*
huː *who*	huː(m) *who(m)*	huːz *whose*	huːz *whose*	(hɪmˈself, hɜːˈself, ðəmˈselvz) *(himself, herself, themselves)*
wʌn *one*	wʌn[2] *one*[2]	wʌnz *one's*[2]	(wʌnz) *(one's)*[2]	wʌnˈself *oneself*[2]

[1] Now restricted to religious and poetic use, as is the even less used plural *ye* which otherwise behaves like *you*.

[2] In some forms of English the forms *him*, *his*, etc., are more common here. The possessive pronoun *one's* is extremely rare.

5. {-self} 'reflexive/emphatic'

{-self} combines with all the personal pronouns, including *one* but not *who*, as illustrated in the table on p 91. Words like *myself* do not look particularly like inflected forms of *me*, etc., but, on the surface, more like compounds consisting of possessive determiner plus noun.[1] However, from the point of view of function and meaning they cannot be interpreted in this way in typical uses like *I made myself do it*; here *myself* contrasts not with *my arm, mind, son*, etc., but simply with *him, you, George*, etc. – nor does it contrast with *me*, of which it may therefore be regarded as an inflectional variant. In *I did it myself/I myself did it, myself* functions like subject modifiers such as *alone, with my colleagues*.

{-self} pronouns have, in fact, two quite separate roles which are usually termed 'reflexive' and 'emphatic'. The REFLEXIVE pronoun must be used in the following positions, whenever the person referred to is identical with the subject:

(a) object	*I hurt myself.*
(b) indirect object	*I did myself a favour.*
(c) predicative	*He isn't himself.*
(d) subject of downgraded ('infinitivized') clause	*I told myself to do it.*
(e) object of downgraded ('infinitivized') clause with zero subject (= identical with main subject)	*His wife threatens to kill herself.*
(f) nominal element in prepositional phrase provided it is not a clear locative	*She has no confidence in herself.* *Are you staying by yourself?* *They saw it for themselves.*

Contrast (f) with (g):

    (g) *I looked behind me,*
        He took his camera with him.
        He felt his blood tingle inside him.

---

[1] Except for *himself, themselves*, which represent the older pattern.

Variable cases include some prepositions of direction:

> I pulled the bedclothes over me/myself.
> He moved the chair towards him/himself.

In its EMPHATIC uses, {-self} may accentuate any pronoun or noun phrase in the sentence. These emphatic uses differ from the others in that the pronoun is an optional modifier (meaning something like 'as opposed to others') and if omitted leaves behind a grammatical sentence, e.g.

> *The King himself made the request.*
> *The King made the request himself.*
> *Did they give the present to you yourself?*
> *In the house itself were a number of nice items.*

When the subject is thus modified, the pronoun may either directly follow it, as in the first example, or appear at the end of the sentence, as in the second.

A final use of the {-self} pronouns is as simple replacements for *I/me*, etc., wherever there is vacillation between subjective and oblique form. Compare these examples with the ones quoted above for *I/me*.

> *We looked for a job, Tom and myself.*
> *It was myself they were looking for.*
> *You know John better than myself.*

C. *VERBAL INFLECTIONS*

1. {-Z₄} '3rd person singular present'

This morpheme is used to form the 3rd person singular form of the present tense of all verbs, including verbal auxiliaries except the modals *will (would), shall (should), may (might), can (could), must, ought* (and sometimes *need* and *dare*), all of which use the bare stem in such cases. The form of this morpheme is consistently /-Z/ with a mere four verbs having a change of stem viz. *is* /ɪz/, *has* /hæz/, *does* /dʌz/, *says* /sez/.

The functions of {-Z₄} are manifold:

(i) It marks the verb as finite through its concord and sequential relationship to the subject, which is thus limited to a third person pronoun or noun phrase.

(ii) It marks the verb as singular.
(iii) It marks the verb as present tense.

$\{-Z_4\}$'s marking of 'singularity' is of course usually redundant, since the singularity of the subject is usually clear by itself.[1] However, when this is not so, the normally redundant $\{-Z_4\}$ may assume a distinctive role; cf.

His sheep grazes in the meadow.
His sheep graze in the meadow.

$\{-Z_4\}$ also signals the category of present tense; in non-3rd person singular forms this category is of course unmarked. The 'presentness' is actually a matter of non-pastness, since, most commonly, general habits or (relatively) permanent states of affairs are referred to.

2. $\{-D_1\}$ 'past tense' $\{-D_2\}$ 'past participle'
As with $\{-Z_1\}$ and $\{-Z_2\}$, the regular forms of the past tense and past participelle morphemes are identical in form. However there are more irregularities and more cases of differences for $\{-D_1\}$ and $\{-D_2\}$. It is true that the two morphemes do not usually come into opposition since $\{-D_2\}$ must normally be preceded by an auxiliary or copular verb to make it finite, whereas $\{-D_1\}$ is finite in its own right. However the two morphemes may contrast in such sentence pairs as:

I can imagine the boy *hid/froze*.
I can imagine the boy *hidden/frozen*.

In these two cases two different types of grammatical construction are involved, and it is the occurrence of $\{-D_1\}$ or $\{-D_2\}$ respectively that signals which construction it is.

We now come to the complex question of the forms of these suffixes. We shall deal with both morphemes together, mentioning specially all cases where they differ.

---

[1] $\{-Z_4\}$ may also have a subsidiary distinctive role in other cases, e.g. with collective nouns like *committee* in such a sentence as *The committee finds it acceptable*, compared with *The committee find it acceptable*.

I: /-D/

The regular form for both suffixes is morphophonemic /-D/, e.g. *called* /kɔːld/, *passed* /pɑːst/, *waited* /'weɪtɪd/. This form of the affix occurs with the vast majority of English verbs and is automatically taken by all new verbs entering the language.

IA: Some verbs take /-D/ but vary the vowel of the stem, e.g. *say-said* /seɪ-sed/, *sell-sold* /sel-sɔʊld/, *hear-heard* /hɪə-hɜːd/, *sleep-slept* /sliːp-slept/, *weep-wept* /wiːp-wept/.

IB: Some verbs take /-D/ but are subject to a consonant change (loss) in their stem, e.g. *have-had* /hæv-hæd/, *make-made*, /meɪk/meɪd/.

IC: Some verbs take /-D/ having first undergone both vocalic and consonantal change (devoicing), e.g. *leave-left* /liːv-left/, *lose-lost* /luːz-lɒst/.

II: /-t/

A whole group of verbs which ought regularly to have /-d/, in fact take /-t/. These verbs mainly end in /-n/ and /-l/, e.g. *burn-burnt* /bɜːn-bɜːnt/, *learn-learnt* /lɜːn-lɜːnt/, *smell-smelled/smelt* /smel-smelt/, *spell-spelt* /spel-spelt/, *spoil-spoilt* /spɔɪl-spɔɪlt/, *dwell-dwelt/ dwelled* /dwel-dwelt/.

IIA: Some verbs change their vowel and add /-t/, e.g. *feel-felt* /fiːl-felt/, *lean-leant* /liːn-lent/, *dream-dreamt* /driːm-dremt/, *buy-bought* /baɪ-bɔːt/.

IIB: Some verbs make both vocalic and consonantal changes in their stem, then add /-t/, e.g. *bring-brought* /brɪŋ-brɔːt/, *think-thought* /θɪŋk-θɔːt/, *catch-caught* /kætʃ-kɔːt/.[1]

III: Devoicing

This only applies to some verbs ending in /-d/; their past form ends in /-t/, e.g. *bend-bent, build-built, lend-lent, spend-spent.*

---

[1] Some of these verbs end in a voiceless consonant in their present form, but the /-t/ is still irregular in the content of the past form base which ends in a vowel, e.g. /(θ)ɔː-/ in *thought*. This irregularity, like most others, can of course be explained historically.

IV: Vowel Change
This is the major irregular category for English verbs, and it is anything but homogeneous. There are many classes and subclasses which we try now to present in an organized way. We shall classify these verbs firstly according to whether the vowel of the past participle agrees with that of the past tense, with that of the present, or with neither; and secondly according to whether the past participle has the ending -(*e*)*n* /-(ə)n, n̩/. Within each group we list the various vowel alternation patterns, some of which only apply to a single verb.

(1) Past Participle agrees with Past Tense, i.e. {-D₁} and {-D₂} are homophonous:

/iː-e-e/	*bleed, meet, read,* etc.
/e-ɒ-ɒ/	*get* (not in American)
/ɪ-ʌ-ʌ/	*dig, win, fling, stick,* etc.
/ɪ-æ-æ/	*spit, sit*
/æ-ʌ-ʌ/	*hang*
/uː-ɒ-ɒ/	*shoot*
/aɪ-ɪ-ɪ/	*slide, light* (also regular)
/aɪ-ʌ-ʌ/	*strike*
/aɪ-ɒ-ɒ/	*shine* (also regular)
/aɪ-ɔː-ɔː/	*fight*
/aɪ-ɑʊ-ɑʊ/	*find, bind, grind, wind*

(1a) Past Participle has same vowel as Past Tense but adds -(*e*)*n*, i.e. {-D₂} = {-D₁} + -(*e*)*n*:

/iː-əʊ-əʊ/	*steal, speak, freeze,* etc.
/e-ɒ-ɒ/	*tread, forget* (*get* in American)
/uː-əʊ-əʊ/	*choose*
/eɪ-əʊ-əʊ/[1]	*break, wake*
/aɪ-ɪ-ɪ/	*hide, bite,* etc.
/aɪ-eɪ-eɪ/	*lie* ('recline')
/ɛə-ɔː-ɔː/[1]	*bear, swear, tear, wear*

(2) Past Participle has same vowel as Present stem, i.e. {-D₂} has a zero value or is absent. There are two examples of this without -(*e*)*n*, viz. each has a different vowel in the past tense:

---

[1] For speakers of dialects with postvocalic /r/, these two groups would form a single class.

/ʌ-eɪ-ʌ/	come (also be-, overcome)
/ʌ-æ-ʌ/	run

(2a) Past Participle has same vowel as Present stem, but adds -(e)n; thus {-D₂} is realized simply as /-(ə)n, -n̩/:

/iː-e-iː/	eat (ate = /et/)
/iː-ɔː-iː/	see
/ɪ-æ-ɪ/	bid ('command') forbid
/ɪ-eɪ-ɪ/	(for)give
/ɔː-e-ɔː/	(be)fall
/ɔː-uː-ɔː/	draw (also over-, withdraw)
/eɪ-ʊ-eɪ/	shake, forsake, take, undertake, etc.
/eɪ-uː-eɪ/	slay
/əʊ-uː-əʊ/	grow, blow, throw
/əʊ-juː-əʊ/	know

(3) Past Participle has a vowel different from both the Present and the Past Tense. Only one pattern exists without -(e)n:

/ɪ-æ-ʌ/	drink, ring, swim, begin, etc.

(3a) Past Participle has individual vowel and in addition -(e)n. Only two types occur:

/aɪ-uː-əʊ/	fly
/aɪ-əʊ-ɪ/	write, ride, drive, (a)rise, etc.

V: /-D/-(e)n

A category of 'mixed' verbs also exists which have a regular past tense but which normally have a past participle in -(e)n (-ed is a less frequently used alternative). Examples are mow-mowed-mown /məʊ-məʊd-məʊn/, hew-hewed-hewn hjuː-hjuːd-hjuːn/, saw-sawed-sawn /sɔː-sɔːd-sɔːn/, cf. also sow/sew, show, strew.

VA:
One verb is of this pattern but has vowel change in the past participle, viz. shear-sheared-shorn /ʃɪə-ʃɪəd-ʃɔːn/.

VB:
One verb has a different vowel in all three forms, viz. do, did, done /duː-dɪd-dʌn/; it is thus a blend of types IV and V.

VI: Zero

A complete series of verbs has no difference at all in form between present tense, past tense and past participle. We may say either that these verbs take a zero variant of the $\{-D_1\}$ and $\{-D_2\}$ morphemes or we can say (perhaps more realistically) that these verbs simply do not take $\{-D_1\}$ and $\{-D_2\}$. Most of them end in /-d/ or/-t/, e.g. *bet, bid* (at an auction), *burn, cast, cost, cut, hit, hurt, let, put, rid, set, shed, shut, slit, split, spread, thrust.*

VIA: A special case is *beat* which has an unchanged past tense but a past participle *beaten* /'biːtn̩/. Thus while $\{-D_1\}$ is not realized overtly, $\{-D_2\}$ has the form /-n̩/.

VII: Suppletion
Our final category contains two verbs which use a completely different form in the past tense compared with present and past participle. They are:

be – *was/were* – *been* /biː/ (unstressed: /bɪ/) —/wɒz, wɜː/ (unstressed: /wəz, wə/) – /biːn/
go – *went* – *gone* /gəʊ – went – gɒn/

The verb *be* is idiosyncratic in other ways too: it is the only verb to have a special form for 1st person singular present tense, to have a different form for all singular as against plural past tense forms, and to have separate forms for plural present and infinitive. Its full conjugation is:

	PRESENT	PAST
1st. Sing.	*am* /æm, (ə)m/	*was* /wɒz, wəz/
(Obsolete and Sing.	*art* /ɑːt, ət/	*wert* /wɜːt/)
3rd Sing.	*is* /ɪz, z, s/[1]	*was* /wɒz, wəz/
Plural	*are* /ɑː, ə/	*were* /wɜː, wə/
Participle	*being* /'biːɪŋ/	*been* /biːn (bɪn)/
Infinitive	*be* /biː, bɪ/	

---

[1] This behaves as though it were morphophonemic /-Z/, except that it is always /ɪz/ when stressed. We have thus observed six different morphemes with the forms /s, z, ɪz/, viz.:
   (1) (noun) plural
   (2) possessive
   (3) noun substitute (with possessive pronouns)
   (4) (verb) 3rd sg. pres.
   (5) verb *be* 3rd sg. pres.
   (6) *his* (unstressed)

The function of {-D₁} is simply to mark PAST TENSE. The function of {-D₂} is slightly more complex. Its most important functions are in its combining:

    (1) with *have* to produce 'perfect'
    (2) with *be* to give 'passive'.

Alone it acts as an adjective, occurring both attributively and predicatively, when it usually carries with it the meanings of 'perfect' and/or 'passive', e.g.

> The illustrated article was rather protracted.
> He looked exhausted.

3. {-ɪŋ} *'participle-gerund'*

Although the functions of this morpheme are varied and complex, its form is simple to describe: it consistently has the form /ɪŋ/.[1]

We have glossed {-ɪŋ} as 'participle-gerund', but it has other important functions:

    (1) In conjunction with the verb *be*, it produces the 'progressive' forms, an integral part of the tense-aspect system of the verb.
    (2) It functions as an affix which is partially or wholly derivational in character.

In fact the range of functions of {-ɪŋ} is unusual, in that it is neither wholly inflectional nor wholly derivational; it forms words which are neither wholly adjectival (participles) nor wholly substantive (gerunds): hence the common use of the neutral expression *-ing* form'. Other major European languages have no comparable single form.

The unequivocally inflectional occurrences of *-ing* forms include the usual nominal and adjectival slots, e.g.

(1) NOMINAL   (a) **subject**: Winning (matches) helps team morale.
                (b) **object**: He loves winning (matches).
                (c) **prepositional object**:
                         He succeeds through winning (matches).
(2) ADJECTIVAL   (a) **prenominal attribute**:
                         His winning shots were superb.

---

[1] However we should note that, as with all other cases of /ŋ/ following an unstressed vowel, {-ɪŋ} is realized as /-ɪn/ in most local and regional dialects, and in the rapid colloquial style of many RP speakers. We should also note the occurrence of /r/ in stem-final position.

> (b) **postnominal attribute of subject:**
> He spent hours in the Casino winning (pounds) every time.
> (c) **postnominal attribute of object:**
> I saw him winning (the race).

However, in all these cases the *-ing* form retains its verbal character, and, except in prenominal attributive position, it may always take a noun as object, as indicated in parenthesis above.[1] Moreover, while the subject of the *-ing* verb may be understood in a general sense (1a) or construed from the context (1b), (1c), (2b), it may also be made explicit by the use of nouns and pronouns (sometimes in the possessive form), e.g. *us/our, John('s)*, in all nominal cases. In cases like (2c) the subject is obligatorily expressed.

The *-ing* form is very similar in one of its uses to the infinitive with *to*: indeed *to smoke* is nearly interchangeable with *smoking* in a verbal complex such as *I like ... a cigar after dinner*. While some verbs such as *like, intend, start*, do not discriminate between infinitive and *-ing* form, others require the one (e.g. *hope, manage*) or the other (e.g. *finish, risk*). An interesting subclass including *want* and *need* makes a contrast between the active use of the infinitive and the passive use of the *-ing* form, e.g.

> The girls will need to scrub.
> The girls will need scrubbing.[2]

When the *-ing* form has lost its characteristic verbal qualities of taking a subject, object (transitive verbs only), adverbial modifier, etc., and has become a pure noun or adjective, then we can say that {-ɪŋ} is acting as a derivational morpheme. In these cases {-ɪŋ} occurs with some lexical items but not with others. Examples are: *warning, meeting; coating, ironing; gardening*, which are all nominal in character. Different in nature is the adjectival {-ɪŋ} of *a frightening affair, an interesting scheme*, where the form may, like ordinary

---

[1] As a result, the sequence *-ing* form + noun may represent either (i) a noun modified by the *-ing* form or (ii) an *-ing* form used nominally followed by its object, or (iii) an *-ing* form used adjectivally followed by its object, as in:
   (i) He played tiring games.
   (ii) He played (at) driving trains.
   (iii) He played wearing gloves.

[2] In this example *the girls* is simultaneously the subject of *need* but the object (or passive subject) of *scrub*. Some Northern English speakers extend this use of the *-ing* form to cases where there are two different noun phrases filling these roles, e.g. *I want it cleaning* instead of *I want it cleaned*.

adjectives, be modified by *very, more*, etc., but may be derived fairly regularly from verbs which take a human object and designate mental processes.

We have so far left aside the uses of $\{-D_1\}$, $\{-D_2\}$ and $\{-\text{ɪŋ}\}$ within the voice-tense-aspect system of the English verb. $\{-\text{ɪŋ}\}$ combines with *be*, while $\{-D_2\}$ may combine with either *have* or *be*; these combinations along with $\{-D_1\}$ give us four optional modifications for any verb viz. PROGRESSIVE, PERFECT, PASSIVE and PAST, of which any one, two, three or even all four may be selected, to give such forms as: *has been seeing, has seen, has been seen.*

D. *OTHER INFLECTIONS*

We mentioned earlier that apart from nominal and verbal inflections there exist some others which are of more debatable inflectional status:

(a) **adjectival comparison** – the two morphemes $\{-\text{ə}\}$ 'more' and $\{-\text{ɪst}\}$ 'most' as in *weaker, weakest.*

(b) **adverbial** $\{-\text{lɪ}\}$ as in *quickly, strangely.* Let us examine the status of each of these in turn.

$\{-\text{ə}\}$ and $\{-\text{ɪst}\}$ may be said to be derivational in the sense that they form new adjectives, the COMPARATIVE and SUPERLATIVE forms, which may occur in many ordinary adjectival positions, e.g.

> The tall boys had an advantage in the line-out.
> taller
> tallest

In such contexts $\{-\text{ə}\}$ and $\{-\text{ɪst}\}$ are clearly derivational in character, since they can be replaced by a single form. On the other hand, such sentences as:

> Michael's boy is *taller* than his teacher
> Michael's boy is the *tallest* in his form

illustrate clearly inflectional uses of *taller* and *tallest*, since each is occurring in a context where the other is impossible, as is also the simple form *tall*.

The forms of the two morphemes are simple to state and have been given in our name for them. The comparative is regularly manifested as /-ə/ (/-ər/ before vowels). The superlative is regularly realized as /-ɪst, -əst/.[1] Some changes in the final phonemes of the stem take place:

(i) final /-ŋ/ in *long, strong, young* alternates with medial /-ŋg-/in *longer, longest,* etc. It might be most appropriate to regard the /g/ as part of the comparative/superlative inflection, since it is not required in this position by the phonological system. Moreover other formations from these adjectives do not take /g/, e.g. /'lɒŋɪʃ/ *longish.*
(ii) syllabic /l̩/ alternates with non-syllabic /l/ in *simple, able,* beside *simpler, abler,* etc.
(iii) as always before a vowel the potential linking /r/ of the adjectival stem itself occurs, e.g. *dear* /dɪə/, beside *dearer, dearest* /'dɪərə, 'dɪərɪst ('dɪərəst)/.
(iv) *far* inserts /ð/, with an optional change of vowel i.e. *far* /fɑː/, *farther/further* /'fɑːðə, 'fɜːðə/, *farthest/furthest* /'fɑːðɪst, 'fɜːðɪst/ (also /-əst/).

{-ə} and {-ɪst} may not be used with all adjectives: they are restricted to monosyllabic and common disyllabic forms. The alternative is a phrase *more/most* + adjective, which is used whenever a longer or less common adjective is involved, either alone, or in company with the {-ə}/{-ɪst} forms, e.g.:

He is the most honest man I know.
She is prettier and more intelligent than her sister.

Two sets of comparative and superlative forms correspond to a pair of adjectives rather than a single one:

good, well[2]	better	best
bad, ill	worse	worst

A similar phenomenon is apparent for two pairs of determiner-like adjectives of quantity which distinguish (mass) singular and (count) plural in the simple form but not in comparative and superlative forms:

---

[1] The variation between /-ɪst/ and /-əst/ for the superlative form is not merely a result of the lack of an /ɪ/≠/ə/ contrast in unstressed position: some speakers pronounce the superlative *oddest* as /'ɒdəst/ but the plain adjective *honest* as /'ɒnɪst/.
[2] Both adjectival *well* ('in good health') and adverbial *well. Soon, cheap,* and a few other de-adjectival adverbs also have comparative and superlative forms.

little, (a) few[1]	less	least
much, many	more	most

As Jespersen points out, the difference between comparative and superlative is not a difference between a comparison with one and a comparison with many or all; nor does the superlative indicate a higher degree. Consider the sentences:

Margaret was happier than all of her six sisters put together.
Jean was the happiest of the three girls.

The criterion for choice of comparative as against superlative is whether the entity compared is thought of as separate from the group with which it is compared or as part and parcel of it.[2]

ADVERBIAL $\{-lı\}$ is our other border-line inflection – border-line in the sense that it might also be thought of as a derivational affix. If we apply the test of replaceability by a simple word with the same function, we shall see that our attitude will depend on how strictly we insist that the function must be the same. The adverb is a complicated, even amorphous word-class containing widely-differing subclasses which nevertheless have just about enough members in common to justify setting up a single class ADVERB, e.g. *naturally* (sentence adverb and manner adverb), *slightly* (degree adverb and adjective intensifier).

Some types of adverb have most or all members without -*ly* (e.g. place adverbs like *here, down, near*), but within the major subclass of MANNER ADVERBS only *well, hard, fast, loud, right*, and a few others regularly occur wthout -*ly*. If we regard these as cases of suppletion or zero realization, -*ly* could be regarded as obligatory for manner adverbs and therefore akin to an inflection.

The phonological form /-lı/ is used absolutely consistently, subject to the following modifications:

---

[1] The form *fewer* is used by some speakers and indeed insisted upon by pedants, but in colloquial English *less* tends to replace it, presumably under the analogical influence of *more*, i.e. *more/less beautiful, more/less cheese → more/less books*.

[2] It is therefore quite natural for speakers of English to use the superlative when there are only two members in the group, so long as the entity compared is one of them, e.g.
Jean was the happiest of the two girls
although such sentences are usually condemend as 'incorrect'.

(i) after syllabic /l/ just /ɪ/ is added, and the /l/ loses its syllabicity – there is no doubling of /l/, e.g. *possibly* /'pɒsəblɪ/, *nobly* /'nəʊblɪ/. After ordinary non-syllabic /l/ the doubling is optional, e.g. *coolly* /'kuːl(l)ɪ/, *wholly* /'həʊl(l)ɪ/; but *fully* can only be /'fulɪ/.

(ii) after the etymological ending -*ic* /-ɪk/ (which often does not have morpheme status) the written language requires -*ally*; this is sometimes pronounced /-əlɪ/ although /-lɪ/ is more normal, e.g. *linguistically* /lɪŋ'gwɪstɪk(ə)lɪ/.

The suffix {-lɪ} may be used with virtually any adjective with the exception of those mentioned above which form adverbs unmodified or by suppletion. An odd case is the word *difficult* which seems to have no adverbial equivalent except phrases like *with difficulty*. An unusual use of {-lɪ} is with noun stems, e.g. *namely, partly, purposely*, where there is no adjective equivalent and the adverb seems equivalent to a prepositional phrase involving the noun, i.e. 'by name', 'in part', 'on purpose'. Apart from these cases the meaning of {-lɪ} might be glossed as 'in a —— way'.

III

DERIVATION

A. *GENERAL*

Derivation differs from inflection in a number of ways, the chief one being, as we have said, the grammatical role of the affixes involved. Whereas inflectors are predominantly grammatical in character, most derivers stand closer to the vocabulary and its root morphemes. The inflectional affixes of English are relatively few in number and fairly regular in their use, having a very general application; English derivational affixes, on the other hand, are greater in number and, with few exceptions, much more limited and sporadic in their distribution. Although the slightly more lexical character of derivers might be expected to give them more semantic precision, in fact their meanings are often vaguer and more diffuse than those of their inflectional fellows; indeed derivers frequently overlap and compete with each other.

The different nature of derivers necessitates a difference in their treatment. Rather than consider their form and function one by one, we intend to discuss in a general way the important characteristics of derivational affixes as a group.

B. *FORMS OF DERIVATIONAL AFFIX*

1. *Prefixes*

Derivational prefixes in English are either monosyllabic or di-syllabic, with the sole exception of the /n-/ of *neither, never, nor, none* (and archaic *nought*).

Monosyllabic prefixes may be exemplified by: /ə-/ *ahead*, /riː-/ *re-occupy*, /priː-/ *pre-arrange*, /ʌn-/ *unhappy*, /nɒn-/ *non-payment*.

Disyllabic prefixes may be exemplified by: /ɔːtəʊ-/ *auto-suggestion*, /semɪ-/ *semi-conscious*, /ɪntə-/ *inter-city*. There are fewer disyllabic than monosyllabic prefixes; amongst the former rare and learned words tend to predominate.

Stress. Prefixes either take the stress or leave the stress of the stem undisturbed. In particular:

(i) The prefixes /ə-/ as in *afire*, /bɪ-/ as in *befriend*, and /ɪn-, en-/ 'put into a; make into a', as in *enrol/enslave*, are always unstressed.

(ii) Some prefixes occur both stressed and unstressed, e.g. /priː/ in *preconception* (stem stressed) *preview* (prefix stressed), *prehistory* (variable).

(iii) Some prefixes are generally stressed when they occur with a noun stem, especially if it is short, e.g. /baɪ-/ *by-product*, /kaʊntə-/ *counter-attack*, /fɔː-/ *foreshore*, /aʊt-/ *outpatient*.

Prefixes have no important effect on the phonemic structure of the stems they occur with.

2. *Suffixes*

English has asyllabic, monosyllabic and disyllabic suffixes, and one that is trisyllabic.

Asyllabic suffixes are limited to /-θ/, /-t, -d/ and /-ŋ/. /-θ/occurs only[1] in the words *warmth, strength, length, breadth, width, depth* (all except the first having vowel alternation) and now seems incapable of being extended. A morpheme which may be referred to as {-D$_3$}[2] has /-t/, /-d/ and /-ɪd/ as allomorphs, e.g. *moustached, moneyed, spirited*. /-t/ is also found as a noun-forming suffix in *height* and *weight*. /-n/ occurs as a variant of the suffix *-n/-an/-ian*, e.g. *Zambian*.

---

[1] *Health* and *wealth* are probably best viewed as simple morphs.

[2] It differs from the homophonous {-D$_1$} and {-D$_2$} in that it forms adjectives from nouns.

Monosyllabic suffixes may be represented by: /-ə/ *runner*, /-ɪdʒ/ *wastage*, /-aɪz/ *localize*, /-ənt/ *contestant*, /-sɪ/ *captaincy*, /-ʃɪp/ *friendship*, /-səm/ *quarrelsome*, /-mənt/ *establishment*.

Disyllabic suffixes may be represented by: /-ɪtɪ/ *sincerity*, /-'ɛərɪən/ *authoritarian*, /-əbl̩/ *debatable*.

The only **trisyllabic** suffix found in English is /-ɪ:'ɑːnə/ *-iana* as in *Shakespeariana*.

Stress. Derivative suffixes seem to fall into three main categories with respect to stress:

(i) The majority of suffixes are unstressed and leave the stressing of the stem unchanged, e.g. /-ɪdʒ/ in *anchorage*, *percentage*, / fl̩, -fəl, -fʊl/ in *beautiful, successful*.

(ii) Some suffixes are unstressed but shift the stressing of the stem, generally to the last syllable. Among others there exist the suffixes /-ɪtɪ/, /-ɪk/, /-əl/, /-jən/ as in *agile-agility, metal-metallic, accident-accidental, assimilate-assimilation*. A different pattern is observable in a few cases with /-əbl̩/ and /-əns/, which can shift the stress back to the first syllable as in *comparable* beside *compare, preference* beside *prefer*.

(iii) Suffixes which are usually stressed include: /-'ɛərɪən/ (*Parliamentarian*), /-'eɪʃn̩/ (*exhortation*), /-'ɪə/ (*mountaineer*), /'iːz/ (*Japanese*), /-'esk/ (*statuesque*).

Affixal combinations. Certain suffixal sequences seem to be analysable from the point of view of function, although there is not a straightforward realization of the two components. The following morph equations would seem to hold good:

/-'ɪsɪtɪ/ = /-ɪk/ + /-ɪtɪ/ e.g. *electric-ity*
/-ɪʃn̩/ = /-ɪk + /-ɪən/ e.g. *electric-ian*
/-ɪfɪ'keɪʃn̩/ = /-ɪfaɪ/ + /-'eɪʃn̩/ e.g. *electrify-electrification*

Stem variations. Certain stems, particularly those of Latin origin, vary in their final consonants before particular suffixes. Stems with final /-k/ in their free allomorphs have /-s/ before Latin-type suffixes beginning with /ɪ/, e.g. /əʊ'peɪk/ *opaque* /əʊ'pæsɪtɪ/ *opacity*, but contrast *opaquish* with /k/. We can formulate tentative rules like:

/-Vt/[1] + /-jən/ → /-Vʃn/ as in *translation*
/-Vd/ + /-jən/ → /-Vʒn̩/ as in *persuasion*
/-Vnd/ + /-jən/ → /-Vnʃn̩/ as in *suspension*
/-Vz/ + /-ɪv/ → /-Vsɪv/ as in *abusive*

but these generalizations apply only to words of Latin origin.

Vowel variations also occur in some stems before suffixes. Many are concomitant with the alternation between stress patterns. Vowels and diphthongs are likely to be reduced in unstressed syllables as follows:

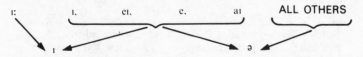

The unreduced syllables may have either primary or subsidiary stress. Examples of such alternation are

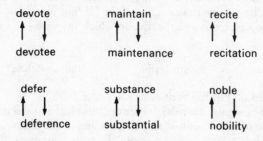

Other stems vary in their vowel phonemes even though the stress pattern remains constant. Certain suffixes, notably /-ɪtɪ/, /-ɪk/, /-ʃn, /-tion*) seem to prefer preceding vowels to belong to the short series,[2] cf. these variations: /iː-e/ *redeem-redemption*, /eɪ-æ/ *tenacious-tenacity*, /aɪ-ɪ/ *bronchitis-bronchitic*, /əʊ-ɒ/ *ferocious-ferocity*, /(j)uː-ʌ/ *resume-resumption*.

Common to all stems (native and Latin) is the principle, found equally in inflection and compounding, that the vowels /ɜː, ɑː, ɔː, ɪə, ɛə, ʊə, ə/ take a following /r/ before a vowel. Examples are /stɑːrɪ/ *starry*, /ˈkjʊərəbl̩/ *curable*. But wherever there is no

---

[1] Here, and in the other transcriptions, V means 'any vowel' (but V alongside a word in conventional spelling means 'verb').

[2] viz. /ɪ, e, æ, ʌ, ɒ, ʊ/.

historical justification for the /r/ – and no *r* in the spelling – it is avoided by many educated speakers, e.g. /'rɔːɪʃ/ not /'rɔːrɪʃ/ *rawish*, /'sɔːəbl̩/ not /'sɔːrəbl̩/ *sawable*.

3. *Final replacives*

Certain word-final consonantal differences between otherwise identical words correlate with the difference between grammatical classes. In one important type we find a noun ending in a voiceless fricative and a related verb ending in the homorganic voiced fricative, e.g.:

-f/-v	-θ/-ð	-s/-z
belief-believe	mouth (N)-mouth (V)	advice-advise
half-halve	teeth-teethe	house (N)-house (V)
proof-prove		use (N)-use (V)
shelf-shelve		

The two most common meaning relationships are for the verb to mean (1) 'have, experience, give—', or (2) 'put into/on to a—'.

In some cases it is an adjective to which the verb is related:

-f/-v	-θ/-ð	-s/-z
safe-save	lo(a)th-loathe	diffuse-diffuse

The meaning of the verb is in each case factitive.

There is a similar alternation between voiceless and voiced sounds in the case of a few noun-verb pairs, ending in the plosives /t/ and /d/, e.g. *intent-intend, ascent-ascend*. In some instances the noun ends instead in /s/, e.g. *expanse-expand, pretence-pretend*. All these types seem to be restricted to cases where /t, d, s/ follow /n/.

A rather different category is formed by adjective-noun pairs like *violent-violence, different-difference*. The /-s/ of such nouns may be analysed in two ways: as a final replacive; or as a suffix added to adjectives in /-ənt/, this latter solution being possible because pronunciations like /'vaɪələns/ and /'vaɪələnts/ are in free variation for many speakers.

The words *speak* and *speech* now seem to provide the only example of alternation between /k/ and /tʃ/. This was formerly a quite common pattern.[1]

---

[1] Cf. *bake-batch, drink-drench*, etc., where the members of each pair are no longer felt to have a close semantic relationship with each other.

4. *Medial replacives*

Vowel alternation also used to play a much more significant role in English, but is now limited to verb inflection and the derivational relationship between certain verbs and (usually) nouns. The marginal nature of medial replacement in derivation is illustrated by the fact that only a couple of vowel patterns have more than one representative, and that the meaning-relationship between the members of some pairs is becoming less close. Examples are: *abode-abide, band-bind, seat-sit, shot-shoot, song-sing, drop-drip, stroke-strike, sale-sell, blood-bleed, food-feed.* The noun meaning may be defined in terms of the verb as 'an instance of -ing', or 'that which − s', or 'where one − s'.

A few factitive-non-factitive verb pairs are still related in this way e.g. *fell* 'cause to *fall*', *lay* 'cause to *lie*'.

One adjective-verb relationship is indicated in this way, viz. *full-fill*. A similar pair is *hot-heat*, where the latter may be either noun or verb. An adjective-noun pair also occurs: *proud-pride*.

Some monosyllabic words exhibit a combination of final and medial replacements, in that both the final consonant and the vowel alternate. The group includes *glass-glaze, grass-graze, bath-bathe, choice-choose, breath-breathe.* We may note that the consonant alternations involved here, viz. /s-z, θ-ð/ are also found in the cases of final replacives we discussed above.

5. *Stress shift*

A whole set of pairs of related words have their members differing from each other solely in respect of their stress pattern. Most usually, again, the related words are noun and verb. They are usually disyllabic with the noun taking its stress on the first syllable, the verb on the second. The following are examples:

abstract, digest, discount, import, increase, inlay, insult, offset, over-hang, torment, transfer, transport.

The word *prostrate* is stressed initially when an adjective and finally when a verb.

It is, however, more common for the members of a pair to be differentiated by stress shift with simultaneous vowel alternation. Vowels are reduced to /ə/ and /ɪ/ in unstressed syllables in the manner described above for stems under the influence of suffixation. Examples are:

NOUN or ADJECTIVE		VERB
absent	/ˈæbsənt/	/əbˈsent/
combine	/ˈkɒmbaɪn/	/kəmˈbaɪn/
conduct	/ˈkɒndəkt/	/kənˈdʌkt/
contrast	/ˈkɒntrɑːst/	/kənˈtrɑːst/
export	/ˈekspɔːt/	/ɪksˈpɔːt/
perfect	/ˈpɜːfɪkt/	/pəˈfekt/
produce	/ˈprɒdjuːs/	/prəˈdjuːs/
progress	/ˈprəʊgres/	/prəˈgres/
rebel	/ˈrebl̩/	/rɪˈbel/
record	/ˈrekɔːd/	/rɪˈkɔːd/
survey	/ˈsɜːveɪ/	/səˈveɪ/

This stress patterning, whether with or without vowel alternation, is typically found in two-syllable words of Romance origin. Yet many words of the latter type now have (or have always had) fixed stress for noun/adjective and verb, either on the first syllable, e.g. *comment, exile, process*, or on the second, e.g. *advance, concern, display, preserve, respect, content* (the latter group being larger). All of these words are both noun/adjective and verb, and exemplify zero difference between the two grammatical classes.

6. *Zero affixes and back-formations*

When we meet two words of different grammatical class which are identical in form and closely allied in meaning, for instance the noun-verb pairs *love-love, fish-fish*, it is possible, as we remarked earlier, to describe them in terms of ZERO-derivation. But, since most users of a language are unaware of its history, this kind of derivation is generally out of place in a synchronic account. In fact the semantic relationships between verbs which are historically derived from nouns can be quite similar to those between original verbs and nouns later derived from them, e.g. *to mother—a mother* beside *to cheat—a cheat* or *to loan—a loan* beside *to look—a look*. We feel that the best synchronic approach to such pairs of words is to regard them simply as instances of MULTIPLE CLASS MEMBERSHIP, whereby one lexical item belongs to two (or more) grammatical classes.

In some cases, however, there is only a partial extension of grammatical role. As examples of adjectives occurring in positions which are generally occupied by nouns, we may cite *the poor, the French*, etc.; examples of verbs in a position which has some nominal characteristics are *have a shave/listen/try/chat, go for a walk/run/drive*. In neither case does the word under scrutiny have the full attributes of a (count) noun: it is just as unEnglish to say *the poors* or *a French* as it is to say *have the shaves* or *you have my listen*. In such cases it may be best to say that certain noun positions may be occupied by (a particular subclass of) verbs or adjectives.

BACK-FORMATIONS are another phenomenon for which we must distinguish sharply between the synchronic aspect and the historical. From the diachronic standpoint it is clear that *beg* has been derived from *beggar*, and *donate* from *donation* by so-called back-formation, i.e. an originally simple word has been reinterpreted as a derived word, or, looking at it differently, a so-called UNIQUE MORPHEME (*begg-*, *donat-*) has been given full morphemic status. But what do we say about the state of the language once the process of back-formation has been completed? In point of fact *beg-beggar* is then in no way different from *run-runner, read-reader*, or any other such pair. The native speaker is no more aware of the established backformation than he is of any other fact of linguistic history. There is no place here for subtractive morphemes.

C. *FUNCTIONAL TYPES OF DERIVATIONAL AFFIX*

1. *Principles of classification*

To achieve an adequate description of derivation in English we must classify affixes according to their function as well as to their form. The range of grammatical functions of derived words is the same as that of simple words. In some cases the derived word is of broadly the same grammatical class as its stem, e.g. *lioness-lion, re-enter-enter*; in other cases the class of the derived word is clearly different from that of its stem, e.g. *enrich-rich, happiness-happy*. On this basis a distinction is usually made between CLASS-MAINTAINING and CLASS-CHANGING affixes. While recognizing this division, we should be aware of one or two difficulties.

Firstly some affixes are both class-maintaining and class-changing. An example is *-ist*, which may derive a noun either from a noun stem, e.g. *isolation-ist*, or from an adjective stem, e.g. *traditional-ist*. Similarly *-ly* may form adjectives either from nouns (*friendly*) or from other adjectives (*kindly*). We should note, however, that while it is quite common for English affixes to derive the same word-class from different stems, it is less common for the same affix to have words of different classes as derivatives.[1] It would

---

[1] One example is *-ary* which produces *evolutionary* (adjective) beside *revolutionary* (noun or adjective).

appear, therefore, that the more significant property of affixes is the word-class they produce rather than the kind of stem they combine with.

The second question à propos of the class-maintaining versus class-changing distinction is how widely we define our classes. If it were argued that *whitish* is different in class from *white* because it does not form a comparative in *-er* (**whitisher*) but prefers *more whitish*, we would probably dismiss this difference as superficial, since it is determined mainly by the phonetic form of the adjective, in particular the number of syllables. If, on the other hand, we consider the difference between *manhood* and *man, priesthood* and *priest*, etc., we recognize that *-hood* combines with nouns denoting ANIMATE beings but forms ABSTRACT nouns. Moreover it seems to be a regularity of English that simple abstract nouns never serve as the direct stem for the formation of other nouns.

We shall find it useful, then, in our survey of suffixes to distinguish between animate, inanimate concrete, and abstract nouns.[1] We shall make our primary division of prefixes into class-maintaining and class-changing, but classify suffixes principally according to the class of word they derive. We give a fairly full but not exhaustive list of the affixes in each case: we include only the more widely-used of the learned affixes.

2. *Prefixes*

(1) **Class-maintaining** prefixes may be grouped simply according to their grammatical class, which is naturally the same for their stem and their derivative.

(a) NOUN: arch- (*arch-enemy*), demi- (*demi-god*), ex- (*ex-mayor*), micro- (*microgroove*), mono- (*monotone*), mid- (*mid-summer*), step- (*stepfather*), sur- (*surtax*), vice- (*vice-chancellor*).

(b) VERB: re- (*re-adjust*).

(c) ADJECTIVE: bi- (*bilateral*), extra- (*extra-marital*), hyper- (*hyper-sensitive*), intra- (*intra-molecular*), pan- (*pan-African*), uni-(*unilateral*).

(d) NOUN and VERB: counter- (*counter-attack*), fore- (*forefront, forewarn*), mis- (*misfortune, misspend*).

(e) NOUN and ADJECTIVE: anti-[2] (*anti-communist*), auto- (*autosuggestion,*

---

[1] We could go on to make other divisions such as PROPER-COMMON, COUNT-MASS, but we lack the space here. Even the division we have adopted gives us difficulties when we come to describe some noun-forming suffixes. Consider the range of different meanings exhibited by *-age* in *orphanage, postage, acreage, drainage*, or by *-(e)ry* in *yeomanry, jewelry, snobbery, creamery*.

[2] *Anti-* and *pro-* may also form adjectives from nouns, e.g. (*He's very*) *pro-Labour, anti-liquor*.

autobiographic(al)), in- (*inexperience, inhuman*), multi- (*multi- millionaire, multilateral*), neo- (*neo-Catholic*), non- (*non-smoker, non-existent*), pro- (*pro-Consul, pro-British*), pseudo- (*pseudo-Liberal*), semi- (*semi-circle, semi-skilled*), trans- (*trans-Pennine*).

(f) NOUN, VERB and ADJECTIVE: inter- (*interrelate*, etc.), post- (*postnatal*, etc.), pre- (*preconception*, etc.), sub- (*subpostmaster*, etc.), super- (*supercharged*, etc.).

(2) Prefixes which are solely **class-changing** are only three in number. Two always convert NOUNS or ADJECTIVES to VERBS; they are:

be- (*befriend, belittle*), en-/em- (*enslave, embitter*). The third prefix is a- which has three slightly different functions; it may derive
—PREDICATIVE ADJECTIVE from NOUN (*ablaze*).
—PREDICATIVE ADJECTIVE/ADVERB from NOUN (*aground*).
—ADVERB from ADJECTIVE (*aloud*).

(3) Three prefixes are both **class-maintaining and class-changing**. They all convert VERBS or NOUNS to VERBS. Examples are:

de- (*decompose, defrost*), dis- (*disbelieve, disillusion*), un- (*unwrap, unhorse*).

In addition *dis-* and *un-* may form ADJECTIVES from ADJECTIVES, (*dishonest, uncertain*), and *dis-* may form NOUNS from NOUNS, e.g. *distaste*.

3. *Suffixes*

The most revealing way to categorize suffixes is according to the class of word they derive. Within this grouping we subclassify the suffixes, according to the word-class(es) to which the majority of the stems belong. In some cases the stem is not a word, but a BOUND ROOT, i.e. a morph that belongs to a root morpheme which has only bound allomorphs. For example, the *horr-* of *horror, horrid* is a bound root, having no free variant; whereas the *metall-* /mɪ'tæl-/ of *metallic*, although a bound morph, is not a bound root, since it has the free variant *metal* /'metl̩/.

(1) Derivers of animate nouns

(a) from an ANIMATE NOUN stem: -ess (*baroness*),[1] -ette (*usherette*).

---

[1] With the exception of *lion* and *tigr-* all stems with which *-ess* combines denote human beings. Such words as *murderess* might be regarded as being derived either from the male agentive, *murderer*, or from the root itself, *murder*.

(b) from a NOUN stem of any kind: -arian (*Unitarian*), -n/-an/-ian (*Syrian, historian*), -eer (*engineer*), -ite (*Labourite*), -ster (*songster*).

(c) from a VERB stem: -ant (*informant*), -ee (*employee*).

(d) from an ADJECTIVE or NOUN stem: -ie/-y (*brownie, Johnny*), -ist[1] (*nationalist, Marxist*), -ling (*weakling, duckling*).

(e) from a VERB or NOUN stem: -er/-or (*rider, actor, jeweller*).

(2) Derivers of inanimate concrete nouns

(a) from an INANIMATE CONCRETE NOUN stem: -ade (*orangeade*), -ing (*towelling*), -let (*booklet*), -ette (*kitchenette*).

(b) from an ANIMATE NOUN stem: -iana (*Victoriana*), -y (*stationery*).

(c) from a VERB stem: -ant/-ent (*consultant*), -ing(s) (*savings, building*).

(d) from a NOUN or VERB stem: -age (*vicarage, package, shrinkage*), -er (*freighter, boiler*).

(3) Derivers of abstract nouns

(a) from an ANIMATE NOUN[2] stem: -dom (*kingdom*), -hood (*motherhood*), -ship (*directorship*).

(b) from a NOUN or ADJECTIVE stem: -ism (*Calvinism, expressionism, colonialism*).

(c) from an ADJECTIVE stem: -ce (*violence*), -ness (*boldness*), -th (*warmth*).

(d) from a VERB stem: -al (*denial*), -ance/-ence (*assurance*), -ation (*temptation*), -ion (*assertion*), -ment (*establishment*), -ure (*failure*).

(e) from a NOUN or VERB stem: -age (*peerage, storage*).

(f) from a NOUN or BOUND ROOT stem: -itis (*tonsilitis, gastritis*), -(o)logy (*Kremlinology, sociology*).

(g) from an ADJECTIVE or BOUND ROOT stem: -itude (*exactitude, gratitude*), -ity (*agility, credulity*).

(h) from an ADJECTIVE, NOUN or BOUND ROOT stem: -(a)cy/-(e)sy (*sufficiency, infancy, adequacy, piracy, courtesy*).

(i) from a BOUND ROOT stem: -or/-our (*horror, splendour*), -y (*economy, scrutiny*).

(4) Derivers of verbs

(a) from a VERB stem: -le (*sparkle, crackle*).

(b) from an ADJECTIVE stem: -en (*darken, sadden*).

(c) from a NOUN or BOUND ROOT stem: -ate[3] (*assassinate, equate*).

---

[1] In some cases a word in -*ist* derived from a noun stem is in free variation with one derived from an adjective stem, e.g. *educationist-educationalist, agriculturist- agriculturalist.*

[2] Exceptionally, these suffixes are added to adjectives, e.g. *freedom, falsehood, hardship.*

[3] Pronounced /-eɪt/, as compared with the adjectival suffix -*ate* pronounced /-ɪt, -ət/ as in *passionate.*

(d) from a NOUN, ADJECTIVE or BOUND ROOT stem: -(i)fy (*glorify, simplify, quantify*), -ize (*computerize, legalize, colonize*).

(5) Derivers of adjectives

(a) from a NOUN stem: -ate (*passionate*), -en (*wooden*), -esque (*statuesque*), -ful (*sorrowful*), -less (*careless*).

(b) from a NOUN or ADJECTIVE stem: -ary (*fragmentary, secondary*), -ish (*bluish, boyish*), -ly (*masterly, deadly*).

(c) from a NOUN, VERB or ADJECTIVE stem: -some (*awesome, tiresome, wearisome*), -y (*draughty, cuddly, greeny*).

(d) from a NOUN, ADJECTIVE or PARTICLE stem: -most (*topmost, outermost, inmost*).

(e) from a NOUN or BOUND ROOT stem: -al/-ial/-ual (*cultural, substantial, factual, federal, social*), -ese (*Japanese, Maltese*), -ic (*alcoholic, economic*), -ical (*farcical, identical*), -ous/-eous/-ious (*poisonous, gaseous, superstitious*).

(f) from a VERB or BOUND ROOT stem: -ive/-ative (*creative, informative, emotive*), -ory/-atory/-itory (*contradictory, auditory, confirmatory*).

(g) from a BOUND ROOT stem: -id (*horrid, candid*).

(h) from a NUMERAL stem: -th (*sixth, millionth*).

(6) Derivers of adverbs

(a) from a NOUN or PARTICLE stem: -ward(s) (*forward(s), homeward(s), inward(s)*).

(b) from a NUMERAL stem: -fold (*twofold, hundredfold*).

D. *THE DISTRIBUTION AND SEMANTICS OF DERIVATIONAL AFFIXES*

1. *Irregularity of distribution*
In the previous section we classified affixes according to the types of word they derive and according to the grammatical class of the stems with which they appear. We listed -*eer*, for example, as a suffix which forms animate nouns from noun stems, e.g. *engineer, profiteer*; there are, however, no words *motoreer, *advantageer. Similarly, although it is perfectly acceptable English to say:

I disbelieved what he said

it is not acceptable to say:

I *disaccepted what he said.

The distributions of *-eer* and *dis-* are defective in this respect. Again, although there exists a word *provocative*, 'likely to provoke', there exists no word **incitative* 'likely to incite'. In such cases we may speak of a derivational GAP.[1]

The distribution of derivers is irregular in another way. In many cases a number of them with similar values are in COMPETITION with each other, and it is impossible to give watertight rules for the selection of the correct affix. If we consider the derivation of nouns denoting persons engaged in an occupation, we find words like *conservation-ist*, *petition-er* and *grammar-ian*, all alike in having abstract noun stems, and yet each with a different affix. Another set of affixes with comparable values is to be found in the words *glad- ness, complex-ity, efficien-cy, impertinen-ce*; again we see that, although every stem is an adjective, each one selects a different suffix to form an abstract noun.

A final example is to be seen in the formation of deverbal abstract nouns with the meaning 'act/process of -ing', where the main competitors are *-al, -ance, -ation, -ment, -ion* and zero. The case of *provocative* and **incitative* seemed to indicate that semantically parallel stems do not necessarily select the same affixes. The following examples show that phonologically similar stems (in this case verbs) may select different affixes:

arrive-arrival	derive-derivation
assess-assessment	confess-confession
debate-debate	abate-abatement
deny-denial	defy-defiance
expect-expectation	elect-election
impose-imposition	disclose-disclosure
neutralize-neutralization	chastise-chastisement
perform-performance	deform-deformation
utter-utterance	better-betterment

Yet despite the similar meanings of these affixes and their apparent complementary distribution, we are still faced with pairs like *excitement-excitation, remittal-remittance*.

Although, as we have illustrated, there are many cases where affixes combine with stems in an apparently irregular way, this is not to deny that certain tendencies and, in some cases, even regularities of distribution are to be observed. It is convenient to recognize three types of regularity: PHONOLOGICAL, SEMANTIC and INTER- AFFIXAL (the latter being discussed in our next sub-section).

---

[1] There are very few inflectional gaps. Note that, for example, the vast majority of verbs are inflected for past tense.

One example of phonological regularity is to be seen in polysyllabic verbs which end in the phoneme sequence /-eɪt/: a high proportion of such verbs form abstract nouns by the addition of the suffix *-ion*, e.g. *illustration, creation, alienation, dehydration*. In other cases, stems which select a given affix are characterized by a particular stress pattern: for instance, most verbs taking *-ee* to derive a noun meaning 'one who is -ed' are disyllabic, with the main stress on the second syllable, e.g. *detain, employ*. Features of both stress and phonemic form characterize nearly all stems which select *-eer*: such stems end in /n/ or /t/ and are disyllabic with stress on the first syllable, e.g. *engineer, profiteer, musketeer*.

We can frequently discern phonological features applying only to a smaller subgroup within the stem-class of a particular affix. A considerable number of verbs which select *-ment*, for instance, have a first syllable of the form /ɪn-/ or /bɪ-/ and have stress on the second syllable, e.g. *enchantment, embarrassment, bereavement, bewilderment*. Again, amongst those verbs which add *-al* to form abstract nouns, we find the rhyming group *arrive, deprive, survive, revive*.

The case of a stem-class characterized by common semantic features may be illustrated by stems which derive noun-adjectives with the meaning '(person) of ——' by the addition of *-i*. Most of these stems denote places in the Muslim cultural sphere, e.g. *Iraq, Pakistan, Zanzibar*. As a minor tendency we may cite the semantically akin *haul, cart* and *freight* which all select *-age*.

2. *Inter-affixal relations*

When derivers are added to stems which themselves are already derived, two (or more) affixes may come to stand next to each other. We sometimes find that when stems derived with a particular affix take a second affix, they generally select a particular one out of a number with similar values. In such cases it seems reasonable to speak of a LINK between the two affixes concerned.

A derived adjective in *-less*, for example,[1] may only form an abstract noun in *-ness*, e.g. *carelessness, weightlessness*; the sequence **-lessity* is impossible. Similarly a derived verb in *-ize* must form its abstract verbal noun in *-ation*, e.g. *dramatization, legalization*. There is a strong tendency for verbal nouns in *-ion* to form agentives in *-ist* and adjectives in *-al*, e.g. *exhibitionist, conservationist, exceptional, occupational*.

---

[1] Cf. also *-ed, -ful, -ing, -ish, -ly, -some, -y*, all of which are native English suffixes.

The sequence in which derivers occur relative to each other is of course fixed: a prefixed deriver must precede any prefixes already contained in the stem, and a suffixed deriver must follow any suffixes already contained in the stem. It is difficult to place any upper limit on the number of derivers to be used in a word. The number of prefixes does not usually exceed two, but words like *re-dis-en-tangle* do occur. Suffixal combinations reach larger proportions, but such giants as *(de-)nation-al-iz-ation-ist-ic*[1] tend to be avoided.

3. *Productiveness*

Those affixes which are currently used to form new words are traditionally termed PRODUCTIVE. The suffix *-ism*, for example, is constantly occurring in new formations such as *revisionism,* *Gaullism*, while a suffix like *-th* is limited to a dozen or so words and seems incapable of further extension. We should not, however, give the impression that productiveness is an all-or-nothing matter: affixes might, in fact, be arranged roughly in a rank order of productiveness, e.g. *-ism* > *-hood* > *-th*.[2]

The degree of productiveness of an affix appears to be strongly influenced by its present distribution, i.e. by the number of words in which it already occurs. In general, affixes with a wide distribution tend to have a high degree of productiveness. A further factor is the number of clearly productive competitors an affix has; for instance, *-ster* (as in *pollster*) is limited in its productiveness partly by the fact that it has to compete with suffixes like *-er*, *-ist*.

When a deriver is subject to phonological restrictions on the stems with which it combines, this may be thought of as acting in two ways at once: on the one hand a suffix like *-ion* is limited in that it largely occurs with stems in *-ate*, etc.; on the other hand, whenever a stem in *-ate* needs a noun derivative, it most naturally selects *-ion*.

Affixes which have a clear-cut lexical meaning are influenced by a factor additional to those mentioned above. One stimulus for the coining of new derived words is what Hockett has referred to as 'the need-filling motive'. The productiveness of a suffix like *-ade*, for example, may decrease or increase according to whether or not

---

[1] Observe the class-changes brought about by these suffixes:

nation	—	al	—	iz	—	ation	—	ist	—	ic
NOUN	→	ADJ	→	V	→	N		→ N		→ADJ
								ANIM		

[2] X > Y means 'X is greater (or more plentiful or more productive) than Y'.

society extends its production and consumption of (fizzy) fruit-flavoured drinks.

Since elements with the widest distribution and most frequent occurrences are likely to have very little specific lexical meaning, their function must be mainly grammatical. We would therefore expect the most productive affixes to be grammatical in character, and it is certainly true that inflectional morphemes are virtually 100 per cent productive. It is not surprising, then, that the most productive derivers of all, -er and -ness, are partly inflectional in character. This is most clearly seen in their occurrence in transformations of whole sentences.

If we compare the three sentences:

(1) Mozart composed this symphony
(2) This symphony was composed by Mozart
(3) Mozart was the composer of this symphony

we will notice that whatever changes we make in the subject, verb or object of the first sentence, we can produce not only a corresponding passive sentence like (2), but also an -er sentence of type (3). The -er here seems to be maximally productive.

However, recalling that derived words are by definition replaceable by simple words, we may find it worth asking what words could replace composer in sentence (3). They are virtually all -er-derivatives (e.g. writer, arranger, editor), a partial exception being author. In other words -er in such positions is really inflectional while elsewhere, such as in

Mozart was a great composer (figure/man/Austrian, etc.)

it is derivative in function. We should also observe that whereas the 'inflected' composer could mean 'of a poem, crossword puzzle, etc.', composer as a pure derivative is limited semantically to the field of music (cf. also writer).

Something similar applies to the -ness of I'm worried about Simon's happiness, which is generally equivalent to . . . whether Simon is happy. Moreover, an unusual coining can take place spontaneously as a transform, even when it would be accepted very reluctantly as a normal item of vocabulary:

A. The play's very slow moving.
B. It's the slow-moving-ness of it that I like.

4. *Meaning*

It is difficult to generalize about the semantic value of derivers, because they in some ways form a bridge between syntax and the vocabulary and thus vary in character between these two poles. The more grammatical an element is, the less lexical meaning it has. We are not surprised, therefore, to find that class-changing affixes like *-ness, -er, -ment, -ation, -ic,* have largely abstract or grammatical meanings like 'person, thing, action, etc., connected with . . .'; exceptions include *-ism* 'cult, philosophy of . . .', adjectival *-en* 'made of . . .' and adverbial *-wards* and *-fold.*

Class-maintaining suffixes, on the other hand, must have some lexical meaning if they are not to be redundant. In English they might be classified under headings like:

FEMALE	-ess, -ette
DIMINUTIVE	-ette, -let
COLLECTIVE	.-age, -(e)ry

The *-le* of *sparkle, crackle,* etc., might be regarded as a verbal intensive or iterative, and *-ish* as a kind of adjectival 'diminutive'. The suffixes *-ology* 'study of', *-itis* 'illness' and *-ade* 'drink' have unusually specific meanings.

Prefixes are, as we have observed, mainly class-maintaining and might be grouped under the following semantic labels:

NEGATIVES	a-/eɪ-/, in-, non-, un-
SPATIO-TEMPORAL	pre-, post-, intra-, extra-, mid-,
RELATIONSHIPS	trans-, sub-, super-
NUMERATIVES	hemi-, demi-, mono-, uni-, bi-, tri-, multi-
PREFIXES OF DEGREE	super-, arch-, micro-

Semi- might be placed in either of these latter two categories, since it is not always so literally numerical as *hemi-* and *demi-* (cf.*hemisphere* with *semi-conscious*).

IV

COMPOUNDING

A. *PROBLEMS OF DESCRIPTION*

1. *What are compound words?*

Although differences of distribution and meaning[1] exist between inflectional affixes on the one hand and derivational affixes on the other, the two classes agree in having a strictly limited number of members. Compounding differs from inflection and derivation in that it does not involve affixes at all, but simply the adding together of any two roots or stems. The roots of a language are not subject to the same numerical limitation as its affixes; it is not only that there are more of them, but also that their number may be increased at any time by borrowings from another language or dialect (e.g. *sputnik, hippy*), or by deliberate fabrication (e.g. *ovaltine*).

It is thus impossible to discuss the components of compounds individually, and our approach here must be different from that used in either inflection or derivation. We shall discuss the problems of delimiting and describing compounds in English, and then give a tentative typology.

Our first problem is to decide exactly what we are to understand by the term COMPOUND WORD. We defined compounding as the process whereby two stems (simple, i.e. roots, or composite) are joined to form a word. But most English roots are free and therefore, in a sense, already words: thus *rail* and *way* are words, but *railway* is normally considered a single word, not a sequence of two words. Why is this?

As we indicated earlier, spelling is a poor guide to word status in the case of compounds. Certainly we should like to treat *firewood, fire-engine* and *fire insurance* in a similar way, despite the inconsistent use of word spaces and hyphens in our orthographical system.

Phonological patterning has been suggested as a criterion for distinguishing compounds from free collocations of words. In particular, main stress on the initial component has been taken as the deciding factor: and certainly the majority of what are usually considered compound words exhibit this feature, whereas word sequences like *red apples* or *wooden bench* generally have the main stress on the final element.

---

[1] Another difference is that the number of derivers greatly exceeds the number of inflectors.

However, a purely phonologically based division would make *'blackberry* a compound but *black 'pudding* a free sequence,[1] *'blacklist* a compound but *black 'market* a free sequence; and yet the members of each pair are similar in their grammatical and semantic structure. Equally striking is the fact that whereas *Oxford 'Road* (also *Oxford 'Avenue*, etc.) would be a free collocation, *'Oxford Street* would be a compound. These inconsistencies underline the fact that the category of COMPOUNDS is a grammatical one, and that, although there is a tendency for it to be phonetically marked in a certain way, such marking is not perfectly regular.

What, then, are the defining characteristics of compound words as opposed to free collocations?

If we take the case of adjective-plus-noun expressions, we see that all free syntactic collocations are equivalent to noun-*that*-be- adjective, e.g. *green leaves = leaves that are/were green, cunning plans = plans that are/were cunning.*

The compound word *madman*, however, involves a specialization in meaning of *mad*, limiting it to 'lunatic', while *mad* can otherwise also mean 'enthusiastic', 'angry' or 'frantic'; we may also note that the *mad* of *madman* cannot be qualified by *quite, rather*, etc.

The compound nature of the word *blackhead*, moreover manifests itself both in the meaning specialization of *head* and in the fact that it is not a 'head' at all but a pimple or a bird WITH a black head. Similarly, a *redcap* is not a 'cap' but a person; hence, whereas *cap* is an inanimate noun, redcap is a human animate noun.

Let us go on to consider such noun-plus-noun sequences as *cotton shirt, cotton socks*, which can be glossed as 'shirt/socks made of cotton'. These combinations differ from, say, *cotton mill* or *cotton reel* in being relatively free syntactically. It seems to be a productive pattern of English for a mass noun M denoting a material to precede and modify another noun X with the expression meaning 'X made of M'; further examples are *stone wall, iron bridge*. We may freely exchange the 'material' noun for any given head noun, e.g. *gold/silver/steel watch, brick/stone/concrete wall*. If we compare this state of affairs with compounds like *cotton mill, cotton reel*, we see that **wool mill* and **plastic mill* are just as unlikely as **nylon reel* or **string reel*. Moreover, although it is perfectly possible to expand *gold watch* to *24 carat gold watch* or *steel watch* to *stainless steel watch*, it is impossible to expand *ironmonger* or *goldsmith* in a similar way. We conclude that *cotton shirt, gold watch, brick wall*, etc., are free collocations, while *cotton mill, goldsmith*, etc., are compounds.

---

[1] Cf. *blackcurrant*, which would be a free collocation for most speakers but for some would be a compound according to this test.

In summary we may say that:

(a) **free collocations** have an extensive syntactic potential (in terms of substitutions, transformations, etc.) that is strictly parallel to other collocations of the same grammatical structure. All free adjective-noun collocations, for example, have a similar syntactic potential.

(b) **compound words** usually have components, the meanings of which are more specialized in the compound than in other environments; moreover the syntactic potential of the components is more limited than elsewhere.

2. *Classifying compounds*

In isolating compounds from other morpheme sequences we have mentioned one criterion for distinguishing between different types of compound, namely, whether the compound as a whole is grammatically and semantically equivalent to (at least) one of its parts. When this is the case, we term the part in question its CENTRE and call the compound as a whole ENDOCENTRIC; in all other cases the compound is referred to as EXOCENTRIC. Endocentric compounds may be sub-divided according to whether only one or both of the parts have functions equivalent to the whole compound. Examples of the three types are:

endocentric—one centre (subordinate): *gunpowder* 'powder for guns', *garden party* 'party in a garden'.

endocentric—two centres (co-ordinate): *pathway* 'path which is a way = way which is a path', *hosepipe* 'hose which is a pipe = pipe which is a hose'.

exocentric: *runaway* 'person who runs away', *outbreak* 'a breaking out'.

A special subclass is the so-called BAHUVRIHI[1] type, where there is a modifier- modified type of relationship but the latter is not equivalent in meaning to the whole compound, e.g. *bluestocking*. We shall use the term HEAD in the restricted sense of 'that which is modified', reserving the term CENTRE for an element which is equivalent to the compound as a whole. Thus exocentric compounds have no centre but may have a head. The vast majority of compounds are of the one-centred endocentric type, where the non-centre element (which is a modifier) restricts the meaning of the centre (which is a head) in some way. The ways in which a

---

[1] A term coined by Sanskrit grammarians from one example of this type, *bahu-vrihi* '((man) possessing) much rice'.

modifier affects the meaning are diverse, as is clearly illustrated by some of Jespersen's examples:

> a goldfish = 'a fish *of the colour* gold'
> a golddigger = 'a digger *for* gold'
> a goldsmith = 'a smith *who works in* gold'
> a gold mine = 'a mine *from which people obtain* gold'.

Although we are tempted to agree with Jespersen's conclusion that 'compounds express a relation between two objects but say nothing of the way in which the relation is understood', we feel that it is worth making some attempt to catalogue the types of meaning relationship to be found. It goes without saying that this cannot be done in the limited space available without omissions and over- simplifications.

The main framework for our classification of compounds must, however, be grammatical. In English we find compound nouns, adjectives and verbs, besides a few adverbs and the numerals. Aside from the grammatical class of the compound as a whole, we must also take account of the grammatical classes of its constituents. In the case of endocentric compounds, where the compound and its head word belong to the same class, there may be different classes of modifier.

Before we proceed to our classification we should mention one special type of compound. As we stated in our introductory section, some root morphemes have bound allomorphs; but as roots they form compounds when they combine with other roots. In the learned vocabulary of English some root morphemes may have a special variant in -*o*- /əʊ/ when they occur as the first element of a compound. Examples are: *Franco-German, Anglo-Norman, Anglo-Indian, electro-magnetism, socio-linguistic, politico-economic, astro-physics.*

In most cases only Latin and Greek elements occur as the first element in compounds of this type, cf. *Franco-British* beside *Anglo-French.* All such words may be regarded as having an adjective in first position, whether they are co-ordinated adjectives[1] like *Anglo-German* = *English-German* or adjective-noun combinations like *astro-physics* = *astral physics*. The element *o* is thus in some ways a kind of adjectival pseudo-suffix, being equivalent, for example, to -*ish (English)*, -*ic (electric)*, -*al (political)*.

---

[1] *Anglo-Indian* may be either EQUATIVE (traditionally called APPOSITIVE) e.g. *the Anglo-Indian community*, or ADDITIVE (traditionally called COPULATIVE) e.g. the *Anglo-Indian treaty*.

In some cases we may posit a compounding of two bound roots, e.g. *patri-cide*, since the *-(i)cide* recurs in *suicide, genocide*, etc., and the *patri-* in *patrilineal, paternal*, etc., and since neither form fulfils our requirements for affix status.

B. *TYPES OF COMPOUND*

1. *Compound nouns*

(1) Endocentric – single noun centre, which generally appears in second position[1]:

(a) ADJECTIVE or PRONOUN MODIFIER (Y) + NOUN HEAD (Z): only one semantic type is possible:
—'Z that is Y', e.g. *madman, greenfly, smallpox; he-rabbit, she-wolf.*

(b) NOUN MODIFIER (Y) + NOUN HEAD (Z): various semantic relationships are possible:

    (i) 'Z that is Y'. Noun modifiers are usually more specific in meaning than their head noun, e.g. *fighter-plane, oak-tree.*

    (ii) 'Z that belongs to/comes from Y'. The first noun may be in its plain or possessive form, e.g. *arrowhead, apple core, folksong, cow's milk.*

    (iii) 'Z that has/contains Y', e.g. *picture book, family man, bagpipe.*

    (iv) 'Z that is made (up) of Y'. These differ from free collocations like *gold watch*, both in their grammatico-semantic restrictions and in having initial stress, e.g. *breadcrumb, snowball, fish cake, paper money, lump sugar.*

    (v) 'Z that V-s Y', e.g. *car thief, sheep dog, fire engine, cotton mill*, the verbs understood being something like 'take', 'round up', 'extinguish' and 'spin' respectively.

    (vi) 'Z that is V-ed by Y', e.g. *steamship, air brake, police dog, hayfever, inkblot, Davy Lamp*, where the verbs understood are something like 'drive', 'work', 'use', 'cause', 'invent', respectively.

    (vii) 'Z that V–s or is V–ed in/at/on (etc.) Y', e.g. *gunpowder, Christmas tree, garden party, press conference, footlight, heart attack, aircraft, garage mechanic, cradle song, night club*. The meaning relationships involved clearly vary between time, location and purpose, the three often overlapping.

---

[1] Henceforth the symbol Y will be used to indicate the first element of a compound, and the symbol Z to indicate the second. V refers to an 'understood' verb.

(viii) **'Z in/at/on (etc.) which Y V–s/is V–ed'**, e.g. *football pitch, law court, date line, saturation temperature.* Time or location is the relationship involved, but it is the reverse of the preceding type, in that here the head noun, not the modifier, denotes the time or place.

(ix) **'Z that is like Y'**, e.g. *bulldog, fountain pen, T-square.* Here a particular subclass is distinguished from the rest of the class by comparing it with a different entity with which the subclass has some feature in common.

(c) NOUN MODIFIER (Y) + DEVERBAL NOUN HEAD (Z): these compounds could be thought of as forming a special sub- group of (A). A different set of relationships is possible because Z retains its verbal content. The head noun (usually derived) may be either agentive or abstract. The semantic types are:

(i) **'Z by Y'** (Y being the actor, and only abstract nouns being possible for Z): *population growth, cloudburst, farm production.* (Cf. such sentences as: *The population grows.*)

(ii) **'Z of Y'** (Y being the goal): *shoemaker, pastry cook, sightseeing, cost reduction, book review.* (Cf. such sentences as: *He makes shoes/ Shoes are made by him; The sight is seen.*)

(iii) **'Z in/at/on (etc.) Y'** (Y being the location, destination, time, instrument, etc.): *sleepwalker, babysitter, nightworker, play-going, colour photography, stage whisper.* (Cf. such sentences as: *He walks in his sleep; He goes to the play.*)

(d) VERBAL MODIFIER (Y) + NOUN HEAD (Z): the verbal modifier appears as a plain stem, as an -*ing* form, or as a deverbal noun. Three semantic types seem to occur:

(i) **'Z that Y-s'** (i.e. the noun names the performer(s) of the verbal activity): *dancing team, hangman, watchdog, demolition gang.*

(ii) **'Z that is Y-ed'** (i.e. the noun names the goal of the verbal activity): *blowpipe, plasterboard, eating apple, smelling salts.*

(iii) **'Z in/at/on/with (etc.) which Y-ing takes place'** (i.e. the noun names the location, time or instrument of the verbal activity): *grindstone, playground, filling station, firing pin, freezing point, retirement age.*

(e) PARTICLE MODIFIER (Y) + NOUN HEAD (Z): these only differ from each other in the nature of the understood verb:

(i) **'Z that is Y'**: *outhouse, outpost, inside.*

(ii) 'Z that V.-s Y': *overlord, down train, undercurrent, afterthought* (where the understood verbs might be thought of as 'rule', 'travel', 'flow', 'come').

(f) NOUN HEAD IN FIRST POSITION (Y): this type is extremely rare. The second element is usually a noun, e.g. *tiptoe* 'toe-tip, tip belonging to the toe' (cf. *arrowhead, apple-core,* where the head noun is in second position).

(2) Endocentric – co-ordinate noun centres: two different types are possible:

(a) EQUATIVE:
8'Z that is a Y = Y that is a Z'. This type is not uncommon, e.g. *girlfriend, prince regent, pathway.*

(b) ADDITIVE:
—'Y and Z combined'. This simple type was rare in English except in geographical names like *Schleswig-Holstein,* until the introduction of modern dual purpose machines, e.g. *clock-radio, fridge-freezer.* The traditional form is a fixed *and*-phrase, e.g. *hook-and-eye, bread-and-butter.*

(3) Exocentric noun compounds have no centre but may still involve a modifier-head construction:

(a) ADJECTIVE MODIFIER (Y) + NOUN HEAD (Z):
—'he who or that which has (a) Y Z' (the pure BAHUVRIHI type): *blackhead, bluebell, dimwit, recap.*

(b) NOUN MODIFIER (Y) + NOUN HEAD (Z):
—'he who has (a) Z like (a) Y': *hawkeye, butterfingers, egghead.*

(c) VERB HEAD (Y) + PARTICLE MODIFIER (Z):

(i) 'he who or that which Y-s Z or is Y-ed by Z': *stand-by, go-between, pullover.*

(ii) 'the act of Y-ing Z': *get-together, splashdown.*

(d) PARTICLE MODIFIER (Y) + VERB HEAD (Z):

(i) 'that which Z-s Y or is Z-ed by Y': *income, offprint, offshoot.*

(ii) 'the act of Z-ing Y': *outbreak, afterglow, downfall.*

(e) TYPES WITHOUT A CLEAR HEAD:

(i) Verb (Y) + Noun object (Z):
—'he who or that which Y-s Z': *pickpocket, scarecrow, stopgap.*

(ii) Noun subject (Y) + Verb (Z)

—'that which Y Z-s': *household* (a rare type).

(iii) Noun object (Y) + Adjective object complement (Z):

'**a sufficient quantity to make Y Z**' (a rare type): *mouthful, spoonful.*

2. *Compound adjectives*

(1) **Endocentric – single adjective centre**, which always occurs in second position. Under adjectives we also include present and past participles in their adjectival role. Some types of meaning relationship apply only to participles, some only to non-participial adjectives; this should be clear from the examples cited:

(a) NOUN MODIFIER (Y) + PLAIN ADJECTIVE HEAD (Z): various semantic relationships occur:

(i) '**Z on account of Y**' (i.e. Y is the cause): *seasick, lovesick, snowblind.*

(ii) '**Z in respect of Y**': *homesick, colour blind, waterproof.* These compounds might also be interpreted in terms of the prepositions *for, to, against,* respectively.

(iii) '**Z of Y**': *blameworthy, carefree*

(iv) '**Z like Y**': *sea-green, stone-cold, dog-tired, pitch-black.*

(v) '**Z as far as Y**': *brimful, knee-deep, world-wide.* These are all double-stressed with the nuclear accent on the second element.

(vi) '**Z as found in Y**': *hunting pink, navy blue, Lincoln Green.*

(b) NOUN MODIFIER (Y) + PARTICIPLE HEAD (Z): Different verbal relationships are possible:

(i) '**Z by Y**': (Y the agent of the verb stem of the past participle Z): *man-made, strife-torn, spellbound.*

(ii) '**Z Y**' (Y the object of the verb stem of the participle Z): *soul-destroying, self-denying, all-embracing.*

(iii) '**Z in/at/on/to (etc.) Y**' (Y location or prepositional object of the verb stem of Z): *home-made, factory-produced, seagoing, law-abiding.*

(c) ADJECTIVE MODIFIER (Y) + PLAIN ADJECTIVE HEAD (Z):

(i) '**Z of the subvariety called YZ**': *dark green, light-blue, Roman Catholic, Irish-American.*

(ii) '**Z enough to be (also) Y**': *icy cold, scalding hot, red hot.*

(d) ADJECTIVE (ADVERB) MODIFIER (Y) + PARTICIPLE HEAD (Z): in these cases the construction is equivalent to an adverb + verb construction; in fact sentences containing such a compound adjective might also be expressed by a **verb plus adverb** or **verb plus adverbial phrase** construction, e.g. *he works hard* beside (*he is*) *hard-working*. Other examples are: *high- born*, *clean-cut*. *Ever-* also occurs as an initial element, representing the adverbial *for ever*, e.g. *everlasting*, also with a plain adjective, *evergreen*; *all* also occurs, being equivalent to *for/over all* in adverbial position, e.g. *allpowerful*, *almighty*.

(2) **Endocentric – co-ordinate adjective centres**: these are relatively rare. Both possible types occur, but the line between them is sometimes hard to draw. The EQUATIVE type may be illustrated by *Anglo-Norman*, *blue-green* (cf. *dark green*). The ADDITIVE type is seen in *Franco-Prussian*, *bitter-sweet* (a special case is *French-German (dictionary)* where the order is relevant, a contrast being made with *German-French*).

(3) **Exocentric adjective compounds**. In both of the following types the compound has a head (which is not, of course, the centre since it cannot stand for the whole compound).

(a) NOUN HEAD (Y) + ADJECTIVE ADVERB MODIFIER (Z): this is the adjectival equivalent of the BAHUVRIHI type like *blackhead*, *dimwit*. It is distinguished from the latter by having the adjective or adverb in second position and meaning 'having a Y which is Z' (rather than 'he who . . .'). Examples are: *footsore*, *heartsick*, *heartbroken*, *inside out*, *upside down*.

(b) ADJECTIVE MODIFIER (Y) + NOUN HEAD (Z): this appears to be a fairly recent type which has arisen from noun phrases occurring prenominally as a noun modifier, e.g. *a first-class player*, and then being shifted to predicative use as in *he's first class*. The meaning of the compound in its adjectival use might be described as 'of that type which V-s (a/the) YZ'. Examples are: *commonplace*, *everyday*, *long-distance*, *high church*, *top quality*. A currently very productive model is with the noun *type*, e.g. *Russian-type*, *new-type*, but this is still rare in predicative position.

3. *Compound verbs*

With the exception of a few exocentric types like *coldshoulder* 'give/ show . . . the cold shoulder', compound verbs are all of the single-centred endocentric type. Three kinds of first element occur, giving us three such types:

(a) NOUN MODIFIER (Y) + VERB HEAD (Z): three types of semantic relationship may be distinguished:

  (i) 'to Z (a/the) Y(-s)' (where Y is the object): *househunt*, *thoughtread*, *flagwave*.
  (ii) 'to Z in/at/on (a/the) Y' (where Y is the location or time): *globetrot*, *springclean*, *sunbathe*, *eavesdrop*.

(iii) 'to Z like a Y': *henpeck, manhandle, chainsmoke.*

(b) ADJECTIVE MODIFIER (Y) + VERB HEAD (Z): the meaning is always 'to Z Y' (where Y is the adjectival predicative complement), e.g. *roughride, whitewash.*

(c) PARTICLE MODIFIER (Y) + VERB HEAD (Z): the meaning is again always 'to Z Y' (where Y is an adverbial particle), e.g. *downgrade, overstep, outstretch, underprop, uphold.*

4. *Other types of compound*

The only other substantial group of compounds is to be found in the NUMERALS. Such compounds as *twenty-four* are additive in the strictest sense: they represent straightforward additions. But compounds like *two hundred* are endocentric with a single head, viz. *hundred.* The same contrast is seen at the derivational level in the difference between *forty* and *fourteen*, the suffix *-ty* meaning 'times ten' and *-teen* meaning 'plus ten'. A combination of the two types occurs in more complex numbers, e.g. *two thousand five hundred.*

Apart from the case of the numerals we only find a few compound prepositions, e.g. endocentric *into* and *on to*, and exocentric *out of.* The adverbial sequences *at once, of late*, etc., are probably best considered as full idioms and are therefore best left unanalysed.

5. *Structures formed by compounding*

The linguistic process of compounding may apply in theory to any kind of stem: even bound roots appear in compounds. Most of our illustrations have been of the compounding of simple words either with other simple words or with derived (or inflected) words, e.g. those inflected with $\{-\text{iŋ}\}$, $\{-D_2\}$ and $\{-Z_2\}$ 'possessive'. It is also perfectly possible for complex words (for the most part, derived ones) to be compounded with each other, and for a compound itself to be a constituent of a further compound.

Examples of some of the different types are:

> bound root + simple word: *Franco-German*
> simple word + simple word: *gatepost*
> simple word + derived word: *colour photography*
> derived word + simple word: *retirement age*
> derived word + derived word: *population growth*
> compound word + simple word: *steamship company*
> compound word + derived word: *blackboard duster*
> simple word + compound word: *council workman*
> derived word + compound word: *conference timetable*
> compound word + compound word: *railway timetable*

Thus different layers of word-formation may be built up to produce lengthy composite words, of which an extravagant example is Zandvoort's (the) *Empire Air Raid Distress Fund Flag Day Committee.*

Compounds themselves of course also form constituents of derived and inflected words. Compound words may behave in the same way as simple words with regard to inflection (e.g. *girlfriend, girlfriends, girlfriend's, girlfriends'; springclean, springcleans, springcleaning, springcleaned*); otherwise they are not true compounds. But compounds may also form the stem of a derived word, e.g. *schoolmaster-ly, un-seaworthy, greenfinger-ed.* In some cases where both derivation and compounding are involved, it is not clear whether a word is best regarded as derived or compound. For example, is a word like *householder* better analysed as *household-er* 'one who has a household', than as *house-holder* 'one who holds a house'?

6. *Other factors affecting compounds*
The tendency towards the 'clipping' of string compounds, i.e. omission of one of their elements, gives rise to some interesting semantic developments. The loss of medial elements may produce compounds with unusual semantic relationships between the components: for example, a *newsboy* is a boy concerned with news only in an indirect way; the word is presumably a 'clipped' form of *newspaperboy.* When a final element is lost, the result is that the remaining element acquires a new range of meaning and, in some cases, a new grammatical class, e.g. *Underground* 'Underground railway'. Sometimes a two-morpheme compound is 'clipped' in this way, e.g. *alarm* 'alarm clock', *life* 'life sentence' (whence the new derivative *lifer*).

'Clipping' of a different kind may affect derived words, e.g. *exam(ination), mike* (for *microphone*); this is mere phonological reduction, through omission of a final segment, and can be termed APOCOPE. A kind of double apocope is sometimes used in compounds, e.g. *mo(tor) ped(al-cycle), tel(eprinter) ex(change).* A further variant is SYNCOPE, i.e. omission of a medial phonological segment, e.g. *breath(an)alyser, heli(copter air)port.*

As an alternative to clipping, compounds may be shortened via their written form, especially if they appear as a sequence of orthographic words. A sequence is formed by adding together the initial letters of these written words, and the acronym formed thus may either be pronounced as a sequence of letter names (a so-called ALPHABETISM), e.g. U.F.O., V.I.P., or be given a pronunciation to match the written sequence according to regular phonographic conventions, e.g. *laser, radar.*

Finally, compounds are just as susceptible as other words to the development of multiple class membership. Thus from the adjective *waterproof* a factitive verb *waterproof* has been formed. Further examples are *blackmail, steamroller* (verb from noun), *evergreen* (noun from adjective); this last example may well have involved 'clipping', some such word as *tree* or *bush* having been omitted.

4

SYNTAX: THE STRUCTURE OF ENGLISH

Michael Garman

Syntax, the study of sentence structure and function, lies at the heart of the study of language.[1] If words are the primary form-meaning complexes of language, then it is sentences that constitute the domains within which they are sequenced and interrelated. Language without syntax would constitute nothing more than a vocabulary, and communication in such a language would be carried on by means of a series of single-word utterances.

Because of its importance, syntax has been studied in widely differing ways, in both pure and applied linguistic research. Pure research has focused on such issues as how far syntactic organization is dependent on the semantic characteristics of words, and on establishing the formal properties of the autonomous level of syntactic organization (i.e. those that are not dependent on word meanings). Applied research has examined such issues as the extent of syntactic variation within a linguistic community, the differences in syntax between the spoken and written forms of particular languages, the role of syntax in the organization of normal and disordered language performance, and the use of syntactic parsing systems in machine-based recognition and production of natural language.

What are the basic building blocks of sentences? These are traditionally taken to be words, and within this approach, there is a division between syntax (word-word organization) and morphology (within-word organization of stems and affixes). With the (re-) discovery of the morpheme in structural linguistics in the earlier

[1] Part of this chapter derives from a course of lectures which has been developed in collaboration with Paul Fletcher, from whom many of the ideas have derived, and who also provided many helpful suggestions on an earlier draft. I am responsible for the deficiencies that remain.

part of this century, syntactic accounts have been proposed that see no such division, working with morphemes as the basic units of sentence structure. But it has increasingly come to be recognized that the boundary on this 'lower' side of the domain of syntax is not so simply drawn as either of these accounts would have us believe. On the one hand, there are many stem-affix complexes that are susceptible of wholly regular, semantically-transparent statement (e.g. the relationship between singular and plural noun stems in English), and syntactic rules provide the ideal means of making such statements. On the other hand, the view that all morphology can be handled within syntax seriously underestimates the degree of within-word structuring that requires statement within the lexicon (where the lexicon is conceived as a list of morphemes, a set of word-formation rules allowing for certain combinations of these, and an output listing of the lexical items, or words of the language, as form-meaning complexes).

Given that sentences are made up of morphemes and words, what sort of higher constructional units do sentences themselves enter into? Syntax has traditionally recognized that sentences may be made up of constituent sentences, in formations that are either compound (i.e. Sentence 1 in coordinate relationship with Sentence 2) or complex (i.e. Sentence 1 in superordinate-to-subordinate relationship with Sentence 2). There are counterparts to this view in current approaches also (as we shall see), although it has increasingly been recognized, on this 'higher' boundary of the domain of syntax, that sentence-sentence constraints are generally much looser, of a different order, and are not susceptible of the same sort of distributional statements, compared to those governing words or morphemes within sentences. 'Text', as higher domains of sentence-structure have come to be called, is an area of study in its own right.[1]

In the brief overview of syntax provided in this chapter, we shall first concentrate on some aspects of the formal procedures employed in establishing the categories of syntactic analysis; then we shall illustrate some aspects of transformational-generative syntax, one of the dominant trends in the formal study of the subject, due to Chomsky and his associates; finally, we shall ex-

---

[1] TEXT LINGUISTICS and DISCOURSE ANALYSIS are terms that are sometimes used interchangeably for this study area; but the former term perhaps is best reserved for the more formal aspects of the study ('syntax beyond the sentence'), while the latter is also concerned with the underlying processes by which speakers produce, and listeners comprehend, extensive sequences of language.

amine a less formal and more descriptive approach, in the work of Quirk and his colleagues. In each case, our survey will be necessarily selective and quite brief.

I

FORMAL SYNTAX

SENTENCES AS UNITS OF ANALYSIS

Our characterization of syntax so far has taken for granted that we know what a sentence of English is. As far as the written English of educated native users of the language is concerned, there is no problem in pointing to such units, in order to demonstrate the fact that they are crucially involved in the organization of this type of linguistic performance. But the same is not true of the spoken language.

In a recent introduction to the study of syntax[1], Brown & Miller provide the following passage, in illustration of the point 'that much of the data actually used by linguists to establish grammar is "regularized". In informal conversation we do not typically speak in units that can easily be recognized as grammatical sentences. Here is an extract from a transcription of part of a radio phone-in discussion on police pay. The speaker is a serving policeman. The items in brackets indicate interpolations from the Chairman of the programme. The symbol + indicates a pause. The symbols *eh, um* indicate "filled pauses".

First of all + I would say that + I don't think any policeman wants a + wants a medal for + for eh the profession which he's in + (No) every person + eh decides + how his eh life is going to + be run (um hum) We we'd work seven days shifts we'd be going to have our two days off (Yes) + and + I don't think + eh + the people realise about shift allowance in England we will receive no shift allowance for this (um hum) um I feel that the press eh eh in a lot of cases give us a bad publicity (Yes) + eh the article in fact that you have written + you + read this morning about the + the + Strathclyde eh (Yes) the press reported that + the + this would + mean a loss of wages about the overtime + about thirty five pounds a week (Yes) well in our local force here in the county area + eh we're not actually

---

[1] See the item by E. K. Brown & J. E. Miller referred to in the Bibliography, p 347.

allowed to be paid for overtime we're told that if we want to do overtime then we must + take time off for it.'

Brown & Miller suggest three points for consideration here: first, how would one derive from this transcription a suitable text for publication, e.g. in a newspaper report?; second, how far can we be precise about how we 'process' the data in order to achieve such a 'cleaned up' version?; and, finally, what sort of units appear to figure in this transcription, and what relation do they bear to 'sentences'?

The last point is the really important one for us. Concealed in the innocuous-seeming expression 'what sort of units appear to figure in this transcription' is a fundamental problem: how does one define one's analytic units, given this sort of data? One can find WORD units, certainly, but what higher-order units can one point to? And what criteria for establishing them would one apply? Using, for instance, the occurrence of pauses (filled and/or unfilled) would not lead to a coherent result. One's impression is that much of this data is built around phrases of just a few words (less than a sentence), with occasionally a much longer unit occurring (rather larger than a sentence). But this is, after all, only an impressionistic judgement, till we establish our criteria for recognizing units.

This consideration leads us to the reason for setting up sentences: they are convenient units of grammatical description, which can be given a precise definition. The grammarian's paradox, then, is the necessity to set up units such as these which are not directly represented in naturally-occurring speech data, in order to describe what is happening in the data. The nature of this paradox is not so far removed from our everyday experience, however. Consider the analogy of such conventional measuring units as feet and inches, or pounds and ounces; these are defined as certain standards, and do not appear directly in the natural world. There are no obvious feet in the height of a tree, or the depth of a pond. Nevertheless, we can express the size properties of such natural phenomena in these standard terms. It is this sort of function that concepts such as SENTENCE fulfil in grammatical description. We shall say, then, that SENTENCES belong to the world of GRAMMAR, while UTTERANCES belong to the world of people; and we need sentences in order to highlight certain properties about utterances. We must bear in mind, however, that this does not imply that people either DO, or SHOULD, speak in sentences. Having said this, we of course allow for the possibility that utterances may under certain conditions more closely approximate to, or depart from, the general properties associated with sentence units. Writing (as I am doing now) permits time for reflection, revision and the setting of fairly precise boundaries on utterances, so that the writer can closely approximate to certain standards of form; these standards are taught at school, in a way that is fairly uniform throughout the educated community. In this respect, much written language is sharply different from what is observed in speech, which tends to be more spontaneous, and produced under greater time pressures, under most conditions. We shall return to the issue of characterizing the syntactic organization of spontaneous speech data in the final part of this chapter.

FORM CLASSES

Traditionally, sentences have been described in terms of word-based 'parts-of-speech'; that is, words in the language have been classified into a small number of abstract types such as noun, verb, adjective, and so on, and sequences of these types, or parts of speech, have been documented as representing different sorts of sentence pattern.

Modern approaches are broadly similar, but they have made an issue of (i) the FORMAL criteria needed to establish these classes, and (ii) the nature of the elements that can be so classified. Under (i), syntacticians in the structural linguistics tradition have criticized earlier approaches for being excessively reliant on inexplicit meaning-based or 'notional' criteria: the most often discussed example is that of the Noun, defined as 'the name of a person, place or thing' in those school grammars (in the days when they were used) which derived from the older tradition. How, then, structural linguists ask, do we classify *sympathy* (assuming that by 'thing', we refer to a concrete object, rather than an abstract concept). It has been suggested[1] that there is a way of reconciling the ancients and moderns if we distinguish between (a) the formal establishment of such classes (the modern way is right) from (b) the secondary issue of providing a revealing label for the form class thus set up (the older tradition was well-motivated). Thus, where (as is often the case) a form class contains a large proportion of items that can be characterized in simple notional terms, then the whole form class can be so characterized, notwithstanding that certain items within it

[1] In J. Lyons, 'Towards a "notional" theory of the "parts of speech"', *Journal of Linguistics*, **2** (1966), pp 209–236.

(by formal criteria) will not satisfy this notional description. It is interesting to note that this sort of position appears to have been well understood by Petrus Hispanus in the thirteenth century (whom we may take as an example of the more sophisticated practitioners in the older tradition).[1]

Concerning (ii), syntacticians today use the term FORM CLASS (rather than word class), in recognition of the fact that elements below the word (stem and affix morphemes) may constitute syntactic classes, and that groups of word and morpheme elements (i.e. larger than the word), generally referred to as PHRASE STRUCTURES also represent syntactic classes (as of course does the largest unit, the sentence).

Formal procedures

The procedures used to establish form classes are basically few in number and fairly simple.

SUBSTITUTION is the simplest of all, establishing, for example, that *the dog from number 23* belongs to the same form class as *Fido* in respect of their equivalent substitutability by the pronoun *it* (actually, 'pronoun' is a misnomer, as this example shows: so-called pronouns actually substitute for whole noun phrases, not nouns alone).

CO-OCCURRENCE is another fundamental criterion, used in a number of ways. It can show the PERMUTABILITY of noun phrases within a sentence, such as:

> Fido bit the cat
> The cat bit Fido.

helping to establish that both *Fido* and *the cat* are similar types of element, both as form classes, and in respect of their relations with *bit*; on this last point, compare

> Fido bit the biscuit
> ★The biscuit bit Fido.

These two criteria together can show quite revealing properties about certain items, such as the complex character of *one* (the proform, not the numeral):

---

[1] My understanding of Petrus Hispanus is entirely derived from F. P. Dinneen, *An Introduction to General Linguistics* (New York, 1967), pp 132–141.

John has a red *motorbike*, and I'd like a blue one
John has that *red motorbike*, and I'd like this one
John has *a red motorbike*, and I'd like one too

where the italicized portions of the first sentence in each case indicate the different replacement functions of the element *one*. Are there three *ones* here, or only one, with three functions?

Verb forms

Most older parts-of-speech analyses looked on noun and verb as the fundamental distinction in syntax, allowing for the most basic sort of predication function that is essential to sentencehood:

John   ran
(Noun)   (Verb)

More recent approaches also treat this opposition as fundamental: Chomsky, for example, recognizes four major syntactic categories, in terms of the dimensions ± noun, ± verb:[1]

	Noun	Verb	Adjective	Preposition
Noun	+	−	+	−
Verb	−	+	+	−

Syntactically, verbs are perhaps more interesting, at least at first sight, inasmuch as the nouns that may appear in a sentence may be said to occur there by virtue of the syntactic properties of the verb. Thus in

⋆John elapsed
⋆The biscuit bit the dog
⋆Mary arrived the book

we may account for the ungrammaticality of the sequences in terms of noun phrases violating certain CO-OCCURRENCE REQUIREMENTS of the verbs; *John* is the wrong sort of noun phrase to act as subject of *elapse*, and so on. The centrality of the verb is also seen in the fact that most definitions of sentences rest, in one way or another, on the presence of a verb constituent.

We shall therefore consider verb forms as a convenient starting point for our illustration of some formal procedures here; and we

[1] N. Chomsky, *Lectures on Government and Binding* (Dordrecht, 1981), p 48.

shall try to link this section to the next, on transformational-generative syntax, by referring there again to the treatment of these forms and their associated elements. The following
examples of verb forms are taken from the passage quoted earlier:

> I *would say* . . .
> we*'d work* . . .
> we *will receive* . . .
> this *would mean* . . .
> we *must take* . . .
> you *have written* . . .

In each case, the extracted form has the verb forms italicized, and
these terminate in a MAIN VERB, a concept which we shall take to be
given for purpose of our discussion.

This leaves us with certain PRE-(MAIN) VERBAL elements, which
are of interest to us. What other pre-verbal elements appear in the
data, and may appear generally in the language? Is it possible to find
examples where these elements occupy positions other than immediately before the main verb? And how far can these individual
elements combine with each other, preceding a main verb (i.e. to
form a complex preverbal constituent)? English has the following
verb elements which may occur as pre-verbal elements in the sense
above, or, as we shall call them, as AUXILIARY VERBS:

Full forms:

will	shall	can	may	must	ought to	dare	need
would	should	could	might				

have	am	was	do
has	are	were	does
had	is		did

Contracted forms:

've	's	're
'd	'm	'll

They can occur other than immediately before the main verb in
NEGATIVE and INTERROGATIVE constructions:

NEGATIVE:
e.g. *will not* . . .

Contracted forms:
(no change in stem)   wouldn't, couldn't, etc.
(with stem change)   won't, shan't, can't, don't

INTERROGATIVE:
e.g. *will you* . . .?

Contracted forms: some of these are not easy to determine, partly no doubt because they are not well recognized in the standard written language.
d' (e.g. *d'you know* . . .?)
'll, sh'll (e.g. *'ll you ring him, or sh'll I?*, where *you* and *I*
          are stressed)
c'n, 've, 's, 'm, d's, 'd (you might like to try to observe these
                          in your own speech)

The set of forms that is emerging here is fairly distinctive; it excludes, for instance, verb forms such as *like, want, go*. The reason for this is that these forms behave differently under negation and interrogation, e.g.

NEGATIVE:
He *could*n't go vs. He didn't *want* to go (*He *wanted*n't to go)

INTERROGATIVE:
Could he go? vs. Did he *want* to go? (**Wanted* he to go?)

So far, we have just considered single auxiliary elements; but the following permitted combinations of auxiliary verbs are also found in the language (ignoring contracted forms here, for simplicity):

3-ELEMENT SEQUENCES:

Position 1	Position 2	Position 3
will/would	have	been
shall/should	*has	*be, *is
can/could	*had	*am, *was
may/might		*are *were
must		
ought to		

2-ELEMENT SEQUENCES:

Position 1	*Position 2*		
(as above)	(as above)		
	Position 2	*Position 3*	
	have	(as above)	
	has		
	had		
Position 1		*Position 3*	
(as above)		be	
		*been,	*is
		*am,	*was
		*are	*were

The patterning of ACTUAL combinations here is rather complex, and quite restricted when compared .to the number of POSSIBLE combinations that would arise through random sequencing. It is in this sense that syntax is concerned with the CONSTRAINTS that a language imposes, or recognizes, on the sequences of elements that make up its sentences. Position 1 elements are quite stable, but those in subsequent positions show restrictions on which forms may occur, depending on what precedes in the sequence. It is one of the goals of syntactic description to provide coherent accounts of such complex phenomena.

Having introduced, as it were, a problem area, we shall now turn to establishing a framework within which a coherent description can be attempted.

II

TRANSFORMATIONAL-GENERATIVE SYNTAX

PHRASE STRUCTURE

Although linguists have rightly been criticized (by other linguists) for sometimes adopting the 'armchair' approach to data, there is considerable evidence of achievements having been made by the analysis of regularized and decontextualized sentence examples.

What such examples embody is the native syntactician's intuitions about the language, and hence they tap a resource which is more fundamental, and simply much more extensive, than any corpus could be. It is a remarkable and important fact that we can contemplate the structural and relational properties of sentences quite apart from their communicative functions. True, this leads to such 'disembodied' examples as[1]

The farmer killed the duckling,

but, while we may criticize such forms as being hopelessly decontextualized (we should not ordinarily use *the* when referring to *farmer* or *duckling* for the first time), they are importantly convenient from the point of view of formal analysis. The basis for such an approach is this: if we can develop a formal system to accommodate such examples, then we can hope to be in a position eventually to consider the rather less regular data that occurs naturally in communicative contexts.

So let us stay with this example, and see what information it may yield. Pronominalization shows that the italicized portions are each noun phrases:

The farmer	killed	*the duckling*
He	killed	it,

and there is further evidence that the sequence *killed the duckling* constitutes a further phrase unit, based on the presence of the verb, and hence called a verb phrase:

The farmer	*killed the duckling*
He	did

Within each noun phrase here, we may recognize an identical sequence of form classes, article followed by noun.

If, then, we wish to characterize the grammatical constituents of our original sentence, we may do so in the following way:

---

[1] From E. Sapir (in *Language* (New York, 1921), Chapter 5), an early and eloquent critic of the use of such decontextualized data.

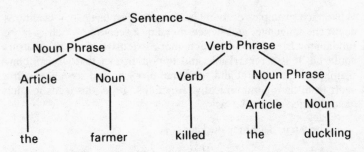

This shows that the sentence unit (S) is the highest order element, the IMMEDIATE CONSTITUENTS of which are the initial noun phrase (NP) and the verb phrase (VP); the VP in turn has as its immediate constituents a verb (V) and a following noun phrase (NP); and the immediate constituents of each NP are an article (Art) and a following noun (N). This description embodies CATEGORY information (i.e. whether an expression belongs to the category NP, VP, Art, N, and so on), and ORDER information (i.e. whether item X precedes or follows item Y). It will be seen also that it is organized along two dimensions, the left-right indicating order in the sequence, while the vertical dimension is probably best described as that of CONSTITUENCY. Thus, as we have already said, the sentence unit S is the highest order element in this constituency chain or hierarchy, since it contains within itself all other constituents, and is not the constituent of any other unit; then we find intermediate constituent elements such as NP and VP, which are both constituents (of S) and comprised of lower order constituents; and finally, we have the terminal, or lowest order constituents, corresponding to the so-called parts-of-speech of traditional grammar, article, noun, verb, etc.

Really, grammar in the sense of SYNTAX stops at the level of these terminal categories or symbols, and our grammatical description would therefore be:

This grammatical description covers a whole range of sentences of the language, including *the chimpanzee kicked the football, the goose laid an egg, the dog bit the man*, and so on. In this sense, the point at which particular words, or LEXICAL ITEMS, are attached to the terminal symbols marks the division between syntax proper and vocabulary. But, as we shall see, there appear to be important links across this boundary, within the field of grammar.

Finally, in this section, we may note that it is possible to provide systems of rules that will yield, or GENERATE, such grammatical descriptions as the one given above: these are known as PHRASE STRUCTURE (PS) rules, and they constitute what are referred to as PHRASE STRUCTURE GRAMMARS (PSG). Let us look first just at the rules required to generate the above structure:

1. S → NP + VP   (this says that a sentence consists of a noun phrase followed by a verb phrase)

2. VP → V + NP   (a verb phrase consists of a verb followed by a noun phrase; notice that we now have TWO noun phrases, one from S, by rule 1, and the other from VP, by rule 2)

3. NP → Art + N   (a noun phrase consists of an article followed by a noun; this rule applies to BOTH the noun phrases we have introduced thus far)

Of course, there are other possible sentence structures in English, and we have to allow for these by appropriate extensions to our rules. A noun phrase possibility that we have already considered is where the whole NP is represented by a 'pronoun', Pron. Another possibility, as in:

The duckling died,

is that the verb phrase may consist of just a verb followed by no noun phrase (the so-called INTRANSITIVE pattern; the TRANSITIVE pattern is where a noun phrase follows the verb, and stands as its object – see further below). Yet another noun phrase possibility is to have a proper noun, PropN, such as *John, Fido, Mary*, in which case no article precedes, as in:

John killed the duckling
Fido bit Mary.

We can accommodate these possibilities (and others we shall not illustrate here) straightforwardly in a phrase structure grammar. We may modify our original rule system, as follows:

1. S → NP + VP   (exactly as before; this is the first rule of the system, and as such has the greatest generality over a whole range of otherwise differing sentence structures)

2. VP → $\left\{ \begin{array}{l} V \\ V + NP \end{array} \right\}$ (curly brackets indicate EITHER-OR options)

3. NP → $\left\{ \begin{array}{l} PropN \\ Art + N \\ Pron \end{array} \right\}$

This rule system will now generate structures such as:

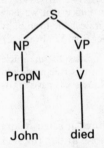
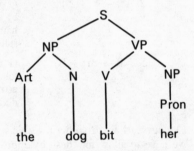

and certain other arrangements of these terminal categories, as allowed for in the rules.

LEXICAL INSERTION

We have just illustrated a phrase structure analysis which is lexically specified, i.e. it has lexical items attached to its terminal categories. It will be appreciated from what we have said thus far that lexical insertion is not a matter that is handled by the PS rules we have specified above. We have no space to go into this issue here, but we shall assume that lexical insertion is achieved by means of lexical items being specified (or SUBCATEGORIZED) for occurrence in certain syntactic frames, and that they are subject to a general insertion statement, or condition, such as:

Insert under any terminal category any word from the lexicon which (i) belongs to that category, and (ii) is subcategorized as permitting insertion into the kind of sentence structure it is being inserted into[1]

We are now in a position to consider the formal statement of the auxiliary verbs in English.

AUXILIARY VERBS

Now let us consider a further example of proform substitution on our sentence.

> *The farmer*   *killed the duckling*
> He   did it.

A moment's consideration will show that, while *he* replaces *the farmer*, *did* is not replacing the verb *killed* here, and *it* is not replacing the noun phrase *the duckling*. Rather more careful consideration will further reveal that the complex proform *did it* represents the BASE form of the verb *kill* together with its following noun phrase *the duckling*, and that *do* (in the form *did*) carries the past tense element. We should also notice that in the proform version we considered earlier,

> *The farmer*   *killed the duckling*
> He   did

the proform *did* is made up of its base form *do* plus past tense *-ed*. But *do* here corresponds with the base form of the verb *kill* and its following NP *the duckling*, yielding the following detailed correspondences·

> *The farmer*   *kill*   *-ed*   *the duckling*
>   1   2   3   2
>   He   do   -ed
>   1   2   3

Here, the numbering of elements should help to make it clear that the past tense element is not actually part of the VP, if by this structure we refer to that sequence which is replaced by the proform *do* (or the complex proform *do it*, in the first example con-

---

[1] From A. Radford, *Transformational Syntax* (Cambridge, 1981), p 120.

sidered here). Such observations support the view that the tense element, whatever its actual position in the OBSERVED form of the sentence, syntactically is to be located outside the VP constituent, such as in:

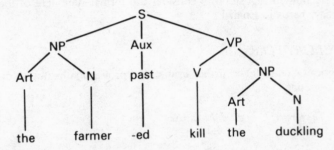

If this sort of analysis is right, then (i) proforms like *do it*, and *do* can replace a whole verb phrase, and (ii) the tense element (in this case, PAST) is not part of this verb phrase. It will be observed that we have given it a separate position in the configuration above, directly under S, under the label AUX (for auxiliary); we shall come to the reason for this in a moment.

Further, if we consider a version of the same sentence with an auxiliary verb, such as

The farmer   *had*   *killed the duckling*
He   had   done it

we can find the same pattern of substitution, with *do it* again replacing the implicit sequence *kill the duckling*, and this time past tense is marked on *had*. Again, we can say that (i) the proform *do it* replaces the verb phrase, and (ii) the tense element, this time also with the auxiliary verb *have*, is not part of this verb phrase. This would require the following framework:

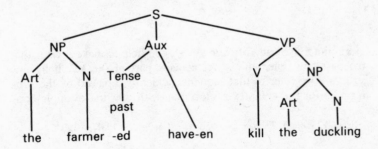

where, in addition to the past tense affix *-ed*, we must also recognize the presence of the *-en* affix associated with the auxiliary verb *have* (and which appears on the verb *kill*, yielding *killed*).

Let us now consider the position when all our auxiliary verb options are taken up, as in:

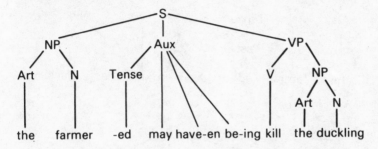

where as well as the obligatory tense element we also have certain optional auxiliary verbs, as set out in positions 1, 2 and 3 of our analysis of verb forms above.

We are now in a position to propose the necessary amendments to our PS rules:

1. S → NP + Aux + VP
2. Aux → Tense (M) (have-en) (be-ing)
(where M refers to the class of verbs in Position 1 of our earlier analysis, traditionally referred to as MODAL auxiliary verbs)

(with the other rules being unaffected). Notice that PS rule 2 says that all the Aux elements are optional (marked as such by being enclosed within parentheses), except for Tense; this amounts to the claim that sentences in English are inherently specified for tense.

Let us see how such a system would derive our example *the farmer killed the duckling*. The appropriate PS configuration would be:

Further possibilities within this framework would be:

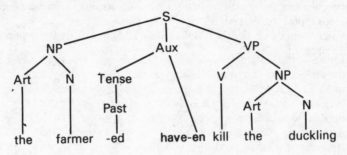

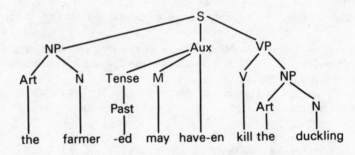

and

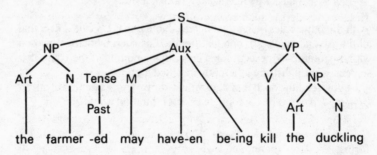

to set out just a few.

What is striking about all these terminal category sequences is the way in which their affixal elements *-ed, -en, -ing* are 'misordered' with respect to their observed positions in sentence structure. What is required, therefore, is a systematic re-ordering of them, in a way that is not simply *ad hoc.* The solution is to test the output sequence for the presence of the following properties:

X – Affix – Verb – Y,

where X and Y may be any element (including zero), Affix is one of the set *-ed, -en, -ing,* and Verb may be one of the elements specified in M, or *have,* or *be,* or any element under the V category in the VP. Whenever such a sequence is discovered, the affixal element must be *applied* to the verb element, in order to yield the appropriate output form (i.e. taking into account the fact that some forms are irregular in the formation). We can show the identification of the sequences involved, and the operation of the affixal procedures, as follows:

the farmer *-ed kill* the duckling
    → killed
the farmer *-ed have -en kill* the duckling,
    → had → killed
the farmer *-ed may* have*-en kill* the duckling
    → might   → killed
the farmer *-ed may* have*-en be-ing kill* the duckling
    → might   → been → killing

The observation that such a single general operation[1] serves to place all the affixes in these (and other) examples correctly may be argued to constitute its own justification for the underlying analysis. But, in considering such an operation, we have clearly gone beyond the sort of phrase structure rules that we have been using hitherto, and this may give rise to the need to seek further justification for what appears to be a quite radical development. In this connection, we should note that there is further support, from a quarter which we have only briefly touched on so far – the case of the auxiliary verb *do.*

Notice that, in our original survey of auxiliary forms, we included *do,* but subsequently left it out of our positional analysis of auxiliary forms. We later mentioned *do* again, when we were discussing its role in the case of *he did it,* and this led us to set up the Tense element in the initial position under the Aux category. Subsequently, we have said nothing more about *do,* till now.

---

[1] First suggested in published form in N. Chomsky, *Syntactic Structures* (The Hague, 1957), and considerably simplified in the account given here.

Now consider what happens when we form interrogative, or negative, versions of our example sentences:

1a the farmer killed the duckling
 b did the farmer kill the duckling?
 c the farmer did not kill the duckling
2a the farmer might kill the duckling
 b might the farmer kill the duckling?
 c the farmer might not kill the duckling
3a the farmer had killed the duckling
 b had the farmer killed the duckling?
 c the farmer had not killed the duckling
4a the farmer was killing the duckling
 b was the farmer killing the duckling?
 c the farmer was not killing the duckling
etc.

The generalization contained in these examples, and others, may be expressed informally as follows: forms of the auxiliary verb *do* are used in interrogative and negative sentences WHEN NO OTHER AUXILIARY VERBS ARE PRESENT.

Why should this be so? For an answer, we again have to refer to the properties of our verb-affix rule above. Consider what happens in the formation of interrogative sentences: the subject noun phrase, in our examples, *the farmer*, and the tense-marked auxiliary verb, *may, has,* or *is*, appear to change places. In the case of the negative sentences, the negative element, *not*, appears immediately after the tense-marked auxiliary verb. Both of these observations are consistent with the following statement:

The noun phrase/negative element is positioned immediately after the Tense element, if there is no auxiliary verb stem following; otherwise, it is placed immediately after the first auxiliary verb stem.

This gives us (illustrating just from the interrogative):

-*ed* the farmer *kill* the duckling
(the verb-affix rule cannot apply; see further below)
-*ed have* the farmer -*en kill* the duckling
→ had   → killed
-*ed may* the farmer have -*en kill* the duckling,
→ might   → killed
-*ed may* the farmer have -*en be -ing kill* the duckling,
→ might   → been → killing

It will be seen that the condition for applying the verb-affix rule in the case of the first example here is not met, since the affix is not contiguous with the following verb: the interposed noun phrase brings this state of affairs about. As a result, the Tense affix is 'stranded', in sentence-initial position, and the function of the *do* auxiliary is to 'rescue' it. The *do* auxiliary is introduced, by rule, just in cases where the verb-affix rule is blocked; and the normal morphological processes apply, to yield *do* + -*ed* → *did*. In this way, we can account for the peculiar distribution of the *do* auxiliary verb.

TRANSFORMATIONS

This discussion has taken us beyond a phrase structure account of this area of English syntax. We have referred to certain rules which ANALYSE the output sequence of the phrase structure configuration and perform certain operations on this sequence, in order to generate the observed forms of sentences. These operations are known as TRANSFORMATIONS, involving, in the cases we have discussed, the attachment of verb affixes to verb stems (the VERB-AFFIX rule), the reversal of the subject noun phrase with respect to certain auxiliary elements in the formation of certain interrogatives (the INTERROGATIVE REVERSAL rule), and the placement of the negative element in the formation of negative statements (the NEGATIVE PLACEMENT rule). We may say that transformational-generative syntax works with two levels of syntactic sequencing, (a) a pre-transformational level, within which certain generalizations may be made about the constituents within a phrase structure analysis of a class of sentences, and (b) a post-transformational level, which converges on the observed forms of those sentences. Central to this approach is the concept that OBSERVED SEQUENCES OF ELEMENTS DO NOT FULLY REPRESENT THE ABSTRACT SYNTACTIC RELATIONSHIPS THAT SENTENCES EMBODY. We must leave our discussion of transformational-generative syntax at this point (although there are many recent developments within this approach that we have not covered), and conclude this chapter by considering a radically different, and complementary, approach to the description of syntax.

III

SYNTACTIC RELATIONS AND SYNTACTIC TRANSCRIPTION

Consider the difference between these two descriptions of our example sentence:

(1)

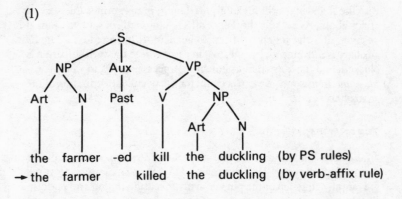

the	farmer	-ed	kill	the	duckling	(by PS rules)
→ the	farmer		killed	the	duckling	(by verb-affix rule)

(2)   *the farmer*   *killed*   *the duckling*

S	V	O	(Clause structure)
Det N	MV	Det N	(Phrase structure)
	-ed		(Word structure).

In (1), the transformational-generative description, the syntactic organization of the sentence is handled in terms of a set of CAT-EGORIES, S, NP, VP, etc., which are set in RELATION to each other by the rules of the system. Thus, the 'Subject of' relationship is expressed in the line that links the leftmost NP to the immediately dominating S category, while the 'Object of' relationship is expressed in the line that links the rightmost NP to the immediately dominating VP category. In this way, we can say that categories have primary status in this description, and relations between categories are derived from the phrase structure configurations that the categories are put into by the rules of syntax.

By contrast, in (2) we have a syntactic description that is organized primarily in terms of relationships, at what is called CLAUSE level. CLAUSE is a term that corresponds to SIMPLE SENTENCE, leaving the use of the term SENTENCE for those units which have more than one clause. Clause (and sentence) structure in this example is set out in terms of the elements S = subject, V = verb (in the sense of verbal element or group; some closely similar systems use the symbol P = predicator for this, which brings out its relational character quite clearly), and O = object. The categorial expression of these relational elements does not affect their identification in these terms: thus, an S element may be expressed as a single noun or pronoun, as a noun phrase, or as a clause. The next level, of phrase structure, helps to specify more categorially what sort of expression is found at each position in clause structure (e.g. main verb (MV) as V element); but even here relational terms are not dispensed with, since, for example, Det = determiner, a relational term which covers such categories as articles, demonstratives and possessive pronouns; thus *the, this* and *our* are all said to 'determine' the head noun. At the next level of structure, the word, it is possible to specify those morphological characteristics that are relevant to the syntax of the clause.

Such a radically different approach to the description of syntax is particularly well suited to the much-neglected function of providing for a system of SYNTACTIC TRANSCRIPTION[1]. It is taken for granted that analysis of, say, the SOUND STRUCTURE of language requires transcription at the level of PHONETICS; but it is often forgotten, apparently, that syntactic analysis is dependent on some syntactic transcription. This need is particularly evident where large corpora are involved, as in the data-base of the Survey of English Usage[2], for example, within which the system of transcription illustrated here has been evolved. As with phonetic transcription systems, the focus of representation may be either relatively narrow, or broad, depending on the demands of the analysis. It is, for example, possible to include stem-lexical information as well as affixal detail in the word-level representation, if one is interested in the relationship between syntactic patterns and lexical choice.

As an example of how such a transcription system might be used to highlight the syntactic properties of spontaneous conversational data, consider the following passage, taken from the Survey of English Usage. It represents a realistic attempt to capture the way that English is actually spoken, by well-educated people who are behaving as naturally as possible (unaware of the fact that they are being recorded). In the passage that is set out here, three adult males who have known each other for some years, are discussing the state of English football. The data is set out as it occurred, except that filled and unfilled pauses, intonational markings and

---

[1] And for such related concerns as the provision of a 'reference' grammar for a language, such as the work of R. Quirk, S. Greenbaum, G. Leech & J. Svartvik, cited in the Bibliography.

[2] Carried out under the direction of Randolph Quirk, and covering spoken as well as written texts of British English. The data was collected with financial support from the Leverhulme Trust and the Calouste Gulbenkian Foundation, and is kept at University College, University of London.

punctuation features, word-repetitions and false starts have been omitted. Incomplete utterances (i.e. those that get off to a true start but are not finished for some reason) are retained. The reason for omitting these features from the original orthographic transcription is to present as clearly as possible the nature of the data on the basis of which a syntactic transcription must proceed. Since the relation, if any, of intonational, pausal, and other fluency characteristics to the determination of syntactic units is unclear, it is preferable to develop a syntactic transcription first on the basis of the sort of data representation that is illustrated here:

(*Participant A*) well what's the failure with the football I mean this I don't really see I mean it cos the money how much does it cost to get in down the road now

(*Participant B*) I think it probably is the money for what you get you know I was reading in the paper this morning a chap he's a director of a big company in Birmingham who was the world's number one football fan he used to spend about a thousand a year watching football you know

(*Participant C*) coo

(*Participant B*) he's watched football on every league ground in England all ninety two

(*Participant A*) [laughs]

(*Participant B*) and he's been to America to watch West Bromwich playing in America he's been to the last two or three world cup things you know tournaments and he goes to all the matches away you know European cup matches and everything that English teams are playing in he's all over the world watching it you see this year he's watched twenty two games so far this year which is about fifty percent of his normal

(*Participant C*) good lord

(*Participant B*) and even he's getting browned off and he was saying that you can go to a nightclub in Birmingham and watch Tony Bennett for about thirty bob something like this a night with Tony Bennett have a nice meal in very plushy surroundings very warm nice pleasant says it costs him about the same amount of money to go and sit in a breezy windy stand

(*Participants A & C*) [laugh]

(*Participant B*) on a wooden bench to watch a rather boring game of football with no personality and all defensive and everything he says it's just killing itself you know

(*Participant A*) yeah

(*Participant C*) m

(Participant B) they're not giving the entertainment they used
to give the conditions have if anything deteriorated and
(Participant C) in what way
(Participant B) they're charging three times what they used to
or four times what they used to

There are a number of interesting aspects concerning the syntactic
organization of this passage. We shall concentrate here on just two,
clause-level, aspects: ADVERBIAL MODIFICATION, and COMPLEX (i.e.
multi-clause) sentences.[1]

ADVERBIAL MODIFICATION

This is a topic which has been neglected in recent treatments of
syntax. The reason for this is partly because it is not easy to capture
the heterogeneous set of relations involved in adverbial modification within a category-based approach such as is used in transformational-generative syntax. Within that approach, it has been
recognized that there are adverbials which modify the VP category
(that is, the adverbial modification is required by the verb), as in

The farmer put the duckling *into the crate*

and there are adverbials which modify the whole S (sentence), as in

The farmer killed the duckling *in the farmyard.*

If all adverbial modification was carried out by means of prepositional phrase categories (PP) as here, it would be a simple matter to
define the adverbial modification relationship as holding between
the category PP and its immediately dominating VP (one type) or
between the PP and its immediately dominating S category (the
other type). However, adverbial modification in English is expressed through not just PP categories but also through single
adverbials (*hurriedly, yesterday, here*), NPs with a head time noun
(*last week, this morning*), and various types of clause sequence (*after
he had got up, having arrived on the scene*). As a result, some such

---

[1] See, for more detailed arguments and analysis on each of these areas, D. Crystal,
'Neglected grammatical factors in conversational English', in *Studies in English
Linguistics for Randolph Quirk*, eds. S. Greenbaum, G. Leech & J. Svartvik
(London, 1980), pp 153–166.

category as 'AdvP' (adverbial phrase) might seem called for, to cover all such possibilities, but this would actually be a RELATIONAL, rather than a strictly CATEGORIAL term. Further, there is reason to believe that a simple division of adverbial modification into the VP- and S-types does less than justice to the data.

Before proceeding with a more detailed analysis of adverbials, we should note that the relational approach to the transcription of English syntax recognizes the following elements at clause level:

S (subject)	controlling concord on the verb;
V (verb)	mutually defined with respect to S;
O (object)	subject to passive-movement, and subdivisible into: O_d (direct object) and O_i (indirect object);
C (complement)	a noun or adjective phrase required by the COPULA verb *be* or other verb of this class. The noun phrase is not subject to passive-movement. C is further subdivisible into: C_s (subject complement) and C_o (object complement);
A (adverbial)	

Using these five basic elements, with their subdivisions, it is possible to state the main canonical clause pattern types in the language as the following:

SV	John was sleeping
SVO	The farmer killed the duckling
SVA	The drunk leaned against the lamppost
SVC	The concert was successful/a success
SVO_iO_d	Mary sent him a note
$SVOC_o$	They built it strong and high
SVOA	She put it in an envelope

In these patterns, it may be said that all the elements that appear are specified in the co-occurrence possibilities of the verb, the central element. Thus, every verb specifies that it 'takes' a subject, S; additionally, *kill* specifies an object, O, *lean* specifies an adverbial, A, and so on. Note that this sort of specification is NOT the same as OBLIGATORINESS of the elements specified in all cases, since *Mary sent a note* is well-formed, where the indirect object O$_i$ is missing, and *they built it* is also well formed, with the object complement C$_o$ missing. What is specified may be said to belong to the NUCLEAR constituents of the sentence. The specification of verbs for the elements that they 'take' in this sense is taken to be their VALENCY in certain analyses.[1]

Having outlined these elements, and the basic clause patterns that they define, it is now possible to make a number of observations about A-elements.

1. First, they are extremely heterogeneous; anything that is not S, V, C or O is a member of A.
2. All the basic clause types can be extended by the addition of further A-elements which are optional, and non-nuclear, and (unlike all other clause elements) not limited in number, e.g.:

   ASVAA   Yesterday, John was sleeping soundly in his own bed.

3. A-elements may appear in a wide range of positions in clause patterns, subject to lexical constraints (particularly, concerning the nature of the head adverbial, and of the head verb in the clause pattern); but one position which is regularly excluded is between V and O:

   *I like very much your English policemen
     S V A   O

   (It may be noted that this restriction would proceed naturally from a VP unit comprising V + NP, tending to resist interruption.)

4. Functionally, A-elements are roughly characterizable in terms of categories such as Time, Manner, Place and Other (the latter including a whole range of functions such as Instrumental, Causal, Benefactive, etc.). They can also be placed into various relational types, depending on their structural relations with other elements in the clause; e.g. ADJUNCTS (required by the specification of the verb), DISJUNCTS (not so required), and CONJUNCTS (serving mainly as clause-boundary or linking elements, close to the function of conjunctions).

Given these major points, it appears that adverbials constitute a rather striking, and challenging, syntactic phenomenon. They are (1) not particularly noticeable in the canonical clause patterns, but (2) form the means of extending these patterns, (3) in a wide range of positions, and (4) in a wide range of structural and functional ways.

---

[1] For example, D. Allerton, *Valency and the English Verb* (New York, 1982).

If we now look at the incidence and distribution of A-elements in the passage from which our extract above was taken, we find some interesting trends. As far as INCIDENCE is concerned, we may illustrate by examining a continuous sequence from our football passage containing 50 occurrences of V, which provides a good approximation to the number of relational patterns or clauses that we must recognize, since there is normally only one V per clause. Of these 50 V-elements, 16 occur in clauses that are clearly internal to another clause, such as the bracketed sequence in

How much does it cost [to get in down the road] now.

The remaining 34 clauses include those that are clearly independent, and some that ought to be regarded as structurally dependent on others while not being clearly internal, e.g.

. . . which is about fifty percent of his normal.

Setting incidence of elements out in terms of internal vs. external clauses in this way, we have (in order of decreasing incidence):

Element		Clause		
		Internal	External	Total
V		34	16	50
S		29	12	41
A	(one)	14	8	22
	(two)	4	—	4
	(three)	2	—	2
	(all)	20	8	28
O		13	4	17
C		7	1	8

The position of A-elements in this table would appear to highlight their importance in the sort of data we are considering – an importance that is not consistent with their position in respect of the canonical syntactic forms that we outlined above. Does this mean that their importance is not primarily a syntactic matter, but rather one of message structure?

This sort of issue may be addressed through an investigation of the syntactically obligatory status of the A-elements concerned. In a more extensive analysis of some Survey of English Usage data (including the passage that we have extracted above)[1] it has been found that syntactically obligatory A-elements occur mainly with the verbs *be, go,* and a few others, and are less numerous overall (in 51 vs. 71 clauses, out of 246), than those A-elements that seem to represent optional modification. The issue as to WHICH A-elements are obligatory or optional in particular contexts is very difficult to determine in many cases, however; consider

I was reading *in the paper, this morning,*

where we might want to say that this clause requires at least ONE of the (italicized) A-elements, but either will do.

As far as distribution is concerned, our passage presents the following picture:

| | | *Position in the clause* | | | |
	Initial	V-A-V	S-A-V	Final	Total
Single adverbs		5	3	2	10
Phrases	3			16	19
Clauses				7	7
	3	5	3	25	36

Note the restricted use made of initial position (where phrases such as *this year,* . . . are found), and of the position represented here as 'V-A-V', denoting the case where an A-element appears in the middle of a verbal group, e.g. between auxiliary and main verb (where adverbs such as *really, probably* and *progressively* turn up). Between subject and verb (S-A-V) also are found single adverbs (e.g. *always*). By contrast, the clause-final position is where the widest range of A-types occurs, although there is a tendency to favour the longer over the shorter types in this position.

This suggests that syntactic constraints on A-elements can be determined, if only in a very gross way; further specification of which adverbials may occur in which positions would appear to require statement in terms of the lexical properties of the clauses concerned, particularly in respect of the verb and, of course, the head adverbial. Concerning the apparently very important functions that A-elements serve in such data as we have been considering, possibly we should say that they are central, or 'nuclear' with respect to MESSAGE structure, even where they are peripheral, or 'non-nuclear' in terms of a purely SYNTACTIC level of description.

[1] In D. Crystal, *op. cit.*

COMPLEX SENTENCES

Within a phrase structure representation, the traditional distinction between COORDINATE and SUBORDINATE sentence types may be configurationally defined, as follows:

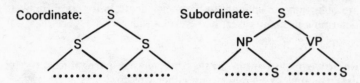

Within the sort of spoken data that we are considering, however, we may find a sequence of clauses whose status with regard to each other has to be determined. We might imagine that we could define a set of linking elements, e.g. *and, but,* and *or,* as marking adjacent clauses that are coordinate, and the rest as marking adjacent clauses that are subordinate. However, this procedure is faced with two practical difficulties. The first is that, where such linking elements occur, their functions may be seen to overlap this attempt at a distinction between coordinate and subordinate types of clause relationship, e.g.:

> I heard his knock at the door *and/so/after which/whereupon* I got up *and* made/*to* make for the back garden as quickly as possible.

The second difficulty stems from the fact that such OVERT clause linkage is not provided in many instances in our data. We find a wide variety of types of inter-clause linkage, and considerable use of stereotyped expressions such as *well, you know, I mean,* etc. in introducing and concluding functions. In the table below, CON-NECTIVES include *and* (especially numerous in this class) and others (e.g. relative pronouns and *to*), PRONOMINAL includes linkage achieved through co-referential pronouns (e.g. *he's all over the world* . . .) where no connective is present; APPOSITIONAL refers to examples such as *European cup matches* . . . and *very warm, nice* . . .; ELLIPTICAL is found in *have a nice meal* . . . and *says it costs him* . . .; and TOPICAL covers a number of more-or-less easily definable cases where the linkage seems to be achieved by maintaining the same topic across a clause boundary (other than in the ways indicated above). Of 37 such instances of all types of linkage in our passage, we find the following breakdown:

Clause linkage over 50 clauses

Connectives	15
(*and*	9
other	6)
Topical	11
Pronominal	7
Elliptical	2
Appositional	2

Regarding clause linkage, then, it would appear that, in this sort of data, the opposition between coordinate and subordinate types is unworkable and too simple; it needs to be replaced by (*i*) some reliable procedure for the recognition of all clause patterns (most readily determinable through the occurrences of the element V, though their BOUNDARIES may be more problematic), and (*ii*) a careful documentation of the many and various ways in which clause patterns thus isolated in the data can be said to stand in relationship to each other.

IV

CONCLUSION

We started this chapter with the observation that syntax is the study of the structure and function of SENTENCES. We then noted that, while sentence units exist in our intuitions about our language, and in such forms of the language as educated and careful written expression, they are not obviously the units in terms of which our everyday spoken use of language is organized.

We have seen how a formal system can be established to derive the observed forms of sentences from quite abstract phrase structure configurations, via processes called transformations, and how this approach allows for the expression of syntactic generalizations that are obscured in these observed forms. We have argued that this approach needs to be complemented by one which provides for syntactic representation at the level of observed forms, in order to understand how language is organized syntactically over longer contextualized sequences than individual sentences.

It appears that this sort of representation must embody both the categorial information of phrase structure elements such as NP and VP, and also the relations that hold between them, since these relations are not regularly derivable from the order of elements in observed sequences.

Finally, we have argued that the inter-categorial relations that have to be recognized in spontaneous speech data are too many and varied to be accommodated within such dichotomies as 'nuclear' vs. 'non-nuclear' modification (in the case of adverbials) or 'coordinate' vs. 'subordinate' conjunction (in the case of clauses). While a clause-based transcriptional approach such as that described here allows such issues to be addressed, many problems remain. Spontaneous spoken syntax still awaits a suitable analytic approach, and much careful investigation, before we can unlock its peculiar syntactic characteristics.

5

LEXIS: THE VOCABULARY OF ENGLISH

Christopher Ball

The *Oxford English Dictionary* has over 450,000 entries. But the words of a living language can never be precisely numbered. Grammar is concerned with closed systems, such as 'number' or 'tense', but the lexical stock of a language is arranged in open sets which, by definition, cannot be finally delimited. The delimitation of the English vocabulary is further complicated by the various lexical dictinctions typical of the different varieties of English. Some words are restricted to a particular dialect of English (e.g. *beck, sidewalk, dinkum*), others to a particular register (e.g. *belly, pussy, teeny*). In another dimension, some words are dropping out of use (e.g. *martial, weary, betrothal*), others are recent innovations (e.g. *teenager, hovercraft, motel*). Even the boundary between languages is partly blurred in the case of vocabulary; by what criteria do we decide whether the following are English words or foreign words quoted in English sentences: *baroque, bourgeois, bouillabaisse?*

The illustration overleaf, showing page xxvii of Volume 1 of the *Oxford English Dictionary*, aptly summarizes the difficulty of delimiting the English vocabulary. But if we cannot draw a line around the vocabulary of English we can certainly indicate its core, the common stock of words which are neither literary nor colloquial, neither foreign nor dialectal, neither novel nor obsolescent, neither scientific nor technical.

'Indeterminacy' is one of the most important features of vocabulary and needs to be discussed a little further. It is a commonplace of language study that two different types of definition are often needed: sometimes we can delimit successive chunks of material much as a cartographer draws boundaries around contiguous countries on a map; at other times the material is indeterminate and can only be usefully analysed by indicating the centre of each chunk, rather than its borders. In the latter case our model might be the definition of a group of partially overlapping magnetic

fields. Clearly, the English vocabulary must be defined in this way –
by indicating its core, rather than by attempting to map its boundaries. But the contrast between determinacy and indeterminacy is
important throughout the study of vocabulary: for instance, we may
say that the opposition between the senses of *male* and *female*, or
sister and *brother*, is determinate, while that between the senses of
large and *small*, or *red* and *yellow*, is not. In general, grammatical
oppositions are determinate: vocabulary is largely indeterminate.

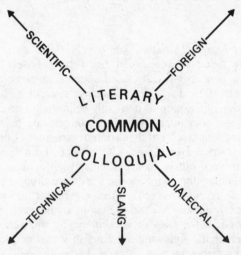

It follows that, while the linguist can usually state decisively
whether a sentence is 'grammatical' or 'ungrammatical', questions
of lexical acceptability are more difficult to answer clearly. *This men
listened musics* is ungrammatical in three obvious respects; *the woolly
hedgehog swore a hearty thought* is lexically unacceptable – or is it? We
find ourselves searching for possible contexts, such as a fairy story,
and conclude that the collocations *woolly/hedgehog, hedgehog/swear,
swear/thought,* and *hearty/thought* are extremely unusual rather than
totally unacceptable. Grammatical questions can be answered 'yes'
or 'no': lexical questions are typically answered by 'more or less'.

Vocabulary, then, is indeterminate, and lexical questions can
often not be answered decisively. A third respect in which the study
of vocabulary differs from that of grammar (and phonology) is that
the synchronic and historical dimensions of language cannot be
altogether separated from one another. Native speakers of English
learn the grammar and phonology of their language during their

early childhood, but they add to their vocabulary throughout their lives. Languages change at all levels, but lexical change seems to occur most freely and frequently, so much so that we all learn and use the processes whereby new words may be formed. Any study of vocabulary must recognize that it is dynamic, not static.

Because of these special problems it is not possible simply to list the items in the English vocabulary, explain the various relations between them, and describe the way in which they refer to the world of experience. The indeterminacy of vocabulary prevents us from even attaining the first step of drawing up an exhaustive inventory of items. All dictionaries necessarily select merely a portion of the theoretically infinite vocabulary of English. Because the internal organization of the vocabulary is so difficult to describe precisely, until recently linguists have been content to compile alphabetical lists of words, treating each one separately and largely disregarding the relations between them. All dictionaries do this, though the best ones give a lot of implicit information about the organization and use of the vocabulary by exemplification. An alternative method of presenting vocabulary is found in the thesaurus, which attempts to display some of the semantic relations of words by arranging them according to their similarity of meaning.

The words we are concerned with are the members of the four great form classes – nouns, adjectives, verbs and adverbs. The remainder of the form classes are within the domain of grammar. (The class of interjections is a special case, not easily handled in either grammatical or lexical terms. Typically, interjections do not contract syntagmatic relations, though forms which may be used as interjections may also be members of other form classes: e.g. *damn*, *God*, *blast*. They require separate treatment, and will be largely disregarded in what follows.) It is one of the interesting features of English that words rarely betray their form class by their structure, and that it is common for the same form to appear as a member of several classes: e.g. *table* (noun, verb), *forward* (noun, verb, adjective, adverb), *round* (noun, verb, adjective, adverb, preposition). As we shall see this feature is exploited in one of the processes of word-formation.

The definition of WORD in English need not detain us, so long as we remember that the word as a grammatical, or phonological, unit will not always or necessarily coincide with the word as a lexical item. The grammar of *Union Jack*, for instance, is noun-modifier + noun-head, but it is convenient to treat it as a single lexical item for the statement of meaning. But this is a special and relatively rare case: most of the time the grammatical word and the lexical word are one and the same. In English, moreover, the word is institutionalized: the convention of showing word-divisions in the written language gives us an obvious and conventional method of definition, and it is in this conventional sense that WORD is used here.

In this chapter I shall attempt in a sketchy way to describe the English vocabulary and to indicate its internal organization and external relation to the world of experience. This will not be done by offering exhaustive lists, but by touching on the sources of the vocabulary, both historical and contemporary, the strata into which it may be divided, the organization of the vocabulary, both formal and notional, and its external reference.

In comparison with many other languages the vocabulary of English is of very diverse origins. Old English was a member of the West Germanic group of languages, which was one of the descendants of Primitive Germanic, itself one of many related Indo-European languages. Historical linguistics cannot reconstruct an earlier form of language behind Indo-European, but there is no doubt that there must have been an earlier history stretching back many thousands of years. Much of the English core-vocabulary is of Indo-European (or earlier) origin: the numerals, kinship terms like *father*, *mother*, *brother*, parts of the body like *arm*, *tooth*, *foot*, personal and other pronouns like *me*, *who*, *that*, animal terms like *hound*, *goose*, *ox*, common verbs like *do*, *sit*, *fall*, and many others. Some words cannot be traced back beyond the Germanic stage, and must therefore have been formed or adopted at that period: *God*, *earth*, *house*, *hold*, *rain*, *sea*, *drink*, and others. A smaller group of words are specifically West Germanic, like *beer*, *sheep*, *learn*. It is a universal feature of languages that they adopt, or 'borrow', foreign words to a greater or lesser extent, and English is no exception. Borrowing has occurred at all periods and continues today. The earliest loan words that can be traced (though there must have been still earlier ones) are some cultural borrowings of the Germanic period, like *hemp*, *rich*, *iron*. A considerable number of Latin words were adopted in West Germanic: *street*, *mint*, *wine*, *cheese*, *mile*, *cup*, *kitchen*, and others. Old English also borrowed from Latin: *school*, *sponge*, *lily*, *disciple*, *offer*, *fiddle*, *paradise*, and others. A small number of words entered Old English from other languages: e.g. (Greek) *devil*, *church*; (Celtic) *bin*, *dun*, *brock*; (Norse) *thrall*, *law*, *fellow*, *wrong*; (French) *proud*, *capon*, *sot*. But most of the new vocabulary which was created in the Old English period was formed by compounding and affixation, rather than by borrowing: *almighty, gospel, shepherd, rainbow, eventide, seaman, Sunday* etc.; *crafty, thankful, friendless, overcome, understand, inward, wisdom,* etc.

These two processes of compounding and affixation have remained the major sources of new words in Middle and Modern English, though there are also other internal methods of word-formation in use which will be discussed later. But English has also adopted a vast number of foreign words from many sources since the Conquest. In the Middle English period the French and Scandinavian loanwords are naturally the most numerous and important. Loanwords are a rough and ready index of the degree of contact between two linguistic communities; the number and direction of the loans also provide a measure of the (real or assumed) cultural superiority of one community over the other. From the Norse settlers in the north and east Middle English adopted a surprising number of words that belong to the core-vocabulary today: *they (them, their), both, ill, die, egg, knife, low, skill, take, till, though, want,* and many more. The complete assimilation of these Norse words into English, so that few native speakers are aware that they are adoptions, can be partly explained by remembering that English is more closely related historically to Norse, a Germanic language, than to French or Latin; it also suggests that the Norse-speaking community must have become fused with the Old English community soon after the Conquest.

The importance of the French element in the English vocabulary is only matched by Latin among the external sources. Many of the French words borrowed into Middle English have been completely assimilated into the core-vocabulary: *aunt, people, debt, lodge, common, pray, war, fruit, table, front, touch, manner, peace,* etc. Others still perhaps betray their foreign origin: *messenger, purchase, pavilion, concord, trespass, challenge, venison, peril, liquor, vengeance, medicine,* etc. French adoptions are found in almost every part of the vocabulary: law, (*justice, evidence, pardon,* . . .), warfare (*conquer, victory, archer,* . . .), religion (*grace, repent, sacrifice,* . . .), rank (*baron, master, prince,* . . .), clothing (*collar, mantle, vestment,* . . .), architecture (*castle, pillar, tower* . . .), finance (*pay, rent, ransom,* . . .), food (*dinner, feast, sauce,* . . .), and many others. As an indication of the tremendous influx of French words in Middle English we may note that, discounting proper names, there are 39 words of French origin in the first 43 lines of the Prologue to Chaucer's *Canterbury Tales.*

Although the French and Scandinavian languages, together with Latin, were the most important sources of Middle English adoptions, they were not the only ones. There are a number of borrowings from Low German (*poll, dote, booze, luff, huckster*, etc.), from Italian (*florin, alarm, million, ducat, brigand* – though some of these seem to have reached English through French), and from Irish (*kern, lough*). In addition we may add a number of indirect borrowings (through other languages, such as Latin or French) from Greek (*centre, fancy, logic, rhetoric, treacle, allegory, comedy, halcyon, theme*, and others), from Gaulish (*gravel, quay, skein, valet*, etc.), and from Arabic (*saffron, admiral, alchemy, cotton, amber, syrup*, etc.).

A large number of words were adopted in Middle English direct from Latin: *diocese, conviction, legitimate, formal, index, orbit, concrete, equator, lupin, locust, implication, compact, admit, discuss*, and many others. Most of these were learned words when they were adopted and have remained outside the core-vocabulary. But already in Middle English we see the beginning of the development whereby Latin, and later Greek, were to contract a special lexical relationship with English. It is an interesting feature of some living languages that they are able to tap the lexical resources of a dead language to create neologisms with the same freedom that they have to produce new internal formations. A number of Indian languages have such a relationship with Sanskrit. In the case of English, not only the vocabulary but also many of the derivational affixes of Latin and Greek are available to create new forms. In the present century English has borrowed from the classical languages, or rather created out of Latin and Greek elements, the following words, among many others: *aerodyne, ambivert, androgen, antibiotic, astronaut, audio-visual, autolysis, barysphere, cacogenics, callipygous, chromosome, cartology, cartophily, cryotron, cyclorama, dendrochronology, dromophobia, ergatocracy, hypnotherapy, hypothermia, isotope* . . . Because the lexical resources of Latin and Greek are treated as if they belonged to English, many neologisms combine elements from different sources: *aqualung, television, microgroove, sonobuoy*, etc. Although all these Latin- and Greek-derived words are distinctly learned or technical, they do not seem foreign, and are very different in this respect from the recent loanwords from living languages, such as *montage, angst, cappuccino, sputnik, kibbutz, vérité, zek*, etc. Thus, for the Modern English period a distinction must be made between the adoptions from living languages and the formations derived from the two classical languages.

Latin has provided English with a large number of productive affixes, such as *de-, ex-, pre-; -al, -ate, -ous*. Many of these can now be used to form new words with roots of any origin. During the modern period a considerable number of words have been borrowed direct from Latin, such as: (16th century) *genius, area, circus, codex, stratum*; (17th century) *premium, squalor, focus, complex, tedium*; (18th century) *ultimatum, nucleus, alibi, extra, prospectus*; (19th century) *opus, ego, animus, aquarium, consensus*; (20th century) *exemplum, gravitas, mores, persona, continuum*. We have borrowed many words from Greek through the medium of Latin, and a smaller number direct, such as: (16th century) *rhapsody, crisis, topic, pathos, stigma*; (17th century) *coma, tonic, cosmos, nous, dogma*; (18th century) *bathos, phlox, philander, triptych, neurosis*; (19th century) *phase, pylon, myth, agnostic, therm*; (20th century) *topos, euphoria, enosis, schizophrenia, hamartia*. From Greek also comes a wide range of learnéd affixes, such as *bio-, chrono-, geo-, hydro-, logo-, auto-, hemi-, hetero-, homo-, mono-, neo-, epi-, meta-, para-, -ism, -ist, -ise, -logy, -graph, -phile, -meter, -gram,* and many others.

While the influence of Latin and Greek on the English vocabulary has been steadily increasing, the number of adoptions from living foreign languages has rather been diminishing in the modern period, although the number of languages which have provided items in the English vocabulary has grown enormously. Naturally enough, apart from the two classical languages, the chief influences have been the major languages of western Europe. French has continued to provide a considerable number of new words, for example (16th century) *trophy, vase, grotesque, machine, moustache*; (17th century) *brigade, unique, attic, soup, routine*; (18th century) *terrain, canteen, brochure, corduroy, police*; (19th century) *acrobat, blouse, beige, chef, prestige*; (20th century) *montage, voyeur, camouflage, questionnaire, chauffeur*. The Italian element is particularly strong in the fields of art, music and literature, for example (16th century) *model, sonnet, madrigal, traffic, bandit*; (17th century) *opera, vista, burlesque, balcony, manifesto*; (18th century) *soprano, quartet, costume, lava, arcade*; (19th century) *flautist, studio, scenario, tirade, spaghetti*; (20th century) *scampi, cappuccino, aggiornamento, timpani, quattrocento*. There is also a considerable Spanish element in English; it is interesting to note how many of these words have their origin in the New World: for example (16th century) *sherry, cannibal, banana, potato, contrade*; (17th century) *cargo, parade, avocado, vanilla, piccaninny*; (18th century) *cigar, hacienda, bolero, stevedore, quadrille*; (19th century) *rodeo, stampede, mustang, patio, canyon*; (20th century) *cafeteria, tango, marijuana, supremo, incommunicado*. Low German, especially Dutch and later Afrikaans, and

High German have been fertile sources of loanwords in the modern period: for example (16th century) *dock, yacht, frolic, beleaguer; landgrave, carouse, younker, kreutzer;* (17th century) *brandy, smuggle, cruise, sketch; plunder, zinc, hamster, sauerkraut;* (18th century) *schooner, roster, mangle, springbok; iceberg, shale, waltz, nickel;* (19th century) *trek, spoor, boss, commander; poodle, lager, yodel, paraffin;* (20th century) *apartheid, autobahn, ersatz, angst, strafe.*

The other European languages have not been nearly so important as sources of vocabulary for English as were French, Italian, Spanish and German. But nevertheless, Modern English has adopted a few words from almost every European language: (the Scandinavian languages) *link, rug, scrub, troll, smut, cosy, ski, fjord, slalom, ombudsman;* (Irish) *brogue, leprechaun, galore, banshee, colleen, céilidhe;* (Welsh) *crag, coracle, cromlech, gorsedd, eisteddfod, hwyl, corgi;* (Portuguese) *padre, flamingo, madeira, buffalo, macaw, caste, pagoda, verandah, albino, commando;* (Russian) *rouble, czar, steppe, mammoth, ukase, balalaika, pogrom, troika, samovar, soviet, commissar, sputnik, intelligentsia;* (Hungarian) *shako, paprika, goulash;* (Finnish) *sauna;* (Lapp) *tundra;* and so on.

The loanwords we have been considering have all, except where otherwise stated, been directly borrowed into English. Many more have reached English indirectly from a wide variety of languages. An example of the intricacies of indirect adoptions is provided by *veneer*, borrowed in the 18th century from German *furnieren*, itself an earlier adoption from French *fournir*, which is derived from a Common Romance word borrowed from Germanic. In the Old and Middle English periods a number of words reached English in this way from non-European languages, and they have continued to do so in the modern period. But, with a growth of international trade and the urge to explore and dominate the unknown world, English has made a number of direct adoptions from languages spoken outside Europe. As with the borrowings from the less important languages of Europe, few of these words have entered the core-vocabulary, and most are material nouns referring to culturally distinct objects. Some examples are: (American Indian languages) *moccasin, wigwam, squaw, mugwump, pemmican;* (Arabic) *sultan, sheikh, roc, hashish, fakir, harem, hookah, ghoul, shadoof, yashmak, bint, shufti;* (Australian languages) *dingo, wombat, boomerang, budgerigar, billabong;* (Chinese) *litchi, ketchup, kaolin, sampan, typhoon, loquat, tong;* (Eskimo) *kayak, igloo, anorak;* (Hawaiian) *hula, lei, ukulele;* (Hebrew) *shibboleth, kosher, kibbutz;* (Hindustani) *guru, pundit, pukka, sari, khaki, swami;* (Japanese) *kimono, tycoon, judo, haiku, karate*; (Indonesian) *proa, amok, sarong, orang-utan, raffia*; (Persian) *cummerbund, purdah, shah, dervish, divan, caravan, bazaar, shawl, houri, howdah*; (Polynesian) *taboo, tattoo, kiwi*; (Sanskrit) *avatar, suttee, yoga, nirvana, swastika, soma*; (Swahili) *bwana, safari, uhuru*; (Tamil) *parash, catamaran, anaconda*; (Tibetan) *lama, sherpa, yeti, yak*; (Turkish) *caftan, yoghourt, kiosk, fez, bosh*; (Yiddish) *schlemozzle, schmaltz*. There are many others.

Two special forms of word-borrowing should be briefly mentioned. The first, loan-translation or 'calque', is exemplified by *loanword* itself, which was formed on the pattern of German *Lehnwort*; other examples are *shock-troops* (German *Stosstruppen*) and *gospel* (Greek *euaggélion*). Internal borrowing is more important: this occurs when one dialect of a language adopts words from another. During the history of English this must frequently have happened, but the details are often unclear. Contemporary Standard British English borrows a large number of words from American English (*movie, jazz, blurb, gimmick, cagey, egg-head, heel* 'cad', *grassroots, rib* 'tease', *sit-in, teach-in, supermarket, tear-jerker, shazam, yuppie,* and many others); *gormless* and *gawp* are recent borrowings from English regional dialects, but dialects of English overseas seem to be more important sources of vocabulary nowadays: e.g. (Australian English) *outback, cobber, bushed, fossick, sheila*.

Loanwords are the most immediately obvious additions to vocabulary, but they are rarely the most important or numerous. Certainly in Old English and in the later Modern English period the internal processes of word-formation have been responsible for the bulk of new words. The two most important processes in English are COMPOUNDING and AFFIXATION (see further, Chapter 3).

Compounds must be carefully distinguished from phrases on the one hand (*greenfinch/green grass*), and from affixed formations on the other (*paratroop/paratyphoid*). As opposed to phrases, compounds typically have a single stress (*'greenfinch*), are inseparable (*green hand-sown grass*), and do not allow modification of the first element (*very green grass*); but *green fingers* and *grass-green* (both of which have two stresses) must be treated as phrase and compound respectively, because, while the first has the two-stress pattern of a normal syntactic group (adjective-modifier + noun-head) as opposed to *'greenfinch*, the latter has the syntactic pattern (noun-modifier + adjective-head) found only in compounds (*'waterproof, 'carefree, 'seasick,* and *'dirt-'cheap, 'pitch-'black, 'brand-'new*). The boundary is, however, indeterminate, as is shown by examples like *ground floor, hand grenade, home town* (*ground-floor*, etc.) which occur variously with one or two stresses. Equally indeterminate is the border between compounds and affixed forms. Typically, affixes are not independent words (*epi-, un-, -ation, -ous*), whereas both elements of compounds are normally free forms. Moreover, it is usually possible to make a generalized statement about the function of an affix, especially if it is still productive, whereas in compounds the same element may function in a variety of ways. Compare *pre-elect, prejudge, prepay, prearrange, precook*, etc., with *puppydog, bulldog, watchdog, policedog, lapdog, sheepdog*, etc. In the first group *pre-* adds the sense 'before' to the verb; in the second no such general statement is possible.

Compounds are usually either nouns or adjectives, although verbal and adverbial compounds are often secondarily derived from primary (nominal or adjectival) compounds: e.g. *to belly-ache, to weekend; sickmakingly, self-importantly*. There are a wide variety of adjectival compounds of the types *carefree* (noun + adjective: *pitch-dark, lovesick, world-wide, self-secure*), *bitter-sweet* (adjective + adjective: *greeny-blue, Franco-Prussian, Indo-European, shabby-genteel*), *breath-taking* (noun + participle: *earth-shattering, self-propelling; hand-made, airborne, self-taught*) and others (e.g. *hard-working, far-fetched*).

The nominal compounds fall into two main groups, EN-DOCENTRIC and EXOCENTRIC. Examples of endocentric compounds are *frogman, atom-bomb, woman-hater*, where each compound has the same grammatical distribution as one of its elements (*man, bomb, hater*); neither element of an exocentric compound (*spoilsport, bighead, fallout*) can replace the compound in this way. There are several different types of endocentric compounds in English: noun + noun (*lipstick, dustman, clothes-line, girl-friend, fighter-bomber, self-contempt, batsman, beeswax, dining-room, inkstand, fox-hunting, shopkeeper, nanny-goat*); verb + noun (*treadmill, flick-knife, sob-sister*); participle + noun (*mocking-bird, serving-woman*); adjective + noun (*blackboard, sick-room*); pronoun + noun (*he-man, she-devil*); noun + adjective (*court-martial, heir-apparent*). Likewise, the exocentric nominal compounds can be sub-divided: verb + noun (*spendthrift, stopgap*); verb + adverb (*diehard, stowaway, setback, frame-up, take-off*); adjective + noun (*redhead, loudmouth, blue-bell, green-shank*). It will be obvious from the examples that several of the sub-types of compounds can be further differentiated; for example, in *lipstick* the first element modifies the second, while in *fighter-*

bomber the two elements are co-ordinate.

Before turning to affixation, we should consider one further, rather odd, type of compound. The reduplicative compound is rare and recent; examples occur in all the main word-classes: noun (*goody-goody, chuff-chuff, never-never*), adjective (*hush-hush, pretty-pretty*), adverb (*fifty-fifty*) and verb (*clop-clop*). Some of these are similar to expressive formations, which will be discussed later. This particular type of compound is especially common in nursery. language: *yum-yum, bye-byes, din-din, woof-woof, ta-ta, Papa*, etc.

English affixes can be immediately divided into PREFIXES and SUFFIXES, for English has no infixes. There are more than 60 prefixes and more than 80 suffixes. Few of these are native forms: of the prefixes, only *a-, be-, un-, fore-, mid-*, and *mis-* are found in Old English, though rather more suffixes have survived (e.g. *-dom, -er, -ful, -hood, -ish, -less, -ling, -ly, -ness, -ship, -y*, etc.). Some suffixes have the effect of converting members of one word-class into another (*laugh/laughable, willing/willingness*); others merely modify without converting (*cartoon/cartoonist, star/starlet*). Most suffixes and some prefixes are confined to particular word-classes. Many affixes are no longer productive, for example *cis-* (*cisalpine*), *preter-* (*preternatural*), *sur-* (*surname*), *-th* (*warmth*), *-ton* (*simpleton*), *-et* (*freshet*), but a surprising number can still be used to create new formations.

Some of the most important productive prefixes are: *anti-* (*anti-Communist, anti-submarine, anti-semitism, antifreeze*); *counter-* (*counter-espionage, counter-demonstration, counter-threat*); *de-* (*deodorize, dehydrate, derate, declutch, decompression*); *dis-* (*disassemble, disincentive, discontinue, disown*); *inter-* (*interracial, interbreed, inter-war, interdependence*); *non-* (*non-skid, non-starter, non-believer, non-stick*); *pre-* (*preshrunk, predigest, prenatal, pre-school*); *re-* (*rethink, repaper, rebirth*); *semi-* (*semi-transparent, semi-skilled, semi-educated, semi-starvation*); *un-* (negation: *unconventional, unfunny, unforeseen;* reversal: *unmake, unfreeze, unsighted*).

Some of the most important productive suffixes are: *-able* (adjectival, from verbs and nouns: *available, adaptable, favourable, marriageable*); *-age* (substantival, from verbs and nouns: *shrinkage, breakage, orphanage, voltage*); *-ate* (verbal, from nouns: *assassinate, vaccinate, chlorinate*); *-ation* (substantival, from verbs: *verification, neutralization, ruination, visitation*); *-dom* (substantival, from nouns: *bumbledom, stardom, muddledom*); *-ee* (substantival, from verbs: *evacuee, examinee, detainee*); *-er* (substantival, from verbs and nouns: *consumer, poser, geographer, probationer, lowlander, honeymooner*);

-ery/-ry (substantival, from nouns: *snobbery, punditry, creamery, rookery, rocketry*); *-ish* (adjectival, from nouns: *Lettish, sheepish, tallish, bluish, fiftyish*); *-ist* (substantival, from nouns and adjectives: *racist/racialist, revisionist, stockist, orientalist, nominalist*); *-ite* (substantival, from nouns: *Bevanite, vulcanite, ammonite, Pre-Raphaelite*); *-ize* (verbal, from nouns and adjectives: *americanize, terrorize, galvanize, bowdlerize, hospitalize, finalize, denuclearize*); *-less* (adjectival, from nouns: *spineless, strapless, humourless*); *-ness* (substantival, mainly from adjectives: *promptness, shortsightedness, willingness, nothingness*); *-ship* (substantival, from nouns: *membership, studentship, censorship, showmanship*); *-y* (adjectival, from nouns, verbs and adjectives: *sexy, spidery, matey, trendy, wriggly, weepy, pinky, crispy*). These lists, long as they are, hardly do justice to the variety or productive affixes and the wealth of affixed formations.

Simple CONVERSION, or 'zero-derivation', is a process of word-formation closely related to affixation. From *tape* (noun) we have produced *tape* (verb, 'make a tape-recording'); from *tease* (verb) we have *tease* (noun, 'one who mocks'). Just as the pattern of root and affixed derivative (*lead/mislead*) can be extended to produce new forms (*derive/misderive, analyse/misanalyse*), so the simpler patterns of *bed* (noun and verb) or *walk* (verb and noun) can also be extended. Adjectives and adverbs seem to resist this type of formation but both nouns and, especially, verbs are often formed by simple conversion. There are four common types and two rarer ones: verbs from nouns (*garage, audition, baby, process, wolf, torpedo*, etc.); verbs from adjectives (*tidy, best, short, gentle, pretty, wise*, etc.); verbs from particles (*up, down*); nouns from verbs (*sweep, bore, sell, must, have*, etc.); nouns from adjectives (*lovely, natural, short, inferior, tiny*, etc.); nouns from particles (*over, down, out, off*). A special type of simple conversion is the process whereby proper names become common nouns. English has a number of words like *wellingtons*, named from the Duke of Wellington, or *cardigan*, named from the Earl of Cardigan. This process, though never very common or important, continues to operate in contemporary English: e.g. *waterloo, boycott, diesel, mae-west, primus, bikini, quisling, sloane, xerox*, etc.

BACK-FORMATION is another related process of word-formation. Just as the relationship between *write/writer, read/reader* encourages the development of new affixed formations like *consumer, trafficker*, so by a reverse derivation we get *scavenge* from *scavenger* and *swindle* from *swindler*. Although this is not a very common process a number of words have been produced by back-formation. The main types are: *scavenger/scavenge (peddle, burgle, hawk, beg, sculpt, ush*, etc.), and *resurrection/resurrect (automate, pre-empt, televize, vivisect, emote, electrocute*, etc.); but there are also a number of other isolated examples, such as *reminisce, enthuse, laze, salve, jell, liaise.*

Affixation, simple conversion and back-formation all have in common the principle of pattern-extension. In a few rare cases the pattern which is extended is itself due to a misconception. The word *hamburger* was borrowed from German where it is a derivative of the city-name *Hamburg*; in English it was misinterpreted as a compound of *ham* (though ham is not used in making hamburgers) and *burger*, and on the basis of this false analysis were formed such new compounds as *eggburger, cheeseburger*, and many others.

ABBREVIATION is a process of word-formation particularly associated with the spoken language. In 1710 Swift wrote a letter to *The Tatler* objecting to the abbreviations *mob (mobile vulgus), rep (reputation), phiz (physnomy*, a variant of *physiognomy*) and *pozz (positive)*. It is instructive to note that of these one (*mob*) has become thoroughly established in spoken and written usage, one (*pozz*) is still found in spoken usage only, one (*phiz*) is only met with in literature from the late 17th century to the 19th century, and one (*rep*) has disappeared altogether, although a new *rep* has been produced from both *representative* and *repertory* (theatre). Three types of abbreviation may be distinguished, depending on whether the beginning, the middle, or the end of the original word is retained. Like *deb* (from *debutante*) are *fan, pub, sub, trog, intercom, mike, polio, perm, bra, prop, mod, pop, prom, pram, zoo, lino, undergrad, exam, prefab*, names like *Al, Ben, Sam*, and many others; sometimes the abbreviated word is provided with a suffix: *cabby, nappy, bolshy, nighty, undies, granny, compo, ammo, aggro*, etc. Like *bus* (from *omnibus*) are *taters, phone, plane, drome, cello, brolly, van*, names like *Bella, Bert, Tina*, etc. Like *flu* (from *influenza*) are *tec, fridge*, and names like *Liz*; this is by far the rarest type. Compounds are also sometimes formed with abbreviated elements: *paratroop, conrod, telegenic, heliport, oxyacetylene, microfilm*, etc.

BLENDING and ACRONYMIC FORMATION are two minor processes of word-formation which arise more from the fancy of an individual than the structure of the language. Lewis Carroll's blends like *slithy* (*slimy* and *lithe*), *mimsy* (*miserable* and *flimsy*), and *chortle* (*chuckle* and *snort*) are well known from *Through the Looking-Glass*; the last one has become completely established as an independent word. Other examples are: *sparson (squire* and *parson), mingy (mean* and *stingy), chloral (chlorine* and *alcohol), motel, brunch, smog, subtopia, chunnel, spam (spiced ham), shamateur, motourist, fantabulous, slanguage, winterim, jumbulance,* etc. *Absquatulate* 'decamp' is a remarkable triple-blend in American English formed from *abscond, squattle* 'decamp', and *perambulate.*

An acronym is a word formed from the initial letters of other words: the classic English example is *radar* (*ra*dio *d*irection-finding *a*nd *r*ange). Most of the new words formed in this way remain proper names (e.g. *Naafi, Unesco, Nato, Zeta, the Raf, Seato, Shape,* etc.), but a few have been assimilated more deeply into the language: *derv* (*d*iesel-*e*ngined *r*oad *v*ehicle), *ufo* (*u*nidentified *f*lying *o*bject) and *radar. Futhorc,* the name of the Old English runic alphabet, is formed from the first six letters of that alphabet. Rather similar to the acronym is the word produced by pronouncing the initial letters of a phrase or compound: *T.V., G.I., Y.M.C.A.,* etc. The development of blends and acronyms is a recent phenomenon in English; no certain example of either is known before the 19th century.

To these seven processes of internal word-formation, compounding, affixation, simple conversion, back-formation, abbreviation, blending, and acronymic formation, must be added one other, EXPRESSIVE FORMATION, which is especially interesting. The forms of words normally have only a conventional relationship with what they refer to, as can easily be shown by a comparison, such as *horse, Pferd, cheval, equus, hippos,* etc. But a small part of the vocabulary is onomatopoeic: the sounds of such words as *cuckoo, ding-dong, swish, buzz,* seem to be appropriate to their senses. As a result of the undoubted existence of the small number of onomatopoeic words speakers of a language tend to associate certain sounds and sound-sequences with certain senses in an expressive relationship. An English example is *-ump,* which has the sense 'protuberance' in *bump, chump, clump, dump, hump, lump, mump(s), plump* (adjective), *rump, stump, tump,* and of 'heavy fall' in *bump, dump, crump, clump, flump, jump, plump* (verb), *slump, stump, thump.* We can therefore distinguish between two types of expressive formation: direct onomatopoeic formation, and the extension of such expressive patterns as *-ump* above. There are many possible, even probable, examples of either type, but it is difficult to find certain examples since in many cases other explanations of the neologism are also admissible, and often multiple origin is to be suspected.

Examples of simple onomatopoeic formations are: *pom-pom* (gun), *plop, ping, whoosh, swish, whoop, coo, twang, thrum, clash,* etc.

The expressive formations are more complex; we may distinguish two types, depending on whether the expressive element is initial or final. For example, initial *spl-* is found in *splash, splodge, splotch, splurge, splutter, splatter, splosh, splat,* all of which have developed in the modern period and are either of directly expressive origin or are expressive variants of other words (e.g. *plash, sputter*); initial *sn-* links a group of words, all probably of ultimate expressive origin, but some very old, having a central meaning 'nasal sound': *sneeze, sniff, snigger, sniffle, snivel, snicker, snore, snort, snuffle.* Of the words ending in *-ump* listed above, more than half are probably of expressive origin; the expressive value of final *-ing* reinforced by *sing* and *ring,* has produced the modern formations *ping, ting,* and *whing.* There are many other patterns, both initial and final, as the following examples indicate: *zoom, scurry, chuff, fizz, fizzle, biff, yatter, squawk, flunk,* etc. In some cases expressive doublets are formed by altering the stem-vowel of a word: e.g. *jibber/jabber, snip/snap, jiggle/joggle, splash/splosh, putter/potter,* etc.

A similar type of formation is seen in words like *chitchat* and *super-duper,* where two elements, which show either vowel-alternation or rhyme, are compounded. Sometimes both elements are independently meaningful (*lovey-dovey, singsong, dripdrop, teenyweeny*), sometimes one (*crisscross, mishmash, fuzzy-wuzzy, rolypoly*), and sometimes neither (*riffraff, zigzag, hurdy-gurdy, hugger-mugger*). Fairly recent formations of this type are: *hifi, pingpong, walkie-talkie, heebie-jeebies, lilo, flower-power, hokey-cokey, itsy-bitsy, swing-wing, wing-ding,* etc.

This brief survey of the history of the English vocabulary and its living processes of word-formation shows very clearly the extreme diversity and variety of English words. Intuitively, we feel that the vocabulary is divided into an indefinite number of different sections, though we would be hard put to it to map them. Although dictionaries make no attempt in their general layout to separate the various strata in the vocabulary, yet they often give helpful labels which classify some words: e.g. *tummy* (nursery), *bread-basket* (colloquial), *guts, belly* (impolite), *viscera* (learned), and so on.

There are many ways in which the vocabulary could be classified, and any classification may be applied broadly (as here) or in more and more minute detail. It is suggested that English words can be located on a number of dimensions stretching from the central core-vocabulary towards extreme neologisms or archaisms, totally foreign words, words confined to a particular regional dialect or appropriate to a particular occupation, medium, or register. We shall consider each of these dimensions in turn, but must remember that some words will be located significantly on more than one dimension: *Franglais*, for instance, is distinctively both foreign and novel; *mike* ('microphone') is novel and more appropriate to the spoken medium than the written; *amelioration* is formal and more appropriate to the written medium; and so on.

The dimension stretching from the neutral core-vocabulary towards extreme NEOLOGISMS can be exemplified by pairs like *gramophone/record-player, reconsider/rethink, complete/finalize, adolescent/teenage*, where in each case the second example still seems distinctly novel. Of course, as with all methods of classifying the vocabulary, we are dealing with a gradation between the unmarked core-vocabulary and the markedly neologistic word, and we can draw up sequences of roughly synonymous terms to show this: e.g. *modern, contemporary, mod, with-it, trendy*. Many examples of recent innovations have been given in the discussion of word-formation, but the following may be added: *grotty, telly, scrounge, supermarket, gimmick, discotheque, groovy, maxi, psychedelic, technocentric, merger, stopover, phoney, drip-dry, aerocrat, computerize, kinky, agism, zap*, and many others. Although much has been said about the processes of word-formation we have not yet discussed its motivation. It is often assumed that new words are created to handle new ideas or objects, but this is only partly true. One of the main functions of neologisms is simply to be new, and it is not surprising that when they are no longer new they often rapidly fall out of use. Words of this sort are time-bound, e.g. *spiffing, erk, lunik, spiv, prang*, etc. The up-to-date all too quickly becomes dated.

The dimension of ARCHAISM is similar to, though not the same as, the dimension of neologism. Again, it is simplest to exemplify archaism by pairs of words: e.g. *feather/plume, warlike/martial, hair/locks* (or *tresses*), *marry/wed* (or *espouse*), *engagement/betrothal, linguistics/philology, tired/weary*, where in each case the second example seems distinctly archaic beside the first. Of course, the relationship between the pairs cannot be explained only in terms of archaism: in the case of *marry/wed*, for instance, we must recognize that in newspaper headlines *wed*, being shorter, is the preferred form. The gradation from the unmarked core-vocabulary towards the extreme archaism can be seen in a sequence such as *hate, loathe, detest, abhor, abominate*. Why do some words become obsolete? There is no single answer to the problem; a number of factors may be involved. Homophony certainly played a part in the gradual loss of *let* ('prevent', cf. *let and hindrance*), *quean* ('woman' – with derogatory sense) and *raze*: the homophones *let* ('allow'), *queen* and *raise* have related, but contrasting, meanings which could easily lead to confusion. Taboo will sometimes cause a word to disappear: *jakes, privy, latrine*, etc. Perhaps one of the most important factors is the tendency for words to fall into roughly synonymous pairs of which one is fashionable and the other unfashionable. We have seen how neologisms can often be paired with neutral words in this way (*teenage/adolescent*); our attitude towards such pairs easily shifts from treating the first member as markedly neologistic, to stigmatizing the second as archaic and obsolescent. Consider *stove/cooker, wireless/radio, cab/ taxi, hasten/hurry, torment/torture, dish/plate, nay/no, hallow/bless, halt/lame, perfidy/treachery, peril/danger*, etc. Any dictionary is full of words which are no longer in active use but which are known from our reading of earlier literature: *abjure, abnegate, accouchement, aestival, afore, ague, ail, alack, amain, ambuscade*, and so on. The archaic element in the vocabulary must be very much larger than the neologistic.

The dimension stretching from the unmarked native vocabulary, which of course includes fully-assimilated LOANWORDS, towards totally FOREIGN WORDS is particularly interesting. The borrowing of a foreign word is not a once-and-for-all matter but a gradual process. At one extreme we have fully-assimilated loanwords like *sky, send, cheese*; at the other the quotation of totally foreign words or phrases in English sentences: *inter vivos, salvete, déraciné, Aufklärung*, etc. Unless an English speaker is bilingual, he will neither use nor understand such foreign quotations. In the gradual transformation of a quotation into a loanword the first step is taken when monolingual native speakers begin to understand and use the new words; examples in contemporary English are *Abseil, cum laude, caritas, bouillon*. In the next stage, the assimilation of the originally unassimilated loanword, three types of change can often be observed.

First the phonology of the word is gradually adapted to conform to English patterns. *Restaurant*, a 19th century borrowing from French, has three common types of pronunciation: /'rest(ə)rɔ̃/ with nasalized final vowel as in French; /'rest(ə)rɔŋ/ with assimilation of the nasalized vowel to the nearest appropriate native pattern; /'rest(ə)rɔnt/ with a new pronunciation deduced from the spelling. In none of the pronunciations, it is worth noting, is the French /r/ retained. Until quite recently English did not have the sound /ʒ/ in final position, though it was common enough medially (*measure, seizure*); but it has established itself in French loanwords: *rouge, beige, collage, camouflage, montage, garage, decolletage, ménage*, and others. Although there are quite a large number of words in this group, there is some evidence that final /ʒ/ is unstable. *Garage*, the most widely-used example, has three pronunciations, /ˈgærɑːʒ/, /ˈgærɑːdʒ/ and /ˈgærɪdʒ/; the last two show assimilation of /-ʒ/ to the more usual English final consonant /-dʒ/, and /ˈgærɪdʒ/ has been further assimilated to conform to the *marriage, carriage* group of words (*montage* also sometimes occurs as /ˈmɒntɪdʒ/). A non-native initial consonant group is found in *schlemozzle*, but the development of the common alternative form *schemozzle* shows that phonological assimilation is in progress. Phonological assimilation sometimes takes the form of a reinterpretation of the spelling according to the usual English conventions: thus we have /ˈspʌtnɪk/ beside /ˈspʊtnɪk/ (*sputnik*), /ˈzɒlvərɑɪn/ and /ˈzwiːbæk/ beside /ˈtsɒlfərɑɪn/ and /ˈtsviːbak/ (*Zollverein, Zwieback*), /kwestɪəˈnɛə/ beside /kestɪəˈnɛə/ (*questionnaire*), and so on.

The second type of change which affects loanwords is that, as they become more closely assimilated into the borrowing language, they become capable of producing derivative formations: from *garage* (noun) have developed *garage* (verb) and *garageman*, from *trek* (noun) we have *trekker* and *trek* (verb). A similar, but rather rarer, process is seen in *au-pair*, which is an adverbial phrase in French but functions in English as a noun; *viva voce*, a Latin adverbial phrase, becomes in English a noun (and derivative verb) in its abbreviated form *viva*.

Thirdly, loanwords often undergo a marked change of meaning as they become assimilated into the borrowing language. *Café* means 'coffee' in French but 'restaurant' in English, the connection being through the sense 'coffee-house'. *Gentle* (13th century), *genteel* (16th century) and *jaunty* (17th century) are three independent borrowings of French *gentil*; *jaunty*, especially, has diverged a long way from the original sense of 'well-born'. *Rodeo* (19th century) seems to have meant 'round-up' when it was first adopted from Spanish, but later it came to refer to the place where the cattle were penned and from this it developed the sense 'cowboy sports'. The frequency with which such changes of meaning take place among newly-borrowed loanwords may seem surprising, since one might assume that a loanword would normally be borrowed to make good a specific deficiency in a language. But loanwords are a type of neologism, and it must be remembered that neologisms are often created as much for their novelty as their particular application. Moreover, a loanword is remarkably isolated: it has no derivational relationships within the borrowing language, nor semantic links with other words, and the network of relationships it contracted with words in the source-language is broken.

Repêchage (20th century) shows this rather well. The French word is a noun derived from *repêcher* 'to fish out again', which can be applied in various circumstances, e.g. to a drowning man, to torpedoes, to a candidate who is given a second chance at an examination. But the various meanings are held together and controlled by the obvious relationship of *repêchage* to *pêcher* ('to fish') and the prefix *re-* ('again'). In English the word is opaque: with the stress on the first syllable it cannot even be related to the common English prefix *re-* ('again'). The word is used for a supplementary race in which the best losers in earlier heats get a second chance to enter the final. A further example, *blank*, was borrowed from French in the 15th century. In French it means 'white, pale, pure, blank', and has a host of derivatives, such as *blanchir* 'whiten', *blanquette* 'veal stew with white sauce', *blanchaille* 'whitebait', and is part of a network of semantic relations with other colour-words, of which the most important is probably its opposite, *noir*. English *blank* has a basic meaning 'empty'; it has completely lost the colour-sense which is primary in French. While it has produced new derivatives (*blank* (noun) and *blankness*) it has lost contact with the words with which it has an etymological relationship (*blanch*, *blancmange*, *Blanche*), and it no longer has a relationship of direct opposition with any other word. These examples should make clear how important to the meaning of a word are its derivational and semantic relationships.

In some languages, such as Vietnamese, recent foreign adoptions constitute a more or less distinct section of the vocabulary for which a separate phonological description is necessary. Is this true of English? There is no doubt that at an earlier period, in Middle English, the French loanwords in particular constituted a distinct section of the vocabulary with a partially different phonology: the diphthong /ɔɪ/ was introduced into English through such adoptions as *choice, joy, join, noise,* etc. But Modern English has fully assimilated these earlier borrowings; and the more recent adoptions from French, though in many cases only partially assimilated, are too few in number to form an independent section of the vocabulary. There are, however, some grounds for claiming that the learned words formed from Latin and Greek elements constitute a special section of the vocabulary: prefixes like *hyper-, meta-, micro-, mono-, para-, poly-, proto-, retro-, ultra-, uni-,* and suffixes like *-ation, -ic, -ician, -ine, -ise, -ory,* are generally found only with elements of Latin and Greek origin. But such words are not phonologically distinct from the rest of the vocabulary, except in as much as they are generally polysyllabic in a language where monosyllables and disyllables are otherwise the majority type. Apart, then, from the possible isolation of a Graeco-Latin element in the vocabulary, the dimension stretching from the core-vocabulary towards fully foreign words cannot be easily broken down into various sections. The gradation from the centre towards the periphery can be exemplified in sequences like: (French) *vogue, valet, valise, velours, voyeur, vécu, vitrail* . . .; or (German) *plunder, poodle, pumpernickel, poltergeist, pretzel, putsch, privatdozent* . . .

The dimension of DIALECT, like that of foreign adoption, is complicated by the fact that there are many dialects of English, just as there are many foreign languages from which we borrow words. Standard British English may be imagined as the centre of a circle, around the periphery of which are ranged Scots, American English, Australian English, and so on. (However, it must be remembered that a similar study could be made of American English, for example, in which case British English would be one of the peripheral dialects.) Although we are once again dealing with a gradation we may distinguish four types of dialect words: words which are not understood by non-dialect speakers, e.g. *ashet* (Scots, 'dish'), *yat* (northern 'gate'), *mullock* (Australian, 'rubbish from a mine'), *meld* (American, 'merge'); the partially assimilated borrowing, which is recognized, but not used by the non-dialect speaker, e.g. *bairn, fash, cookie, checkers, dinkum, cobber*; the more fully assimilated word, which is both recognized and used by the non-dialect speaker, but still retains its dialect association, e.g. *dour, canny, lass, feckless, outback, movie, figure out*; and, finally, the fully assimilated adoption, which is of historical interest only, e.g. *vat, till, hale, raid, blizzard*. It is often forgotten how much of the English vocabulary is produced by intimate borrowing from its dialects. Most of us are aware of the stream of new words from American English, but the following list of Australian English words shows that English borrows from other dialects as well: *aborigine, also-ran, barrack, billy-can, booze-up, bushed, cobber, crook* (adjective), and so on. At present it is clear that British English is adopting many more words from overseas dialects, especially American English, than from the regional dialects of Britain.

In the discussion of the dimension of dialect, I have so far confined myself to spatially separate varieties of English; but the term DIALECT can also be applied to forms of language appropriate to particular social classes. The situation is complicated in English by the fact that the standard language is both a regional and a class dialect at one and the same time. Standard English, defined as the form of language common to its educated speakers, is itself remarkably diverse; both members of such pairs as *mirror/looking-glass, toilet/lavatory, slip/petticoat, costume/suit,* or *notepaper/writing-paper,* in which some see a class-difference, are certainly part of it. But there are a number of words which can be located along the dimension stretching from the standard language to the speech of the uneducated: *chocks, telly, drawers* ('pants'), *bint, skirt* ('woman'), *Ma, fancy* (verb), *fag* ('cigarette'), *tanner* ('sixpence'), *neck* (verb), *char* ('tea'), etc. Some of these are also used in the standard spoken language, but usually with an intentionally humorous or vulgar effect. There are a number of other words in English which have a different social connotation, such as *varsity, footer, togs, Mama,* etc. But these words, which are used by members (or those who affect to be members) of a superior social group, are less common than the vulgarisms.

From the class-dialect it is but a short distance to the occupational dialect. All occupations develop their own vocabulary of technical terms: *hose* ('socks, etc.' in the clothing trade), *battels* ('bill for board and lodging' at an Oxford college), *lexis* ('vocabulary' in specialist books on language), and so on. In such cases, of course, it is very difficult to draw the line between the core-vocabulary and the occupational vocabulary. Once more, we can observe a gradation, as in the following lists of linguistic terms: *pitch, preposition, prefix, paradigm, phoneme, polysemy . . .;* or *dialect, denotation, dative, diacritic, deixis, diathesis . . .* What our dictionaries call learned words can also be grouped with other terms appropriate to particular occupations. Occupational dialects are distinguished almost entirely by their vocabulary; their grammar and phonology are rarely distinctive. When we remember how many occupational dialects may be distinguished it is easy to see that this is one of the more important dimensions by which the vocabulary can be classified.

Occupational varieties of language are roughly halfway between DIALECT, which refers to varieties of language distinguished by user, and REGISTER, which refers to varieties of language distinguished by use. To some extent it is true that each occupational variety is used only by a section of the speech-community as a whole, but most of us command more than one occupational variety – for example, the languages of our profession, our hobbies and sports; and we are able to switch from one to another as appropriate.

The most immediately obvious distinction within the field of register is MEDIUM. We can observe two main types of medium, spoken and written language (though we may note in passing the two intermediate types, reading aloud and scripted language). Clearly, the bulk of the English vocabulary can be appropriately used in both written and spoken English, but there are a number of words which are more often used in one or other medium: *decease, alight, commencement, authorization, appended; hey, ref, oopsy-daisy, telly, teeny, with-it, chewy, twee,* etc. There is a partial, but by no means complete, correlation between the archaic and the written sections of the vocabulary, and between the novel and the spoken portions.

The other dimensions which I have grouped together under the general heading of register are ROLE and FORMALITY. The first of these, role, refers to the various types of language appropriate to different social roles: the language of the commentator differs from that of the lecturer; a letter to *The Times* and a letter to one's wife will not be alike. Some of the differences will be grammatical, but many of them are lexical, e.g. *cleanse* (language of advertising), *pussy* (language of the nursery), *hereinafter* (language of legal documents), *wed* (newspaper headlines). The dimension of role can be exemplified by a comparison of such sentences as: *the damn fool nearly ran over my bloody foot!* and *Darling, you must give me a teeny drink – I've had a simply frightful time!* What makes us think that the first sentence was spoken by a man and the second by a woman? We can distinguish a large number of different roles, and each one will have its own appropriate vocabulary. As before, there is a gradation from the core-vocabulary to the special words associated with each role, for example in this list of nursery words: *grumpy, grizzle, potty* (noun), *gee-gee, bow-wow* (noun). It may be objected that the dimensions of role and occupation are very similar, but the difference can be shown by a comparison of *copy, leader, par* (occupational language of journalism) with *probe, ban, bar* (verb) (role language of newspaper headlines).

The dimension of formality can be exemplified by pairs such as *right away/immediately, think/consider, photo/photograph,* etc. The well-known comparison of *low-income dress for dignified maturity* with *cheap clothes for fat old women* shows that a formal style is more appropriate for such a notice. Once again we must recognize a considerable degree of overlap between the categories of formal and written language and between informal and spoken language, but medium and formality are distinct dimensions. Compare the following notices: *visitors are kindly requested not to walk on the lawns/please keep off the grass*; or these letters – *Dear Bill, Thanks for your note. Next Wed. is O.K. See you then. Yours, Jack./Dear Mr Smith, Thank you for your letter, Wednesday, 4th June, will suit me admirably, and I look forward to meeting you on that date. Yours sincerely, J. Brown.*; or these introductions – *Mrs Johnson, may I introduce a colleague of mine – Mr Jones?/Meg, this is Jimmy: he works with me.*

We have now seen how the English vocabulary may be roughly stratified along a number of dimensions – archaism, neologism, foreign adoption, dialect, medium, role, and formality. Any word may be located in the vocabulary by placing it on a scale stretching from neutral to extreme for each of these dimensions. Thus, *puissance* is distinctively archaic, foreign, formal and appropriate to written English, but neutral as regards neologism, dialect and role; *weskit* is archaic, typical of a particular class-dialect, and more appropriate to spoken English, but it is neutral in other respects; *yum-yum* is more appropriate to spoken English and the role language of the nursery, and is very informal; *hors d'oeuvre* is foreign and typical of the occupational language connected with food; and so on. This is one way in which the organization of the vocabulary may be studied. Another way is to map the derivational relationships of words. We have already seen how the various processes of word-formation produce families of words, derivationally related, such as *father* (noun and verb), *fatherhood, father-figure, fatherland, fatherless*, etc., or *television, televise, telly, T.V., telly-mania*, etc. Most words are members of such word-families, although there are some, especially among the recent borrowings from foreign languages or dialects, which are isolated: *biennale, aficionado, ouzo, quorum, tontine, torso*, etc. But the vocabulary is organized in more ways than the two which have so far been mentioned (derivational relationships and lexical dimensions): we must now proceed to study collocational organization and sense-relationships.

The term COLLOCATION is used to refer to co-occurrence of words. Adjective + noun is a regular grammatical structure, and examples of it may be multiplied: *blank look, molten glass, yellow tie; blank glance, molten butter, yellow wine.* We use the term COL-LOCATION to describe the acceptability of the first group in contrast to the (relative) unacceptability of the second. To some extent the concept of collocation handles what is often called idiom, the apparently inexplicable phrases like *glad eye* or *glad rags*, and equally the non-occurrence of seemingly parallel phrases like *glad ear* or *glad clothes*. But these idiomatic examples are extreme cases of collocational restriction. All words have a range of acceptable collocations, and when we know a word's range of collocations we have gone a long way towards understanding its meaning. It may be objected that in many cases collocations (such as *blue leaf, molten feather, woolly hedgehog*) do not regularly occur for the very obvious reason that leaves are never blue, nor are feathers molten, or hedgehogs woolly. We may feel that it is not so much the words that are incompatible in such cases, as the referents. In other cases, such as *unmarried wife, female father, he ate his beer*, the incompatibility seems to be almost more a matter of grammar than of lexis: *wife* and *father* each belong to subclasses of noun which normally exclude adjectives such as *unmarried* and *female*, respectively; *eat* is one of a number of verbs (such as *chew, munch, gnaw*, etc.) which do not usually select as object such words as *beer, milk, orange-juice*, and so on. But although collocational restrictions sometimes border on grammatical and logical restrictions, the bulk of collocational patterning is clearly within the sphere of lexical organization. Moreover the study of the English vocabulary will be assisted more by an attempt to describe such collocational patterns than by explaining them away by an appeal to common sense.

It will be obvious that the question of lexical acceptability is not a straightforward one. Few collocations can be firmly excluded as impossible; they range from the unquestionably acceptable to the extremely unlikely. Context is often all-important: *woolly hedgehog* will be admissible in a fairy-story, *blue leaf* in some sorts of poetry, while it does not require much imagination to produce an appropriate context for *unmarried wife* or *female father*.

In order to bring out the reality and importance of collocational patterns we must discuss some examples in detail. The dictionary-definition of *hale* is 'healthy'; yet we all recognize that no single example of *healthy* can be replaced by *hale* in contemporary English speech or writing: *healthy child, healthy walk, healthy influence, healthy water, healthy state*, etc. In fact, *hale* probably occurs only in the collocation *hale and hearty* today. The knowledge of its restricted collocation is more important for the understanding of *hale* than is its dictionary-definition. But this is not all. We note that the collocational range of *hearty*, which is anyway considerably restricted, is further reduced by the addition of *hale*. With *meal, laugh, support, welcome, appetite*, for instance, *hearty* is acceptable, but *hale and hearty* inappropriate.

Soft, mild and *gentle* can all collocate with *voice, rebuke,* or *breeze,* for example, but each of them also has exclusive collocations with other words: *soft water, soft ground; mild ale, mild steel; gentle blood, gentle slope.* The example of *soft water* can be used to show how a collocational relationship will often hold good through a series of derivationally-linked words: *water-softener, she softened the water, the softness of the water,* etc.

Another word where collocational pattern is interesting is *rotten.* This has two closely related senses, 'putrid' and 'of poor quality'. How does the native speaker know which is intended in any particular case? *Rotten apples* is clearly ambiguous, but *rotten butter* must be 'butter of inferior quality'; in this case, the appropriate word for 'putrid' is *rancid,* which has a very restricted collocation, virtually confined to *butter, oil, fat (lard,* etc.), *taste and smell (flavour, odour, stink,* etc.). It is easy to see how large a part is played by collocational pattern in distinguishing such virtual synonyms as *putrid, rotten, rancid* and *addled. Addled,* which is confined to *eggs* and *brains (wits,* etc.), is like *hale* and many other, generally archaic, words which have very restricted collocations: *spick and span, chit of a girl, flitch of bacon, rood screen, serried ranks,* etc.

Of course, it is easier to point to the fact of collocational range and restriction, and give a few fragmentary examples, than it is to undertake a full description of the collocations of even a few words. Our dictionaries normally list only the unexpected ones (*glad rags, glad eye*), and only give a full statement in the case of highly restricted words like *addled.* But the commonest words have individual collocational patterns which contribute to their distinctive meaning: *a quick glance* (but not *a fast glance*), *a black mood* (but not *a white mood*), *a new day* (but not *a novel day*), etc.

One of the most easily overlooked types of lexical change is the extension or restriction of a word's collocational range. Recently *key* has considerably extended the range of words with which it collocates: *key man, key component, key move,* etc. Adjectives of value very frequently undergo rapid collocational extension in colloquial usage, simultaneously exchanging their precise sense for a more general one, for example *gruesome party, revolting dress, wicked price, vicious remark, blissful idea, heavenly shoes, divine soup,* etc. The collocational range of words may also be restricted, as the following examples from *Pride and Prejudice* indicate: *happy manners, mean understanding, tolerable fortune, perfect indifference, indifferent imitations,* etc. These, though not impossible, would all be unusual collocations today.

Most of the examples of collocations which have been discussed have been within the grammatical structure, adjective + noun; but it has been stressed that the collocational relationship is not dependent on any particular grammatical structure. One of the problems in the study of collocation is how far a collocation may be extended before it becomes insignificant: e.g. *soft water; the softness of cool, fresh rainwater; use the water from the stream at the end of the field – the softness will be good for your skin.* Are each of these to be counted as collocations of *soft/water*? However, although there are obvious difficulties in making a collocational description of vocabulary, there is no doubt that the range of collocations contracted by any particular word is one of the important elements in its meaning. We must now turn from collocational organization to SENSE-RELATIONSHIPS.

In discussing the meaning of words we are accustomed to assuming that each word will have one single meaning (or, at least, one basic meaning) more or less like proper nouns such as *Chaucer* or *Edinburgh*. I have tried to show that what we call meaning is a complex of different relationships, and we have so far considered the relationships of derivation, dimension, and collocation. Two types of relationship remain, sense-relations and reference. The latter is easily understood: it is the relationship between words and the world of experience. *Edinburgh* and *Chaucer* 'refer' to the city and the poet, respectively. Sense-relations are the semantic relations words contract with one another. Let us consider an example. We may say that *orange* (adjective) refers to the colour of oranges, but we should add that it is part of a lexical system (*red, orange, yellow*, . . .) and that its meaning largely depends on its position between *red* and *yellow*. Similarly, *cow* and *vixen* refer to female cattle and foxes, respectively, but a fuller understanding of their meaning is gained by observing that *cow* and *bull* are incompatible, but the sense of *fox* includes that of *vixen*: in other words, the utterance *I saw a fox today – I think it was a vixen* is perfectly acceptable, but *I saw a bull today – I think it was a cow* seems, at least, facetious.

We may broadly distinguish four types of sense-relationship: identity, inclusion, incompatibility, opposition. Few words contract all four types of relationship, but no word is completely without sense-relations. Identity of sense, commonly called SYNONYMY, is easy to exemplify: *adder/viper, photo/photograph, hide/conceal, just/fair, telegram/cable, gramophone/record-player, football/soccer*, etc. It will be obvious, even from this short list of examples, that it is rash to claim that two words are synonymous without qualification. Two important qualifications must be made. First, identity of meaning commonly depends on context: *do* and *clean* are synonymous in a sentence like *have you done/cleaned your teeth?*, but not often otherwise. Secondly, the concept of synonymy of sense is not intended to handle the type of difference already discussed under the heading 'dimension'. For example, the meaning of *soccer* differs from that of *football* in that the former is both more informal and more colloquial than the latter: they share an identical sense, though once again, one should observe that they will not necessarily be synonymous in all contexts, e.g. *Rugby football is a brutal game.*

Identity of sense is closely related to INCLUSION. The latter refers to the relationship between *red* and *scarlet/crimson/magenta*, etc., or *fruit* and *apple/plum/lemon*, etc. English, like other languages, provides numerous examples of families of more specific words subsumed under a more general cover-term. In some cases the general terms are so general that they are able to embrace most of the rest of the vocabulary, e.g. *thing, do.* Inclusion differs from identity in that, while synonyms may freely replace one another, only the including term can replace the included, and not vice versa. The sentence *there's a plum-tree in our garden* implies *there's a fruit-tree in our garden*, but *fresh fruit for pudding!* does not imply *fresh lemons for pudding!* In some cases, the family of included words lacks a general including term, as, for instance, the group *tree, shrub, bush.* A thesaurus arranges the vocabulary of a language according to the two types of sense-relation so far discussed, identity and inclusion. The fact that the whole of the vocabulary of English can be accounted for in such a scheme indicates the linguistic importance of these sense-relationships.

INCOMPATIBILITY handles the difference in sense between such members of a lexical set as *red, green, yellow, blue*, etc., or *lion, tiger, leopard, panther*, etc. Many words differ in sense without being incompatible; in the sentences *that lion is a joke* and *the sky is wide and blue* the pairs *lion/joke* and *blue/wide*, which certainly differ in sense, are applied to the same objects. Conversely, incompatible words are commonly similar in sense, and make up a family of words which are included in a higher general term. Thus in most contexts *coloured* includes *red, yellow, green*, etc., which are mutually incompatible; in turn *red* includes another incompatible set, *crimson, scarlet, vermilion*, etc.

In cases like *father/mother* or *brother/sister*, which are incompatible sets with only two members, we come to the fourth type of sense-relation, OPPOSITION. This is easily exemplified with pairs like *odd/even*, *wet/dry*, *father/son*. Several different types of opposite may be distinguished. Complementary pairs like *odd/even* or *male/female* differ from opposites like *good/bad* in that there is no gradation between the extremes. If a number is not odd, it must be even; if a person is not male, she must be female. Pairs like *good/bad*, *wet/dry*, *few/many*, *cheap/expensive*, are, however, gradable. This is the commonest type of opposite. A third type is the converse pair like *husband/wife* or *mother/daughter*, where there is a reciprocal relationship between the two terms. In the case of *mother* we may observe that it is a member of a complementary pair (*mother/father*) as well as a converse pair (*mother/daughter*), and that, in turn, *daughter* is a complementary opposite to *son*.

It is worth noting that a word can be in opposition to two or more words in different ways. *Odd* and *even* are, as we have seen, a complementary pair, but *odd* and *normal* are in some contexts gradable opposites. A sentence like the following plays on this double relationship: *you may call eighty-eight an even number, but it's the oddest number I've ever seen.* On occasions complementary pairs may be treated as gradable pairs to gain a particular effect: *John seems rather more married than he used to be.* The flexibility of the sense-relations we have been considering cannot be emphasized too strongly. Certain linguistic contexts, or social situations, will neutralize some relations and generate others. *Red* and *white* are ungradable opposites when collocated with *wine*, though the system is slightly complicated by the third term, *rosé*. *Black* and *white* are two members of a large incompatible set when collocated with *horse*, but are complementary terms when applied to *magic* or *coffee*. *Good* and *bad* have been stated to be gradable opposites, but when a mother says to her child *David, you are not a good boy* she is implying a complementary relationship between them.

With the four types of sense-relation which we have discussed languages are able to map the world of experience. It is important to note that different languages do this in different ways. Even English and French (or German), which are closely related both historically and culturally differ in a number of instances, e.g. *know/savoir, connaître; cousin/Vetter, Cousine.* In the latter case German has a pair of complementary terms distinguishing sex, where English *cousin* is indifferent with regard to sex.

We have now completed our survey of the various ways in which the English vocabulary is organized. I have argued that a word's meaning, far from being a straightforward matter, is a complex of

different relationships. Fully to understand the meaning of a word
we need to know its derivational relations, its place on the various
lexical dimensions, its collocational patterns, the sense-
relationships it contracts with other words, and, of course, finally,
its reference.

Some of these approaches to the study of vocabulary can be
usefully applied to literature. For instance, the words of W. H.
Auden's poem *Who's Who* seem to have been carefully selected
from a particular section of the vocabulary: they are remarkably
informal, colloquial and neologistic.

> A shilling life will give you all the facts:
> How Father beat him, how he ran away,
> What were the struggles of his youth, what acts
> Made him the greatest figure of his day:
> Of how he fought, fished, hunted, worked all night,
> Though giddy, climbed new mountains; named a sea:
> Some of the last researchers even write
> Love made him weep his pints like you and me.
>
> With all his honours on, he sighed for one
> Who, say astonished critics, lived at home;
> Did little jobs about the house with skill
> And nothing else; could whistle; would sit still
> Or potter round the garden; answered some
> Of his long marvellous letters but kept none.

We notice *life* ('biography'), *researchers, pints, jobs, potter, marvellous*.
The vocabulary (and the grammar, though this is not relevant here)
is carefully designed to imitate the language of the potted
biography mentioned in the first line. Not only the selection of the
words but also their collocation is appropriate to this scheme, e.g.
*give/facts, climbed/mountains, weep/pints, astonished/critics, sit/still,
long/letters*. These, and, some of the longer sequences, are markedly
ordinary collocations and give this poem its unoriginal, even banal,
effect. A study of the vocabulary will take us so far: but one needs to
go beyond the words to explain why the poem, with all its clichés, is
yet so moving.

At different periods in the history of English special vocabularies
have developed for certain literary purposes. In Old English the
vocabulary of verse was partially distinct from that used in prose,
which was no doubt closer to the spoken norm. A similar situation
has developed several times in the more recent history of English.

In the 18th century poetry commonly used a rather formal vocabulary: e.g. *abode, bounty, celestial, dread, dirge, dauntless, disdainful, fleeting, fretted, graved, genial, heath, haply, hoary, inglorious, ignoble, jocund, lowly, nigh, pangs, pore, ply, rill, rustic, rugged, sturdy, shrine, strife, strew, sequestered, swain, turf, unfathomed, vale, wan, wonted, wayward, woeful, yon, yonder.* These words, which as a group, if not individually, seem typical of 18th century verse, are all drawn from Gray's *Elegy Written in a Country Churchyard.* But other lists could be produced to exemplify the vocabulary typical of the later 19th century poetry (for example, such adjectives as *sweet, tender, dear, keen,* . . .), or of other periods or other literary kinds. Of course, one can only isolate the distinctive vocabulary of a period or genre in a very rough and ready way. Often a particular author will have his own partially distinctive vocabulary, e.g. Hopkins (*dapple, selve, comb, frond, fretty, juice, whelm, sear,* . . .), or Hemingway (*bastard, crazy, yank* (verb), *bitch, plenty* (adverb), *awful* (adverb), *lousy,* . . .), or Spenser (*ween, puissance, hight, darksome, loathly, doff, mazed, wight, blithe,* . . .). But in the study of the selection of vocabulary one should not concentrate solely on the eccentric at the expense of the more normal. The choice of undistinctive vocabulary, as in this poem by Robert Frost (*Stopping by Woods on a Snowy Evening*), is just as significant a stylistic decision as, for example, Spenser's use of archaic diction in *The Faerie Queene.*

Whose woods these are I think I know.
His house is in the village though;
He will not see me stopping here
To watch his woods fill up with snow.

My little horse must think it queer
To stop without a farmhouse near
Between the woods and frozen lake
The darkest evening of the year.

He gives his harness bells a shake
To ask if there is some mistake.
The only other sound's the sweep
Of easy wind and downy flake.

The woods are lovely, dark and deep,
But I have promises to keep,
And miles to go before I sleep,
And miles to go before I sleep.

Not only the selection but also the collocation of words may be distinctive and interesting. In the Auden poem quoted earlier the collocations were, on the whole, so predictable as to appear (intentionally) trite. In the Frost poem the collocation of, for instance, *little/horse, frozen/lake, easy/wind, downy/flake*, is not predictable, but they are in no way remarkable or unusual. Some of the most startling lines of verse achieve their effect by unexpected collocations, e.g. *Light thickens; A grief ago; Sweet rose, whose hue angrie and brave/Bids the rash gazer wipe his eye . . .*; etc. Some poets, such as Dylan Thomas, use the unexpected collocation almost as a stylistic device:

> How soon the servant sun,
> (Sir morrow mark),
> Can time unriddle, and the cupboard stone,
> (Fog has a bone
> He'll trumpet into meat),
> Unshelve that all my gristles have a gown
> And the naked egg stand straight . . .

In verse like this it is not the selection of words which is distinctive but their collocation. By combining the notions of selection and collocation we can distinguish four lexical styles: distinctive vocabulary in unusual collocations, distinctive vocabulary in usual collocations, undistinctive vocabulary in unusual collocations, undistinctive vocabulary in usual collocations. This is, of course, a greatly oversimplified scheme, since, as we have seen, vocabulary can be distinctive in a large number of different ways, and the scale between the usual and the unique collocation is a gradual one.

A further point of interest is the question of lexical repetition. In Old English prose it was an acceptable rhetorical device to repeat words and their derivative relations in a way which now seems intolerable. The following passage by the homilist Aelfric, with its very literal translation, is a clear example of this practice.

'þæt folc, þa þe þæt wundor geseah, cwædon be Criste, þæt he wære soþ witega, þe toweard wæs.' Soþ hi sædon, sumera þinga: witega he wæs, forþan þe he wiste ealle towearde þing, and eac fela þing witegode, þe beoþ gefyllede butan twyn. He is witega, and he is ealra witegana witegung, forþan þe ealle witegan be him witegodon, and Crist gefylde heora ealra witegunga. þæt folc geseah þa þæt wundor, and hi þæs swiþe wundredon; þæt wundor is awriten, and we hit gehyrdon.

'The people when they saw the wonder, said about Christ that he was the true prophet who was to come.' They spoke the truth, in some ways: he was a prophet, because he knew all things to come, and also prophesied many things which are without doubt fulfilled. He is a prophet, and he is the prophecy of all prophets, because all prophets prophesied regarding him, and Christ fulfilled all their prophecies. The people then saw the wonder, and they wondered at it greatly; the wonder is recorded, and we have heard it.

Now, there is no doubt that such a style seems offensive in Modern English. Far from lexical repetition being an acceptable rhetorical device, some authors clearly strive for its opposite, lexical variation. Consider this passage by Dr Johnson (*Rasselas* chapter 44, 'The dangerous prevalence of imagination'):

'Disorders of intellect,' answered Imlac, 'happen much more often than superficial observers will easily believe. Perhaps, if we speak with rigorous exactness, no human mind is in its right state. There is no man whose imagination does not sometimes predominate over his reason, who can regulate his attention wholly by will, and whose ideas will come and go at his command. No man will be found in whose mind airy notions do not sometimes tyrannise, and force him to hope or fear beyond the limits of sober probability. All power of fancy over reason is a degree of insanity; but while this power is such as we can control and repress, it is not visible to others, nor considered as any depravation of the mental faculties: it is not pronounced madness, but when it becomes ungovernable and apparently influences speech or action.

'To indulge the power of fiction, and send imagination out upon the wing, is often the sport of those who delight too much in silent speculation. When we are alone we are not always busy; the labour of excogitation is too violent to last long; the ardour of enquiry will sometimes give way to idleness or satiety. He who has nothing external that can divert him, must find pleasure in his own thoughts, and must conceive himself what he is not; for who is pleased with what he is? He then expatiates in boundless futurity, and culls from all imaginable conditions that which for the present moment he should most desire, amuses his desires with impossible enjoyments, and confers upon his pride unattainable dominion. The mind dances from scene to scene, unites all pleasures in all combinations, and riots in delights, which nature and fortune, with all their bounty, cannot bestow.

'In time some particular train of ideas fixes the attention; all other intellectual gratifications are rejected; the mind, in weariness or leisure, recurs constantly to the favourite conception, and feasts on the luscious falsehood whenever she is offended with the bitterness of truth. By degrees the reign of fancy is confirmed; she grows first imperious, and in time despotic. Then fictions begin to operate as realities, false opinions fasten upon the mind, and life passes in dreams of rapture or of anguish.

'This, sir, is one of the dangers of solitude, which the hermit has confessed not always to promote goodness, and the astronomer's misery has proved to be not always propitious to wisdom.'

There is obviously much of lexical interest in this passage. We note the selection of distinctive vocabulary – learned, formal, and typical of written rather than spoken English; on the other hand, the collocations, without being predictable, are rarely abnormal. Johnson often uses the sense-relationships of identity or opposition to produce such parallels as *fictions/false opinions* or *to promote/to be . . . propitious to*, and such antitheses as *luscious falsehood/bitterness of truth*. But we are particularly concerned with the repetition of words. In this passage of over 400 words we are immediately struck by the rarity of the lexical repetitions and the variety of the significant vocabulary: *mind* (5 times); *imagination/imaginable* (3 times); *ideas, attention, fancy, reason, fiction(s), conceive/conception, intellect/intellectual* (twice); *will, notions, believe, insanity, mental, madness, speculation, excogitation, enquiry, thoughts, opinions, wisdom* (once). This is an extreme case of lexical variation, but to a greater or lesser extent all modern prose strives to avoid lexical repetition. It is interesting to note that the Old English vocabulary, which was more homogeneous than that of Modern English and contained many more and larger derivative families, was better designed for a style permitting lexical repetition; a style of lexical variation is, however, wholly appropriate to Modern English with its immensely diverse vocabulary providing such partial synonyms as *work, job, toil, employment, occupation, labour,* etc., or pairs like *despise/contempt, mind/mental,* etc. It is perhaps not too much to claim that the structure of the English vocabulary is partly responsible for this feature of modern English prose style.

6

STYLE: THE VARIETIES OF ENGLISH

David Crystal

Many of the terms used in the study of language are 'loaded', in that they have a number of different, sometimes overlapping, sometimes contradictory and controversial senses, both at popular and scholarly levels. The word STYLE is a particularly good example of the kind of confusion that can arise. The multiplicity of meanings which surround this concept – or, perhaps set of concepts – testifies to its importance in the history of English language studies, and indicates the magnitude of the problem facing any student of the subject. On the one hand, there are highly technical definitions of style such as 'the style of a text is the aggregate of the contextual probabilities of its linguistic terms' (Enkvist); on the other hand, there is the loosely metaphorical, aphoristic definition of style as 'the man himself' (Buffon). Style has been compared to thought, soul, expressiveness, emotions, existence, choice, personality, good manners, fine clothing . . . and much more. How, one might well ask, is it possible to sort out such a semantic tangle? For sorting out there must be, if there is to be any clear discussion of this undeniably fundamental aspect of people's use of language.

One useful way into the tangle is to look at the most important senses in which the word STYLE is used at the present time, and see if there is any common denominator, or dominant use. There may be no single answer to the question, What is style?, but it should at least be possible to distinguish the main strands of meaning which would underlie any such answer.

The first, and possibly the most widespread use, is to take STYLE as referring to the distinctive characteristics of some SINGLE author's use of language – as when we talk of 'Wordsworth's style', or make a comment about 'the style of the mature Shakespeare'. There are a number of different areas of application for this interpretation: for example, we may want to clarify some comparative question (as when comparing the 'styles' of two poets in a given tradition), or we may be concerned with the study of some single author as an end in itself, or again we might be engaged in stylistic detection work – 'linguistic forensics', as it is sometimes half-seriously called – as with the investigations into the 'style' of the Pauline epistles, to see whether one man wrote them all. But in each of these applications, the primary task is the same: to pick out from the totality of the language that an author has used those features which would be generally agreed as belonging to him, identifying him as an individual against the backcloth of the rest of the language-using world. And it is these idiosyncratic linguistic markers which are referred to by this first use of the term 'style'. If we beware of the metaphor, 'style is the man' is an appropriate summary of the focus of this view.

A second, and closely related use, is to talk about 'style' in a collective sense, referring to GROUPS of literary figures, as when referring to the 'style' of Augustan poetry, or generalizing about the style associated with one particular genre of drama as opposed to another. This is a more general sense, obviously, but it is to be noted that the procedure for arriving at any conclusions in this area is precisely the same as in the study of individual authors: distinctive linguistic features have still to be identified and described – only this time the use of these features is shared by a number of people, and are not idiosyncratic in the narrow sense of the preceding paragraph.

These two senses are the most common in any discussion about literature, in view of the emphasis in literary criticism on defining the individuality of authors and tracing the development of genres; but in terms of the study of the English language as a whole, it should be stressed that these senses are extremely narrow. They are restricted largely to literary English, and to the written form of the language. But we can – and do – equally well apply the term STYLE to spoken English, whether literary or not, and to written English which has nothing to do with literature at all; and it is this more general use which provides us with a third sense. For example, when we refer (usually in a pejorative tone of voice) to the 'style' of Civil Service prose, or to 'business-letter style', or to the 'formal style' in which sermons or proclamations are given – or even to the 'style' of newspaper and television advertisements – we are referring to an awareness of certain features of English sounds and spellings, grammar and vocabulary, which characterize in a distinctive way these particular uses. And comparably familiar examples could be cited of people referring to the style of individuals, as well as of groups – 'I do like John's lecturing style, don't you?'

In the light of these examples, the term STYLE can be seen to be applicable, in principle, to a great deal of language use other than literature; and on the basis of this we might well generalize and say that style seems to be a concept which is applicable to the language as a whole. The word 'distinctive' has occurred a number of times already in this chapter. If one of the bases of style is linguistic distinctiveness of some kind, then it is very difficult – probably impossible – to think up cases of uses of English in which there is no distinctiveness whatsoever. Even the most ordinary kinds of conversation have the distinctive feature of being 'most ordinary'. Non-literary uses of language must not be decried simply because they are non-literary. To refer to such uses as 'style-less' is to beg the whole question as to what style consists of, and to ignore a highly important perspective for literary study. Without an 'ordinary' style, or set of styles, which we are all familiar with and use, it is doubtful whether we would ever appreciate an extraordinary style, as in literary linguistic originality. This is a point I shall return to later.

Other senses of the term STYLE may be found, but they take us into a quite different dimension. These are mainly variants of a sense of style as a 'quality' of expression. When we talk about someone or something displaying 'style', we are making an intuitive judgment about a (usually indefinable) overall impression – as when Mr X is said to 'have style', whereas Mr Y has not. This is very near to the sense of 'style' as 'powers of lucid exposition or self-expression': Mr Z 'has no sense of style at all', we might say. Then there is a wholly evaluative sense, as when we talk of a style as 'pretty', 'affected', 'endearing', 'lively', and the like. These uses are very different from those described in previous paragraphs, as what we are doing here is making value judgements of various kinds about a particular use of language, passing an opinion about the effect a use of language has had. The difference between the phrases 'Shakespeare's style' and 'affected style', essentially, is that the first is a descriptive statement, referring to certain features of the English language which could presumably be pointed out and agreed upon in a reasonably objective way; the second is an evaluative statement, where a subjective judgement is passed about some aspect of a use of language, and where we are told more about the state of mind of the language critic than about the linguistic characteristics of the author being assessed. Any critical task will involve both elements, descriptive and evaluative, in varying degrees, corresponding to WHAT we respond to and HOW we respond to it.

What must be emphasized is the importance of placing our evaluative decisions in a thoroughly descriptive context: value judgments with no 'objective correlative' to support them may give us a great deal of personal pleasure, but they do not provide anything of permanent critical value. We can only resolve a debate as to the merits or demerits of someone's style if the parties in the debate are first and foremost objectively aware of the relevant characteristics of the language they are discussing. The descriptive, identifying task is quite primary, as it provides the basis for the response which any two critics might be arguing about. Why does X think that line effective, whereas Y does not? The descriptive analysis of a piece of language (I shall call this, whether written or spoken, a text) is in no sense a replacement for a sensitive response to that language, as some critics of a linguistic approach to literature have implied – how could it be? It is simply an invaluable pre-liminary which is likely to promote clear thinking. What such a descriptive analysis might involve I shall outline below.

When such matters are considered, it becomes very clear that there is unlikely to be a single, pithy answer to the question 'What is style'. And perhaps therefore a more constructive question might be: 'What is there in language that makes us want to talk about "style", in any of its senses, at all?' This approach can be revealing: not only does it display the complexity of the concept of style very clearly; it also integrates this concept with that of 'language' as a whole, and thus produces a more general characterization than any of those so far reviewed. The approach is, briefly, to see 'style' in the context of the socially-conditioned VARIETIES a language may be shown to possess – and this is the reason for the title of this chapter.

The idea that the English language can be – indeed, HAS to be – seen in terms of varieties is one of the themes underlying the first chapter of this volume. The phrase 'THE English language' is itself highly misleading, for there is no such animal. If we look at the use of English in all parts of the world expecting to find identical sounds, spellings, grammar and vocabulary on all occasions, then we are in for a rude shock. There is a great deal in common between 'American' and 'British' English, for instance – to take one example that regularly rears its head in the letter-columns of the press – but people are much more aware of the fact that there are differences. The English language is not a single, homogeneous, stable entity: it is a complex mixture of varying structures. The unfortunate thing is that so many people look upon this as an unsatisfactory state of affairs, and try to correct it. The English-speaking world is full of people who want to make everyone else speak as they do, or as Shakespeare did. It is a pity that the fact and fundamental role of variety in the English language cannot be accepted for what it is – an inevitable product of language development.

What, then, are these varieties? The kind of variation which people are most readily aware of usually goes under the heading of REGIONAL DIALECT. It is not difficult to cite examples of people who speak or write differently depending on where they are from. This is one of the most well-studied aspects of language variety. The major rural dialects of Great Britain have all been studied in some detail, at least from the phonetic point of view, as have many of the dialects of the United States. Urban dialects – such as those of London, Liverpool, Brooklyn, and Sydney – have on the whole been less intensively studied, but their distinctiveness is as marked as that of any rural area. Take, for instance, the language of currency heard in parts of Liverpool a few years ago: *og* or *meg* (halfpenny), *two meg* (penny), *joey* (threepence), *tiddler* (silver threepenny piece), *dodger* (eight-sided threepenny piece), *sprowser* (sixpenny piece), *ocker* (shilling piece), and so on. Terms such as *kecks* (trousers), *jigger* (back alley), *ozzy* (hospital) and *sarneys* (sandwiches); phrases such as *good skin* (nice chap), *to get a cob on* (to get into a bad mood) and *that's the gear* (that's fine); sentences such as *don't youse butt in with the men* (don't interfere with what we're doing) and *I'll put a lip on you* (I'll hit you in the mouth): all these illustrate clearly the kind of language variation which can only be explained in terms of geographical place of origin.

Three points should be noted in connection with regional dialects. The first is that this kind of variation is usually associated with variation in the SPOKEN form of the language. The existence of a standardized, written form of English, which all people born into an English-speaking community are taught as soon as they begin to write, means that modern dialects get written down only by their introduction into a novel or a poem for a particular characterization or effect. The speech of the gamekeeper in *Lady Chatterley's Lover*, or that of many of the characters of Dickens, or of the 'regional' novelists such as Joyce, indicates this point abundantly – but even here, only the vaguest approximation to the original pronunciation is made. (After all, if we tried to indicate this pronunciation with any degree of accuracy, it would mean devising some form of phonetic transcription, and this would make the text impossible to read without training.) In non-literary contexts, regional dialect forms are not common, though they are sometimes used in informal contexts, and there are a few predictable examples, such as the differing spellings of certain words between British and American English.

Secondly, despite the association of regional variation with speech, DIALECT is a term which should not be identified with ACCENT. The 'regional accent' of a person refers simply to pronunciation; 'dialect', on the other hand, refers to the totality of regional linguistic characteristics – idiosyncrasies of grammar and vocabulary as well as pronunciation. An accent is usually the most noticeable feature of a dialect. Whenever comedians wish to make a joke using dialect differences, they invariably get the effect they want by simply 'putting on' a new accent, and not bothering to introduce any grammatical or other features into their speech – but in many ways an accent is the most superficial feature also. Changes in syntax and vocabulary are much more relevant for defining the differences between two dialects than are variations in pronunciation.

Thirdly, we must remember that dialects are not just local matters. My only illustrations so far have been from the dialects of one country; but far more important in a way are the dialects of English which operate on an international, as opposed to an intranational scale. Whatever differences exist between the regional dialects of England, they have all a great deal in common when compared with those of, say, the West Indies or the United States. The term 'dialects of English' MUST be allowed to include these areas, whose importance will undoubtedly increase as regional forms of literature develop.

But regional place of origin is by no means the only kind of linguistic variation in a language. Just as important is the variable of SOCIAL place of origin – where we come from in terms of a position on a social scale of some kind. The social background of individuals has a powerful and long-lasting effect on the kind of language they use, and there are certain general linguistic markers of class which occur regardless of the particular region to which they may belong. For example, distinctions can often be pointed out in terms of the choices we make in the use of words referring to particular concepts – such as how we address people or say farewell to them, or how we refer to various meals, relations, or the toilet. Terms like *mate* and *old man* have clear social restrictions in British English. Again, the use of 'Received Pronunciation' normally implies a degree of education which need not be present for any of the other accents used in Britain. 'Class dialects', as they might be called, exist. They are not linguistically as clearly definable as are regional dialects because the social correlates are not as readily delimited and defined as regional ones – it is not simply a question of kind and degree of education. Also, English has far fewer indications of position on a social scale than many other languages: in Japanese, for example, there are distinct, 'honorific' forms of words, which overtly recognize class distinction.

Before going on to relate these points to the notion of style, a third variable in English should be referred to, which is very similar to those already outlined, namely, HISTORICAL variation. Our use of English indicates very clearly our historical place of origin, as well as our regional and social background – our place on a time scale of some kind. Whether we like it or not, the younger generations do not use the language in the same way as the older generations do. This affects vocabulary for the most part, but sometimes also grammar and pronunciation. Parents' complaints about the unintelligibility of their children are perfectly familiar. The macrocosmic counterpart to this is of course the phenomenon of language change over the centuries. 'The English language' can hardly be restricted to that of today, but must be allowed to comprise earlier states of the language. Of course the boundary-line between English and the language from which it came is by no means easy to determine (it is a matter of some delicacy as to whether Anglo-Saxon should or should not be included under the heading of 'English'), but there is no doubt that SOME earlier states can be legitimately included, which is the point to be made here. And just as there are different standards or norms for the various regional and class dialects, so there are different norms for the historical 'dialects' also, though this is often forgotten. We cannot talk about Elizabethan English, let us say, in precisely the same terms as Modern English, or vice versa. The person who tries to read a Shakespeare play without caring about the values that pronunciation, grammar and vocabulary had at that time is being just as unrealistic as the person who cries 'Preserve the tongue which Shakespeare spoke!' in present-day discussions about correctness. Shakespearian English, as the English of any other historical period, must be seen in its own terms, bearing in mind the usage of the Elizabethan period of language development, and no other. Without an awareness of linguistic differences between the various periods of English literature, a great deal which is of literary importance can be missed. To take just one example: without an understanding of the normal personal pronoun system in Elizabethan English (the meanings of the pronouns *thou* and *you*, in particular), our appreciation of Hamlet's remarks to Ophelia (in Act 3 Scene 1), where there is a controlled alternation between the different forms of the second person, is much reduced.

These three types of variation, regional, social, and historical, are very important factors in accounting for the heterogeneity of the English language. There are other factors too, as we shall see shortly; but these three form a group on their own. The basis for this grouping is that they are all relatively permanent, background aspects of any individual's use of English. Most people normally do not talk as if they were from a different area, class or time from the one to which they actually belong. Of course, a few people have the ability to adopt a different dialect for humorous or literary reasons, as we have already seen in the case of regional variation; and there are also cases of people adopting what they believe to be a more 'educated' dialect of English in their quest for social betterment. The case of Eliza Dolittle in *Pygmalion* merely takes to extremes a process which is not uncommon. But these are nonetheless the exceptions: on the whole we do NOT vary our regional, social or historical linguistic norms. They are, essentially, a linguistic background against which we can make ourselves heard. They are, to put it another way, varieties of the language on the largest possible scale.

The relevance of these dialectal features to the study of the phenomenon of style should be clear from this paragraph: they have very much a NEGATIVE role to play. Regional, social, and historical variations in a use of language have to be eliminated before we can get down to some serious study of what we consider to be 'style'. When we talk of 'Coleridge's style', let us say, we are not, in the first instance, thinking of his regional, etc. linguistic background; and people do not in fact generally make use of such phrases as 'the style of the Cockney', 'the style of Elizabethan English', and so on. Dialectal features are uncontrolled, unconscious features of our use of language; many people find it impossible to vary their usage deliberately in these respects. Consequently, if we hope to account for the relatively conscious, controlled use of language which can produce the distinctiveness referred to above, then it must be other elements of language than these which are being manipulated. What other kinds of variation exist in English, therefore, that could account for our awareness of a 'style'?

A few of these other variables have been given detailed study.

Certain aspects of the immediate situation in which language is used have been shown to have a strong influence on the kind of linguistic structures which occur. One of the most important of these is the occupational role that people may be engaged in at the time of speaking or writing: the job they are doing very often carries with it a probability that in normal circumstances certain linguistic structures will be used and others will not be. One way of speaking or writing is felt to be more appropriate to a specific professional activity than another, and the members of a profession tend to conform in their usage to produce a consistent expression. The reasons for this kind of behaviour are sometimes difficult to determine, but its extent is beyond dispute. One very clear example of occupationally-motivated use of language is in the technical vocabulary associated with various fields: scientists, for instance, make use of a range of vocabulary which precisely defines the phenomena they are investigating. This vocabulary does not normally occur outside of a scientific context, and alternative ways of expressing the same ideas do not normally occur within a scientific context – a particular substance may have a quite familiar domestic name, but in the laboratory this name will tend not to be used, because popularity carries with it looseness of meaning, and ultimately ambiguity. Similarly, scientists, when not 'on duty', will not use their technical terminology to refer to everyday objects, for there is no need to introduce such a degree of precision into their language. The comic situation in which a scientist asks his wife at dinner to 'pass the $H_6C_{12}O_6$' is comic precisely because it is an abnormal, unexpected, incongruous choice of vocabulary which has been made.

But it is not only vocabulary which characterizes an 'occupational' use of language – a PROVINCE, as it is sometimes called. The grammar is always important too. In scientific English, there are a number of constructions whose usage is different from other kinds of English. The way the scientist tends to make use of passive voice constructions is a case in point. 'The solution was poured . . .' is generally found in preference to 'I poured the solution . . .'. There are a variety of reasons for this, though probably the most important is the concern to keep the account of the process being described as impersonal as possible. Similarly, legal English, as found in certain documents, displays a highly distinctive and much more complex syntax that can be found elsewhere – unpunctuated sentences that continue for pages are by no means exceptional. And in addition to grammar, the way in which the language is written down or spoken may be further indications of a specific brand of occupational activity. Probably the most immediately distinctive feature of written advertising language is the way in which different sizes and colours of type are made use of, a flexibility not normally seen in other written forms of the language. And a distinctive method of 'speaking an occupation', so to say, can be seen in the 'tone of voice' which may be adopted: those of the lawyer and clergyman (while speaking in court and preaching respectively) are frequently-quoted examples, and in addition the pronunciations adopted by radio news-readers, political speech-makers, and railway-station announcers could be cited – or indeed that of most people who find themselves speaking in public as part of their professional life. There are criteria for successful and unsuccessful uses of English in all these cases; and if we take the successful uses as a norm, then it can be shown that there are certain linguistic features which have a high probability of occurrence on any occasion when a particular province is used. In this way, it makes sense to talk about the 'style' of a legal document, or a political speech, as we can readily refer to the distinctive features in the pronunciation, spelling, grammar, and vocabulary which we would associate with these kinds of English, and which would not appear in the same combination elsewhere.

A second situational variable which conditions particular uses of English is the relationship between the participants in any dialogue: this will be an important factor governing the kind of language we choose to use. If two people are, broadly speaking, separated socially (as in the relationships existing between employer and employee, student and teacher, or old and young member of a family), then it is generally the case that different language structures will be used by the two parties, which will reflect this distinction. The socially 'inferior' person will show deference to the 'superior' in various ways, for example by the form of address, or by avoiding the more slangy words and constructions which might be used in informally talking to social equals; and other linguistic correlates can be found to indicate the dominance of the superior. Children are drilled in these conventions from an early age: 'Don't talk like that to the vicar/Mr Jones/your grandfather . . .' is a common exhortation; and the emergence of social linguistic norms of this kind can be seen in the role-playing which all normal children enter into – 'being' daddy, or the grocer, carries with it the linguistic forms of daddyness, or grocerdom, and children show remarkable powers of mimicry and memory in these matters.

There has been relatively little research into this field of inter-personal relationships – where social psychology and linguistics overlap – but certain types of reasonably predictable variation have been shown to exist, e.g. the different degrees of FORMALITY which occur in English. It makes sense to distinguish a FORMAL from an INFORMAL style in English (with further sub-divisions within both). The kind of language we speak or write on formal occasions (such as in an interview, making a speech, or applying for a job) is simply not the same as that used on informal occasions (such as in everyday conversations with our family, or writing to an old friend). This is almost a truism. What is often ignored, however, is that the linguistic features which indicate formality and informality are not just idiosyncratic, but are common to all members of the speech community. The evidence suggests that people tend to be formal in more or less the same linguistic way: they choose certain words more carefully, they avoid other words like the plague, they become more self-conscious over what they believe to be the 'correct' pronunciation of words, and so on. This kind of situationally-conditioned language variation, then, is yet another element contributing to the general distinctiveness of a use of language: a convenient way of referring to it is to call these variations of STATUS.

There are other situational variables which influence the kind of English we choose to use in a given situation. For example, the PURPOSE for which we are using language generally produces a conventional framework or format for our speech or writing, and this can be highly distinctive. The lay-out of a letter, an advertisement, or a legal document, the organization of a lecture or a sports commentary, are all examples of formats which have be-come to a greater or lesser extent standardized in English. It is not a question of personal choice here: for a commentary or a lecture to be successful, certain principles of 'verbal lay-out' must be followed. Then again, the broad distinction between the spoken and the written medium of the language has its specific linguistic correlates: some words and structures occur solely in speech, others only in writing. Most of the nuances of intonation have to be ignored in the written representation of speech, for example, and most of us are well aware of the social pressures that curtail our freedom to write down 'four-letter words', and the like. And of course the kind of language we use will undoubtedly vary de-pending on whether we speak with the intention of having our words written down (as in dictation or many kinds of lecturing), or write with the aim of having our words read aloud (as in speech-construction, news-writing for radio or television, drama, and, sometimes, poetry).

It is not the purpose of this chapter to give a complete breakdown of all the categories of situationally-conditioned language which operate in English, even if this were possible in the present state of the art. The cases so far mentioned should suffice to show the heterogeneity and fluidity of the English language. What needs to be emphasized, however, is that this flexibility of usage affects each of us individually, and it is this which provides a crucial perspective for understanding the question of style. In the course of one day, each of us modulates through a wide range of varieties of English: the various levels of domesticity, professionalism, and so on, through which we pass carry with them changes in the nature of the language we use. The level of formality, to take but a single example, will vary considerably every day, ranging from the intimate level of family conversation (linguistically very marked, through the frequent use of such things as 'pet' nonsense words and slang which only the family understands) to perhaps the artificial formality of a chaired business meeting (with all the linguistic conventions made use of there – proposals, secondings, etc.). What must be made clear – and it is this which distinguishes province, status, and the like from the dialects discussed earlier – is that these distinctive uses of language are all relatively temporary and manipulable in their use. We do not normally continue at the same level of formality, let us say, for a very long period of time. 'Professional' contexts give way to domestic interchange, which in turn may give way to a receptive appraisal of formality differences, as encountered on television. And, associated with this, these kinds of variation in English are all matters which we can to a very great extent control: the concept of choice is much more relevant here than it was with the dialects. In a given situation, which has clear extra-linguistic indices of, say, formality, it is possible to exercise some degree of choice as to whether appropriate, formal language is to be used, or inappropriate, informal language. Of course, most normal people choose the former, only lapsing into the latter when they are very sure of their social ground – as, for instance, to make a joke. But the point is that, in principle, we have both awareness and control over a number of linguistic points along the formality scale, and the question of which one to use is primarily up to us. Similarly, we all know the conventions for letter-writing; but we may choose to ignore them if we so wish. Whether we do so will depend almost entirely on our relationship to the person we are addressing:

obviously, if we are dependent on someone for advancement, we will restrain ourselves, linguistically, and respect the conventions which we know are expected (e.g. the letter will be neatly laid out, punctuation will be 'correct', formulae – such as 'yours faithfully' – will be appropriately used); on the other hand, a letter to a close friend may carry with it all kinds of differences – loose use of punctuation, use of slang, disregard for regular line-spacing, etc. Such a situation does not apply to the use of dialect features of English because, as we have seen, apart from on rare occasions, we have little awareness of and control over their use.

We may summarize this discussion by saying that the English language can be seen as a complex of (to a greater or lesser extent) situationally-conditioned, standardized sets of linguistic variations: these can be referred to as VARIETIES of the language. A variety is therefore a formally definable, conventionalized group use of language which we can intuitively identify with aspects of some non-linguistic context in which it occurs (and which, as linguists, we try to formalize and explicate). An important qualification here is that we are aware of this relationship 'to a greater or lesser extent'. Some uses of English have a very clear and direct intuitive relationship to a social situation (as when the use of *thou* and related forms automatically associates with a religious set of contexts); other uses are much less predictable (as when an official-sounding phrase might have come from one of a number of different types of context). The concept of language variety is simply a descriptive hypothesis to account for these intuitions of formal-functional correspondences in language; and in this sense it covers many of what were above referred to as 'styles'. Phrases such as 'formal style', 'the style of radio news-readers', and so on, are meaningful because it is possible to suggest clear linguistic correlates for these notions.

To say that a particular social situation has a regular association with a particular kind of English is not to say that other kinds of English may not be introduced into that situation. In principle, this is always possible, for after all we can never be ABSOLUTELY certain that people will behave in a maximally predictable way in a given situation. But there are some language-using situations where the possibility of making simultaneous use of a number of varieties of English is relatively normal, in order that a particular linguistic effect be achieved. Literature and humour are the clearest examples of this happening, but cases of 'stylistic juxtaposition' can be found elsewhere too. For example, a political public speaker may introduce quotations from the Bible into the oration to point a particular issue; or a television advertisement may introduce language from a scientific form of English in order to get some of the scientific overtones rubbed off onto the product; or a sermon may introduce television advertising jingles to make an idea strike home more directly. These are reasonably frequently-occurring examples of language from two or more varieties being used in a single situation, and the kinds of juxtaposition which occur are to a certain extent predictable, especially when compared with the essentially unpredictable juxtapositions which are introduced into literature and humour. Many kinds of joke are successful because they introduce incongruity of a stylistic kind into the punch line; and in literature, it is a standard procedure for an author to incorporate into a work snatches or even extended extracts from the non-literary varieties of English. It is difficult to see how this could be otherwise, but some authors go in for stylistic borrowing of this kind much more widely than others: the chiaroscuro of overtones and association in much of James Joyce is to a very great extent explicable in terms of other varieties of (particularly religious) English; and T. S. Eliot is another who constantly makes use of this technique in a very definite way. Moreover, many of the so-called 'revolutions' in the use of poetic language in the history of English literature can ultimately be reduced to attempts to replace the methods of expression associated with one variety of the language by those associated with another: an example would be the introduction of scientific language by the Metaphysical poets, or by some twentieth-century authors, into a poetic context where scientific language had been almost completely absent for some time. Whether the 'language of the age' is or is not the language of poetry is not a matter for discussion here; but it should be noted in passing that this argument will never be resolved until an attempt is made to clarify the notion of 'language of the age' as such – and in order to do this, SOME reference to a theory of language variety is going to be necessary.

So far I have been discussing aspects of language variation which are basically group uses of language. The remaining factor accounting for linguistic heterogeneity stands apart from all these, in that it is concerned with the language habits idiosyncratic to a person, those which distinguish someone from the other members of a group, as opposed to integrating that person linguistically with them. In one sense, of course, linguistic idiosyncrasy is less important than the dimensions of variety outlined above, as we can only be aware of idiosyncrasy against a background of non-idiosyncrasy: we cannot recognize the individuality of authors until we are first aware of the language habits of their time, i.e. the linguistic features of the various dialects, provinces, and so on, against which background they can display themselves. And this means that any study of individuals requires the prior recognition of the more general linguistic usages contemporaneous with them. (This explains the difficulty of trying to identify the authorship of texts in languages which are no longer spoken – as in the case of the Pauline epistles. Whether the linguistic idiosyncrasies of the epistles are those of one man [= Paul?] or not depends on whether we can first eliminate from the discussion those features common to other letter-writers of the period, and those common to the language as a whole at that time. And in view of the fact that there is so little comparative material extant, it is doubtful whether the problem is solvable.) In one sense, then, linguistic idiosyncrasy is subordinate to the study of shared uses of English; and this is of course the position taken by those who are engaged in teaching the language, where they are in the first instance trying to teach the language 'as a whole', and disregarding those features which belong to individuals. But from the point of view of the study of style, idiosyncrasy – as some of the viewpoints outlined at the beginning of this chapter suggest – becomes of primary importance.

One thing must be made clear at this point. By IDIOSYNCRASY I am not referring to those uncontrolled, and normally uncontrollable features of our spoken or written utterance which are due entirely to our physical state and which will always be present in everything we speak or write. In everything we say, there will always be an idiosyncratic voice-quality, a background vocal effect which identifies us as individuals, and this we do not normally change (unless we are professional actors or mimics, of course). The analogue to voice quality in the written medium is our personal handwriting. Similarly, if we speak with a particular kind of speech defect, or using some psychopathologically-induced set of recurrent images, these may well be idiosyncratic, but this too is a different sense from that intended by the concept of stylistic idiosyncrasy. In the latter case, I am referring to the linguistic distinctiveness individuals can introduce into their language which is not shared by other members of society (i.e. not a variety) and which is capable of conscious control. The author of the language may choose to put something in or leave something out. The important word here is 'may', as very often, depending on someone's experience of using the language, specific linguistic indices of personality may make their appearance with apparently no conscious effort on the author's part. We are all familiar with the linguistic idiosyncrasies of certain public figures or of favourite authors; we talk about an author's name being 'stamped indelibly on every page', and so forth. But in principle this is something over which authors have a large measure of control: they can change words, alter their order, add and delete at will. Theirs is the decision which ultimately controls what we see or hear, and which ultimately defines their individuality in the use of language. The linguist's job here is to identify and explain the idiosyncratic effects which authors have introduced into their use of language, to see whether these form any kind of pattern, and to try to demonstrate their purpose in relation to the work as a whole.

It is important to emphasize, once again, that linguists do not have an evaluative role in this matter: theirs is, basically, a descriptive task. They are not studying an author's work to decide whether it is good or bad, representative of this quality or literary tradition or that: its 'place' in literature is not of primary importance to them AS LINGUISTS – though of course this may well have entered into their decision as to which text to analyse in the first place, a decision not made on linguistic grounds. Linguists are primarily concerned with ensuring that all features relevant to the identification of an author's own behaviour are understood. If some features are omitted through ignorance, they would argue, then there is a very real danger of relevant information for the overall qualitative assessment of the author by the critic being overlooked. The reason why STYLISTICS, the linguistic study of what is considered to be 'style', has become so popular over recent years, it would seem, is precisely that, using the traditional methods of language analysis and literary criticism, so much of importance for this basic assessment DOES get overlooked. Students of literature, or of any use of English, frequently begin their analysis of a text in a highly impressionistic way, relying on their innate sensitivity to produce the results they seek. But sensitive response alone is – apart from very rare cases – an inadequate basis for reaching a clear understanding of the message which is being communicated. Most people do not have the ability to approach the study of the language of a text in any systematic, objective kind of way. The gifted few, it is true, may be able to sum up the relevance of a poem for them without entering into any systematic procedure of analysis, but for the majority, the initial aesthetic response needs to be supplemented by some technique which will help to clarify the meaning of a text. Stylistics, then, hopes to provide just such a technique of comprehensive analysis, so that, once it has been mastered, students of language may find it easier to appreciate the complexity of language use.

This now brings me to the final aspect of stylistics which I want to discuss here, namely, What ARE the techniques whereby the 'style' of a text can be analysed? The kinds of language variation which may be found in any piece of language, we must remember, reduce to three basic types: there are the features I have called DIALECTAL (regional, class, historical) which partition the English language in terms of one set of dimensions; cutting across these, there is a second set of dimensions, relating to specific factors in SOCIAL SITUATIONS, such as occupation, relative status, and purpose; and thirdly, there is the possibility of IDIOSYNCRATIC variation, which allows for the modification of the group norms by individual users. It needs a fairly sophisticated stylistic theory to be able to account for every factor; but from the point of view of specifying a procedure for analysis, ALL these dimensions of language variation can be studied in precisely the same way, using any of a number of possible techniques suggested by General Linguistics. Exactly which technique we use will of course be the outcome of our particular training and predilections, and of the specific theory of language structure we may adhere to. These days, there is a great deal of controversy as to which of the many linguistic theories available provides the best basis for the analysis of any given piece of language, but the existence of certain features, or LEVELS of language structure, seems to be generally recognized; consequently it is probably easiest to illustrate the kind of preconception a linguist might bring to bear in studying a text from the stylistic point of view by outlining what is involved in these levels. The most useful levels of structure to recognize for stylistic purposes have already been discussed in the earlier part of this book: phonetics, phonology, grammar, and vocabulary. (The concepts of phonetics and phonology are primarily reserved for the study of speech: for the study of a written text, the analogous levels could be referred to as GRAPHETICS and GRAPHOLOGY respectively.) I would argue that the distinctiveness of ANY text can be broken down in terms of these levels: whatever distinctive stylistic feature we may encounter in English, it can be described as operating at one or some combination of these levels.

To obtain a clearer picture of what is involved, I shall illustrate the kind of distinctiveness which might occur at each level, taking my examples primarily from literary texts. At the PHONETIC level would be studied any general features of sound which help to characterize a text, such as when a particular voice quality (or set of qualities) is associated with a particular use of language (as in much religious and legal professional speech). The 'clerical' voice is a well-recognized phenomenon, and this principally refers to a quite different 'set' of the vocal organs from that normally used by the clergyman in everyday conversation. Also under phonetics, one would consider those aspects of speech which would normally be referred to under the heading of SOUND SYMBOLISM – a hypothesized capacity of sounds to intrinsically reflect objects, events, and so on, in real life. This view may be illustrated by people who claim that there is something in the nature of an [i:] sound, for instance, which makes it necessarily relate to smallness in size, or whiteness, or something else; or that onomatopoeic words – such as *splash* or *cuckoo* – could have no other shape because they contain the sounds of real life ('biscuits are so called because of the sound they make when you break them'). These arguments have been generally shown to be unfounded. Even such clearly onomatopoeic words as *splash* vary in their form from one language to the next, showing evidence of non-naturalistic influence; and there are always counter-examples to any generalization we might care to make about the 'inherent meaning' of sounds such as [i:]. But it is nonetheless the case that various uses of language (poetry being the clearest example) do try to make use of speech sounds in as evocative a way as possible. If poets consider a particular sound to have a powerful atmosphere-creating potential, then they may well make use of it (i.e. words containing it) more frequently than usual. Of course we have to remember that in general we can only interpret sounds in a given way once we know the theme being expressed by the words: [s] sounds in a poem about a swan may well reflect the noise of the water, but in a poem about evil might equally appropriately be intended to conjure up the noise of serpents, and the like – in other words, there is no 'general meaning' for the [s] sound in language, or even in English. But having said this, we may still plot the way the poet manipulates specific sounds, seen as individual, atmosphere-setting sonic effects, to reinforce a particular theme, and this would be studied at the phonetic level of analysis. In the written medium, we would be referring on similar grounds to such matters as the general size and shape of the type being used (as in the distinctiveness of posters, newspapers), and the lay-out of a text on a page (as when Herbert writes a poem about an altar in the shape of an altar). The PHONETIC and GRAPHETIC levels of analysis, then, to a certain extent overlap with non-linguistic considerations (e.g. matters of colouring), but the point is that from the stylistic point of view, even such non-linguistic matters as choice of colour might have a contribution to make to the definition of the distinctiveness of a particular use of language – and thus would have to be allowed for in any stylistic theory.

The PHONOLOGICAL and GRAPHOLOGICAL levels are easier to illustrate as they relate to more familiar matters. There are, broadly speaking, two areas of potential distinctiveness: what I would refer to for speech as the SEGMENTAL and the NON-SEGMENTAL areas. Segmental characteristics of style would cover the use of specific vowels and consonants within a particular language's sound system in combination in a distinctive way, as when we make use of reduplicative effects such as alliteration, assonance, and rhyme in English. It is important to note that these devices have a major structural, as well as aesthetic, function – that is, they are the province of phonology, as opposed to phonetics. Alliteration, for example, may well have an important aesthetic appeal; but from the point of view of its overall function in a poem, it has an equally important – and sometimes a more important – role as an organizing process, linking words more closely than would otherwise be the case. For example, when we read such a line as 'Thron'd in the centre of his thin designs' (from Pope's *Epistle to Dr Arbuthnot)*, the major function of the alliteration is to force the words 'thron'd' and 'thin' together, and thus produce a juxtaposition of the concepts 'mediated' by the words, which in the present context produces an ironic contrast. This kind of thing is presumably one of the factors underlying phrases such as 'fusion and meaning', or when we talk about a poet's 'intensifying' meaning. And similar illustrations could be found for the other reduplicative segmental processes. In passing, we should note that it is difficult to generalize about phonological distinctiveness for more than one language. Such matters as alliteration and rhyme are essentially deviations from the normal ways of distributing consonant and other phonemes in English. That is why these effects are so noticeable: they are not normally encountered in our contact with English. In a language where initial reduplication of phonemes WAS normal, however – where prefixes were the routine way of indicating cases, for instance – then much less effect would be gained by alliteration, and we could anticipate that other phonological features than this would be used to produce dramatic and other effects. Similarly, in a language like Latin, where – because of the inflectional endings – it is difficult NOT to rhyme to some extent, we do not find rhyme being used as a literary device with anything like the same frequency as in English.

The other aspect of phonology is the non-segmental; that is, the features of intonation, rhythm, speed, loudness of articulation, and other vocal effects we introduce into speech in order to communicate attitudes, emphasis, and so on. Spoken English is highly distinctive from this point of view. Taking intonation patterns alone, there would be good grounds for distinguishing between most varieties of spoken English currently in use. There is the characteristically wide range of pitch movement in the public-speaker as opposed to the narrower range in everyday conversation; the 'chanting' effect of the sermon; the restrained, regular movement of the news-reader; and so on. And when we consider features other than pitch, our classification can become very precise: compare the varying speed and loudness of the sports commentator with the measured speed, loudness and pause of the professional reader; the many vocal effects (such as increasing and decreasing the tension of the muscles of the vocal organs for stretches of utterance, which produces a tense, 'metallic' effect and a lax effect respectively) which are introduced into the use of English for television advertising; or the primary role of rhythmic variations in establishing the linguistic basis of poetry. It should be clear from these examples that a great deal of our awareness of stylistic distinctiveness in speech derives from the perception of 'prosodic features' of this kind. When we vaguely hear speech in the distance and say 'That sounds like . . .', we are generally basing our judgement on the dominant prosodic variations we can hear.

The analogous features to phonology in the writing-system of a language can be roughly summarized as the spelling and punctuation of that language. I say 'roughly', because a great deal more is covered by graphology than is traditionally understood by these labels, e.g. the difference between upper and lower case symbols is of systematic importance in English (and not just a matter of aesthetic appeal): it can be used distinctively, as when we write something out in capitals to achieve extra prominence, or when we introduce a graphological change in order to indicate a change in context (without actually having to say so), as when Eliot writes

> I didn't mince my words, I said to her myself,
> HURRY UP PLEASE ITS TIME
> Now Albert's coming back . . . (*The Waste Land*)

In English, variations in spelling for special effects are uncommon, though we do find archaic spellings introduced into poetry, or notices printed in an old-fashioned way. An example of this, again from Eliot (*East Coker*), is a good example of the impact of the visual medium which could not possibly be translated into spoken form:

> And see them dancing around the bonfire
> The association of man and woman
> In daunsinge, signifying matrimonie –
> A dignified and commodious sacrament.
> Two and two, necessarye coniunction,
> Holding eche other by the hand or the arm
> Whiche betokeneth concorde.

More commonly in English, we find variations in punctuation, even to the extent of occasionally omitting this altogether (as in the final pages of Joyce's *Ulysses*, for example).

Vocabulary, a language user's 'choice of words', or DICTION, as it is sometimes called, is presumably so familiar an aspect of a person's style that it does not need detailed illustration here. At this level, stylistics tries to determine the extent to which certain words, combinations of words, and types of word are part of the distinctiveness of a use of language. All varieties of English make use of a restricted kind of vocabulary, e.g. the learned, technical vocabulary of scientific English, the loosely colloquial vocabulary of informal conversation, the formal, precise vocabulary of legal documents, the archaic vocabulary of much of religious English, and so on. Sometimes a variety can be identified merely on the basis of certain items of vocabulary, as in the use of such words as *heretofore*, which is used only in legal English or attempts to simulate it. More often than this, however, a style is lexically distinctive due to certain words being used more, or less, frequently than in other varieties or individuals – authors may be said to have their 'favourite' words, for instance. Or there may be a particular distribution and proportion of various categories of word in a text, e.g. the highly distinctive mixture of technical, slang, formal and informal vocabulary in sports commentary, or the parallel use of technical terms and non-technical glosses in many kinds of lecturing. Again, an individual may produce stylistic effects by coining new words (e.g. *theirhisnothis*, Joyce) or by putting unexpected words in a standardized context, as in Thomas's *a grief ago* (where the expectation of a noun of time imbues the notion of grief with temporal associations) and similar examples. The choice of a specific word is one aspect of style; the placing of that word in a specific context is another, quite different aspect.

In studying vocabulary, we are of course studying meaning to a certain extent, but meaning is not restricted to single words or small combinations of words. Of relevance for stylistic study is the way in which the overall meaning of a use of language is organized, and it is this more general study of meaning which takes place at what is often referred to as the level of DISCOURSE. For example, when we talk about the 'theme' of a poem or novel, or discuss the 'progression' of ideas in a play or an income tax form, we are referring to the most general patterns of meaning that we have been able to discern in a text, and there is a great deal of stylistic significance to be said here, if this is done systematically. The discourse organization of a lecture, for example, with its steady development interspersed by passages of recapitulation and anticipatory summary (e.g. 'there are three things I'd like to say about this . . .') is quite different from the regular, alternating flow of descriptive narrative and background comment which characterizes a sports commentary, and this is different again from the near-random progression of ideas in conversation. I take my examples here from the less familiar (spoken) varieties: in the written medium, the concept of the paragraph, which is a semantic unit (cf. the notion of 'topic sentence', and so on), has long been with us, as have such visualist devices as sub-headings, spacing variations, and diagrams, which make the movement of thought relatively unambiguous and easy to perceive.

Finally, there is the grammatical level of analysis, which is probably the most important component of any stylistic description. There is invariably more to be said about the grammar of a text than about any other level, and in order to make a successful study here it is essential to have fairly clear ideas about the general nature of English grammar, as suggested by some grammatical theory. It is impossible even to outline what would be involved in a complete grammatical description of a text here: some further reading on this question is given in the Bibliography on p 349. But if we consider merely the kind of variations which occur at ONE point in English grammar, it might be possible to get an impression of the overall complexity involved, and so not underestimate the scope of grammatical analysis. The TYPE OF SENTENCE one may find in a text is often a reasonably unambiguous diagnostic indication of its provenance. There is nothing like the long complex sentences of legal documentation elsewhere in English. The language of instructions

structions has a very restricted range of sentence structures at its disposal (high frequency of imperatives and imperative-like elements, absence of questions). Newspaper reporting generally makes use of relatively short, uncomplicated sentences. News-reading (and most other forms of radio narrative) never uses anything other than statements. In scientific English, equations and formulae can replace elements of sentence structure and sometimes whole sentences. In commentary, conversation and advertising, there is a very frequent and varied use of MINOR sentences (i.e. structures which function as sentences, but which do not have the subject-predicate structure characteristic of the majority of English sentences – as in *hello, sorry*, and so on). The traditional distinction between SIMPLE, COMPOUND, COMPLEX and MIXED sentence types is relevant for categorizing the kinds of distinctiveness we find in texts, and these categories can be further subdivided – the number and type of subordinate clauses, for example, varies considerably from variety to variety as would be clearly shown by a comparison of political public speaking (where they are very frequent, tending to pile up on each other in rhetorical climaxes) with radio news broadcasting (in the latter, subordinate clauses are common, but their distribution is more sporadic, and they rarely are used in anything approaching a 'cumulative' way). In literature, changes in the direction of the plot, or the theme, can be indicated by altering the kind of sentences generally being used; and this device is of course extremely common as one index (often the most noticeable) of character – Dickens, for example, regularly gives his characters a predictable linguistic basis, and sentence structure usually has an important distinctive role to play in this. Again, the absence of clear sentence boundaries may be a major way of communicating a particular effect, as with certain stream-of-consciousness techniques. And there is a great deal else which can be manipulated to make sentences work in a distinctive way (e.g. the devices that may be introduced in order to LINK sentences to each other, such as cross-referencing, repetitions of words, the use of adverbs like *however* and conjunctions).

This has been a very brief outline of a possible method of discovering some principle(s) of organization in the mass of linguisitc features which constitute the distinctiveness of a use of English. It should be clear that ALL levels of analysis enter into this distinctiveness, though some (the grammatical and lexical in particular) have a more dominant role on most occasions. The concept of 'style' which emerges from this approach, when seen within the perspective of language varieties as presented earlier, is thus very much a cumulative, developing, dynamic one: it is essentially a descriptive convenience which summarizes our awareness at any given moment of the controllable linguistic features that distinguish one use of English from any other. The specification of these uses is in terms of the dimensions of variation outlined in the first half of this chapter: the features are identified and inter-related in terms of the levels of analysis outlined in the second half. It is in such attempts to provide a relatively objective way of talking about and analysing language variation systematically, precisely, and comprehensively, that linguistics hopes to be able to make a permanent contribution to the study of English style.

7

THE EARLY HISTORY OF ENGLISH

W. F. Bolton

I

We do not know when, how, or where language began. It was in any case immeasurably long before written documents, and beyond the earliest recollections of surviving folk-memory. Some students have argued that this or that kind of datable edifice or tool could not have been made or used except by human creatures capable of speech. The argument is subjective. Nor can we say that the progress of language in mankind was like the progress of language-learning in an infant; almost surely it was not. And we do not know whether language began in a single place on the globe and spread through the world, diversifying from region to region until its common origin became completely disguised, or whether it grew up as an independent development at various times and places when different societies reached the stage that would initiate and support it. The latter is more probable. All of our knowledge is based on written records, a comparatively recent development, and on what the written records enable us to infer: half a dozen surviving words in related languages may suggest a hypothetical formula for the lost original from which all derive.

This comparative method, however, enables us to push back only a little further than the earliest written records to their immediate antecedents. Now the earliest documents in some western language families are about 4,000 years old, but those in others little more than 1,000 years. It is plain that we cannot get uniform results with uneven evidence like this. And of course the results are most uncertain just when they are most interesting, that is, when they are pushed back the furthest beyond written evidence. But one feature of language as it passes from one time and place to another is of great help: we know that the alterations of linguistic sounds are regular, that is, the same sound in language A will not become two or three different sounds as it passes into language B, so long as other conditions remain the same. We are thus enabled to study the history of sounds rather than the history of words, and we are not obliged to find the same word in all the languages under study before we can make a start. Sound, for the historian of language, is the basic material just as it is for the analyst of our contemporary language, although for somewhat different reasons. Historians are also like modern analysts in that they go on to classify the further categories of language as morphology (shapes of words), syntax (shapes of sentences), and vocabulary. They differ from their colleagues in depending wholly on what they can learn from surviving written records – and the ones that survive are not always the ones they would have chosen for their purposes.

In fact, the written records are at once essential and inadequate for the historian of any language, and it is best to take a page or two at this point to say what the inadequacies are: these general considerations must be applied to almost everything that follows, for they have much the same force in every age of the English language before the invention of printing. Incompleteness of survival is the first difficulty. We may take it as an axiom that no historian of language ever has sufficient documents old enough to satisfy him. Of course the employment of writing goes back much further than the beginnings of English, but as it happens the first speakers in England of what was to become our language were almost certainly unlettered when they arrived in the middle of the fifth century. Literacy arrived about 150 years after, but it was Latin literacy; and the earliest surviving records in English – which used and adapted the Latin alphabet – are another 150 years later, that is mid-eighth century. And the late date of these papers is only one feature of their unrepresentativeness; language exists in time AND space, and the distribution of the evidence in space is as poor as that in time. We find a feature or form in the south-west of England, for example, but we are very fortunate indeed if we find anything to compare it with in the north-east, so we are unable to say that 'X is distinctive and restricted to the south-west' but usually only that 'X is found in the south-west'. For a linguistic level like sound it is not perhaps so disastrous, because the stock of sounds in any one dialect is small and therefore most sounds will be represented in even a restricted body of evidence. But it becomes a different matter for morphemes and even more so for words.

The second difficulty is that of the relation of spelling to sound. If a thousand years from now a linguistic historian found English *confection*, French *confection*, and German *Konfektion* in several documents, he would rightly conclude that they were connected, especially as the only difference was constant, that is, the German represents English and French *c* with *k* on both occasions. But he would not know that this regularity corresponded to a spelling habit rather than a speech habit, and that in fact the *c* or *k* in the three forms of the word represents the sound which is most alike in the different languages, and that the word is otherwise almost unrecognizably varied in the way English, French and Germans pronounce it. The only way he might arrive at this important differentiation would be by hearing tapes or records made a thousand years before, or by reading what writers said the words sounded like – especially if those writers described the sounds in terms of their articulation (unvoiced velar stop, etc.) instead of using subjective or relative terms ('the hard *c*' uses both). The historian in the far future will have these two kinds of evidence to work with, for they are being produced in profusion today; but the historians today have nothing of the sort with which to investigate the English of a thousand years ago. They must depend on inferences drawn from the previous and later history of the language insofar as they know it, and they always run the risk of circular reasoning.

The third difficulty relates to the first, the matter of adequate records from every point in time and space, but we can illustrate it with our hypothetical future historian. We must presume that he recognizes that his documents are written in three different languages, but he cannot write linguistic history with only that information. It would be very difficult for him to make much historical use of his documents unless he also knows whether they represented American or British English, Parisian or Marseilles French, Hamburg or Munich German, and so forth; and if British, whether that of London or Liverpool, and if London whether that of Belgravia or Battersea. Nor – unless a title page, or the dateline on a letter, or the like survived – would he know within several hundred years when the documents were written, and whether his copy was perhaps made at a place and time far removed from the original; if so, the writer of the late copy would very likely have mixed a large number of his own speech forms and spelling conventions with those of his source. Once again there is evidence . . . handwriting, binding, references to historical events, etc. . . . . that will help when explicit statements about time and place are missing, but it is relatively uncertain. During much of the time we are studying, the kind of documents that often begin with a date and a place, like deeds, were usually written in Latin.

Our history of the early stages of the English language, then, can be realistically written – and realistically read – only if writer and reader make the following admission: that a term like 'early West Saxon' does NOT refer to the language spoken in Wessex up to the year about 900, but rather to the linguistic agreements among the sounds, forms and words as they are reflected in the few surviving documents which, although of uncertain date and origin, appear to represent that time and area. Of course this is putting the case at its worst, and in fact careful work over the last century and more has produced and is still producing results of remarkable solidity on which the following pages are based. But almost none of these results is so solid that it might not be changed by the addition of new evidence, in some cases the discovery of only one more document, or by the application of new methods, especially the mechanical or computer analysis of existing material.

II

With so much at our disposal, we can say a few things about the pre-history of English – the story of what it was before it appears in the oldest surviving documents. We know that the natural history of any language or language family is that of continual differentiation: that is, in the course of time one language becomes two or more, and they in turn divide again. Some aspects of modern communications have a superficial levelling effect, so that features of different dialects sometimes appear to coalesce; but such changes are few, and the causes that bring them about are very recent. In the main, language tends the other way, and the migration of people makes such change more rapid and extreme, both because it isolates them from other speakers of the same mother-tongue, and because it exposes them to the influences of other linguistic communities.

The very existence of variety in any one language proves this view. If we take several of the many present-day varieties of English, we may account for the differences among them in one of three ways:

(1) The differences go back to the very beginning of language, that is, several varieties of English existed from the first moment humanity began to speak, and continue to exist today. OR

(2) English is the point of convergence of many different languages, and the varieties of modern English are merely the

descendants of even more different tongues all on their way to becoming English. OR

(3) English is merely the general name for a variety of linguistic practices, the differences among which are the result of the natural tendency of languages to diverge from common originals over the course of time.

The first explanation sees the varieties as parallel in their development: ↓ ↓ ↓

The second sees them as convergent: ↘ ↓ ↗

The third sees them as divergent: ↗ ↓ ↘

No other explanation fully accounts for the situation of variety which we confront today, and of the three, the first two are obviously impossible. The third therefore stands demonstrated, proving that languages change over time in the direction of greater differentiation.

On this principle, what we should expect – and what we find – is that the various forms of English now spoken go back to a relatively few originals of which we have record, and that they in turn go back to a single original of which we have no record. This original likewise is one of several branches from a single stock, some others of which still survive or leave descendants. The image of a tree implied in words like 'stock' and 'branch' will serve well enough for a visual model of this development (so long as we do not think that the process involved in linguistic change is anything like that which makes a tree grow as it does). As far back as we can go by hypothetical reconstruction – 'ground level' – is the common language spoken about five or six thousand years ago, perhaps somewhere in central Europe. Because the speakers of this tongue who went eastward gave rise to some of the languages of modern India, and those who went westward brought the parent of most of the languages of modern Europe, the language of the stock is usually called Indo-European. It had nine main branches: Indian (which gave, among others, Sanskrit and Hindi); Iranian; Armenian; Albanian; Baltic-Slavonic; Celtic; Greek; Latin; Germanic. Not all of these branches sprang from the parent stock at the same point, so that some branches are more distantly related than others. English is a member of the Germanic branch, and its closest external affinities are with the Greek and Latin branches. By the time the earliest surviving documents in English were written, classical Greek and even more classical Latin had altered and vanished. We are consequently unable to make direct comparisons between these related languages in the same state of their development. Even so, some Old English words can, when compared with Latin words, suggest a great deal about the relationship between them. Old English *hwæt*: Latin *quod, fæder: pater, heafod: caput, fotes: pedis*.

Not much here strikes us at first, but after a bit we notice that Old English *t* regularly appears as Latin *d*, Old English *f* as Latin *p*, and – if we recall that Latin *quod* begins with a *kw-* sound – Old English *h* as Latin *k*, spelled with a *c* or *q*. These generalizations can be extended in our description of Old English and Latin, and other different ones could be formulated for Old English and other languages. But the point to remember is this: it is not the similarity of individual words which shows the relation of two languages. Modern Arabic is unrelated to English, but has borrowed a number of English words. It is rather the pattern of the sounds in corresponding words that shows the relationship. Grammar too – another kind of pattern – tells us a great deal about related languages, and we shall see that Old English retains many similarities with Latin that Modern English has long lost. Our word *consolation*, on the other hand, although it is closely akin to a Latin word, tells us nothing about the relation of English and Latin to their common stock, because it is borrowed directly from Latin, not a collateral descendant of it.

Just as a number of branches radiate from the common stock of Indo-European, so a further number spring from the branch we have called Germanic. They are three: East Germanic, which has no survivors and was represented chiefly by Gothic; North Germanic, of which the modern Scandinavian languages are the survivors; and West Germanic, including modern Dutch, German, and English. (A sub-branch of West Germanic, 'Ingvaeonic', included all the languages but Old High German.) These groupings can all be traced in each category of language: sound, vocabulary, morphology, and syntax. We have seen how a certain sound-change sets the Germanic languages apart from the others in the Indo-European family. Sound changes give the clearest evidence, but the distribution of vocabulary is significant too. Some words, in one form or another, are common to all members of the Indo-European family, and some to only one branch or sub-branch or language, thus:

English: Old English *acan* ('ache')
Common Ingvaeonic: Old English *bysig*, Old Dutch *bezich* ('busy')
Common West Germanic: Old English *gast*, Old Low German *gêst*,
   Old High German *geist* ('ghost', 'spirit')
Common Germanic: Old English *sæ*, Old Icelandic *sær*, Gothic
   saiws, etc. ('sea')
Common Indo-European: Latin *pater*, Old English *fæder*, Sanskrit
   pitar, etc. ('father')

Hence we may talk of common 'levels' of vocabulary which, along
with the other features of sound, morphology, and syntax, enable us
to   distinguish   the   branches   and   sub-branches   of   the
Indo-European language stock. We can observe that Old English
has a pre-history, a period of development which is older than our
oldest records. We have no written records of Common Indo-
European, Germanic, West Germanic, Ingvaeonic, or early Old
English (although Greek, Sanskrit and Latin records give us
evidence of languages contemporary with and related to Germanic
and its descendants). We can judge, from the late surviving records
in related languages, something of what this pre-history was, and
we shall need to do so in order to understand the surviving records
properly; but we can never reconstruct the earliest days of the
English language fully.

III

The Germanic tribesmen from northern Europe who settled in
Britain in the mid-fifth century were not the first invaders of the
island: the Romans in 55 B.C. and, long before them, the Celts had
come – the Romans for an occupation that lasted five hundred years
and the Celts as permanent inhabitants who survived both the
Romans and the Saxon invasions. The departed Romans left little
linguistic heritage except in some place-names and in a few words
taken over from Latin by the Celts. The Saxon invaders, when they
came, likewise brought a few words of Latin taken over from the
Romans who occupied territory near the Saxon homeland on the
Continent. And of course when the Saxons subjugated the Celts in
Britain, the resulting mixture of races left a Celtic imprint on the
Saxon vocabulary, but again it was a very slight one, largely restricted to place-names. All in all there was little language mixture in
England between the coming of the Saxons around 450 and the
coming of the Roman missionaries 150 years later.

As Bede tells us, the Germanic tribesmen whom we have been calling 'Saxons' for convenience were in fact from three tribes, the Saxons, Angles and Jutes, and they settled in different parts of the country: the Jutes in Kent and the Isle of Wight, the Saxons in the southwest, and the Angles in the Midlands and north. Doubtless, for the reasons already mentioned, the tribes spoke different dialects of the Ingvaeonic branch of West Germanic, and these differences became accentuated in England. As a result there are four chief dialects of Old English, two of which correspond to tribal origins: Kentish in the Jutish area and West Saxon in the Saxon; the Anglian area divided linguistically into Mercian between the Thames and the Humber, and Northumbrian northwards.

Among the varieties of speech, we can sometimes mark a difference in rate of change: many features of American English, for example, are more conservative than British English. But all languages change, and no tongue represents fully and faithfully the features of its antecedents. Those derivatives of a common original which are relatively more conservative than others have, in any case, no claim to be 'better' because of their conservatism: conservatism in language neither results from nor imparts linguistic superiority, and in fact 'superiority' is not a notion that relates to any demonstrable feature of language.

We have no way of knowing which of the three Germanic dialects brought by the invaders was most like Ingvaeonic, and in any case the isolation of the settlers in various parts of England prevented any one from gaining the ascendancy over the others. It was only much later, probably during the ninth century, that the increasing political unity of the country brought the dialects into contact and hence, in a manner of speaking, into competition: and then the event was not decided on the basis of the comparative adequacy of Kentish, West Saxon, Mercian or Northumbrian, but on the dialect origins of the men who had brought about the unification, who were in the main West Saxons. Hence it was for entirely non-linguistic reasons that West Saxon became the premier dialect of Old English. But because our written records for the most part do not go back further than the century of this linguistic domination, they reflect it. We have scant evidence for any Old English dialect but West Saxon, and the study of Old English must concentrate on the forms of that variety, much as the study of Old Norse comes down to the study of Old Icelandic because the literary survivals in that language dominate the documents in early Scandinavian. Some of the features we are going to describe are therefore common features of Old English over the six hundred years it was spoken in England, but some may be only West Saxon, especially West Saxon of the last century and a half before the Conquest, when our documents are most plentiful.

Let us have a look at some literary Late West Saxon. This passage comes from the opening lines of Blickling Homily IX:

We gehyrdon oft secggan be þam æþelan tocyme ures Drihtnes, hu He Him on þas world þingian ongan, þæt heahfæderas sægdon and cyþdon, þæt witigan witigodan and heredon, þæt sealmsceopas sungon and sægdon, þæt se wolde cuman of þam cynestole and of þæm þrymrice hider on þas world ... 'We have often heard say regarding the noble advent of Our Lord, how He commenced to reconcile Himself with this world, which the patriarchs said and made-known, which the prophets prophesied and praised, which the psalmists sang and said, that He would come from the royal throne and from the realm of glory hither into this world ...'

A number of the words are still perfectly familiar, with the same form and meaning: *We, oft, he, him, on, world, and, of.* A further number have changed in spelling but not very much in form and meaning: *þæt,* 'that', *hider* 'hither', *wolde,* 'would', *ures,* 'our, ours', *hu,* 'how', *cuman,* 'come', *be,* 'by, regarding'.

But some words from this passage which still survive have changed much more radically in form: *gehyrdon,* 'heard', *secggan,* 'say', *sægdon,* 'said', *sungon,* 'sang', *þas,* 'this', *þam* or *þæm* (pronounced 'tham'), 'the'. Finally, there are a number of words which have disappeared from the language entirely, or which survive only in distantly related forms or in dialect words: *æþelan,* 'noble' (cf. the name Ethel); *Drihtnes,* 'Lord's'; *þingian,* 'reconcile'; *ongan,* 'commenced' (cf. 'began'); *cyþdon,* 'made known' (cf. 'uncouth', 'not familiar'); *witigan, witigodan,* 'prophets', 'prophesied' (cf. 'wit', 'witty'); *heredon,* 'praised', *se,* 'he'. A special group of these lost words includes the compounds *tocyme,* 'advent', *heahfæderas,* 'patriarchs', *sealmsceopas,* 'psalmists', *cynestole,* 'royal throne', *þrymrice,* 'realm of glory'. It is noteworthy that in translating the words and compounds that have disappeared from the language, I have almost always used modern words which are of Latin or Greek origin: 'noble', 'reconcile', 'commenced', 'prophets' and 'prophesied', 'praised', 'advent', 'patriarch', 'psalmists', 'royal throne', 'realm of glory'. When the native Old English words passed out of use after the Norman Conquest, their place was taken by words the

Normans brought with them, Latin words or French words taken from the Latin, and many of these are the words we use today.

Now if we look at these four groups of words more carefully, we shall see that they have something more in common than their resemblance to or difference from their modern equivalents. The words that changed least include three pronouns, two prepositions, and one conjunction, as well as one adverb and one noun. Most of these words, that is, are 'grammatical' words, words which help form the backbone of the sentence but are not full of referential meaning in their own right. They are called CLOSED-CLASS words, because they are relatively few in number, and because they change in membership and form very slowly. The next group, the words which have changed only a little, are mostly other closed-class words: two conjunctions, a preposition, a modal auxiliary verb, as well as another adverb and a verb. When we move on to the third class, the words that have survived but only in a deeply changed form, we find there are only two closed-class words, the definite and demonstrative articles, but there are three verbs (including two tenses of one of them). The verbs are common ones in everyday use: 'hear', 'say', 'sing'. When finally we come to the group in which the changes have replaced the Old English words entirely, we find only one closed-class word, *se*; but five verbs, seven nouns, and one adjective. Many of these words are of less common use than 'world', 'come', 'say', 'hear', and 'sing', and some of them are very specialized.

These observations on the survival of words from Old English into Modern English hold pretty well for all the vocabulary of Old English. Of course we must not jump to conclusions about the familiarity of Old English words. Some of them changed a great deal in form, like *þæt* which we now spell 'that', but not much in sound; others changed more in sound than spelling – *we* was pronounced 'way', *he* 'hay', *world* rather like 'whorled'. Even when we are dealing with such old texts, the spelling is more stable over the years than the sound, and our passage would sound very unfamiliar if we heard it spoken aloud as the Anglo-Saxons heard it. A number of the sounds in Old English, like a number of the words, do not survive into our modern speech: one in particular is represented in the spelling of 'eight', 'high' and other words with 'gh', and sounded much like the 'ch' in German *ach*, but here the modern spelling commemorates a sound lost soon after the spelling became fixed. The Anglo-Saxons, indeed, pronounced all the letters in the words they spelled, so *ward* kept the 'r' it has lost in many modern forms of

English, and even trilled it. *Hwær* (modern 'where') sounded the *h* clearly, as did *hring* ('ring'), *hnecca* ('neck') and *hlinca* ('link'). On the other hand, some sounds of Modern English were absent from Old English: they are the ones that English took over from other languages after the Norman Conquest, or that came about as the result of sound-changes since then. They include the vowel sounds in 'house', 'proud'; 'joy', 'join'; 'my', 'might'.

But many of the changes that influenced the sound so greatly did not come about until five hundred years after the passage was written, and they are a later part of our story. We should not go on, however, without remarking on some common features in the sound and spelling changes that have taken place. You will have noticed how the symbol *þ* is replaced by our 'th'. Other changes are regular as well. The *d* in *hider* and *heahfæder*, for example, have both become 'th' in 'hither' and 'father'. And just as the symbol *æ* in *fæder* has been replaced by *a*, so it has too in *þæt*. The *u* in *ures* and *hu* has been replaced by 'ou' where it does not end the word ('our') and 'ow' where it does ('how'). So even though modern spelling is not entirely systematic, it has some regularities in its relation to the sound and spelling of Old English.

The words which have vanished from standard Modern English include five compounds. Old English was very fond of compounds, and often used them where we would use two words ('royal throne') or a phrase ('realm of glory'). Those two examples are made up entirely of native, that is Germanic, elements in the Old English vocabulary. Sometimes Old English writers would use native elements to render a Latin or other foreign word part by part, much as Modern German still often does when, for example, it writes *Fernsehe* 'far see' for *television*, a word whose Greek and Latin elements mean just what the German word does. Such renderings – element-for-element translations, if you like – are called CALQUES. Both *tocyme* and *heahfæderas* are calques on *adventus* and *patriarchos* respectively: *to* = *ad*, *cyme* = -*ventus*, *heah* = *archos*, *fæder* = *patri*-. (Actually, as we have already seen, *fæder* and *patri*- come from the same Indo-European source, as so, for that matter, do *cyme* and -*ventus*.) Yet another kind of compound which is charac-teristic of Old English word-formation is *sealm-sceopas*. The first element is Greek (by way of Latin) *psalm*; the *ps*- sound simplified in Old English pronunciation, as it is in Modern English, but they were more honest about the spelling. The -*a*- has become -*ea*- by the influence of the following -*lm*, a sound-change which – though perhaps not of great importance itself – shows how early the word came into Old English, for the intermediate change of *-a-* to *-æ-* took place at a very early date indeed, when English was only just becoming English. To this now well-naturalized word the Old English writer has added *sceop*, 'poet or singer', and created a compound of foreign plus English word. Such compounds were not so common in Old English as those in which both elements were native, and were largely restricted to foreign words which, like *sealm*, had become familiar and naturalized. The great period of combining foreign and native elements was the Middle English.

Even after this discussion and the aid it brings in recognizing what are at first unfamiliar-looking words, you might not be able to read the sample passage by yourself. That is because Old English differs from Modern English not only in the membership of its vocabulary, and in the sounds and spellings of its words: it differs also in the way it relates words one to another in a sentence. There are three main ways of doing this in Modern English; we can alter the shape of a word, usually by adding an '*-s*' to denote the plural or the possessive ('father', 'fathers', 'father's'); we can alter the order of the words ('Father sees Jim', 'Jim sees father'); or we can introduce prepositions ('The father of Jim', 'The Book of Albert'). Clearly all three ways work together to form a system, and if one of them changes, the others will too.

Now in Old English the first way was easier and more flexible to employ, because there were many meaningful endings to words in addition to the '*-s*' of plurality or possession. They had the '*-s*' as well, of course: you see it in the plural *heahfæderas* (singular *heahfæder*) and *sealmsceopas*, the possessive *Drihtnes* (nominative *Drihten*). There are also plurals in *-an*, like *witigan* (cf. modern 'oxen', 'children', 'brethren'), and a number of others; but a variety of ways to signal 'plural' does not really add to the number of things you can signal, merely to the ways you can do it. Old English gained its flexibility in being able to signal, in addition to the nominative and possessive, the direct and indirect object, singular and plural, masculine, feminine and neuter, all with word endings; and these word-endings applied not only to nouns, as the plural and possessive do today, but to adjectives as well, with a few changes, and to the definite articles. When, a few lines after the passage quoted, the writer says

> Þa ealra fæmnena cwen cende þone soþan Scyppend and
> ealles folces Frefrend,
> 'the queen of all women gave birth to the true
> Maker and Comforter of all people',

we can follow him only if we know that *ealra fæmnena* is possessive plural, *ealles folces* possessive singular, and *þone soþan Scyppend* accusative singular; and we can make the distinction in the case of *Scyppend* only because the definite article is present, for as it happens *Scyppend* has no distinctive accusative ending, and the *-an* ending of *soþan* is shared with a number of other signals, of which the plural *witigan* noted above is only one (the dative *æþelan* is another). A literal translation of the short example would be

> The of-all of-women queen gave-birth-to the
> true Maker and of-all of-people Comforter . . .

We do not need to spell out all of the many variations in Old English word-ending to see how they signal the relation of one word to another in a way that word-order or the use of prepositions might otherwise be called on to do.

Of course prepositions and word-order do enter into the signalling system of Old English: the writer of the Blickling Homily used them extensively, more so than some other writers whose style was mainly dependent on word-endings. The Blickling writer has *be* ('by', 'regarding'), *on*, and *of* in important places, and his word-order is not altogether strange; but a measure of its variety is the placing of *þingian ongan* ('to reconcile commenced') at the end of its clause but of *wolde cuman* ('would come') near the beginning of its clause, and the reversal of the relative position of the finite and infinite verbs in the two phrases.

So the supply of word-endings for nouns was greater by far in Old English than in Modern English, and adjectives and articles – which are today completely without even the reduced word-endings of our nouns – had a full range too. What is more, verbs were capable of equally wide variation. In our example, *seccgan*, *þingian* and *cuman* are all infinitives, marked with the termination *-an*. Sometimes today we mark infinitives with a signal borrowed from the prepositions, 'to': 'he commenced to reconcile . . .,' but often we do not: 'we have heard say', 'would come'. The forms of the Old English infinitives are thus more regular and more distinctive. The passage includes a number of finite verbs, two past singular (*ongan*, *wolde*) and many past plural (*gehyrdon*, *sægdon*, *cyþdon*, *witigodon*, *heredon*, *sungon*). We may take note of two features of these finite verbs. One is that the plural verbs all have a distinctive ending *-on*, which the singular verbs lack. In Modern English, only the verb 'to be' distinguishes in the past between singular and plural; in the rest, one form caters for the past of all numbers and persons. Here again

Old English has a greater range of signals built into the grammar of the language. We should also note that many of the verbs in the past tense have a -d- in them, but *ongan* and *sungon* have not. Here the situation is unchanged in Modern English: we still observe a difference between verbs that take a -d in the past, like 'heard', 'said', 'made', 'praised', and those that do not, like 'began' and 'sang'. The only difference is that Old English had many more verbs of the kind that do not take -d in the past, and a somewhat more elaborate system of signalling the past tense in the absence of -d. As in so many things, the variety of the Old English system has been lost. Old English had many forms of the noun: we have only the possessive and plural. Old English could signal possessive and plural in a number of ways: we rely almost entirely on the ending '-s'. Old English could make distinctions between several persons and both numbers in the past: we cannot. Old English had many verbs that could show, in a variety of ways, the past tense without recourse to -d: many of these, including 'help', 'climb', and other ones in frequent use, we have lumped together with the ordinary conjugation in -d.

So two things stand out about the vocabulary and grammar of Old English. One is that its stock of words was a rich one, and capable of increase from its own resources in the face of new needs; and that this stock underwent change and replacement over time, with some kinds of words more vulnerable than others. The other is that the grammar provided a wealth of inflectional capabilities that have since declined, and the decline has resulted in an increasingly rigid word-order and dependence on lexically-empty words like prepositions.

IV

Old English did not become Middle English the moment William the Conquerer set foot on the beach at Hastings in 1066. In some ways, in fact, the classification of Old English as 'English before the Norman Conquest', and of Middle English as 'English from the Norman Conquest to the beginning of the Renaissance in England', is inconvenient and misleading. For one thing, it is entirely the result of hindsight. Although we have relatively few statements of the ideas that medieval Englishmen held about their language, we can be sure that our present ways of looking at medieval English would be utterly strange to them. It is unlikely that an Englishman in the year 1100 would have seen such a difference between his own language and that of his grandfather that he would have called it by a different name.

For another thing, the divisions 'the Norman Conquest' and 'the Renaissance' are not very helpful. They are quite unlike each other: anyone near the scene would have recognized the Norman Conquest, an identifiable event that took place at a fixed point in time. But not so the Renaissance, which is another relatively modern way of describing a gradual change that altered a number of human activities, political, cultural, and – least of all – linguistic. Indeed neither the Conquest nor the Renaissance were linguistic events, and so they are even more inconvenient for classifying language.

How then can the classification proceed? It must follow the categories of language, obviously, and not those of politics, warfare or culture. As we have remarked, it is often helpful, at least in the case of English, to analyse language in terms of its sounds, its word-shapes, its sentence-shapes, and its vocabulary. We have reviewed Old English with special reference to these categories. Now, if we turn to Middle English, we shall notice several things about the categories as they appear in the later form of the language.

1. There are marked changes in all of them.
2. Such changes are all in evidence during the late Old English period, but they accelerate rapidly in the centuries following the Norman Conquest.
3. Some of the changes (notably vocabulary) begin earlier and go further than some others (notably sound).
4. The changes are continuous, and although they can be traced in early documents, they are most obvious in late ones.

Let us look again at a sermon for our evidence. Of course no one document is going to give us testimony to everything we need to know about, but sermons are a particularly satisfactory source of information. They are abundant in every age; they are not so conservative as translations of the Bible, nor so influenced by considerations of style as poetry; but they have a stylistic unity all the same which helps us to compare them.

Here is part of a twelfth-century sermon on the parable of the bad servant:

Ða yrsode ðe laford, ant læt hine bitæcen
þam stiðum witnerum, þe hine witniæn
sceolden, oð ðet he forgylde al ðæt feoh
him seolfum. . . . Her is mucel andgit eow
monnum to witenne; and we nimæð her to
ðissere trahtnunge Augustinum ðone wisæ.
'Then became-angry the lord, and caused
him to-be-committed to-the cruel torturers,
who him torture should, until that he
repaid all that money unto-him self. . . .
Here is (a) great significance for-you
men to understand; and we take for this
exposition Augustine the wise.'

A few changes from Old English have taken place in the century
since the Conquest: *þe laford* would have been *se hlaford* before, but
the definite article *se* has altered to resemble the other definite
articles that finally all became modern 'the', while the initial cluster
hl- has simplified to *l*. On the other hand, the verbs still show their
full complement of endings: plural present (*nimæð*) in *-æð*, past
(*sceolden*) in *-en* (Old English *-að*, *-on*); infinitive (*betæcen, witniæn,
witenne*) in *-en* or *æn* without the marker *to* and in *-enne* with it (Old
English, *-an*, *-anne*); past singular (*yrsode, forgylde*) in *-de*. The
pronouns still observe a difference between the direct and indirect
object (*hine, him*), later levelled to 'him' for both. The definite
articles are inflected likewise (*ðone, þam*), as are the demonstratives
(*ðissere*, feminine dative singular), the adjectives (*stið-um*, dative
plural) and nouns (*witner-um, monn-um*, even – with a Latin ending
but following the English syntax – *Augustin-um*). This full inflectional system is reflected in the relatively light use of prepositions; the translation into Modern English has to insert them in a
number of places where the passage under study can omit them
without ambiguity. And (aside from the name Augustinus) there is
not a single word of non-Germanic origin.

We have already noticed that a number of Old English words did
not survive into Modern English, and some of these are still in use
in this passage: *yrsode* (as a verb, but cf. modern 'ire'); *stiðum*;
witnerum and its associated *witniæn; forgylde, andgit, nimæð;
trahtnunge*. But there was another kind of change that went with this
loss, and that is the way vocalic verbs and nouns often crossed over
into the consonantal class. The example *læt* in this passage is a bit
untrustworthy, because the scribe obviously uses *æ* in a number of
different ways: but in Old English the present was *læt-* and the past
was *let*. Here the difference between the two vowels seems to be

ironed out. 'Let' never got beyond this point, because it ends with 't', and English usually doesn't add a '-ed' suffix to verbs ending with 't' or 'd'; but the reduction of the Old English vowel contrast has left us with an ambiguity in phrases like 'I let him out', which does not appear to be obviously either past or present. In a word like 'help', the Old English contrast between the present *help-* and past singular *healp* (the past plural was *hulpon* and the past participle *geholpen*) was similarly neutralized, and the modern form 'helped' emerged, although for a time both the vocalic and the consonantal systems operated side-by-side in this word, as they continue to do today with 'hang' (past 'hung' or 'hanged'), 'shine' (past 'shone' or 'shined'), and 'dive' (past 'dived' or 'dove', although in fact this was a consonantal verb in Old English and the past 'dove' is a relatively modern creation in imitation of 'drove').

A similar situation obtained with nouns and, to a lesser extent, adjectives. We still say 'man', 'men' and 'goose', 'geese', but a host of other nouns of the same sort have changed over to the 'boy', 'boys' class: otherwise we should now say 'book', 'beek'; 'goat', 'geat', and so forth. Similarly we can still say 'old', 'elder', but not 'long', 'lenger', as we should if the Old English forms still persisted. In none of these cases did the Middle English period begin with the change to the modern form, but rather the change took place during the centuries following the Norman Conquest and was frequently incomplete by 1500 or even later.

At least the written language, then, kept much of the characteristic features of Old English for several lifetimes after the Norman Conquest, and we should not go far wrong to describe this passage as late Old English of the twelfth century, basing our terminology on the linguistic facts rather than the date of the text. Conversely, some of the characteristics that do distinguish Middle English can be traced sporadically in texts from before the Conquest.

Even in this early example of post-Conquest English, for example, we have seen that Old English word-endings like *-an* for the infinitive and *-on* for the past are both being spelled *-en*. That is a loss of one kind of distinction, and if it continues, another kind of distinction – with prepositions, word-order, or both – will have to take its place. We have also seen that a distinction was lost when *let* and *læt* became the same. And we have noticed that Old English differs from later forms of the language in its all but exclusively Germanic vocabulary, which is inclined to form calques on foreign words rather than to borrow them. If we then go on to list these points, we would have a catalogue of the chief ways in which Middle English differed from Old English:

1. Old English is the period of full inflections in final syllables, Middle English the period of levelled inflections (in most cases, Modern English is the period of lost inflections).
2. Old English also preserves more vowel distinctions WITHIN the word than does Middle English, as well as those distinctions in the word-ending mentioned under (1).
3. As a result of (1) and (2), Old English depends less on prepositions and word-order than Middle English.
4. Old English has a vocabulary almost entirely Germanic; Middle English, especially among the open-class words, makes much use of words borrowed from non-Germanic languages.

We have already had a great deal to say about (3) and (4), and their consequences in any given text are relatively easy to identify. We have also seen how, in the twelfth-century text under discussion, (1) and (2) make an appearance, but not to a dramatic degree. Looking backward, we must ask whether even those hints of levelling are new in a text of the twelfth century. We shall find that they are not. Not only do tenth-century texts, written at least a full hundred years before the Conquest, reveal many cases of the weakening of -*an* to -*en* (e.g. *nesen* for *nesan*) and similar levelling of other inflections (e.g. *þances* for *þancas*); they also reveal a loss of the -*n* or -*m* altogether (*cyðe* for *cyðan, gode* for *godum*), and – even more significantly – mistaken cases of the fuller form where the weaker was required (*sceawedon* for *sceawede, þendan* for *þenden*), sure evidence that these endings are no longer playing a fully meaningful role. If we bear in mind that at every stage of the medieval language the scribes were prone to employ archaic forms that were decades behind the real speech-habits of the time, we shall realize how important these occasional 'mistakes' in tenth-century manuscripts really are.

The same can be said for (2). One of the distinctions lost in Middle English was the one Old English made between the vowel of the past singular and that of the past plural in some verbs. 'Bite', for example, had *bāt* in the past singular and *biton* in the past plural; similarly, 'ride' had *rād* and *ridon*. In Middle English, the ending of the plural, as we have seen, weakened to -*en* and finally vanished. But another change took place, even earlier: the distinction between the two vowels of the past was levelled, and while the past of 'bite' became *bit* (the vowel of plural), that of 'ride' became *rād* (the vowel of the singular). There is no way of telling which vowel will predominate, but the levelling was universal. Thus 'find' had *fand* (past singular), *fundon* (past plural), and we can tell by our modern 'found' that the plural vowel persisted. Yet even before the Conquest the levelling in this verb has begun: there is late Old English *fund* alongside *fand*. Here, too, then, a Middle English characteristic is anticipated in Old English. If we turn to a text of the early thirteenth century, however, what were mere stirrings in the tenth, eleventh or twelfth centuries now begin to appear as profound changes.

Hise deciples hedde gret drede of þise tempeste, so hi awakede hine and seiden to him, 'Lord, save us, for we perisset' . . . þo aros up ure lord and tok þane wynd . . . þis is si vaire miracle þet þet godspel of te day us telþ. 'His disciples had great dread of this tempest so they woke him and said to him, "Lord, save us, for we perish." Then our Lord rose up and rebuked the wind. . . . This is the fair miracle that the Gospel of the day tells us.'

Words like 'disciple' and 'miracle' are the kind that Old English was most likely to borrow when its own vocabulary did not provide an adequate term: recall 'psalm' in *sealm-sceop*. So we need not take such words by themselves as evidence for the wholesale penetration of foreign vocabulary into English writing. So 'tempest' and *perisset* (i.e. *perisheth*; the *ss* represents 'sh', and *th* often appears as *t* in this text, for example in *te*, 'the') are another matter, and 'save' clinches the question. The vocabulary of the piece is in a different linguistic world from that of our twelfth-century example.

The form of words differs too. Old English *hlaford*, itself already a simplification from unrecorded Old English *hlaf-ward*, 'guardian of the loaf', became *laford* in our last text and now 'lord' in this one. Old English *godspel*, 'good story', a calque on *evangelium*, a Latin form of the Greek word meaning 'good story', was soon to follow the way of *hlaford* and simplify to 'gospel'.

The Old English practice of compounding that we see in *hlaf-ward* and *god-spel* took a new turn in the Middle English period, when the stock of French and Latin words became available for compounding with native English forms. Our examples show that whereas *Augustinus* was felt as a foreign word in Old English and accordingly inflected with a Latin accusative ending, *Augustinum*, the present passage gives *deciples* and *perisset*, among others, as instances of foreign words whose terminations are English. It is as though we first said *musea* and *rhinocerotes* as plurals of *museum* and *rhinoceros* until we became accustomed to them and began to treat them as fully English words. From there it is but a step to taking other kinds of suffix besides plural and adding those to foreign words, giving *martyrdom*; or adding a full foreign word to an English one, to get *gentleman*. This kind of combination appears quite early in Middle English, as the Old English example *sealm-sceop* would lead us to expect; but naturally enough, its fullest effect is delayed until the period of greatest borrowing from French and Latin, in the thirteenth and later centuries.

The inflections are simpler than in the twelfth-century example, but not so simple as they were to become. There is no longer a distinctive past plural (*hedde, awakede*) except in *seiden*; it appears that the *-on*, now weakened to *-en*, is optional. But there is at least the possibility of a distinctive present plural in *-eth*, represented here as *-et*, and the third person in *-(e)þ* remains (*telþ*) as it did at least in some writing on into the eighteenth century. The definite article *se* is preserved (as *si*), and *þæt* (as *þet*), and so is the accusative form in *þane*; but against these survivals we must note *þise* (a greatly simplifed form of *ðissere*, as in the former passage) 'this', and *te* 'the'. The nouns show no inflection at all, nor do the adjectives *gret, vaire*; but *hise* has the plural *-e*.

The pronouns, indeed, retain fairly full inflection, as they do to the present day. The function of the pronoun in the sentence is such that its inflectional simplification will always lag behind that of nouns. Here the nominative plural is still *hi* as it was in Old English, and the distinction between accusative *hine* and dative *him* is still observed. On the other hand, the force of the dative *him* is not sufficient for it to stand alone as it did in the previous example from Middle English; here it is 'helped' by the preposition, *to him*, and similarly *of þise, of te day*, instead of genitive forms like *þissere* and *þæs dæges*. Accusatives like *hine, us* and datives like *us telþ* do not require prepositional aid even in Modern English. Word-order, consequently, is much like that of our own language, except in the last sentence where the finite verb in a subordinate clause is, as before, in final position, and in the second sentence where an adverb in initial position displaces the subject to a place after the verb. Both of these differences from Modern English practice can be paralleled in Modern German, and they show the continuing influence on Middle English syntax of the Germanic descent of Old English.

For our last example of Middle English sermon prose we may go ahead to the year of Chaucer's death, 1400, or thereabouts:

þe hethen philosofres skorned hym, for oure feygthe may not be preved by reson; and þei, þe philosofres, granted no þinge but þat reson enformeþ hem.
'The heathen philosophers scorned him, for our faith may not be proved by reason; and they, the philosophers, granted nothing but that (which) reason informs them.'

The translation is hardly needed, so close – save in some details of spelling – is the language of the passage to Modern English; yet it is well over five hundred years old, only a century or two younger than the other Middle English passages we have been looking at. So we can say that Middle English was not the instant and distinctive development in the years that immediately followed the Norman Conquest; its characteristics, on the contrary, developed most rapidly and positively in the centuries beginning two hundred years after the Conquest, that is, from the mid-thirteenth century onwards.

The vocabulary of this example, to begin with, is heavily French, Latin, or Greek through Latin, in origin. Nouns, ordinary verbs, adjectives and adverbs not of Old English stock are *philosofre, skorned, feygthe, preved, reson, granted, enformeþ*; only *hethen* (itself a calque on *paganus*) and *þinge*, of the open-class words, are not imports. On the other hand, the personal and possessive pronouns can almost all be traced back to Old English: *hym*, the objective form now common to accusative and dative; *oure*, the new spelling for *ure* as in the previously examined passage; *þei*, a replacement under Norse influence of the previous *hi*, leading to Modern English 'they'; *hem* still showing the influence of the Old English form that accompanied *hi*, not yet brought into line with *þei*. So also the article *þe*, the special verbs *may* and *be*, particles *not* and *no*, the prepositions *for, but*, and *by*, and the relative *þat*. The grammatical framework of the sentence is English, and the 'meaning' words are not – which is, as we have already seen, much the modern distribution of our vocabulary.

Only the plural word-ending marks the nouns, although of course the possessive was available as well. The article and adjective *þe hethen* are unmarked as plurals. The verb inflections too are simplified: no past plural on *skorned* or *granted*, although of course the third person present singular retains its *-eþ* ending. The infinitive *be* is unmarked. With the loss of noun, article, adjective and verbal inflections, the word-order has become fixed. Only in one place in the translation, the relative pronoun, is any supplementation needed. It was another century before this construction took its modern form.

V

The conclusions we have reached about the history of the four categories traced in these passages of Middle English gave cause for reflection. How is it that the steady change of language seems to have increased so abruptly over a period of two centuries, and how is it that – the superficialities of spelling aside – it has changed so little in the five hundred years since?

The answer is twofold: the kind of evidence we have for making this study at all, and the history of the reputation of English. We have already looked at the first question, and seen how our reliance on the surviving documents influences the kind of study we can make. The second has a great deal to do with the first, for when a language has a high reputation as a literary and offical medium, it will be used in many documents, and the documents will stand a good chance of preservation. It is difficult at this distance of time to imagine an England in which English was not the habitual language for literature and official writing, yet for much of the early Middle English period it was in fact eclipsed by French and Latin. The French and Latin vocabulary of English begins to grow rapidly in the mid-thirteenth century when English begins to make its come-back: the vocabulary, it might be said, is the spoils of that victory.

The English that emerges in the greatly increased number of vernacular documents that survive from about 1250 until about 1350 is undergoing the turmoil of this contest. It is purely figurative, but not perhaps altogether misleading, to regard the English that we find in documents of the thirteenth century as something that has been hibernating since the influx of French-speaking conquerors in 1066. Of course the spoken language of England among the middle and lower classes remained English, but the people who mattered – by and about and for whom the documents were made – were French-speaking. The new awakening of official and literary Middle English shows the effects of the hibernation: it is remarkably like the Old English of two centuries before. In the hundred years up to 1350, it undergoes a period of rapid accommodation to its new role, making up for lost time. And when, in 1350 or 1400 onwards, it begins to enjoy the rewards of having established itself, it does what any other estab-lished person or institution does – it settles down and becomes conservative.

But language itself is not an institution: literature is. It is the literature of England whose history most nearly relates to the figurative account just completed. And it is to the growth of English literature in the second half of the fourteenth century, particularly in the hands of Chaucer, Gower, Lydgate, Wycliff, and their literary successors, that the stabilization of the literary language is largely attributable. Literature is traditional: once it has models, it seeks to follow them. The models for literary English were, until the mid-fourteenth century, few, scattered, and of uncertain reputation. With the coming of a consolidated school of English prose and poetry, the English language gained a literary embodiment that guaranteed its continuity as nothing before could have done.

We speak of the superficialities of spelling as the element of Middle English that has changed the most. Because we are so carefully drilled in spelling, we are supersensitive to anything that goes against what we have learned. In fact, many of our spellings go back to Middle English, even though we – unlike our forefathers then – are allowed only one 'correct' spelling. The 'ea' in 'weather', the 'o' in 'love', the 'gh' in 'night', and very many others, represent various special conditions of Middle English that did not last beyond 1500. Yet they survive in our spelling because the linguistic traditions of 1400 command a large following even today.

Indeed, the superficialities of spelling, as we can even better call them in view of these considerations, did not change anything like so much as did the sound-patterns of English – that is precisely why spelling is so out of step with pronunciation today. The chief change in sound was one that sets Middle English apart from Modern English rather than from Old English, and it is consequently a subject for the next chapter. The point is, however, that the appearance of stability following the great changes of the late Middle Ages is in some ways only an appearance. It relates to conditions of interruption, renewal and conservatism that apply chiefly to the written, literary language. Spoken Middle English would reveal something different. But it is spoken Middle English that we cannot recover, although we can study its modern descendants. We must rely on what was written, but we must avoid taking all it tells us as the whole truth.

VI

The changing role of English in the centuries that followed the Norman Conquest had other effects then on the dialects and now on our knowledge of them. Dialects already existed, as we have seen, and do so today; but in a time when literacy and education are not widespread, there is no medium to give currency to any one dialect in preference to others. So much has the situation in this respect changed since the coming of universal literacy, general education and, most recently, radio and television, that we are prone to look upon the preferred dialect of English as the English language itself, and on all other varieties as deviant or substandard. But the 'received' form of English is a dialect like any other, one of the parts that make up the whole, and its reputation is a historical accident that has nothing to do with its linguistic adequacy.

As we have seen, such accidents gave preference to West Saxon among the dialects of Old English, at least for the purposes that brought into being the documents on which our study of Old English is based. The accidents arose from conditions that, generally speaking, went out of being with the Norman Conquest, and so West Saxon lost the basis for its preeminence. So long as French and Latin remained the languages of authority and literary reputation, the dialects of English lacked a national preferred form of the sort West Saxon had been: all English dialects were out of the kind of fashion that West Saxon had enjoyed. As a result, such documents as were written in English might be in any one of several dialects. All had the same standing and hence the same chance. Naturally enough, there is an early preference for the English of the London region, and the preference becomes more marked as time passes, until London English assumes the role that West Saxon had formerly held. But in the meantime, other kinds of English found record in documents.

The documents tell us a great deal about dialects that already existed but that had little trace hitherto. For example, the Viking occupation of East Anglia and parts of the North must have resulted in a large number of Old Norse words coming into Old English. We have an early record of some of them, like *call*, and very late in the Old English period, *take*; but most of them, like *window, sky*, and many others, appear only in Middle English, by which time the source of the influence was long departed from England and the Vikings themselves almost forgotten. This comes about probably because the 'classical' form of Old English was from an area of minimal Norse influence, and because during the period of the occupation, Norse words were regarded with a measure of hostility. In Middle English the 'underground' vocabulary of Norse finds expression in the absence of the restraints which obtained in Old English, and even the pronouns, as we have seen, are affected, first in the North and then gradually towards the South.

This example of dialect-mixing, the spread of a local – even a foreign – characteristic to other dialects, brings us to another point. So far as we know, the dialect situation in Old English was relatively stable. Of course the language changed, and as we have seen, change brings an increase in dialect differentiation: the three-fold tribal distinctions were already made four-fold by the division of the Anglian dialect into a northern and a southern variety by the time records begin. But the appearance of a distinctive dialect for the London region is a Middle English phenomenon, as is the splitting of the southern Anglian dialect into two further varieties, West Midlands and East Midlands. Northern Anglian, the Old English Northumbrian dialect, retained something like its old borders, but in Middle English historians call it Northern; West Saxon too underwent little alteration of geography, but its Middle English successor is called South-Western; and Kentish Middle English goes by the name of South-Eastern.

The identification of these areas depends on the discovery of contrasting items in two neighbouring dialects, and the mapping of the frontier between them. The contrasts can be in any of the four linguistic categories we have already discussed: we have seen how the distribution of the various early Germanic dialects can be illustrated by means of vocabulary, for example. But even though vocabulary is convenient for purposes of illustration, and may be the kind of contrast that is most noticeable in our experience of dialect variety today, it has certain important drawbacks for the discovery of dialect frontiers. For one thing, there are very many words in a language: English has perhaps ten thousand times as many words as it has sounds. Thus the likelihood of a given word turning up at the time and place you need it to give you the evidence for a dialect frontier is ten thousand times slighter than the chances of a given sound turning up. For another thing, people can easily use two words for the same thing, particularly if they live near a dialect border, or have biographical reasons for doing so: as an American who lived in England for twelve years, I mix what should be contrasting items of the two forms of English, and no one really knows what part of my car I mean by the 'hood'.

As we have seen, grammatical forms can be distinctive of dialect, for the replacement of the ending in 'he goeth' by 'he goes' began as a northernism, and the distribution of the various forms of grammatical words like 'she' is an important clue to Middle English dialect borders. To some extent, syntax is also a matter of dialect: even today the use of negatives, for example, differs between 'he won't go' and 'he'll not go', largely according to the area. But it is in sound that most stable contrasts are to be found. Both British and American speakers of English are aware of areas in their parts of the world where historical 'r' after a vowel is pronounced, and other adjacent areas where it is not: some speech communities say 'harder' so you can hear both 'r's, and some so you can hear neither. And so forth. Whatever the local practice, it is almost certain to be consistent in ALL cases involving the sound in question. Now of course modern English spelling gives us very little to go on in such cases, because, as we have seen, it is more uniform than the varieties of speech are ... in fact, with very few exceptions, it is entirely uniform throughout the English-speaking world, masking a wide range of differences in the spoken language. In Middle English, however, spelling had only begun to become uniform toward the very end of the period, and the surviving spellings give us a far better guide to the actual sounds than do their modern equivalents. Of course the problems that were mentioned at the outset of this chapter, regarding the localization and dating of documents, still hinder investigators, but they can come to some important conclusions, and these are being perfected continuously.

We are able to say, for example, that the Old English long *a* as in *rād* became long *o* everywhere outside the Northern region. Now *rād* is only one example; all instances of the vowel underwent the same change except in the North. Sometimes we get a result that survives in dialects, such as non-northern 'home' against Scots 'haim' (Old English *hām*). Sometimes it survives in place-names, such as non-northern Stonton (Leicestershire) against northern Stanton (Northumberland), or Stonebury (Herefordshire) against Stanbury (Yorkshire), from Old English *stān*. In the case of *rād*, the result is more complex but still consistent. The Old English word was both a verb, the past of 'ride', and a noun, 'a riding'. In the South the long *o* duly appeared, but two different solutions were found for the problem of how to spell it: the verb became 'rode', although the final '-e' has nothing to do with the history of the word and only serves to mark the sound of the 'o'; and the noun became 'road', although the 'a' once again is just a notation to mark the sound of the 'o' and doesn't reflect the long *a* that was its ancestor. In the North, the long *a* remained, and the marker that was chosen to indicate its length was *i*, giving 'raid' (like 'haim'). In due course of time this vowel, which sounded like that of 'father', changed to that of – well, 'change'. But unlike 'haim', the new 'raid' did not remain a dialect word. It came into use in Scotland and elsewhere to mean 'the object of a riding, an attack', just as 'road' came to mean 'that on which a riding takes place'.

The border between the *a* that became *o* and the *a* that remained *a* provides us with a dialect frontier, called an isogloss. Other contrasts provide still others: the *y* sound in Old English *hyll*, 'hill', *'byrig'*, 'bury', and so forth, became variously 'e' (mostly in Kent), 'u' (in the South West and South West Midlands), and 'i' elsewhere. Such an outcome enables us to divide up the area south of the Humber in a way that the *a/o* test does not; on the other hand, the *a/o* test helps us divide the area in which Old English *y* becomes 'i'. And so it goes. Not all the isoglosses coincide, and that is a good thing, for between wide-spread isoglosses we can identify usefully confined dialect areas. But where there is an overlap of several isoglosses, we have a major dialect frontier.

Like the continuity of language in time that we remarked on when talking about the change from Old English to Middle English, the continuity of language in space – for language exists in both – means that our dialect frontiers are to some extent falsifications: dialects alter gradually, not at borders. But the schematic results obtained by the discovery and comparison of isoglosses do provide a useful way of analysing the past and present varieties of English.

The area that was the source of the London dialect differs from some of the others in its eclecticism. Linguistically as well as geographically it is an extreme south-eastern corner of East Midlands, but Kent is on its southern border and the easternmost tip of South Western – the old West Saxon – approaches to within a few miles. Thus the rule, that one or another but not more than one development of a given sound will be characteristic of a dialect, breaks down in the London dialect as we observe its outgrowth in modern English. For example, the development of Old English *y* which we spoke of above gives us modern English 'hill', the Midlands and Northern form, but alongside it modern English 'bury', spelled in the South Western form and pronounced in the South Eastern: all three possibilities are illustrated in these two words alone. Or notice the early Middle English *vaire* in the thirteenth-century Kentish text above on p 241. It illustrates the rule that says Old English initial *f-* became *v-* in Southern, and particularly South Eastern, texts. If we look at modern 'fox', 'vixen', we can see that 'vixen' (Old English *fyxen*) has this Kentish characteristic but 'fox' hasn't. And to conclude, while 'vixen' has a Kentish initial consonant, it has a Midland *i* following it. Such cases show clearly the mixed or eclectic nature of the London dialect.

Thus in place of the four Old English dialects, we have five in Middle English, with an emergent sixth in the London region, an amalgam of the characteristics of East Midlands with some of those of South Eastern and a few of South Western, as well as such northernisms as became general throughout the country by 1450 or 1500: the plural pronoun 'they', and the third person present singular verb ending in '-s' ('loves' displacing 'loveth') chief among them. So it is not only in the evidence for the Middle English dialects that the change in the role of English had its effects: it is in the dialects themselves. The descendant of West Saxon, South Western, is not the premier dialect of Middle English. It is only a minor component in that dialect. Vocabulary and grammar too show the influence of the Norsemen, who came and went during the Old English period but whose linguistic heritage becomes disseminated only in the Middle English. The way that the survivals of Old English were handed on by Middle English to our modern language is fundamentally affected by the changes in status that English underwent after the Norman Conquest.

8

THE LATER HISTORY OF ENGLISH

Charles Barber

The English language since about 1500 is called Modern English, or New English. I shall call it Modern English, and use the abbreviation ModE. The abbreviation ME will stand for Middle English (c. 1100–1500), and OE for Old English (before 1100). There is of course no sudden change in the language at 1500, but if a text from 1400 is compared with one from 1600, the differences between ModE and ME can be seen clearly enough. These differences are numerous, but we can well begin by noting just a few of the major ones. In phonology, the most striking difference is in the pronunciation of the long vowels, a difference produced by the change known as the Great Vowel Shift. In grammar, the loss of inflections begun in the ME period has continued in ModE, and a relatively small number of inflectional endings have been standardized; the personal pronouns have been reduced in number; and there has been extensive development of the use of auxiliaries (words like *will, must, should*), a development facilitated by the rise of the 'dummy' auxiliary *do*. In vocabulary, the ModE period has been one of great expansion; in the earlier part of the period, a common method of word-formation was the borrowing or adaptation of words from Latin, but throughout the Modern period great use has also been made of affixation, conversion, and compounding.

During the ModE period, too, the language has spread widely over the world; in 1500 it was spoken by perhaps five million people in England and southern Scotland; today (1987) it is the first language of more than 350 million people, and the largest English-speaking communities are of course in North America. This spread of the language has encouraged divergent development, and there are now distinctive varieties of English in different parts of the world. However, the improvement in communications may now be putting a brake on this divergence; the different forms of English are influencing one another, and the influence of American English is particularly potent.

In enlarging on these topics, it will be convenient to deal separately with Early Modern English (eModE), from 1500 to 1700, and Later Modern English (lModE), since 1700. Within each sub-period, we shall consider in turn vocabulary, grammar, and phonology.

I

EARLY MODERN ENGLISH, 1500–1700

The Expansion of the Vocabulary: Loan-words

In the late medieval period, English had been re-established as the language of administration, government, and literature in England, and a standard literary language had arisen, based on London usage. But, even after the disappearance of French as a living language in England, the English language was not entirely without a rival: Latin was still the language of international scholarship, and it was only in the course of the eModE period that it finally fell out of use in England. As late as 1689 a major scientific work, Newton's *Principia*, could be published in Latin, though it is interesting to notice that his *Opticks*, fifteen years later, was published in English. In the 16th century many people believed that learning was not learning at all unless it was written in Latin, and this attitude was often reinforced by the vested interests of those who wished to preserve their position as an élite: physicians for example were bitterly hostile to the publication of medical works in English, which might undermine their monopoly. But there were also strong forces making for the use of English: patriotic feeling, typical of the new nation-states of Europe; the religious disputes during and after the Reformation, in which controversialists wished to be read by a wide audience; the importance attached by Protestants to the reading of the Bible in the vernacular; the increasing importance of social groups which lacked the classical education of the gentry, but which were eager for instruction; and, behind all these, the introduction of printing, which had expanded the reading-public.

But when translators or popularizers produced works in English for this new reading-public, they often found the language deficient in technical terms for the subjects they wished to handle (geometry, rhetoric, medicine, and so on), and were obliged to invent new

English words or expressions. The following passage illustrates both the concern with a new technical vocabulary and the necessity that the popularizers felt to defend their English writings against the traditional academics; it is taken from the preface to the first English translation of the *Logic* of Ramus, made by a Scot but published in London in 1574:

Heare I will speake nothing of the enuious, that thinkethe it not decent to wryte any liberall arte in the vulgar tongue, but woulde haue all thinges kept close eyther in the Hebrewe, Greke, or Latyn tongues. I knowe what greate hurte hathe come to the Churche of God by the defence of this mischeuous opinion: yet I woulde aske them one thing that thou mayest knowe their deceiptfull policie, and that their saying hathe no grounds of veritie. Whether wrote Moyses (the Hebrewe and deuyne) and after him Esdras in the Hebrewe and vulgar tongue or in some other strange tongue? Did Aristotle and Plato Greke Philosophers, Hipocrates and Galen Greke Phisitions, leaue the Greke tongue, because it was their natiue language, to seke some Hebrewe or Latin? Did Cicero who was a Latinist borne write his Philosophie and Rethoricke in the Greke tongue, or was he content with his mother tongue? and suerly as he testifiethe hym self he had the perfecte knowledge of the Greke tongue, yet he wrothe nothing therin which we haue extant at this daye. Shall we then thinke the Scottyshe or Englishe tongue, is not fitt to wrote any arte into? no in dede. But peraduenture thou wylt saye that there is not Scottyshe wordes for to declare and expresse all thinges contayned into liberall artes, truth it is: neither was there Latin wordes to expresse all thinges writen in the Hebrewe and Greke tongues: But did Cicero for this cause write no philosophie in Latin? thou wilt not saye so, lest I take the with a manifest lye. What then did Cicero? he laborethe in the Latin tongue, as Aristotle before hym did in the Greke, and thou enuious felowe ought to do in thy mother tongue what so euer it be, to witte he amplified his natiue tongue, thinking no shame to borrowe from the Hebrucians and Grecians suche wordes as his mother tongue was indigent of. What, shall we thinke shame to borrowe eyther of the Latin or Greke, more then the learned Cicero did? or finde some fitt wordes in our owne tongue able to expresse our meaning as Aristotle did? shall we I saye be more vnkynde to our natiue tongue and countrey then was thiese men to theirs? But thou wilt saye, our tongue is barbarous, and theirs is eloquent? I aunswere thee as Anacharsis did to the Athenienses, who called his Scithian tongue barbarous, yea sayethe he, Anacharsis is barbarous amongest the Athenienses, and so are the Athenienses amongest the Scythyans, by the which aunswere he signified that euery mans tongue is eloquent ynoughe for hym self, and that others in respect of it is had as barbarous.

The translator here advocates the method of borrowing words from Latin and Greek to remedy the deficiencies of the English vocabulary, and also mentions the possibility of finding 'fitt wordes in our owne tongue', i.e. adapting existing words to new uses. In fact there were in the 16th century opposing schools of thought about vocabulary-expansion, and three main methods were advocated: (1) The borrowing of words from other languages, especially the classical languages; (2) The coining of words from native elements (by affixation, compounding); (3) The revival of obsolete words, and the adoption of dialect-words into the standard language. The whole process was highly conscious; Spenser, for example, was not just acting on individual whim when he used archaisms and dialect-words in his poetry: he was part of a whole movement. The preface to *The Shepherd's Calendar* (1579), in which one of Spenser's friends ('E.K.') attacks the borrowing of words from foreign languages and justifies the use of archaisms, is just one document in a controversy that raged for decades.

The disadvantage of words borrowed from Latin or Greek was that they were likely to be opaque to the reader lacking a classical education – precisely the reader aimed at by the translators and popularizers. The coiners and early users of new learned words are therefore often careful to paraphrase them. There is a well-known passage in Sir Thomas Elyot's *The Governour* (1531) in which he speaks of 'an excellent vertue where vnto we lacke a name in englisshe', and thereupon coins a name for it:

Wherfore I am constrained to vsurpe a latine worde, callying it *Maturitie*: which worde, though it be strange and darke, yet by declaring the vertue in a fewe mo wordes, the name ones brought in custome, shall be as facile to vnderstande as other wordes late commen out of Italy and Fraunce, and made denizins among vs.

He then explains at length what he means by the word, and concludes: 'And this do I nowe remembre [i.e. record, mention] for the necessary augmentation of our language'.

The defenders of native coinages could argue that their new words were more easily comprehensible to the ordinary reader. This argument was used by Ralph Lever in his book on logic, *The Arte of Reason, rightly termed, Witcraft* (1573). Lever puts his principles into practice by coining new compound words to translate the technical terms of logic found in Latin. Examples of his coinages are *endsay* ('conclusio'), *foresays* ('premissae'), *ifsay* ('propositio conditionalis'), *naysay* ('negatio'), *saywhat* ('definitio'), *shewsay* ('propositio'), and *yeasay* ('affirmatio'). None of these has survived, and today we in fact use anglicized forms of the Latin words that Lever was translating – *conclusion, premises, negation, conditional proposition*, etc.; some of these indeed already existed in

Lever's time, though not all of them were yet used as technical terms of logic. And in general it is true that, in the eModE period, the usual way of coining technical and scientific terms was by borrowing words from Latin or Greek, or inventing words from Latin or Greek elements. In form, such coinages are often influenced by earlier English borrowings from French; for example, Elyot says that his new word *maturity* is borrowed from the Latin, presumably meaning *maturitas* (though the only Latin word he actually quotes in his discussion is *maturum*); but *maturity* has the ending -*ity* typical of words borrowed from French, and could well be from the French *maturité* (itself of course derived from Latin). Indeed, it is often difficult to say whether a word has been borrowed from Latin direct, or whether it has come from French. In the Ramus passage quoted earlier, there are four words which the Oxford English Dictionary does not record as being in use before the 16th century. Three of them are coined from Latin elements: *barbarous* (1526), *Latinist* (1538), and *extant* (1545), though the ending -*ous* of *barbarous* shows the influence of French. The fourth, *decent* (1539), while ultimately deriving from Latin, has probably come via French. However, it also happened that words which had been borrowed from French in the ME period were reshaped in the eModE period under the influence of Latin. Two examples in the Ramus passage are *perfecte* and *peraduenture*; the ME forms are *parfit* and *perauenture*, derived from the French; the modern forms are Renaissance remodellings under the influence of Latin *perfectum* and *aduenire*.

Of course, not all the new words derived from Latin were the coinages of translators and popularizers. The expansion of knowledge and the rise of the natural sciences inevitably led to word-formation; there are many new scientific words, like *pollen* (1523), *vacuum* (1550), *equilibrium* (1608), and *momentum* (1699), and the mathematical terms like *area* (1538), *radius* (1597), *series* (1611), and *calculus* (1672); though the earliest uses of such terms are not always the technical ones. There are also Latin loans in other spheres, for example legal terms like *alias* (1535), *caveat* (1557), and *affidavit* (1622), and even relatively ordinary words like *miser* (1542), *circus* (1546), and *album* (1651). Moreover, many Latin loans, far from being utilitarian, were an expression of linguistic exuberance, a love of the high-sounding or pompous word. Richard Mulcaster, writing in 1582, speaks of the words which the English language 'boroweth daielie from foren tungs, either of pure necessitie in new matteres, or of mere brauerie, to garnish itself withall', where *mere brauerie* means something like 'sheer ostentation'. Even writers who approve of Latin loans often attack the extravagances of such coinages, which are condemned as 'ink-horn terms'; and dramatists ridicule the pompous affecters of Latinisms, like Holofernes in Shakespeare's *Love's Labour's Lost*. But ridicule of excesses did not of course stop the great influx of Latin loans, which was at its peak round about 1600.

While Latin was the main source of new loan words in the eModE period, other languages were also drawn on. From classical Greek came especially technical terms of rhetoric, literary criticism, and the natural sciences; examples are *phrase* (1530), *rhapsody* (1542), *larynx* (1578), *pathos* (1591), and *cosmos* (1650). Of the living languages, the most influential was French, followed by Italian, Spanish, and Dutch. Many of the French loans were military or naval, but there were also many words connected with the arts, fashion, and social life, especially in the late 17th century; examples are *pioneer* (1523), *sally* (1542), *bourgeois* (1564), *volley* (1573), *stockade* (1614), *parterre* (1639), *crayon* (1644), *ballet* (1667), *commandant* (1687), and *denim* (1695). The Italian loans too were often military, like *squadron* (1562), *parapet* (1590), and *barrack* (1686); there were also words from commerce, like *traffic* (1506) and *mercantile* (1642), and from the arts and architecture, like *cupola* (1549), *stucco* (1598), and *opera* (1644). Fewer words were borrowed from Spanish, but here too warfare and commerce were prominent, as in *cask* (1557), *comrade* (1591), *parade* (1656), and *cargo* (1657). Of the Dutch words, many are to do with seafaring, like *dock* (1513), *sloop* (1629), and *cruise* (1651); there are also words to do with the visual arts, especially in the 17th century, e.g. *easel* (1654), *stipple* (1669).

The Expansion of the Vocabulary: Word-formation

It was the flood of loan-words which caught the attention of Shakespeare and his contemporaries, and led to bitter arguments, but in fact an even greater expansion of the vocabulary took place in the Early Modern period by means of affixation, compounding, and conversion. Indeed, the examination of a 2% sample of entries in the Oxford English Dictionary suggests that more new words were produced by affixation alone than by borrowing from all languages put together. The common productive suffixes included *-ness* and *-er* for forming nouns, *-ed* and *-y* for adjectives, *-ly* for adverbs, and *-ize* for verbs. Active prefixes included *be-*, *counter-*, *dis-*, *en-*, *fore-*, *inter-*, *re-*, and *under-*; by far the commonest prefix, however, was *un-*, which was used freely with nouns, adjectives, verbs, adverbs, and participles. Enormous numbers of such coinages are recorded in the OED, which attributes to Shakespeare alone the first use of no fewer than 164 words beginning with *un-*. In many cases the elements used in affixation had originally been loans, but had since become naturalized in English: the adjective *comfortable* had been borrowed from the French in the fourteenth century; in 1592 the adjective *uncomfortable* was formed from it by means of the native prefix *un-*. And almost any adjective borrowed from abroad will eventually have an adverb formed from it, using the suffix *-ly*, as with *immature* (1548), *immaturely* (1620).

Compounding was especially used to produce new nouns, often everyday practical words to do with such things as agriculture, the mechanical arts, seamanship, plant-names, and names for people (especially opprobrious ones). Examples are *bawdy-basket* ('hawker of indecent literature') (1567), *Frenchwoman* (1593), *heaving-net* (1584), *lung-flower* (1597), *pinch-fart* ('miser') (1592), and *sheep-brand* (1578).

Conversion (or zero-morpheme derivation) is the process whereby one word is created from another without any change of form, as when, in the opening speech of *Henry IV Part 1*, Shakespeare takes the noun *channel* (a Middle English loan) and converts it into a verb ('No more shall trenching Warre channell her fields'). The formation of verbs from nouns was the commonest type in the Early Modern period, but it was also reasonably common to form nouns from adjectives and from verbs, as when the noun *brisk* ('a fop') (1621) was formed from the adjective, and the noun *scratch* (1586) was formed from the verb.

All in all, the influx of words during the eModE period was enormous. An examination of the *OED* suggests that, during the Early Modern period, the vocabluary of English more than doubled. This enormous expansion of the vocaculary sets a problem for the reader of eModE literature. When we meet a word in the literature, it is often difficult to judge how it struck the original readers: a word that to us seems quite ordinary or neutral may then have sounded affected, or startling, or delightfully new. Some of the words that were condemned by contemporary critics as pompous or affected now sound quite unobjectionable; for example, words ridiculed by Ben Jonson in *Poetaster* include *strenuous* and *spurious*, which to us are not self-evidently absurd.

Another difficulty for the reader of Renaissance literature, of course, is the fact that many words have changed their meanings since that time. Examples can be seen in the Ramus passage already quoted. The word *decent* there means 'suitable, decorous'; *close*, as often in this period, means 'secret, hidden'; *straunge* means 'foreign'; and so on. Particularly difficult are the words that have behind them a whole way of looking at the world which has now passed away; such is the word *vnkynde*, which means 'unnatural', and implies a whole view of what constitutes naturalness in human behaviour.

The Grammar of Early Modern English

With vocabulary, we are concerned with what are sometimes called 'open-ended' word-classes (nouns, verbs, adjectives and adverbs) whose members cannot be listed exhaustively – since, after all, any speaker of the language can invent a new one at any time. In grammar, by contrast, we are dealing with closed systems containing relatively few members, which can be listed exhaustively: word-classes like pronouns, determiners, conjunctions, auxiliaries; sets of inflections; permissible phrase- and sentence-patterns; and so on.

In eModE the system of determiners had reached very much its present-day form. DETERMINERS are the grammatical words used to mark nouns, like. *the, a, each, any, my.* One important group of determiners in English is formed by the DEMONSTRATIVES. Modern English has a three-term system of demonstratives, *the/this/that*; Old English on the other hand had a two-term system, *se/þes*. The two OE demonstratives had a large number of different forms, which were selected according to the gender, number, and case of the following noun. The three ModE demonstratives, on the other hand, have few forms: *this* and *that* have plural forms *these* and *those*, and *the* has a single invariable form. The modern situation was reached in about 1500. In Early Middle English, there were still numerous forms of *se*, like *þone* (accusative singular masculine) in the passage quoted by Professor Bolton, on p 238, but in the course of the ME period *the* established itself as the normal form, though even at the end of the ME period we sometimes find a plural form *tho*. But in the early 16th century even *tho* disappears from the standard language, and *the* becomes the sole form. The demonstrative *that* (OE *þæt*) was originally the neuter of *se*, but in Early Middle English it broke away and became a contrasting demonstrative; in Late Middle English it appropriated to itself the plural *those*, which originally had been the plural of OE *þes*. From other forms of *þes* comes the ModE plural *these*, which spread from the Midland dialects and was in general use by about 1500.

We perhaps ought to say that in eModE there was in fact a four-term system of demonstratives, for in addition to *the/this/that* it had *yon*, as in Shakespeare's 'see how yon Iustice railes vpon yon simple theefe' (*King Lear* IV. vi). There is an OE form *geon*, but it is rare, and its grammatical status is uncertain. Its descendant *yon* (with a ME variant *yonder*) occurs as a determiner in ME and eModE; like *that*, it means 'the one over there' or 'the one further away', but it carries the additional implication 'and in sight'. Outside Scots, it does not survive in lModE except as an archaism.

The remaining determiners were also in much their present-day form by the 16th century. One difference, however, is that the form *its* is not found in the 16th century, *his* being used instead, as in Old and Middle English; *its* is not found before the 17th century, is very rare in Shakespeare, and does not occur in the A.V.; so in the A.V. we find 'But if the salt haue lost *his* sauour, wherewith shall *it* be salted?' (*Matthew* V.xiii). Throughout the eModE period, the determiners *my* and *thy* have alternative forms *mine* and *thine*, which occur only before vowels; so we find *my father* but *mine uncle*. But *my* and *thy*, orignally used only before consonants, tend more and more to occur also before vowels, and to displace *mine* and *thine*. In Shakespeare, both types are found before vowels, as in *mine eye, my eye*.

Although the system of determiners was in very much its present-day form by the 16th century, the phrase-structures in which the determiners occurred sometimes differed from ours. Shakespeare for example has 'At each his needlesse heauings' (*Winter's Tale* II.iii), 'of euery/These happend accidents' (*Tempest* V.i); the A.V. has 'Art thou that my lord Eliiah?' (*I Kings* XVIII.vii); these all have sequences of determiners not now possible. And in vocatives we find phrases like 'Dear my lord', 'O poor our sex', where the determiner comes between the adjective and the noun.

In the Ramus passage, the word *who* occurs as a relative pronoun ('the Athenienses, *who* called . . .'); this usage is not found before Modern English times. Earlier, *who* (OE *hwā*) was interrogative or indefinite, never relative. In the course of Middle English, the inflected forms *whom* and *whose* came to be used as relatives, but the nominative *who* was not used in this way until the 16th century. The common relatives in Middle English were *that*, *which*, and *the which*; these continued to be used in eModE alongside *who*, as can be seen from the Ramus passage, where all three occur. In eModE, *which* could be used to refer to persons, a use which is not now possible; Shakespeare writes 'The Mistris which I serue' (*Tempest* III.i), and in the A.V. the Lord's Prayer begins 'Our father which art in heaven' (*Matthew* VI.ix). The present-day regulation of *who, which,* and *that* is not reached until the lModE period.

In the Ramus passage, nouns regularly form their plural by adding -*s* or -*es* (*thinges, tongues, Phisitions,* etc.). In ME, the plural ending -*n* or -*en* had been general in the south, but it was gradually displaced by the northern -*(e)s*. In Chaucer, -*(e)s* is the most frequent plural ending, though the -*(e)n* plural occurs sometimes, as in *eyen* 'eyes', *foon* 'foes', *eldren* 'ancestors', *doghtren* 'daughters'. In eModE, the -*(e)s* plural has become the normal form (in the early 16th century often spelt -*ys*). There are indeed a few -*(e)n* plurals in eModE, like *shoon, peasen, hosen, housen,* though they occur only sporadically; a few vestiges remain today, like *oxen* and *children*; but the regular Modern English plural is -*(e)s*, pronounced /s/ or /z/ or /ɪz/ according to the preceding phoneme, and this pattern is established in the standard language in Early Modern times. There are indeed some deviations from the pattern. There are some uninflected plurals descended from OE neuter nouns, like *sheep, deer, swine*; eModE retains rather more of these uninflected plurals, and we sometimes meet plural forms like *horse, thing, winter, lamb*. And throughout the Modern English period we have complicated things by introducing Latin and Greek loan-words complete with their plurals, like *formula/formulæ, phenomenon/phenomena, stratum/strata, nucleus/nuclei*. However, if such words are used frequently, they tend to go over to the regular -*(e)s* plural; an example is *formula*, which has a plural *formulas* beside *formulae*. If a loan-word of this type is used in the plural more often than in the singular, its plural form may come to be used as a singular, since it does not bear the expected mark of the English plural. This seems to be happening to the word *datum*, for *data* is now often treated as a singular ('this data'), and given an -*(e)s* plural ('these datas'). In the 18th century the same thing happened to *strata*, which was given a plural *stratas*, but this has died out.

By Early Modern times, the old dative inflections of the noun had disappeared, and the ending -*(e)s* had been standardized for the genitive, both singular and plural. Since this genitive ending is identical with the plural ending, most ModE nouns have only two forms: *boy* has the baseform /bɔɪ/, and a form /bɔɪz/ which serves for genitive singular and plural and for non-genitive plural. In lModE, of course, we distinguish the three functions of the second form by having three different spellings (*boy's, boys', boys*); and there are in fact a few nouns that have four separate forms, e.g. *man, child*. In the 16th century, there are occasional examples of nouns being uninflected in the genitive: *my father and mother soules; our Lady Day last*. Indeed, *Lady Day* has survived as a set phrase in lModE (cf. *the Lord's Day*), as has another example of the uninflected genitive, which occurs in the Ramus passage, namely *mother tongue* ('mother's language'). In the 16th century there are also numerous examples of the use of *his* after the noun instead of a genitive inflection: 'in a sea-fight 'gainst the Count his gallies' (*Twelfth Night* III.iii). Broadly speaking, however, the inflection of nouns had reached its present state by the 16th century.

Adjectives, which in Old English had been inflected for number, case, and gender, had reached their present state, in which there is a single invariable form, well before the Modern period opened. Changes have continued, however, in the comparison of adjectives. In Old and Middle English, a number of adjectives change the stem-vowel in the comparative and superlative, and occasional examples of these 'mutated' forms are still found in the 16th century, like *long/lenger/lengest* and *strong/strenger/strengest*. However, these died out in the course of the eModE period, and the only relics today are the forms *elder, eldest*. In eModE, comparatives and superlatives often have *-er/-est* where today we use *more/most*: we invariably use *more/most* with polysyllabic words, but in the 16th and 17th centuries we meet forms like *delicatest, notoriousest*; we also select *more/most* with certain disyllabic adjectives, for example those ending in *-ous* or *-ect*, but in eModE there are forms like *perfecter, famousest*. The Modern English tendency for *more/most* to supplant *-er/-est* is still going on. Moreover, in eModE it was possible to use double comparatives and superlatives, and we meet expressions like *more swifter*, and Shakespeare's 'This was the most unkindest cut of all' (*Julius Caesar* III.ii).

As for verb-inflections, many Middle English endings have disappeared by eModE times: whereas Chaucer had infinitives like *to expressen*, the Ramus passage has *to expresse*; Chaucer has imperatives like *Gooth!*, where Shakespeare uses forms like *Go!*; and Chaucer has plural forms like *they diden*, where eModE has *they did*. However, the old northern present-plural in *-(e)s* is still found in the 16th century, and Shakespeare uses it not infrequently, as in 'His teares runs downe his beard' (*Tempest* V.i). It will also be noticed that the Ramus passage has some verb-inflections that are no longer used: it has special forms for concord with *thou*, like *mayest* and *wylt*; and in the third-person singular it does not use *-(e)s*, but *-(e)the* as in *thinkethe, hathe, laborethe*. (The final *-e* was not of course pronounced in eModE, and *-ethe* is merely a spelling-variant of *-eth*.)

However, *-(e)th* was not the universal third-person singular inflection in the 16th century, as is illustrated by the following extract from Shakespeare:

OL. What thinke you of this foole *Maluolio*, doth he not mend?

MAL. Yes, and shall do, till the pangs of death shake him: Infirmity that decaies the wise, doth euer make the better foole.

CLOW. God send you sir, a speedie Infirmity, for the better increasing your folly: Sir *Toby* will be sworn that I am no Fox, but he wil not passe his word for two pence that you are no Foole.

OL. How say you to that *Maluolio*?

MAL. I maruell your Ladyship takes delight in such a barren rascall: I saw him put down the other day, with an ordinary foole, that has no more braine then a stone. Looke you now, he's out of his gard already: vnles you laugh and minister occasion to him, he is gag'd. I protest I take these Wisemen, that crow so at these set kinde of fooles, no better then the fooles Zanies.

OL. O you are sicke of selfe-loue *Maluolio*, and taste with a distemper'd appetite. To be generous, guiltlesse, and of free disposition, is to take those things for Bird-bolts, that you deeme Cannon-bullets: There is no slander in an allow'd foole, though he do nothing but rayle; nor no rayling, in a knowne discreet man, though hee do nothing but reproue.

CLO. Now Mercury indue thee with leasing, for thou speak'st well of fooles.

Enter Maria

MAR. Madam, there is at the gate, a young Gentleman, much desires to speake with you.

OL. From the Count *Orsino*, is it?

MAR. I know not (Madam) 'tis a faire young man, and well attended.

OL. Who of my people hold him in delay?

MAR. Sir *Toby* Madam, your kinsman.

OL. Fetch him off I pray you, he speaks nothing but madman: Fie on him. Go you *Maluolio*; If it be a suit from the Count, I am sicke, or not at home. What you will, to dismisse it.

Exit Maluo

Now you see sir, how your fooling growes old, & people dislike it.
(*Twelfth Night*, I.v)

In that passage, the normal third-singular ending is *-(e)s*, as in *decaies, takes, has, desires, speakes, growes*; there are only two occurrences of *-(e)th*, both in the word *doth*. In Chaucer, by contrast, the normal ending is *-(e)th*. The *-(e)s* ending spread from the north, and it was only in the course of the 16th century that it became the predominant form in the standard language. In the A.V. of 1611, it is true, the -*(e)th* forms are still normal; but the A.V. is archaic in style, and closely follows earlier translations. In Shakespeare, -*(e)s* is decidedly more frequent than -*(e)th*, and the latter is especially found in a few favoured forms, notably *doth* and *hath*. There is indeed evidence to suggest that, in the later 16th century, -*(e)s* was often pronounced even when -*(e)th* was written. For example, William Camden, in 1605, gives an account of Sir Thomas Smith's proposals for spelling-reform, including the use of *z* instead of *s* to represent the pronunciation /z/:

Z; he would haue vsed for the softer S, or eth, and es, as *diz* for dieth, *liz* for lies.

This clearly implies that the spelling -*eth* represents the pronunciation /z/. In any case, the ending -*(e)th* was obviously on its way out in the 16th century, and had disappeared from the normal standard language by the end of the eModE period.

Some third-singular verbs in the passage, however, have no inflection at all: *though he do, if it be*. These are subjunctive forms, which are merely vestigial in lModE but still quite common in eModE. They are found especially in subordinate clauses of condition and concession, and in noun clauses after verbs of requesting and commanding, as in the following sentence from *The Taming of the Shrew*: 'Tell him from me (as he will win my loue)/He *beare* himselfe with honourable action' (I.i.).

In both the Ramus and the *Twelfth Night* passages, all past tenses and past participles of verbs are in their present-day form (disregarding minor differences of spelling): past participles like *kept, come, sworn, gag'd*, past tenses like *wrote, called, saw*. Historically, English verbs can be divided into two main classes: strong verbs, that form their past tense by changing the vowel of the stem (*give, gave*); and weak verbs, that form their past tense by adding a dental suffix to the stem (*walk, walked*). In Old and Middle English, strong verbs had different stem-vowels for the past singular and the past plural: Chaucer writes *he rood* ('he rode'), but *they ryden* ('they rode'). In Modern English, this distinction between past singular and past plural has disappeared, with the sole exception of *was/were*. Sometimes the modern form has the vowel of the old singular, as in *rode*; sometimes it has the vowel of the old past participle, as in *bore*; sometimes it has a vowel that could come either from the past participle or from the old plural, as in *found*. In general, the strong verbs had reached their present form by the 16th century, but eModE does show some divergences from present usage, and in such cases there are usually alternative forms: *he wrote, he writ; he smote, he smot; he flung, he flang; he spoke, he spake;* and so on. In the piece of Sir Thomas Elyot quoted on p 254 above there occurs the past participle *commen* 'come'; this preserves the Old English ending -*en* which was once standard for the past participles of strong verbs but now survives in only a few, like *given*. However, in some cases where lModE preserves the -*en* ending, it is not uncommon in eModE to find an alternative past participle modelled on the past tense, as in *I have wrote*. The prefix *y*- found on past participles in Middle English disappears in eModE; when Spenser, in the late 16th century, uses forms like *ygoe* ('gone') and *ybound* ('bound'), these are intentional archaisms for literary effect.

In general, there has been a tendency in all periods of English for strong verbs to become weak, and for newly formed or borrowed verbs to be declined weak, so that today there are fewer strong verbs than there were in Old English. An example of a strong verb that became weak in the Early Modern period is *climb*; the old strong past tense *clomb* is still found in the 16th century, alongside various other forms like *clam*; but weak forms *climmed* and *climbed* also occur in the 16th century, and *climbed* is the predominant form by about 1600.

The eModE system of personal pronouns shows some changes from Middle English, but is not yet that of lModE. In Middle English, the pronoun of the second person plural was *ye*, of which the accusative form was *you* (originally, like the other accusatives of personal pronouns, a dative form). This distinction between *ye* and *you* is still found in the early 16th century, and is usually maintained in the A.V. of 1611, as in the following passage:

Ye cannot serue God and Mammon. Therfore I say vnto you, Take no thought for your life, what yee shall eate, or what ye shall drinke, nor yet for your body, what yee shall put on. . . . Which of you by taking thought, can adde one cubite vnto his stature? And why take ye thought for raiment?

(*Matthew* VI.xxiv)

There, *ye* and *you* are regularly distinguished in a way exactly parallel to *he* and *him* or *we* and *us*: the form *ye* or *yee* is used for the nominative, and *you* for the accusative (*vnto you, of you*). But, as we have seen, the A.V. is archaic in style, and in fact in ordinary usage the distinction between *ye* and *you* had broken down by the middle of the 16th century, and both forms were used in free variation for either nominative or accusative. For example, the distinction is still preserved in Sir Thomas Elyot's *Governour* (1531), but in Roger Ascham's *Toxophilus* (1545) the two forms are used indiscriminately for the nominative, though *you* is the preferred form for the accusative. In the second half of the 16th century, *ye* tends to be replaced by *you*: it will be noticed that, in the passage quoted from *Twelfth Night* (c. 1600), Shakespeare regularly uses *you* both for nominative and for accusative. However, *ye* continued to occur as a variant until the second half of the 17th century, when it disappeared from the standard language.

Beside *ye/you*, eModE had the pronoun *thou/thee*, as can be seen in the Ramus and Shakespeare passages. Originally, *thou* was singular and *ye* plural, but in the 13th century *ye* came to be used as a respectful singular form for addressing a superior. In Early Modern English, *ye/you* is of course used if more than one person is addressed: it has never been possible to use *thou/thee* as a plural. Among the polite classes, if only one person is addressed, *thou/thee* is used to intimates, to children, and to inferiors; *ye/you* is the polite form used to superiors or to non-intimate equals. To use *thou/thee* to a superior or to a non-intimate equal is insulting; in *Twelfth Night*, Sir Toby advises Sir Andrew to insult Cesario when he writes him a challenge:

taunt him with the license of Inke: if thou thou'st him some thrice, it shall not be amisse.

(III.ii).

It will be seen that the distinction between *thou* and singular *you* is very similar to the difference today between addressing a person by their first name ('Mary', 'Jim') and addressing them formally by their title ('Miss Jones', 'Mr Smith'). However, even in Shakespeare it can be seen that the *thou/you* distinction was beginning to break down, and speakers sometimes switch from one form to the other for no obvious reason. In fact, *thou/thee* was beginning to give way to *you* as the sole second-person pronoun, though *thou/thee* continued in common use to the end of the 17th century. Indeed, the distinction between *thou* and *you* must still have been felt quite strongly in the mid-17th century, or there would have been no point in the Quaker habit of using *thou/thee* to everybody indiscriminately. Originally, it is plain, this was a subversive gesture, a refusal to pay due respect to those in secular authority over you, rather like refusing to remove your hat in the presence of a social superior; indeed, George Fox himself links the two pieces of behaviour when he describes in his *Journal* how in 1652 a Justice was scandalized 'because I did not putt off my hatt and saide thou to him'. However, *thou* fell out of use in the standard language in the 18th century, though it has persisted in regional dialects, and as a literary/poetic form, and also in the special register of prayer.

The third-person plural pronouns *they*, *them*, *their* are Scandinavian loan-words which spread from the north in the course of the ME period. The nominative *they* spread faster than the other two, and we find that Chaucer uses *they*, but not *them* and *their*, in place of which he has *hem* and *hire*, from Old English. But in eModE the spreading process is complete, and *they/them/their* are the normal forms in the standard language. However, *hem* has survived as an unstressed form down to the present day, now written *'em* and pronounced /əm/.

A final point about eModE grammar is more important than it appears at first sight. This is the development of the auxiliary *do*. In the *Twelfth Night* passage there are two different ways of asking questions: Olivia says 'What thinke you?', simply inverting the order of subject and verb, whereas today we say 'What do you think?'; but in the same speech she says 'Doth he not mend?', where the question is formed by putting some part of *do* in front of the subject, in the present-day manner. There is a similar variation in affirmative statements: beside 'the pangs of death shake him' we find 'Infirmity . . . doth euer make the better foole'. In that last sentence, the *doth* is not emphatic: 'Infirmity doth make' is simply a stylistic variant of 'Infirmity maketh'. We find a similar free variation in negative sentences: Maria says 'I know not (Madam)'; but it will be remembered that Hamlet says 'I doe not know/Why yet I liue to say this thing's to doe'. So we see that in eModE there is an auxiliary *do*, but its regulation is not as it is today: whereas today we use *do* in questions and negations, but not in unemphatic affirmations, in eModE it could be inserted or omitted at will in all three types of sentence.

To see the importance of this situation, let us digress for a moment and consider the auxiliaries in Present-day English (PresE). In PresE the auxiliaries are a class of grammatical words, i.e. they form a closed system. There are two types of auxiliary, the non-modals (*be*, *have*, *do*), and the modals (*can*, *could*, *may*, *might*, *shall*, *should*, *will*, *would*, *dare*, *must*, *need*, *ought to*, *used to*). The modals are distinguished by not having the *-(e)s* inflection of the third-person singular: we say *he does* but *he can*. They are also distinguished by position: when modals and non-modals occur together in a verb-phrase, the modal always comes first (*he might have gone; you ought to be going*). Both kinds of auxiliary are of great importance in PresE grammar (see further, chapter 4).

One function of the auxiliaries is in the forming of negative statements. The normal way of negating a sentence in PresE is to put *not* (or its weak form /nt/) after the auxiliary: *She may not come; It isn't raining.* In some cases the auxiliary has a special form when it precedes /nt/: *will* becomes *won't*, *shall* becomes *shan't*, and so on. Another function of the auxiliaries is in the forming of questions. The normal way of asking a question in PresE is to put the subject of the sentence after the auxiliary: *Can she come?; Is it raining?* It will be noticed that this has the effect of preserving the word-order subject-verb (*she come*) which is an important feature of PresE.

The auxiliaries are also used for sentence-emphasis. This is achieved when the auxiliary is given the main stress in the sentence and ordinary falling intonation is used ('John *can* come', 'They *won't* know'). This gives a different effect from stressing any other word in the sentence. If I say '*John* can come' I mean 'John and not somebody else'. If I say 'John can *come*' I mean 'come but not do something else'. In both cases the emphasis singles out just one part of the sentence for contrast. But if I say 'John *can* come' I am not contrasting *can* with some other possible auxiliary, but am under-lining my belief in the truth of the whole sentence, rebutting an assertion to the contrary. (Though a contrast with the auxiliary alone can be achieved by using a rise-fall-rise intonation, giving the meaning 'can but won't'.)

The importance of auxiliary *do* in PresE grammar is that it is the DUMMY auxiliary: it performs the various functions of an auxiliary, but is empty of meaning. So we use it when no other auxiliary has an appropriate meaning. If we want to negate a sentence, or to ask a question, or to achieve sentence-emphasis, and none of the other auxiliaries is required in our sentence, we use auxiliary *do*: 'We didn't go'; 'Do you know him?'; 'But John *does* live there'. These uses of *do* are often found queer and puzzling by foreign learners of English, but in fact they are not queer at all, but entirely in accord with PresE sentence-patterns.

The establishment of the dummy auxiliary *do* was essential for the existence of the system of auxiliaries as we know it. In the absence of a dummy auxiliary, Chaucer has sentences like the following: *I pray yow that ye take it nat agrief* ('I pray you that you do not take it amiss'); *Seyde he nat thus?* ('Did he not say thus?'); *Ware the sonne in his ascencioun/Ne fynde yow nat repleet of humours hoote* ('Beware that the sun in its rising does not find you full of hot humours'). There we have sentences negated and questions asked without an auxiliary being used. Auxiliaries, therefore, lacked the central function that they have today, for they were not the normal means for forming questions and negatives. Indeed, it is not entirely clear that there was a system of auxiliaries in English before the invention of the dummy auxiliary; for, until that event, the items that later became auxiliaries behaved very much like ordinary lexical verbs, and perhaps just were ordinary lexical verbs.

The full establishment of *do* as a dummy auxiliary took place in eModE, but the present-day regulation of its use was not reached until about 1700. The use of *do* followed by the infinitive of a verb is not uncommon in Middle English, but there it is not usually a dummy auxiliary, but has a causative sense. The ME sentence *Wrightes he did make haules & chambres riche* means 'He caused carpenters to make rich halls and chambers'. In the south-western dialects there was a variant of this construction, in which *Wrightes* or the corresponding word is omitted. An example is *a kastelle he did reyse*, which means 'he caused a castle to be built' (it is in fact a translation of the French *Chastel fet lever*). But sentences of this last type are potentially equivocal. If we say *He built a castle*, there is already a causative element in the meaning of *built*, since we do not necessarily mean that he built it with his own hands. So ME sentences like *He did build a castle* would be identical in meaning with sentences like *He built a castle*. Speakers would equate *did build* with *built*. At first the equation would only take place in causative contexts, but before long it would be transferred to non-causative contexts. And at that point *did* had become a semantically empty word, a dummy auxiliary, and *He did build* was merely a stylistic variant of *He built*.

The development of this non-causative use of *do* took place in the south-western dialects round about 1300, and spread from there. At first it was used mainly in poetry, because it was a convenient device for putting a verb into rhyme-position at the end of the line. Then it spread to prose, where it is first found about 1400. It spread slowly in the 15th century, and rapidly in the 16th century, and at the same time the old causative use of *do* died out, its place being taken by *make* and *cause*. In Shakespeare's time, as we have seen, *do* is commonly used as a dummy auxiliary, but its use is not regulated as it is today. This regulation takes place during the 17th century: *do* gradually drops out of affirmative sentences (except for the emphatic use), and comes to be used more and more regularly in negative and interrogative ones, until the present-day situation is reached in about 1700.

The Phonology of Early Modern English

In eModE, just as today, there was great variety of pronunciation. There were regional variations, and even though the educated pronunciation of the London area had great prestige, and was on the way to being recognized as a standard, it was not at all uncommon or disgraceful for gentlemen or noblemen to speak with a regional accent: Sir Walter Raleigh, that eminent courtier, retained a Devon accent to the end of his days. And even within the speech of a regional or social group there were variations of pronunciation, just as there are today. I shall have to confine myself to the pronunciation of the educated classes of the Court and of the south-east of England (which I shall call STANDARD pronunciation). When I refer to ME phonology, I shall mean that form of ME from which the standard form of eModE descended. When I make comparisons with PresE pronunciation, I refer to the British accent known as Received Pronunciation (RP), and in particular to RP in the first half of the 20th century, as described by Daniel Jones.

The long vowels: the Great Vowel Shift

One of the striking changes between Middle English and eModE is in the pronunciation of the long vowels, a change often called the Great Vowel Shift. In Late Middle English there were seven long-vowel phonemes, which we can denote by the symbols /iː/, /eː/, /ɛː/, /aː/, /ɔː/, /oː/, and /uː/. (The dots after each symbol indicate that the vowel is long.) In the Great Vowel Shift these seven long vowels underwent a systematic transformation, which can be illustrated diagrammatically (Fig. 8.1) the arrows showing the direction of change. The diagram is a conventionalized cross-section of the mouth-cavity seen from the left-hand side. Vowels are marked on the diagram as dots, which represent the position of the highest point of the tongue when the vowel is uttered. It will be seen from the arrows that all vowels became progressively closer in quality, i.e. made with the tongue higher. However, this could not happen to /iː/ and /uː/, which were already as close as they could be, and these two vowels became diphthongized; the progressive change in position of the starting-

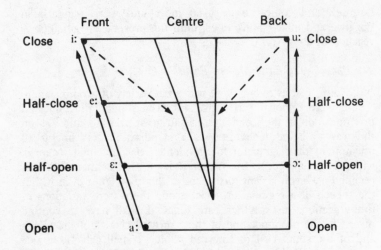

Fig. 8.1. The Great Vowel Shift

point of these diphthongs is suggested by the dotted arrow. The changes involved will perhaps become clearer if we consider each vowel in turn.

Late ME /u:/ was a close back vowel, resembling that of Modern French *vous*, or of PresE *who*. It was usually written *ou* or *ow* (*found, hous, now*). By about 1500 it had become diphthongized to /ʊu/, and in the 17th century it became the /aʊ/ diphthong which it is in PresE. In Shakespeare's time it had not developed quite so far as this, and was probably /əu/, not unlike the vowel in PresE *home*. (The symbol ə represents a central vowel, like that in the *er* of PresE *father*.)

Late ME /ɔ:/ was a half-close back vowel, resembling that of Modern French *chose* or Modern German *wo*. It was written *oo* or *o* (*food, who*). In the 15th century it became closer in quality, and by 1500 it had become /u:/, which it remained.

Late ME /ɔ:/ was a half-open back vowel, resembling that of PresE *law*. In ME it was spelt *oo* or *o* (*goot, hope*), but in Modern English the words that had ME /ɔ:/ are usually spelt with *oa* or *o* (*goat, hope*). In the early 16th century the vowel became closer in quality, until it reached the half-close position /ɔ:/, where it remained until the 18th century.

Similarly with the front vowels, except that here we have to deal with four long vowels where PresE has only three.

Late ME /iː/ was a close front vowel, resembling that of PresE *machine* or Modern French *si*. It was usually spelt *i* or *y* (*tide, tyde, why*). By 1500 it had become diphthongized to /ɪi/, and in the 17th century it became the /aɪ/ diphthong which it is in PresE. In Shakespeare's time it had not developed so far as this, and was probably /əɪ/, starting from a central position.

Late ME /eː/ was a half-close front vowel, resembling that of Modern French *thé* or Modern German *zehn*. It was spelt *ee, e* or *ie* (*green, grene, field*). In the 15th century it became closer in quality, and by about 1500 it became /iː/, where it remained.

Late ME /ɛː/ was a half-open front vowel, resembling that of Modern French *même*, or the first element of PresE *air*. In ME it was spelt *e* or *ee*, but in Modern English the words that had ME /ɛː/ are most often spelt with *ea* (*clean, meal*). In the 15th century it became closer in quality, and round about 1500 it had become /eː/, where it remained throughout the Early Modern period. In PresE, ME /ɛː/ has of course fallen together with ME /eː/, and we have the same vowel in *clean* as in *green*; but in eModE this was not so, and Shakespeare distinguished between *see* /siː/ and *sea* /seː/, between *meet* /miːt/ and *meat* /meːt/. For the modern reader, a good guide (though not an infallible one) is the spelling: the spelling *ea* is characteristic of words which in eModE had the opener vowel, while the spellings *ee* and *ie* are characteristic of words that had the closer vowel.

Finally, Late ME /aː/ was an open front vowel, with a quality like that of the vowel of Modern French *la* or Modern German *Vater*. It was usually written *a* (*bake, dame*). In the 15th century it became closer in quality, and by about 1500 had become /æː/ (like the vowel in PresE *bad*). It continued to become closer during the 16th century, and in Shakespeare's time was probably /ɛː/. However, unlike the other long vowels it did not then remain stable, but continued to become closer, and there is considerable evidence to suggest that, in the second half of the 17th century, it became /eː/, and therefore fell together with ME /ɛː/, so that the same vowel was used in *bake, dame, clean, meat*. This obviously raises problems, since the two phonemes have NOT fallen together in PresE, and we shall return to the point when we deal with Later Modern English phonology.

The following table will serve as a summary of the Great Vowel Shift. It gives the probable pronunciation of seven words for Chaucer, for Shakespeare, and for PresE (RP).

ME Phoneme	Chaucer	Shakespeare	20th Century	Modern Spelling
iː	tiːd	təid	taɪd	tide
eː	greːn	griːn	griːn	green
ɛː	mɛːt	meːt	miːt	meat
aː	maːk	mɛːk	meɪk	make
ɔː	gɔːt	goːt	gəʊt	goat
oː	foːd	fuːd	fuːd	food
uː	huːs	həus	haʊs	house

The short vowels

In contrast to the long vowels, the short vowels have been relatively stable. However, one change occurred in the system of short vowels in eModE: a new short-vowel phoneme arose, giving seven short vowels as compared with the six of Late Middle English.

The six short vowels of Late ME can be denoted by the symbols /ɪ/, /e/, /a/, /ə/, /ɔ/, and /ʊ/. The first of these, /ɪ/, has remained unchanged to the present day; it is the vowel of *bid* /bɪd/, *chin* /tʃɪn/. The second, /e/, is also practically unchanged, though perhaps it has become a little closer in quality since ME times; it is the vowel of *bed* /bed/, *fresh* /freʃ/.

The third, /a/, was a front open vowel, resembling that of Modern French *la*; it occurred in words like *hat* /hat/, *black* /blak/. In the course of the 16th century it became closer in quality, and by 1600 it was /æ/, and there it has remained, giving the PresE pronunciations /hæt/, /blæk/. However, the older quality of the vowel has been retained in Northern England and in much of the Midlands, and there the pronunciations [hat] and [blak] are still normal.

The fourth, /ə/, was a central vowel, like the *er* of PresE *father*. In Late Middle English it occurred only in unstressed syllables, where it arose as the weakened form of various ME short vowels (which explains why we have no regular representation for it in ModE spelling). Throughout the ModE period there has been a tendency for unstressed vowels to become either /ə/ or /ɪ/, but the process had already begun in Late ME, and the /ə/ phoneme was probably well established by the opening of the eModE period. In the course of eModE, /ə/ also came to be used in stressed syllables; in about 1600, the groups /er/ and /ɪr/ both became /ər/ when they preceded a consonant, and later in the 17th century the group /ʊr/ also became /ər/. This situation has not of course persisted in Later Modern English, since the /ə/ has been lengthened in such posi-

tions, and today we once again have /ə/ only in unstressed positions. So at the beginning of the eModE period, *herb* was /herb/,
and *bird* was /bɪrd/; in the early 17th century the pronunciations
were /hərb/ and /bərd/; but today they are /hɜːb/, bɜːd/; and we
have /ə/ only in words like *about* /ə'baʊt/, *father* /'faːðə/.

The fifth, /ɔ/, was about half-open in quality, like the *o* of
Modern German *Sonne*, or like a shortened version of the vowel of
PresE *law*. It occurred in words like *dog* /dɔg/, *fox* /fɔks/. Today,
however, it is /ɒ/, a vowel of much opener quality, very nearly fully
open, as in *dog* /dɒg/, *fox* /fɒks/. The change to an opener quality
took place in the course of eModE, and the very open vowel was
fully accepted in standard speech by the middle of the 17th century.
In some forms of American speech, /ɒ/ is unrounded to [ɑ], giving
pronunciations [dɑg], [fɑks], in which the vowel is rather like the *a*
in RP *father*.

The sixth and last short-vowel phoneme of Middle English,
/ʊ/, had a quality like the vowel of PresE *put, full*. In Later
Modern English it has split into two phonemes, /ʊ/ and /ʌ/. The
phoneme /ʌ/ is the one that occurs in PresE *cut* /kʌt/ and *luck* /
lʌk/; in the 16th century these were /kʊt/ and /lʊk/. To understand the process by which this split probably took place, we must
pause a moment to distinguish between PHONEMES and
ALLOPHONES.

A phoneme is one of the basic units in the sound-system of a
language, like /p/ in PresE. It is contrasted with the other
phonemes of the language, and it is by these contrasts that different
words, different meanings, are distinguished. So, in PresE, /p/
contrasts with /b/ (*pin, bin*), with /f/ (*pin, fin*), and so on. But /p/ is
not always pronounced in the same way in PresE, even by a single
speaker. For example, it is usually followed by an aspiration, a kind
of [h] sound, giving the pronunciation [pʰ]: and *pin* (if you listen
carefully) is in fact pronounced [pʰɪn]. But when the /p/ is preceded by an /s/ belonging to the same syllable, this aspiration is
absent, and the pronunciation is [p]; so *spin* is pronounced [spɪn].
These two variants, [pʰ] and [p] are called ALLOPHONES of the
phoneme /p/. Allophones are contextual variants of a phoneme;
they can never contrast with one another, and hence are never used
to distinguish different words or meanings, which is why the native
speaker is usually unconscious of them (see further, chapter 2).

To return to /ʊ/ and /ʌ/: it is probable that the bifurcation of
/ʊ/ into two phonemes began by its developing two allophones, and
that later these achieved the status of phonemes. In the early part of

the 17th century, the /ʊ/ phoneme developed an allophone [ʌ], which was used in a large number of words like *cut* [kʌt] and *luck* [lʌk]; but in other words, especially in the neighbourhood of certain consonants like /p/ and /l/, the allophone [ʊ] continued to be used, as in *put* [pʊt], *full* [fʊl]. At this stage [ʊ] and [ʌ] were merely contextual variants, but in the mid-17th century other changes occurred which brought them into positions where they contrasted with one another, so that they now constituted two separate phonemes. As an example we can take the words *luck* and *look*. In the 16th century, *luck* was /lʊk/, but it was one of the words where the [ʌ] allophone came to be used, so in the early 17th century it was pronounced [lʌk]. In the 16th century the verb *look* (from OE *lōcian*) quite regularly had a long vowel, and was pronounced /luːk/ (as it still often is in the north of England). But in the 17th century the vowel of *look* underwent shortening, as happened with many monosyllabic words in eModE, and it became /lʊk/. But the shortening of /uː/ produced [ʊ], not [ʌ]; so at this stage there were in English the words *look*, pronounced /lʊk/, and *luck*, pronounced /lʌk/; and so /ʊ/ and /ʌ/ were now separate phonemes, since they served to distinguish these two words.

This may seem a little complicated, but it is worth making an effort with it, because it illustrates an extremely common way in which change takes place in the sound-system of a language: a phoneme develops two or more allophones, contextual variants; then other changes in the language bring these allophones into positions where they contrast with one another, and they become separate phonemes.

Diphthongs

Late ME also had a number of diphthong-phonemes. A DIPHTHONG is a glide-vowel, in which the speech-organs change their positions while the vowel is produced. It can be represented by a digraph, of which the first symbol shows the starting-position of the diphthong, and the second symbol the position towards which the speech-organs move. So the diphthong /ai/ begins with the speech-organs in the position for [a], but almost immediately they glide away in the direction of [ɪ] (though they may not go the whole way).

There were seven diphthongs in Late Middle English: /ai/, /au/, /ɛu/, /iu/, /ɔi/, /ʊi/, and /ɔu/. They underwent various changes in eModE, but there was a general tendency for them to be monophthongized, i.e. to change from diphthongs to pure vowels.

Late ME /aɪ/, which resembled the vowel of PresE *die*, was found in words like *day, nail, rain*. In the 16th century it became /ɛɪ/, and in the first half of the 17th century was monophthongized to /ɛː/; it therefore fell in with the /ɛː/ from ME /aː/, so that we now have the same vowel in *day* and *rain* as in *bake* and *dame*.

Late ME /ɑʊ/, which resembled the vowel of PresE *how*, was found in words like *claw, hawk, cause*. It had a similar history to ME /aɪ/. In the 16th century it was retracted to /ɒʊ/, and in the first half of the 17th century was monophthongized to /ɒː/. In Later Modern English its quality became closer, and it is now the half-open vowel /ɔː/.

Late ME /ɛʊ/ and /ɪʊ/ were still kept distinct in the 16th century; /ɛʊ/ occurred in words like *few, dew, ewe, beauty*, and /ɪʊ/ in words like *new, true, blew, view*, and the two pronunciations were still distinct in Shakespeare's time. However, in the first half of the 17th century /ɛʊ/ became /ɪʊ/, and the two diphthongs fell together. In the second half of the 17th century /ɪʊ/ became /juː/, i.e. with a pronunciation like PresE *you*, and in many positions this still remains, as in *new* /njuː/, *view* /vjuː/, *few* /fjuː/. However, in some positions /juː/ has been simplified to /uː/ in Later Modern English. In PresE we invariably find /uː/ after /r/, as in *rule* /ruːl/; after /dʒ/, as in *June* /dʒuːn/; after /tʃ/, as in *chew* /tʃuː/; and after Consonant + /l/, as in *blue* /bluː/. But in some positions we find alternative forms with either /juː/ or /uː/: so *suit* can be /sjuːt/ or /suːt/; *lute* can be /ljuːt/ or /luːt/; and similarly with *enthusiasm, absolute, resume*. It seems likely that in such positions /uː/ is now in process of displacing /juː/; the younger generation certainly seem to favour /uː/.

The Late ME diphthong /ɔɪ/, found in words like *choice, joy, noise*, has remained unchanged in the Modern English period. However, some words now pronounced with /ɔɪ/, like *boil, destroy, poison*, had alternative pronunciations with Early Modern English /ʊɪ/. In the later 17th century, /ʊɪ/ developed into /aɪ/, and so fell together with the /aɪ/ from ME /iː/. This accounts for early 18th century rhymes like Pope's *join/divine*. However, in the course of the 18th century the /ɔɪ/ pronunciation displaced the /ʊɪ/ pronunciation in such words, the process no doubt being aided by the influence of the spelling.

And finally the Late ME diphthong /ɔʊ/, found in words like *know, own, low*, remained in the early part of the eModE period, but in the 17th century was monophthongized to /ɔː/; this was raised to

/oː/, and so fell together with /oː/ from ME /ɔː/; so that today we have the same pronunciation in *know, own, low* as in *goat, hope.*

The shortening of long vowels

As we have already seen in the case of the word *look*, long vowels were frequently shortened in the Early Modern period. The shortening is sporadic, so that it is difficult to lay down rules for it, but it is particularly common in monosyllabic words ending with a single consonant, like *sieve, grit, dead, sweat, blood, cook, hot.* As can be seen, it is often (but not always) possible to detect these shortenings from the spelling: as the spellings suggest, *sieve* had ME /eː/, *dead* and *sweat* ME /ɛː/, *blood* and *cook* ME /oː/. But we could not have guessed from the spellings that *grit* had ME /eː/ and *hot* ME /ɔː/.

The vowel that results from the shortening may depend on the date at which the shortening took place. If ME /eː/ was shortened during the Early ME period, it resulted in /e/: the words *friend, depth, fellow, kept* all had /eː/ in Early Middle English, but Early ME shortening produced /e/. But at the beginning of the eModE period, ME /eː/ became /iː/, and the shortening of this is ModE /ɪ/; examples are the words *riddle, nickname, sieve* and *grit*, all of which had ME /eː/, and which underwent shortening in late ME or Early Modern English. Again, the words *blood* and *cook* both had ME /oː/ (= eModE /uː/), but one has PresE /ʌ/, the other /ʊ/. The earlier shortening is *blood*; it changed from /bluːd/ to /blʊd/ before the allophone [ʌ] had developed, and so shared in this development; but *cook* was shortened from /kuːk/ to /kʊk/ after the distinction between [ʊ] and [ʌ] had already been established, and therefore remained /kʊk/.

Many words fluctuated in eModE, some people using a long vowel, others a short. The spelling is a good guide to the most frequent eModE pronunciation.

The consonants of Early Modern English

Two new consonant phonemes arose in eModE, namely /ŋ/, the phoneme that occurs in PresE *sing* /sɪŋ/ and *sink* /sɪŋk/, and /ʒ/, the phoneme that occurs in words like PresE *vision* /ˈvɪʒən/. The pronunciation [ŋ] did indeed exist in Middle English, but it was not an independent phoneme: it was simply an allophone of the phoneme /n/, the variant of /n/ that occurred before /k/ and /g/.

In ME the pronunciation of *sing* was [sɪŋg], but in the 16th century the final /g/ was lost in such words, giving the PresE pronunciation /sɪŋ/. When this happened, /ŋ/ became an independent phoneme, for there were now contrasting words like *sing* /sɪŋ/ and *sin* /sɪn/, where the contrast depends solely on the distinction between /n/ /and /ŋ/. The /g/ was not lost in medial position, however, as can be seen in words such as PresE *finger* /'fɪŋgə/ and *longer* /'lɒŋgə/. PresE words in which the medial /g/ is missing are re-formations: for example the word *singer* /'sɪŋə/ is a new formation from the verb *sing*. The simplification of final /ŋg/ to /ŋ/ did not occur in some regional dialects, and pronunciations like /sɪŋg/ are still commonly heard in an area stretching from the West Midlands to South Lancashire.

The phoneme /ʒ/ arose from earlier /zj/. In the course of the eModE period, the word *vision* developed from /'vɪzjʊn/ to/ 'vɪʒən/; and similarly with such words as *azure, measure, leisure, transition,* and *visual*. In ME, the group /zj/ normally occurred only in a medial position after a stressed vowel; in consequence, the phoneme /ʒ/ in ModE is largely restricted to this position. In recent French loans, however, it is now also sometimes heard in word-final position, as in *beige, garage, rouge,* and *prestige*.

Otherwise, the consonant-system of eModE differs from that of ME mainly in the distribution of the consonant-phonemes; in particular, the positions which some consonants could occupy became more restricted in eModE. An example is the phoneme /h/. In late ME this had an allophone [h] which occurred in syllable-initial position, as in *hawk, behind,* just as in PresE. But /h/ (written ȝ or *gh*) could also occur in syllable-final position (*plough, ploȝ* 'plough', *laughen, lauȝen* 'to laugh'), and before /t/ (*light, liȝt* 'light', *doughter, doȝter* 'daughter'). In these positions it had allophones [ç] and [x] (as in Modern German *ich* and *ach*), which occurred after front vowels and after back vowels respectively. But at the beginning of the eModE period the /h/ phoneme disappeared in all positions except the syllable-initial one (though before it did so it often lengthened the preceding vowel). In most cases, PresE has no consonant at all in these positions (*light, daughter, plough, high*), but in some words we have /f/ (*enough, draught, dwarf*), which stems from a dialectal variant.

Another example of restrictions on consonant position is provided by /g/ and /k/. In Middle English these could occur initially before /n/, as in *gnawen* /'gnɑʊən/ 'to gnaw' and *knelen* /'kneːlən/ 'to kneel', but in the course of the Early Modern period the initial plosive disappeared, leading to the PresE pronunciations /nɔː/ and /niːl/. It was also common for clusters of three consonants to be simplified by the loss of the middle one; an example of this is /t/, which disappeared when the preceding consonant was /s/ or /f/and the following consonant was /l/ or /m/ or /n/, as in *bristle, chestnut, Christmas, soften*. The semivowel /w/ also disappeared from certain positions in eModE: in the initial cluster /wr/, as in *write, wrap*; between a consonant and a back rounded vowel, as in *sword* and *two*; and in the first syllable of the second element of compound words, as in *boatswain, Greenwich*. It will be noticed that when consonants are lost in eModE our present-day spelling tends to preserve the evidence of the earlier pronunciation. In some cases the influence of the spelling has led to the restoration of the lost consonant in Later Modern English pronunciation, as in *awkward, forward, housewife*, in which a lost /w/has been restored in the standard language (though *hussy* and *hussif* still exist alongside *housewife*).

Stress, rhythm, intonation
It is difficult to be certain about features like stress, rhythm, and intonation, when we are dealing with a stage of the language before the invention of the gramophone and the tape-recorder; but on the whole it seems likely that in these respects the system of eModE was not markedly different from that of PresE. But there are of course differences of detail. It is clear, for example, that in eModE many individual words had stress-patterns different from their present ones. When Hamlet refers to the Ghost as clad 'in compleat steele', we can be pretty sure that the adjective was stressed on the first syllable. And the attentive reader of Renaissance poetry will soon be familiar with words like *re'venue, en'vy* (verb), *ad'vertising, auth'orize, char'acter (*verb) *'commendable, 'confine* (noun), *con'jure, 'construe* – words where, either regularly or sporadically, the stress-pattern is different from ours.

Moreover, many words had an alternative form with one more stress than today. This was especially the case with polysyllabic words, such as *argument, ignorance, immediately, majesty, pilgrimage* and *temperate*, all of which could have a secondary stress on the final syllable. What is more, when the final syllable was stressed it had a full vowel, so that these six words were exact rhymes to *went, advance, fly, sky, age*, and *date*. In some cases, words of this type had an extra syllable when they had the secondary stress. This happened when there was a syllable consisting of the vowel /ɪ/ immediately before the vowel with the secondary stress. If the secondary stress was lost, the /ɪ/ became /j/, and ceased to be syllabic. So *imagination* could have six syllables (*i-ma-gi-na-si-on*), with stresses on the second, fourth, and sixth; but if the stress on the final syllable was lost, the word had only five syllables, as today.

II

LATER MODERN ENGLISH

By the 18th century, English had reached very much its present form, as the following passage illustrates; it is an extract from a letter from Swift to Pope, written in 1736:

Pray do not use me so ill any more . . . I have nobody now left but you. Pray be so kind as to outlive me, and then die as soon as you please, but without pain; and let us meet in a better place, if my religion will permit, but rather my virtue, although much unequal to yours. Pray let my Lord Bathurst know how much I love him. I still insist on his remembering me, although he is too much in the world to honour an absent friend with his letters. My state of health is not to boast of; my giddiness is more or less too constant; I have not an ounce of flesh between skin and bone; I sleep ill, and have a poor appetite. I can as easily write a poem in the Chinese language as my own. I am as fit for matrimony as invention; and yet I have daily schemes for innumerable essays in prose, and proceed sometimes to no less than half a dozen lines, which the next morning become waste paper. What vexes me most is, that my female friends, who could bear me very well a dozen years ago, have now forsaken me, although I am not so old in proportion to them, as I formerly was, which I can prove by arithmetic, for then I was double their age, which now I am not. Pray put me out of fear as soon as you can, about that ugly report of your illness; and let me know who this Cheselden is, that has so lately sprung up in your favour. Give me also some account of your neighbour who writ to me from Bath . . . Farewell, my dearest friend, ever, and upon every account that can create friendship and esteem.

In vocabulary, that seems thoroughly familiar to the present-day reader. In grammar it differs little from PresE: the sole second- person pronoun is *you*; the third-singular inflection is invariably *-(e)s* (*vexes, has*); and auxiliary *do* is regulated in the present-day manner (*do not use me*). There is indeed one past tense of a strong verb which is archaic (*writ* for *wrote*); and a present-day writer would probably put *badly* instead of *ill*, and would probably not use the construction *is not to boast of*. But such differences are minor.

Swift's spelling, too, is standardized in accordance with present-day conventions. In the 16th century, spelling varied a good deal from writer to writer, and even within the work of a single writer. But there were forces making for standardization (like printing), and there were a good many generally accepted spelling- conventions. Those conventions, however, often differed from our own. For example, *u* and *v* could both be used either for the consonant or for the vowel, and it was normal to use *v* at the beginning of a word (*voice, vnto*) and *u* elsewhere (*cause, giue*). Standardization did not take place until the second half of the 17th century, and the spellings then established were on the whole the ones we still use.

In 'polite' circles in the 18th century there were also ambitions to 'correct' and 'fix' the language in other ways – to remove what were considered corruptions and deficiencies, and then to establish its vocabulary, grammar, and pronunciation once and for all, possibly by means of an Academy. Such ambitions are delusive: no language which is being used can be prevented from changing. But it is from this period that we inherit the prescriptive attitudes towards the language which have been so influential in the last couple of centuries.

Although the Swift passage looks extremely modern, change has of course continued to take place during the lModE period, in vocabulary, in grammar, and in pronunciation.

The vocabulary of Later Modern English

During the Later Modern period, the vocabulary of English has continued to expand, and indeed at the present time the expansion seems to be going on at a prodigious rate. As in the Early Modern period, we have continued to form numerous words from Latin and Greek elements; this method is used especially for learned words, and in particular for the vocabulary of science, which has expanded at an ever-increasing rate. Much of the vocabulary of the sciences, of course, never moves outside the narrow specialist sphere, but some scientific words gain a more general currency, like *gene, oxygen, molecule, hibernate, conifer, metabolism, isotope*. Words will move into general use if they bear closely on everyday problems of health and the treatment of disease (*vitamin, penicillin, antibiotic*), or if they are connected with widely used products of technology (*nylon, transistor, television*). When they do move into general currency, they are quite likely to change their meanings: to the man in the street, a *transistor* is a kind of wireless-set; *atomic* often means 'powerful, shattering'; *allergic* is commonly used to indicate a disinclination or dislike; a man who tells you that he has a *complex* may have no psychological theories about repression; and *syndrome* is now going the same way.

In contrast to ME and eModE, borrowing from living languages has played only a small part in the expansion of the lModE vocabulary. French has remained the most popular source for borrowings, especially for words connected with the arts (*critique, connoisseur, montage*), with clothes and fashion (*rouge, blouse, suede*), with social life (*etiquette, parvenu, élite*), and more recently with motoring and aviation (*garage, hangar, chauffeur, fuselage*). We have borrowed a few more nautical terms from the Dutch (*schooner, caboose*), and from Italian a few more words to do with the arts (*studio, replica, scenario, fiasco*). From German come scientific words, especially in chemistry and mineralogy, like *paraffin, cobalt*, and *quartz*, and a few wartime words like *strafe, blitz, ersatz*. Because of Britain's active part in world trade, we have also borrowed odd words from distant and exotic countries, like *pyjamas* from India, *budgerigar* from Australia, and *raffia* from Indonesia. And we continue to borrow words from abroad when there is some special reason, like *sputnik* from Russian (though *lunik*, surprisingly enough, was not borrowed from Russian, but coined in the United States on the analogy of *sputnik*, and then borrowed back by the Russians).

More important for word-formation in lModE has been affixation – the making of words by the use of prefixes and suffixes. This has been important throughout the history of English, and continues to be so. For example, the prefixes *un-* and *de-* are freely used to create words like *unsympathetic, unfunny, deration, decontrol*. Other prefixes very much alive in the lModE period are *dis-, pre-, anti-, pro-, mis-*; and recent additions to the list include *neo-, pseudo-, crypto-*, and *mini-*. An example of a living suffix is *-ize*, which can be added to adjectives (*national, miniature, tender*) or to nouns (*carbon, vitamin, vapour*) to form new verbs; and from these in turn can be formed abstract nouns in *-ization*, like *nationalization*. Other active suffixes include *-er* (*bumper*), *-ee* (*trainee*), *-ist* (*stockist*), *-y* or *-ie* (*civvy, goalie*), and *-wise*, used for forming adverbs (*computerwise, examinationwise*).

We have also continued to form words by compounding, conversion, and shortening. In compounding, two words are put together and given a single main stress, as in *oilcloth, nosedive, airscrew, postman, paperback*; later, it often happens that changes take place in the pronunciation of the word, and one element ceases to be a free morpheme; this has happened with *postman* (a 16th century formation), which in RP is /ˈpəʊstmən/, not /ˈpəʊstmæn/. Conversion is the process of transferring a word from one grammatical category to another, for example from noun to verb, or from adjective to noun; it has gone on all through the Modern English period, and is particularly active in the present century, producing new verbs like *to feature, to film, to process, to service, to audition, to garage*, and new nouns like *a highup, a must, a handout, knowhow* (the last two being formed from the phrasal verbs *to hand out* and *to know how*). Shortening in Modern English usually consists in dropping the end part of a word, giving forms like *photo, cab*, and *telly*, but sometimes it is the first part of the word that is lost, as in *bus* and *plane*. Sometimes it is not a single word that is shortened, but a phrase, as in *prefab* ('prefabricated house') and *nylons* ('nylon stockings'). The shortened forms sometimes have a spelling-pronunciation, as with *photo* /ˈfəʊtəʊ/ (from *photograph* /ˈfəʊtəɡrɑːf/) and *bra* /brɑː/ (from *brassière* / ˈbræsɪɛə/).

There are other ways in which lModE has acquired new words: by blends (*brunch, motel*); by taking over proper nouns (*cardigan, mackintosh, bikini*); by taking over proprietary trade-names (*thermos, primus*); by means of acronyms (*radar, Nato*); but these are minor sources. Words also move into general currency from regional dialects or from the language of specialized groups within the speech-community; such borrowings are called 'internal loans'. The Industrial Revolution brought a few words from regional dialect into wider circulation, like *bogie* (on railway rolling-stock), *bank* ('hill, gradient'), and *trolley* (originally a Suffolk word). There are also words from lower-class speech and from the language of occupational groups: *gadget* is first known as sailors' slang in the 19th century; *wangle* began as printers' slang; *spiv* has come from the language of race-gangs; and the word *square* ('unaesthetic') has come in from jazzmen's slang. These particular words, perhaps, are not yet fully respectable, but they may become so; we have many words which were once considered low or vulgar, including respectable words like *coax, flimsy, flippant, fun, sham*, and *snob*, all of which were frowned on as vulgarisms in the 18th century.

The grammar of Late Modern English

There have been no major changes in the grammar of English since the 18th century, but a few minor developments. We saw in the Swift passage the use of a past tense *writ*, where we use *wrote*, and there are other examples in the 18th century of past tenses differing from PresE ones – forms like *choosed, creeped, swum, sung, grinded*. Past participles, too, sometimes have different forms in the 18th century, and we meet expressions like *he had spoke*; other examples include past participles like *arose, drove, rode, ran*, and *shook*. Some of these forms persisted into the 19th century.

In the system of auxiliaries, some changes in usage have been going on. The modal auxiliary *can* has been encroaching on the territory of *may*, and it is now common to use *can* in asking or giving permission ('Can I go now?'). In its turn, *may* is encroaching on the territory of *might*; for many of the younger generation in England, the auxiliary *might* hardly exists at all, its place being taken by *may* or *could*; and a few years ago I read in a national newspaper an account of a football-match which had ended in a goalless draw, in which occurred the surprising sentence 'Just before half-time, Leeds United may have scored a goal' (meaning 'they might have scored a goal, they had a chance of scoring a goal'). Similarly, *will* and *would* are encroaching on *shall* and *should*, and the old school-book rule that *I/we shall* denotes futurity while *I/we will* denotes volition is certainly not true; it is common to use *will* with the first person pronouns to denote simply futurity, as in *We will all die some day*.

It seems likely that some of the modal auxiliaries are ceasing to be auxiliaries, and turning into ordinary lexical verbs. The clearest cases are *need* and *dare*; sometimes these are used as auxiliaries (*Need he go? He dare not go*), and sometimes as lexical verbs (*Does he need to go? He doesn't dare to go*); and it seems likely that they are moving into the latter class. The same process is seen in *ought to* and *used to*; these are normally auxiliaries (*Oughtn't he to go? He usedn't to go*), but nowadays they are sometimes used as lexical verbs (*Didn't he ought to go? He didn't used to go*), though these are perhaps still substandard. As lexical verbs, of course, *ought to* and *used to* are odd: their lack of the third-singular inflection *-(e)s* can be explained by saying that they have the past-tense inflection *-(e)d*, but then this inflection ought to be dropped after auxiliary *did* (cf. *he walked*, but *he didn't walk*).

Changes continue in the comparison of adjectives. In the lModE period it has been normal for monosyllabic adjectives to be compared with *-er/-est (ruder, rudest)*, and for polysyllabic adjectives to be compared with *more/most (more beautiful, most beautiful)*. Dissyllabic adjectives have been variable, some taking *-er/-est (clever, narrow, profound, cloudy, common, pleasant,* etc.), and the others *more/most (thoughtful, pleasing, famous, sheepish,* etc.). The tendency during the lModE period has been for *more/most* to encroach on *-er/-est*, and it is now normal to say *It's more common than I thought*, and *He is the most clever of the three*. Among the younger generation, it is even becoming normal to use *more/most* with monosyllables, and you hear things like *He was more rude than I expected*. The trend from *-er/-est* to *more/most* is in line with the broad development of

English over the last thousand years: it is a change from the synthetic to the analytic, from the use of inflections to the use of grammatical words and word-order.

Another development of Modern English which is in the same direction is the proliferation of phrasal verbs, formed from a lexical verb followed by an adverbial particle, like *try out, let on*. They are of course found before Modern English times, but there has been a great expansion of them in the ModE period, and new ones are still being formed. They may be transitive, like *shrug off* or *fall for*, or intransitive, like *lose out* or *butt in*. Sometimes the phrasal verb can be followed by a preposition, giving forms like *walk out on, gang up against, face up to, fix up with, get away with, meet up with*.

However, one change going on in recent times is in the opposite direction: it is becoming more normal to use the -'s genitive inflection of nouns instead of constructions with the preposition *of*. Earlier in the lModE period, people said *the man's face*, but *the face of the clock*. Broadly speaking, the -'s genitive was confined to nouns referring to animate creatures, though there were also other types (*a week's holiday, the water's edge*). However, the recent tendency, at any rate in the written language, has been for the -'s genitive to be used with all types of nouns, and we meet expressions like *the clock's face, the pound's devaluation, evil's power, the game's rules, London's East End*.

The system of determiners has remained stable in the lModE period, but there has been a tendency recently for the definite article to be omitted in a number of positions where formerly it was inserted. In the 19th century, children caught *the mumps* or *the measles*, but nowadays they are more likely just to catch *mumps* or *measles*. People now talk about being *at university*, or of going *to grammar school*. They discuss the *art of theatre* (though they still go *to the theatre*); and similarly with *cinema*. And they enquire whether there has been any change *in Bank Rate*. The similar tendency to say *Government* instead of *the Government* is probably an Anglo-Indianism.

The phonology of Later Modern English

In Later Modern English, there has perhaps been some reduction in the amount by which pronunciation varies. Inside England, for example, the old rural dialects have been dying out, as a consequence of improved communications, greater mobility of population, the establishment of universal education, and more recently the rise of the mass media. Of course there are still class and regional accents in England, but the range of variation is perhaps less than it used to be. One of these accents has continued to be considered standard inside England; in the 18th century, indeed, it was still possible for a self-respecting country gentleman to speak with a regional accent, but this has become rarer. One of the forces making for the propagation of a standard pronunciation has been the public school, the boarding school for the sons of the rich, which has been the favoured means of education for the English gentry at least since the time of Arnold of Rugby in the early Victorian age. The public schools have propagated a pronunciation which, inside England, is non-regional, and is used by upper-class speakers from all parts of the country. This is the pronunciation which, earlier this century, was described by Daniel Jones in his *Pronouncing Dictionary*, and called by him Received Pronunciation (RP). There are signs, however, that nowadays the educated speech of south-eastern England is regarded as a standard, rather than the speech of the public schools. Moreover, as a result of the social changes of the last half-century, educated regional speech has risen in prestige in England, and is quite common among the professional classes. So RP in the old sense seems to be losing its monopoly.

Outside England, of course, RP has no special status. The Scots, the Irish, the Americans, the Australians, and all the other national groups in the English-speaking community, have their own accents, and see no particular virtue in the pronunciation of the English upper classes. During the colonial period, indeed, the language of England had prestige and influence throughout the English-speaking world; but that age is past, and RP is now merely one accent among many. However, it is one of the accents that has been fully described, and whose history has been examined in detail; and in my brief account of lModE phonology I shall concentrate on the standard language of England.

The long vowels

It will be remembered that we were left with a problem about the long vowels at the end of the eModE period. In the late 17th century, ME /aː/ and ME /ɛː/ had fallen together as /eː/, so that *bake* and *mate* had the same vowel as *clean* and *meat*, and were in contrast to ME /eː/, which had become /iː/, as in *green* and *meet*. Whereas in PresE it is not so: on the contrary, it is ME /ɛː/ and ME /eː/ that have fallen together (*clean, meat, green, meet*), and are in contrast to ME /aː/ (*bake, mate*). But if two phonemes have once fallen together, there is no means of unscrambling them again: ordinary speakers do not know the histories of the pronunciations that they use, and are unable to restore distinctions that have vanished in their own speech. So what are we to think? One possible view is that after all ME /a:/ and ME /ɛ:/ did not fall together in the late 17th century, that *bake* and *mate* never did have the same vowel as *clean* and *meat*; and that, on the contrary, at that date ME /ɛ:/, became /i:/, thus falling together with the /i:/ from ME /e:/. This may be right, but it must be said that the evidence for the falling-together of ME /a:/ and ME /ɛ:/ is quite considerable, and is not too easily disposed of. An alternative view, which accommodates this evidence, is that there were two variant styles of pronunciation in eModE: in the style which was standard at that period, ME /a:/ and ME /ɛ:/ fell together in the late 17th century; but there was also a substandard style of speech in which ME /ɛ:/ had fallen together with ME /e:/, perhaps even before the Modern Period had begun, and in which the resulting phoneme was kept distinct from ME /a:/. The modern pronunciation would then result from a change of fashion: in the 18th century, the style which had formerly been substandard became standard, and the old standard style fell out of use. Such a change of style might be explained by regional movements of population, or, more probably, by social changes: the modern style of pronunciation may have been characteristic of the London middle classes, who carried it into the standard language when they rose to positions of power and prominence in English society. If this view is accepted, certain aberrant pronunciations in PresE (*great, steak, break, yea*) can be explained as vestiges of the older style.

In the later 18th century, then, there was a phoneme /i:/ (from ME /e:/ and ME /ɛ:/), and a phoneme /e:/ (from ME /a:/, and also ME /aɪ/). At the end of the 18th century, the /e:/ was diphthongized to /eɪ/, which remains in PresE, as in *bake* /beɪk/, *mate* /meɪt/; but in some styles of speech, like Scots, the pure vowel has remained.

The long back vowels in the 18th century were /u:/, /o:/, and /ɒ:/. At the end of the 18th century the /o:/ was diphthongized to /oʊ/, and in the 20th century this became /əʊ/, as in *goat* /gəʊt/, *home* /həʊm/. The /ɒ:/ phoneme, which was an open rounded back vowel, has become progressively closer during the lModE period, and is now /ɔ:/, a half-open vowel; it is the vowel heard in PresE *law* /lɔ:/, *cause* /kɔ:z/.

During the present century, the close long vowels /i:/ and /u:/

have become diphthongized; Daniel Jones, earlier in the century, described them as long pure vowels, but in educated speech today they are usually pronounced [ii] and [ʊu], especially when the vowel is in final position, as in *see* and *who*. In substandard speech the diphthongization has proceeded further, and one hears pronunciations like [əi] and [əu].

Later Modern English, as we shall see, also has two new long-vowel phonemes that did not exist in eModE. They are /ɜ:/, the vowel that occurs in PresE *bird* /bɜ:d/ and *turn* /tɜ:n/; and /ɑ:/, the vowel of PresE *pass* /pɑ:s/ and *father* /'fɑ:ðə/.

The short vowels
The short vowels have remained reasonably stable. The new short vowel /ʌ/ (as in *cut* and *luck*), which probably began as a moderately close back unrounded vowel, has become opener and moved further forward during the lModE period. Early this century it was still in the back half of the vowel-diagram, but was fairly open; and in recent years it has been moving forward, so that in the speech of the younger generation it is now a central or even front vowel, moving towards the quality of the vowel of Modern French *la*.

There has been a tendency for /æ/ to be lengthened; the lengthening is sporadic, occurring in some speakers but not others, in some words but not others; but it is particularly common in monosyllables ending in a voiced consonant, and some speakers regularly use a fully long [æ:] in words like *bag*, *bad*, and *man*.

In unstressed syllables, there has been a recent tendency for /ə/ to spread at the expense of other vowels, especially /ɪ/. Typical PresE pronunciations are *system* /'sɪstəm/, *ability* /ə'bɪlətɪ/, *kitchen* /'kɪtʃən/, where formerly the pronunciations were /'sɪstɪm/, /ə'bɪlɪtʃ/, /'kɪtʃɪn/. This development is bringing RP more into line with other forms of English speech, like American and Australian, where such /ə/ pronunciations are common.

Lengthening before voiceless fricatives
At the end of the 17th century, the short vowels /æ/ and /ɒ/ were lengthened, in one style of speech, when they occurred before the voiceless fricatives /s/, /f/ and /θ/. The lengthened forms were accepted as standard in the 18th century, but the short vowels have continued to exist alongside them in some varieties of English.

The lengthening of /æ/ was /æ:/, which was later retracted to /a:/, and then to /ɑ:/. So *ask* was early 17th century /æsk/, late 17th century /æ:sk/, 18th century /a:sk/, and 19th century /ɑ:sk/, which it has remained. And similarly *staff* and *bath*, which had early 17th century /æ/, have become PresE /stɑːf/ and /bɑːθ/. The lengthening did not take place if another vowel followed, so we have *class* /klɑːs/, but *classic* /ˈklæsɪk/. The development of 17th century /æ/ to 18th century /aː/, and later to /ɑː/, also took place in some other cases, as in the words *father* and *answer*. As a consequence of the process, we have in lModE a new phoneme, /ɑː/. (Middle English /aː/, it will be remembered, had become /eː/ by the late 17th century, and is now /eɪ/.) However, some forms of English have retained a short vowel before the voiceless fricatives; in northern England you often hear pronunciations like [ask] and [baθ] (where [a] corresponds to RP /æ/). And some forms of English have retained the older lengthened forms: pronunciations like [æːsk] and [bæːθ] are heard in some varieties of American English and pronunciations like [aːsk] and [baːθ] are normal in Australia and New Zealand.

The lengthening of /ɒ/ was /ɒː/, which fell together with the /ɒː/ from ME /au/, and with it developed into PresE /ɔː/. The pronunciation with the long vowel was accepted as standard in the 18th century, but the forms with a short vowel have always continued to exist alongside those with a long, and both pronunciations exist in PresE, as in *cross* /krɔːs, krɒs/, *off* /ɔːf, ɒf/, *broth* /brɔːθ, brɒθ/. At the present time, the pronunciations with the long vowel are dying out, and sound rather old-fashioned.

The loss of /r/

The biggest change in the consonant-system of lModE has been the loss of /r/ when it occurs before a consonant or a pause. In eModE, /r/ was still pronounced in such positions, as in arm /ærm/, *dare* /dɛːr/. But during the 17th century the /r/ was weakened in such positions, and in the mid-18th century it disappeared. At the end of a word, the /r/ was lost only if a pause or a consonant followed; if a vowel followed, the /r/ was retained. So in PresE the word *father*, pronounced in isolation, is /ˈfɑːðə/; *father could* is /ˈfɑːðəkʊd/; but *father and mother* is /ˈfɑːðərənˈmʌðə/.

However, although this change is characteristic of RP, it has not taken place in all forms of English, and indeed the majority of the English-speaking community retain pre-consonantal and final /r/. It is retained, for example, by most American speakers, though there are a few areas where it is lost (the coastal South, eastern New England, New York City).

The consonant /r/ has exercised considerable influence on

preceding vowels during the ModE period. Many of these changes began in the eModE period, and some even in ME; but their full consequences for the phonemic system of English were not apparent until the loss of final and pre-consonantal /r/ in the 18th century, so it has been convenient to defer their consideration until this point. The changes were far-reaching and of many kinds. We can consider briefly three of them: changes of quality, lengthening, and diphthongization.

One of the changes of quality, that of /er/ to /ar/, goes back to Late Middle English. It occurred especially before consonants, and accounts for PresE forms like *farm* and *star* from ME *ferme* and *sterre*. But it occurred somewhat sporadically, and in eModE there are many words which retain /er/. There are also words in which both pronunciations are recorded in eModE; and a few doublets have survived to the present day, like *person/parson, perilous/parlous, university/varsity*.

In the words in which /er/ was retained in eModE, this developed in about 1600 into /ər/, so *herb*, which had been pronounced /erb/, became /ərb/. At about the same date, the group /ɪr/ before a consonant also became /ər/; so *bird*, which had been pronounced /bɪrd/, became /bərd/. In the course of the 17th century, /ʊr/ also became /ər/; *curse* was first /kʊrs/, and then /kʌrs/, and finally /kərs/. In the early 18th century /ə/ was lengthened before /r/ in stressed syllables, and then the /r/ was lost; this gave us the new long-vowel phoneme /ɜ:/ of lModE, as in PresE *herb* /hɜ:b/, *bird* /bɜ:d/, *curse* /kɜ:s/.

In the 17th century, /æ/ and /ɒ/ were lengthened before /r/ when another consonant followed, so *arm* developed from [ærm] to [æ:rm], later [a:rm], and *corn* from /kɒrn/ to /kɒ:rn/. In the case of /æ/, the lengthened vowel must in the first place have been a mere allophone, the variant of /æ/ which appeared before /r/; but when the /r/ disappeared in the 18th century, the long /a:/ became an independent phoneme, since for example the distinction between *am* and *arm* no longer depended on the /r/, but on the vowel, /æm/ as compared with /a:m/. The long /a:/ fell in with the one which had arisen before voiceless fricatives (and which until this time was presumably also only an allophone), and with it developed at the end of the 18th century to /ɑ:/, giving the PresE pronunciation /ɑ:m/. In the case of /ɒ/, the lengthened vowel fell in with /ɒ:/ from ME /aʊ/, and with it developed into PresE /ɔ:/, so that we now have the same vowel in *corn* /kɔ:n/ as in *cause* /kɔ:z/.

And finally diphthongization. In the eModE period, the long

vowels had special allophones which occurred before /r/. These allophones were opener in quality than the normal allophone of the phoneme in question. In the 17th century, we can postulate that *here* /hiːr/ was actually pronounced [hɪːr]; *dare* /deːr/ was [dɛːr]; *roar* /roːr/ was [rɔːr]; and *poor* /puːr/ was [pʊːr]. However, in the course of eModE, an [ə] glide developed between the long vowels and the following /r/, giving the pronunciations [hɪər], [dɛər], [rɔər], and [pʊər]. At this stage, the diphthongs were still only allophones: [ɪə] for example was merely the variant form of /iː/ which happened to occur before /r/. But when the /r/ vanished, in the 18th century, these diphthongs became phonemes in their own right, and are the centering diphthongs of PresE, /ɪə/, /ɛə/, /ɔə/, and /ʊə/. The PresE pronunciations of the four words are /hɪə/, /dɛə/, /rɔə/, /pʊə/.

A similar [ə] glide developed between diphthongs and /r/, so that *fire* and *flour*, which were eModE /fəir/ and /fləur/, have become PresE /faɪə/ and /flaʊə/.

English as a World Language

The expansion of the English language over the world began in the 17th century, with the first American settlements, but it is in the Later Modern English period that this expansion has been really spectacular, and that English has become the principal international language. Until about a century ago, the major speech-area of the language was still Britain, but in about 1850 the population of the United States overtook that of England, and then shot far ahead, so that North America is now (1987) the main centre of the English-speaking community, with some 15 million native speakers in Canada and over 220 million in the United States. The British Isles remain the second most important area (nearly 60 million), followed by Australia (15 million), New Zealand (3 million) and South Africa (over 1 million). English is also important as a second language in many parts of the world, especially in former British colonial possessions like Nigeria and India.

With this expansion, divergent development has taken place, so that there are now distinctively American forms of English, Australian forms, and so on. The most striking differences are in pronunciation, but there are also differences in vocabulary, and small differences in grammar. When a speech-community expands geographically, there is a tendency for the peripheral areas to be the most conservative linguistically, while the original homeland of the language tends to be the most innovative area. And in fact we have

already noticed cases where standard British English has innovations not shared by most peripheral areas: most American
forms of English retain preconsonantal and final /r/, which is lost in
RP; and Australian English retains the 18th century pronunciation
[aː] for the phoneme /ɑː/ (though in this case the speech of
northern England is even more conservative, preserving the even
earlier unlengthened [a]). In grammar, American English preserves
a past participle *gotten* which is more archaic than *got*, the only form
found in standard British English. Even in vocabulary, where the
peripheral areas are most likely to innovate, some items are retained
which have been lost in England; in Australian English, for example, we find old dialect words which no longer survive in England, like *dinkum* 'genuine', *larrikin* 'hooligan', and *fossick* 'seek'.

On the whole, however, the peripheral areas tend to innovate in
vocabulary, because they encounter new objects, new flora and
fauna, new situations. Australian *outback, stockman, swagman,* and
American *rapids, cowboy, groundhog* are the products of a new
geographical setting and a new way of life. Speakers in the
peripheral areas may also encounter speakers of other languages,
from whom words are borrowed. The Australians borrowed words
from the local aboriginal languages, like *dingo, gunyah, billabong.*
North American English has borrowed from Amerindian languages
(e.g. *chipmunk, totem, pow-wow*); from Spanish (e.g. *canyon, ranch,
stampede, desperado);* and from French (e.g. *prairie, rapids, pumpkin*).
And of course similar processes of word-formation – using
affixation, shortening, conversion and so on – go on independently
all the time all over the English-speaking area. Sometimes, as a
consequence, different areas have different words for the same
object: American *railroad, auto, sidewalk, subway,* beside British
railway, car, pavement, underground. But, with the improvements in
international communications, there has come a tendency for such
vocabulary items to become common property; speakers will know
both forms, even if they uses only one themselves; and in some
cases the local form will ultimately be displaced by a more distant
one which is conquering the whole speech-area. American influence, as could be expected, is particularly powerful, and the
English language all over the world now has an enormous number
of words and phrases of American origin, many of which are no
longer thought of as specifically American at all.

If we consider the formal literary language, differences in
grammar between the regional varieties of English are very small.
We have already noticed that American English has a past participle

gotten beside *got*; it also has a past participle *strived* beside *striven*. In the Northern dialects of the United States, the verb *dive* has a past tense *dove*, but in the Midland and Southern dialects it is *dived*, as in Britain. Americans can use impersonal *one*, and then continue with *he* and *his*, as in *If one loses his temper, he should apologize*, where the English would replace *his* and *he* by *one's* and *one*. The English can use a plural verb and plural intensive or reflexive pronoun after a collective noun, as in *The government are considering the matter themselves*, whereas Americans prefer singular forms. There are also differences in the use of prepositions. For example, the English would live *in* King Street, but most Americans would live *on* it (though *in* is heard in New York City, and also in Canada); and the English cater *for* somebody, while the Americans cater *to* them. But, while points of this kind could be multiplied, they are all very minor.

If one turns from the literary language to familiar speech, and especially to less educated speech, the differences in grammar become greater. Even so, one can say that the different regional varieties of English have essentially the same grammatical system.

Differences in pronunciation are greater still. Some varieties of English have the same system of phonemes as RP, but the actual realizations of some phonemes are different. Educated Australian has the same phoneme system as RP, but has rather different qualities for the vowels: for example, the Australian /ɑ:/ is pronounced [a:], much further forward than in RP, somewhat like the vowel in German *Vater*; while the Australian /ɪ/ phoneme is pronounced [i], closer than that of RP, so that to an Englishman it often sounds like /i:/. In some varieties of English, the actual system of phonemes differs in some ways from that of RP; for example, where RP has two phonemes, /ʊ/ and /ʌ/, the speech of northern England has only one, usually realized as some kind of unrounded [u]. In yet other cases, the system of phonemes is the same, but their distribution in actual linguistic forms is different. For example, RP and educated Australian both have an /ə/ phoneme and an /ɪ/ phoneme, but Australian frequently uses /ə/ where RP has /ɪ/: RP *waited* and *loaded* are /'weɪtɪd/ and /'ləʊdɪd/, but in Australian are /'weɪtəd/ and /'ləʊdəd/; and similarly *boxes* is RP /'bɒksɪz/ but Australian / 'bɒksəz/ (which in RP could only be *boxers*). Differences of all three kinds – of realization, of system, of distribution – are found between RP and American English, and also between the different regional varieties of American English. The vast majority of the differences are concerned with the vowels; the consonant-system of English is pretty much the same in all present- day varieties of the language.

During the lModE period, then, English has become a multi-centred language, whereas in eModE (despite the Scots) it was to all intents and purposes single-centred, with London as its focus. It has taken the English a long time to recognize this situation; through most of the lModE period they have tended to assume that their own form of the language is the only 'correct' one, and that other varieties, like the American, are in some way inferior and corrupt; and it is not surprising that the arrogance and provinciality of this attitude have provoked violent nationalist counterblasts, especially from Americans. Things are changing, however, and even the English are at last realizing that the Queen's English has no special divine right. A tolerant acceptance of all regional varieties of English, an accordance of parity of esteem, may not quite have come yet, but at any rate it looks as though it may be on the way.

9

THE SOCIAL CONTEXTS OF ENGLISH: A SOCIOLINGUISTIC APPROACH TO THE LANGUAGE AND LITERATURE

Dick Leith

I

'I have resisted the term sociolinguistics for many years, since it implies that there can be a successful linguistic theory and practice which is not social.' Labov's words, published in 1972, have not only been an inspiration to a generation of linguists unsympathetic to the idealising tendencies of much linguistic theory, but have also prompted a considerable amount of empirically-based research attempting to show the relationships between language and social structures. One result of this research is that we now know more about varieties of English, in different parts of the world, than of any other language. More specifically, our knowledge of BRITISH English has been greatly enriched by recent research into the speech of the great conurbations such as Belfast, Glasgow, Newcastle, Liverpool and London, as well as that of smaller towns and cities like Norwich and Reading. We are now much more aware of the ways in which English usage is affected by such variables as gender, age, social class, and ethnicity. In this chapter I shall attempt to outline some recent advances in our understanding of these matters before going on to suggest how sociolinguistics can be of value in the study of the history of English and in the study of its literature. Central to the chapter is a discussion of the standard variety – its status at the present time, its historical development, and its relationship with literary style (as exemplified in the fiction of D. H. Lawrence).

Throughout their research, sociolinguists have concentrated on spoken varieties of English rather than on its written forms, and more especially on the non-standard speech of the powerless and under-privileged in society. Such research has increased awareness not only of the differences between speech and writing – these are much greater than many people think – but of wider patterns of variation in general, the extent of which can hardly be over-estimated. It could therefore be said that sociolinguists tend to operate with a conception of language that is different from those held by others, non-linguists and linguists alike. Variation, so distrusted by the pedant, is meat and drink to the sociolinguist, who always insists on the importance of social, regional and stylistic dimensions – the who? what? when? where? and in what situation? – affecting usage. This emphasis also exposes the reliance of theoretical linguists on standardized written forms for their arguments (despite their claim to privilege speech over writing). But it is also likely to embarass anybody who embraces the popular mythology about the standard variety. Not only has there been no widespread adoption of the standard variety, as is often assumed; sociolinguistic research reveals how ill-defined the notion of the standard actually is, especially in its spoken manifestations, and how no general statement about its superior richness, complexity or range of distinctions can be made. On the contrary: recent studies show how complex and subtle the patterns in non-standard English are, and how it is the peer-group, rather than the media or formal education, that is most influential in shaping speech-habits, especially in childhood and early adolescence. Young children, in fact, are more aware of the social symbolism of particular varieties – something which the sociolinguist considers to be of vital importance in the description of a language – at a much earlier age than has often been thought. And it is because local, non-standard usages often have profound social values for their users that sociolinguists have tended to use the term VERNACULAR, rather than the more negative NON-STANDARD, when referring to them. VERNACULAR covers not only the linguistic forms themselves, but the social attitudes and norms surrounding their use.

The popular tendency to identify a particular language with a nation or race is, again, less easy to sustain in the light of sociolinguistic inquiry. There has been a marked inclination within English studies – both literary and linguistic – to equate the English language with something called the 'spirit', or 'soul' of Englishness – a tendency derived from the eighteenth-century idea that languages are the pedigrees of nations. The history of English has accordingly often been presented as the 'organic' growth of a language which 'flowered' during the period of 'national' consciousness (often identified with the so-called Early Modern period). From this it is only a short step to the widespread view today that the subsequent history of the language is a narrative of degeneration. Such positions are less tenable once we remember that today English is a world language, that in many parts of the world (e.g. India) our culture-bound distinction between 'native' (or 'first') and second language is less easy to make, and that in some cases (in, for instance, the so-called Afro-Caribbean varieties) the line between dialect and language is a highly controversial matter.

Sociolinguists sometimes take pride in the vast amount of empirical linguistic data that they have amassed, usually by means of the tape-recorder, 'in the field', in contact with 'real' speakers of English. It is certainly true that there is much that is positive and fruitful to emerge from this research. Detailed attention to linguistic variation at a particular time and place, for instance, may help us understand some of the mechanisms of linguistic change. It can also alert us to the importance of distinguishing between what people actually say, what they think they say, and what they think they ought to say; as mentioned above, ATTITUDES to usage must never be overlooked. And we are more likely to gain a greater understanding of problems and issues in education if we know something of the linguistic habits and attitudes of children in schools. However, the practices of sociolinguistic fieldwork generate their own particular problems which sociolinguists are only just beginning to appreciate. One of these is the possible effects of fieldworkers themselves on the informants with whom they interact – an issue particularly likely to be salient when the relationship between language and gender is explored. Another aspect of this research that has often been criticised is the tendency to concentrate on the smallest – and therefore, perhaps, the most trivial – units of linguistic structure, such as sounds. It is units of this kind that are most amenable to quantification – another strong emphasis within sociolinguistic study – and most susceptible to variation; but one outcome of these tendencies is that it is the differences among vernacular varieties that are highlighted rather than what, at other levels, they might have in common. Finally, it is one thing to CORRELATE linguistic items with such sociological categories as class, gender, and ethnicity, and quite another to EXPLAIN such correlations, as some critics have recently pointed out. Many attempts at explanation are sociologically naive, as indeed is the uncritical acceptance of dominant definitions and even stereotypes of social class and gender.

Labov's own pioneering study of the English of New York City, based on the speech of a random sample of its population, showed how certain usages varied according to the socio-economic status of the informant and the situation in which he or she was placed by the field-worker. The well-known New York pronunciation of words like *three* and *thing* with initial /t/ rather than /θ/ was most likely to be produced by lower-status groups in situations where attention was less on the FORM of an utterance (as it would be, for instance, when reading from a list of isolated words) than on the content of what was being said (as when relating a narrative of personal experience). ALL social groups, however, used at least a few /t/-pronunciations, and likewise all groups tended to shift away from this usage when placed in more 'formal' situations. Labov concluded from this that the population of New York city generally shared the same ideas about 'correctness' in pronunciation, and that certain usages were not only identified in the popular imagination with particular social groups, but were also sensitive to shifts in situation. Thus /t/ in *thing* etc. was both an INDICATOR of low social status and a MARKER, in that its incidence fluctuated in a predictable way according to the situation.

Another variable, the presence of /r/ in word-final or preconsonantal position as in *car* and *card*, was found to be socially salient in other ways. To sound the /r/ in these phonological environments was not traditional in New York speech, but since the Second World War it has been considered prestigious. The speech of the higher socio-economic groups is most likely to show this feature since it is among these groups that the usage has been introduced to the city. What Labov classifies as lower middle-class speakers, however, appear to be so anxious to identify with this usage that in the most 'formal' situations their speech contains a HIGHER proportion of '/r/-pronunciations' than the group above them in the status hierarchy. Lower middle class usage has accordingly been described as 'hyper-correct'. One conclusion that Labov drew from this finding was that the spread of certain linguistic items through time could be related to the behaviour of particular social groups. Sociolinguistic research could therefore offer insights into the processes of change affecting English in the past.

Why was it, however, that even though all the interviewed speakers in New York appeared to agree on what usages counted as prestigious, many of them persisted with usages that they knew were socially stigmatized? One answer to this is that the stigmatized usages themselves carried their own, 'covert' prestige, because they formed part of the vernacular of local peer-groups. A possible generalization is that people appear to accept at one level the ways in which their own speech is defined by the education system and other official institutions, but at another level they find compensatory ways of valuing it. Thus in Britain in a number of interviews and tests, non-RP speakers have shown that although they may rate RP speakers highly for their 'intelligence' and social standing they do not necessarily regard them as friendly or sincere. In short, the less privileged social groups remain most loyal to the vernacular culture of their local communities.

Recent sociolinguistic studies of British English have sought to investigate more fully the notion of vernacular culture. A major problem, however, has been that definitions of such cultures tend to be based on a popular imagery that is male-centred. The concept of the vernacular culture has been linked with a masculine stereotype of physical toughness associated with heavy industries of the traditional kind such as mining and shipbuilding where collectivism and solidarity are allegedly strong. These cultures are often thought of as generating attitudes that are antipathetic to both so-called 'white-collar' aspirations and to standardised speech (regarded as 'effete'), and which encourage vernacular forms of language, whether dialectal, slang, or taboo. To complete the stereotype, women are seen as isolated from the culture of the work-place, their social status defined by the OCCUPATION of their husbands, and as vulnerable, therefore, to the pressures of linguistic standardization. This model provided an easy explanation for the common observation that the more traditional forms of dialect and the more stigmatized vernacular variants are less likely to be used by women than men, particularly working-class men. Thus, in a sociolinguistic survey of Norwich (Norfolk) during the late 1960s it was the WOMEN informants who told the fieldworker that they used the RP-type /juː/ pronunciation of words like *tune* and *dew* (rather than the local /uː/ variant) more often than recordings of their actual speech indicated; and this could be explained as a desire on their part to identify with the more prestigious pronunciation. Male informants in Norwich, on the other hand, preferred to think of themselves as using the local vernacular variants.

A study of Belfast speech in the 1970s which concentrated entirely on the vernacular of working-class communities found, however, that the model described above actually applied in only one of the city areas investigated – Ballymacarrett, a Protestant community in which a high proportion of the male population was employed in shipbuilding. In contrast with their womenfolk, the men were more likely to work in the same district as they lived, one with which they closely identified and where their (often over-lapping) social networks of kin, friendship, and work-place were strongly based. In this community the norms of Belfast vernacular were most clearly associated with the males. Thus, monosyllabic words like *bet* and *peck*, in which /ɛ/ is followed by a voiceless plosive, tend to have [æ]-type vowels among the men, [ɛ] among the women. The vowel in words like *hat, man* and *back* is subject to a process of raising, retraction, and rounding among working-class men in Ballymacarrett, so that vowels ranging from [ɛ] to [ɔ·ə] can be heard; women, on the other hand, are more likely to use the [a] variant found among middle class people. Men there are also more likely to delete intervocalic [ð] in *mother* and *brother* and to use the strongly local unrounded [ʌ] pronunciation in certain words like *pull, took, look* and *would*. Although in Ballymacarrett the correlation between usage and gender seems clear and stable, it is much less so in areas of West Belfast such as the Catholic Clonard and Pro-testant Hammer districts where the traditional linen industry has declined in the course of the present century and where there is not such a strong distinction between men and women with respect to patterns of work and leisure. Clonard usage is noteworthy, however, in that there it is the older women who tend to use the vernacular [ʌ] vowel in *pull*, etc. more than the men; and it is YOUNGER women there who are introducing the vernacular pronunciation of /a/ – the raised, rounded and retracted variants – into the area. One con-clusion suggested by this data is that it is by no means easy to generalize about the ways in which language patterns with gender: age, for instance, tends to be an interlocking variable, as we shall see more clearly later.

The complexity of Belfast pronunciation suggests a greater range of variation between standardized and vernacular usage than in New York City. In this respect the situation in Belfast is probably similar to that found in other northern British cities such as Newcastle, Glasgow and Edinburgh, each of which could be said to have a sub-stratum mix of regional dialects far removed in structure and historical development from the standard variety. In the case of Belfast, much Protestant usage actually reflects the patterns of Scots, while Catholic speech is related to variants found in the south and west of Ulster and beyond, and brought more recently into the city. In such a community there is no uniform attitude about correct usage. However, Belfast speech in one respect may be said to have become more standardized in recent years in that the distribution of phonemes in individual words has tended to follow the RP pattern. The older rural dialects of Ulster sometimes have a long [iː]-type vowel in words like *brick*; the short vowel, also characteristic of RP, is now more common in Belfast itself. The vowel in *want, wasp*, etc. is traditionally [a] (as in many northern British dialects, where /w/ has not had the rounding influence it has had in the south), but is now giving way to a rounded /ɒ/-type variant. On the other hand, Belfast vernacular differs markedly from RP in the scope of allophonic variation. While middle-class speakers tend to use the short open front [a] vowel in *bad, bag, man* etc., working-class speech shows a tendency towards a rounded vowel in these words, so that front raised vowels, as used by such people as television announcers, are actually stigmatized in the local vernacular.

The complex patterning of language and gender noted in Belfast has also been found in a survey of local adolescent usage and attitudes in the southern English town of Reading in Berkshire. Adolescents there tend to use a high proportion of certain morphological and syntactic items (several of which are also, incidentally, common throughout England in vernacular usage). Many of these usages show patterns of regularity greater than is found in the standard variety (in contrast to those Belfast pronunciations discussed which could be said to be LESS regular than those of RP). The forms include:

1. A present tense -*s* verbal suffix with non-third person singular subjects, e.g. *we goes* (whereas standard English restricts this suffix to the third person singular).
2. A second person form of the verb *be* in *was*, e.g. *you was* (in contrast to standard English *you were*).
3. Multiple negation, as in *I don't know nothing* (in contrast to standard English *I don't know anything*).

Use of these forms is strongly linked with the cultural norms of adolescent males, among whom fighting skills, minor criminal activities, 'blue-collar' jobs, certain styles of dress and haircut, and swearing were highly prized. Those boys who identified closely with these behaviours and attitudes made extensive use of the linguistic items listed. Other non-standardisms, such as the use of *never* as a negative marker of past tense (e.g. *I never kicked him*, cf. standard *I didn't kick him*) and the use of *what* as a relative pronoun (*the man what saw me*, cf. standard *the man who saw me*) were less strongly linked with the vernacular culture, and were used quite frequently among other boys.

Adolescent girls, on the other hand, did not participate in this culture to the same extent, and among those who did usage of these variants was not so marked. But there are still some interesting correlations to be noted with respect to the girls' usage of the listed features. For girls, non-standard *never* and *what* were actually used more often by those who explicitly shunned the vernacular culture. Furthermore, two other non-standardisms not previously mentioned, *come* as a past tense (as in *I come*, cf. standard *I came*) and *ain't* (a negated form of both *be* and *have*) appeared to be avoided by the same group of girls whereas they were used quite extensively by girls who identified with the vernacular culture. Thus, these two features could be said to mark vernacular loyalty for girls rather than boys. If we also include another feature, non-standard *do* as in *how much do he want* (cf. standard *how much does he want*), which is used more often by girls than boys, it seems safe to conclude that in respect of at least some linguistic features the different genders in Reading have different norms, and that it is too crude to say that in general the speech of the girls is more 'standard'. Furthermore, the foregoing analysis leaves out the possibility that there may be some non-standard variants which are used by girls as a marker of a different kind of peer-group from the vernacular one postulated in the survey.

The discussion of Reading speech highlights the importance of age, as well as class and gender, in the study of variation in English. Sociolinguistic inquiry has become interested in age as a variable for a number of reasons. First, it has been able to confirm a widely-held impression that the usage of individuals is likely to vary in the course of their own life as they are exposed to the early pressures of peer-group and education system, and later on to those of employment and retirement. It is a common observation, for instance, that vernacular usage is most strongly evidenced in the speech of adolescents and the elderly. Secondly, sociolinguists might be able to show the earliest age at which children learn the SOCIAL significance of different usages – clearly a vital factor in language development. It has been found, for instance, that children in both Edinburgh and London have acquired this knowledge at primary school age (considerably earlier than had been assumed). Thirdly, if a certain linguistic usage in a particular community can be correlated with a particular age group, it might be possible to study the mechanisms of linguistic change in 'apparent' (as distinct from 'real') time. For an example of this we can turn to the work of Peter Trudgill, whose survey of Norwich speech in the late 1960s was the first attempt to apply the Labovian approach to a speech community within the British Isles.

In Norwich the traditional Norfolk vowel in words like *top* and hot, an unrounded [ɑ]-type vowel similar to that used in many varieties of English in the USA, is gradually being replaced by a rounded [ɒ] similar to that found in RP and most other British English accents. Trudgill's finding from a random sample of the population, that the rounded variant was much more frequently used by younger speakers than older ones, suggested this development. This is what is meant by the 'apparent time' dimension; and if a usage appears to be clearly linked to age, it ought to be possible to predict the direction of a linguistic change over a number of years (i.e. in 'real' time). Before discussing this possibility, however, it is necessary to point out that this particular example shows how difficult it is to base sociolinguistic generalizations on a single social variable: not only is it younger speakers who tend to use [ɒ], but it is also more commonly used among WOMEN categorized in the survey as middle-class and MEN categorized as working-class. According to Trudgill, the former group identify with [ɒ] because it is found in RP, and the latter because it is associated with the accents of London and the Home Counties, apparently a source of 'covert prestige' for working-class men in Norwich. Age, class, and gender therefore interlock in rather complex ways.

It has actually been possible to study linguistic change in 'real time' in Norwich by undertaking a second survey of the city twenty years after the original research. The results show that while some changes may have been predictable others seem to have occurred in a rather random and haphazard way. Thus, whereas in the late 1960s the glottal realization of /t/ as [ʔ] was stigmatized, the proliferation of its use even into the more 'formal' styles of pronunciation since then suggests that it has lost much of its stigma (a conclusion that squares with much impressionistic observation during the last decade or so). More surprisingly, perhaps, is the introduction into Norwich speech of the [v]-realization of /r/, a pronunciation sporadic in English speech generally and one which is often characterized as a speech defect. Since however this is also found in London English, and since another innovation in Norwich speech, the substitution of /f/ and /v/ for /θ/ and /ð/ has a similar association, the influence of the metropolis is not an unlikely explanation – adequate, at any rate, it seems, for the older generation in Norwich who now describe the speech of youngsters there as 'Cockney'.

From the preceding paragraph it should be clear that any attempt to explain linguistic change must take account not only of social and stylistic variation but of the regional dimension as well. Traditionally, the study of regional variation in language has been the preserve of the dialectologist. In contrast with sociolinguistics, however, dialectology has tended to reify the notion of dialect as a set of forms authenticated by history and highly vulnerable to the pressures of standardization. What is interesting for the dialectologist is what can be related to antiquity; from this flows the assumption that 'genuine' or 'pure' dialect exists, and that it is the fieldworker's task to record it before it is lost forever. In practice, this means selecting a particular kind of informant who is thought to best preserve such usage; accordingly, the norm for selection is, as has been appropriately and wittily proposed elsewhere, a NORM – the non-mobile, older, rural male. Dialect forms, moreover, are usually collected using a questionnaire, foregrounding thereby the distinction between dialects as something seen as an aspect of verbal interaction and, on the other hand, as isolated exotica of special interest to the antiquarian. For sociolinguists, however, the regional dimension is only one facet of the linguistic repertory of a particular area. They would accordingly seek to correlate dialectal usage with all the social variables discussed above, and, recognizing that a given individual – 'NORM' or otherwise – is unlikely to use it consistently, seek to explore the social attitudes surrounding its use. As something capable of change, moreover, dialect is not to be identified exclusively with a highly unrepresentative part of the population.

This is not to say, however, that the findings of dialectology can be simply dismissed. One outcome of the work of the *Survey of English Dialects* in the 1950s and 1960s has been to promote the study of regional Englishes outside England itself, and we now have valuable data on English as it is spoken in Wales, Ireland and Scotland (if we are not to label the usage of that country as Scots), as well as varieties of English beyond the British Isles. One aspect of these varieties of great interest to the sociolinguist is the extent to which certain patterns in the usage of these areas are influenced by the 'substratum' of other languages such as Welsh and Gaelic (of both Ireland and Scotland). In some varieties of Welsh English, for instance, the vowel in the final syllable of *export, expert*, etc. is short /ɔ/ or /ɔr/ and /ə/ or /ər/ respectively, depending on whether or not the accent is one in which postvocalic and preconsonantal /r/ is sounded) since in Welsh long vowels only occur in stressed syllables. At the lexical level, it is possible to explain the southern Irish idiom *I let a shout* as originating from the influence of Irish *ligim* which can mean both *utter* as well as *shout*. And at the level of syntax, the influence of Scottish Gaelic may underlie the fondness for clefting in Hebridean English, as in *Is it this here you want me to read?* (as opposed to *Do you want me to read this?*)

For a more detailed example of how the fruits of dialect research can be used by sociolinguistics we can return to the study of linguistic change in East Anglia, the area which includes Norwich. The example shows how the sociolinguist needs to be concerned with the SYNCHRONIC aspects of linguistic structure as well as the diachronic one (the dominant focus of dialectology: indeed, it is often claimed that sociolinguistics is able to break down the Saussurean insistence on keeping the two distinct). A sound-change currently taking place in East Anglia is the merging of two sounds originally distinct (but since merged in other varieties): one the reflex of Middle English $\bar{\varphi}$ (from Old English $\bar{a}$) as in *road* and *go*, which is [ʊu], the other the reflex of ME *ou* (OE $\bar{a}w$), as in *flow* and *know* (pronounced [ʌʊ]). Thus *moan* and *mown* have now begun to sound alike, as in RP and most other accents. Evidence from dialect surveys from the 1930s up to the present time shows that the merger has gradually been spreading north-eastwards from the London area towards the Suffolk/Norfolk border (see map). North of this point it has spread in a kind of pincer movement amongst urbanized areas along the Norfolk/Cambridgeshire border to the west of Norwich as far north as the coast, and, on the east, among the similarly urbanized centres of Lowestoft and Great Yarmouth. In most of Norfolk however the phonemic distinction has been maintained, although in Norwich itself it seems to have died out altogether within the last decade or so. It is apparently the middle class that is leading the merger, and evidence suggests that the pressure for change, as in the case of the vowel in *top* (see above), comes from different sources. In Norwich, middle class speakers tend to use a pronunciation intermediate between the two vowels, and in this they are perhaps guided by the existence of a similar pronunciation in RP. In the southern part of East Anglia, however, the merger is effected by GENERALIZING the [ʌʊ] vowel throughout all the relevant words (a change occurring first in certain phonetic environments only, then spreading to others). This may be because the [ʊu]-type vowel in *boat* etc. stands out as being very different from both the RP [ɔu] sound and the wider Cockney diphthong, which, being often realized as [ʌʊ], is similar to the East Anglian vowel in the *mown* class of words. Since Cockney influence in the southern part of East Anglia and also the north-western towns like Kings Lynn (where there is overspill population from London) is growing, it is among WORKING CLASS speakers that the [ʌʊ] diphthong has been spreading at the expense of [ʊʊ].

Unmerged			Merged	
Rural East Anglia	RP	Norwich middle-class speakers	Colchester working-class speakers	Cockney
moan [ʊu]	əʊ	θə	ʌʊ	ʌʊ
mown [ʌʊ]	əʊ	θə	ʌʊ	ʌʊ

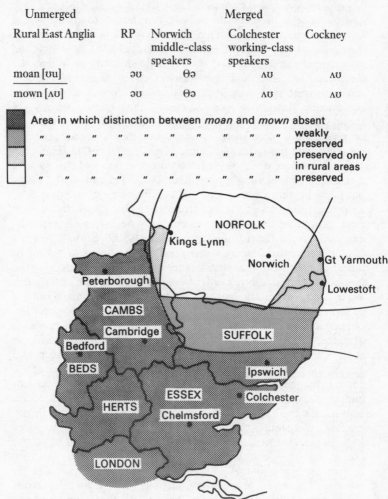

Area in which distinction between *moan* and *mown* absent
" " " " " " " " " " weakly preserved
" " " " " " " " " " preserved only in rural areas
" " " " " " " " " " preserved

Fig. 9.1. Map Showing Merger of Vowels in MOAN, MOWN, etc.

We must now turn to the last social variable to be discussed, the issue of ETHNICITY. Predictably enough, our treatment of this must also take account of all the other parameters – class, gender, age and region – so far discussed. Ethnicity, however, is of particular importance when we attend to certain varieties of English which have attracted a great deal of attention in recent years, and not only from linguists. 'British Black English' is the term sometimes applied to the varieties used by descendants of West Indian immigrants who were born in English cities and towns such as London, Manchester, Bristol, Bedford, and the West Midland conurbation which includes Birmingham and Wolverhampton. The development of these varieties is complex, since the histories of their antecedents, the Caribbean creoles which in turn derived from the pidgins of coastal West Africa, remain largely conjectural. Pidgins can be defined as simplified varieties arising from a process of intermittent contact among speakers of different languages; their grammars tend to be morphologically simple, their vocabulary reflects their multilingual roots, and they tend to be used only for certain specialized uses, such as trade. Once a pidgin becomes the first language of a community, however – as happened when pidgin-speaking West African people were taken to the Caribbean plantations during the slave trade – it becomes a creole: a fully-developed language, though one that at first lacks both writing system and status. (Some, however, like Surinam Creole, have been promoted in these respects.) Processes of pidginization and creolization are widespread throughout the world, and can be seen as an inevitable outcome of contact situations among languages: indeed, it is arguable that many of the major European languages (including English) developed in a not entirely dissimilar way.

The Caribbean creole most influential in the linguistic backgrounds of West Indians is that of Jamaica. Known as PATOIS among people of Caribbean descent, this variety is difficult to describe as a discrete linguistic entity since throughout its history it has been officially denoted as 'English' by the British-instituted education system in Jamaica. As a result, it has been for a very long time implicitly compared with standard English, and, not surprisingly, it has been found wanting. Terms such as 'monkey-talk' or 'broken' or 'bastard' or 'impoverished' English continue to be used to refer to it even at the present time; West Indian usage today could therefore be said to attract the same kind of pejorative descriptions as were used of English dialects, particularly urban ones, fifty and more years ago. West Indians in the Caribbean have accordingly been made to feel ashamed of their speech and have learned, as a consequence, to 'code-switch' in the direction of Standard English when they feel the need arise. The description of Jamaican usage therefore poses a challenge to the linguist in that there exists a continuum between creole in its 'deepest' forms at one end of the scale and more standardized forms at the other. Of great importance and interest to the sociolinguist is the fact that such variability manifests itself not only in the speech of the community at large but also in that of the individual even within a single utterance. Thus, in *When me sister loses her temper* **mi gaan so** the speakers show the same kind of switching as occurs among bilingual speakers in societies as widely distributed as Ghana, India, and the USA – linguistic behaviour that is constrained by a variety of psychological and social factors associated with interaction such as hesitation, topic, and audience, and which should not be casually dismissed as the inability to keep two languages apart.

It is necessary to devote some space to the description of Jamaican creole since this inevitably influences the way we see British Black English. Such a description, however, is very difficult because so many of its features resist analysis in terms of the linguistic categories postulated for English. Thus, it has recently been suggested that Jamaican creole is not, for instance, a stressed language, like English, but is more like the sub-Saharan tone languages from which it is partly descended. Other features such as lexical items e.g. *jook* (pierce) and syntactic patterns such as the use of serial verbs such as *dat will teach dat gal ti* **come try muck** *up my scene* have cognates in African languages and similarly encourage, therefore, an 'Africanist' perspective (which is not without its ideological implications). But there is much that can be identified as European in origin. The presence of the now somewhat archaic Portugese-based form *sabi*, for instance, as in *mi no sabi* ('I don't know') might encourage the view that Jamaican creole, like many other pidgins and creoles, is descended from an original Portugese-based pidgin that has since been 're-lexified'. This form now co-exists, however, with the more recent *mi no nuo* and *ai duon nuo*, showing a Jamaican creole version of English *know*, and also demonstrating the potential for shifting between 'deep' usage and the more 'English' end of the continuum. But that 'English' is not always the standard variety: from the earliest times, it seems, English dialect forms such as *aks* (itself a direct reflex of the Old

English variant *acsian*, 'ask', beside *ascian*) have been present in the creole, and it is by no means easy to establish the geographical origin of such items as they occur in a number of non-standard varieties on the 'periphery' of the British Isles – Ireland, the north of England, and the West Country.

Despite its history of stigmatization, Jamaican Creole has considerable prestige among young people of Caribbean background in Britain. Before we examine the reasons for this, it is necessary to point out that there is sufficient evidence to suggest the existence of a version of the creole within Britain itself. British Jamaican Creole, as some linguists have termed this variety, preserves many of the grammatical features of Jamaican Creole, such as its tendency not to inflect the verb for tense: *I see John last week* (rather than *saw*). Creole grammar has other ways, however, of specifying time-relations, particularly that of ASPECT (habitual versus non-habitual actions, completed versus ongoing). Thus in Jamaican Creole the particle *a* shows an action in progress: *Mary a go home* means Mary is going home; *Mary en go home* means Mary went home. The copula verb is often deleted before predicative adjectives, e.g. *she wicked*, as in many Caribbean creoles. But British Jamaican Creole differs from the Caribbean variety with respect to vocabulary, at least in the view of its users. Speakers report forms such as *dunseye* (money) which are not used in the Caribbean.

Although British Jamaican Creole provides a reference-point for the Afro-Caribbean community in Britain, many younger Blacks born in Britain use speech-forms which are closer to standard English. This is particularly the case regarding the syntactic examples mentioned above. But certain lexical items such as *tief* ('steal'), morphological tendencies (no past-tense markers, no third person singular *s*-inflection in the verb) and pronunciations (the vowel in *pot*, etc. is often an unrounded [a], that in *cut* [ɔ] – a vowel which in Jamaican Creole is also used in RP /əʊ/-and /ɜ:/-words such as *go* and *bird*) are widely enough used to suggest the existence of yet another variety, British Black English. Of particular importance to the sociolinguistic description of this variety, however, is the range of contexts in which it is used. British Black English seems to be clearly associated with certain 'performance' styles of speech which in turn are an important component of adolescent street-culture. The variety accordingly enjoys a great deal of covert prestige – so much so, in fact, that White children and adolescents sometimes introduce it into their own speech.

Knowledge of Black varieties of English is important not only for the linguistic description of the language as a whole, but also for assessing the educational prospects of Black children themselves. The fact that children of West Indian origin appear to be among the lowest achievers in British schools suggests that many teachers may be unaware of the linguistic background of such children and continue to judge their language according to the pejorative stereotypes noted above. The response of many Black children is accordingly predictable – they EXAGGERATE Black usages, since these afford them a sense of their own distinctive identity in the face of what is seen as an oppressive culture of dominance. Central to that identity is the notion of a distinctive ETHNICITY which, like Rastafarianism, reaches back towards Africa for its roots.

II

Within what might broadly be called the Anglophone world the construction of a link between language and ethnicity has been by no means limited, of course, to speakers of Caribbean descent. Inside the British Isles itself the maintenance of the minority Celtic languages such as Welsh and, in Scotland, Gaelic, owes in part to similar gestures of defiance. It is arguable that the link develops and flourishes in contexts of dominance, in which one group feels that its interests and cultural identity are not fully realized within society. Such links were also made in the past among native speakers of English, the forebears of those who today find the language-attitudes of many Black, Welsh, and Scottish people so puzzling. What sociolinguists today call language-loyalty seems to have developed, for instance, during the later Middle Ages when the use of French in England had attracted a great deal of opprobrium. In this section, however, I want to deal with a later period in English history when an association between language and something akin to 'Englishness' was forged amongst certain powerful and influential sections of society.

At certain periods of history the notion of ethnicity may be conflated with that of nation. This seems to have occurred with respect to English during what historians call the Early Modern period (c. 1500–1700). Certain writers at this time wrote about an 'English nation' unified and symbolized by the English language. During the Tudor period in particular a dominant linguistic issue was the relationship between English and another language, Latin. At this time nationhood was an issue impossible to separate from the desire of certain European monarchies to demonstrate their independence from the unifying – to some, smothering – influence of Roman Catholicism; and the language of that religion, of course, was Latin, with its fixed writing system, codified grammar, long and glittering history, and guaranteed audience of international scholarship. Latin exemplified a kind of timelessness and also spacelessness; it occupied what was felt to be the history of the intellect throughout the civilized world. To the autonomy-seeking power elites of Renaissance France, Italy and England, Latin had all the wrong connotations. Autonomy needed some kind of justification, based on difference from other groups; and one sure way of marking difference was to insist on the integrity of a language that only your own group spoke. The relative merits of Latin and English as media for scholarship and literature were accordingly debated by many writers in Tudor England, and part of this process was a growing awareness on the part of some of the extent of writing in English since Anglo-Saxon times – some of which could afford useful ammunition in debates about religion or the development of 'native' legal traditions – and, in consequence, of the separate history of what came to be called the national language.

Such attention to the English language in general inevitably focussed on the particular variety to be used for 'serious' and scholarly writing. This variety, of course, is what comes to be known as the standard, and for the development of this variety the Early Modern period is of crucial significance. Before exploring this matter in detail, however, it is necessary to make a few general points about the process of standardization and the status of the standard variety at the present time.

Standardization can be seen to proceed in four distinct but overlapping stages. The first of these involves the SELECTION of a particular variety in preference to all others. In the case of English, where the whole process of standardization has taken a very long time, the variety selected was the south-east midland dialect of the merchant class based in London. Its origins, then, were already marked for region and social class. Another stage is ACCEPTANCE of that variety, first by those involved in various kinds of official and public discourse, later by the population at large (where among certain strata in particular places at different times acceptance can only be described as grudging). A third stage is FUNCTIONAL ELABORATION, where the standard is developed as an omnifunctional variety. In the case of English this meant displacing Latin and, to a certain extent French, from such domains as scholarship, government and law. Finally, there is the stage of CODIFICATION, in which the standard is 'fixed' in grammars and dictionaries by recommending certain usages and stigmatizing others. It was in the eighteenth century that this process was systematically begun with respect to English.

The foregoing account does however mask an important ambiguity in the term STANDARD. On the one hand it is commonly used to denote a kind of lingua franca – a variety indispensible for those who speak mutually incomprehensible dialects, and essential for the purposes of 'national' communication. On the other hand it also means a kind of yardstick or ideal against which all usage can be measured. The standard accordingly comes to be seen as the 'best' variety, and the other English dialects are increasingly stigmatized and demoted from their earlier status as autonomous varieties with their own writing systems. This second attitude towards the standard also inspires what has recently been called the tradition of 'complaint' on the part of observers, many of them established literary figures, who ritually denounce the 'state of the language'. This tradition can be seen to stretch from Caxton in the late fifteenth century to John Rae, headmaster of Westminster School, in the 1980s.

One final point to make about the process of standardization in general is the importance of writing. Unlike speech, writing needs to be taught by explicit instruction, and is therefore much more easily standardized. Similarly, writing does not betray to anything like the same extent as speech the regional and social characteristics of the user. If, moreover, a piece of writing is destined for printed circulation – a possibility that has existed ever since the introduction of printing in the 1470s made possible the widespread dissemination of the standard – there are the extra controls exerted by publishing houses and printers. And once the written standard has been fixed – especially in regard to spelling – there is the other constraint associated with the fact that a writer's potential audience may be far removed in time and space from the one he or she may have had in mind. In general, it is possible to say that since the beginning of standardization the process of writing itself has gradually come to mean writing in the standard variety (and therefore either consciously or unconsciously promoting it).

Today, with the standard firmly entrenched as a taught variety in schools ever since the Education Acts of the 1870s, the process of standardization is probably as complete as it ever will be. In fact to some the standard has become so thoroughly naturalized that it is synonymous with the English language itself. As a result, it has become identified with 'ordinary' English, the norm against which other varieties (including, interestingly enough, regional dialects and Black English) seem vital and exotic. As we shall see, this view is of special relevance for the study of literature, which throughout much of the twentieth century has been seen by Formalist theorists as depending for its effects on the systematic distortion of the 'norm' of the language.

This is not to say, however, that the standard today has attained the goal of fixity. Codification remains the most problematic and sensitive aspect of standardization, not least because usage continues to be constantly changing. While the spelling system is today the most fixed aspect of the standard, the level of structure represented by spelling, that of sound, is the least. This is partly because pronunciation, being part of speech, is inherently difficult to codify: learned early (and largely unconsciously) in life, it is subject to enormous variability and change, as we have seen. It is accordingly possible to speak standard English with any accent, but this is not to deny that Received Pronunciation still preserves much of its status as either a prestige accent or as a model (its influence on vernacular usage in this latter respect has already been noted). Vocabulary is also in one sense difficult to codify since it is the most open-ended and expansible level of linguistic structure. The line between standard and non-standard however can often be drawn clearly with respect to dialect (*play*, rather than northern *laik*) and slang (*pig* denotes a four-legged animal rather than a policeman). Morphology is fixed (*themselves* rather than *theirselves*, *I did it* not *I done it*) in contrast with the massive variation in the dialects. Syntax however is fixed only with respect to certain constructions (e.g. avoidance of the cumulative negative); others (such as *It is I* rather than *It is me*) have been codified in deference to the spurious example of Latin and can be described only as pedantic rather than standard; but the vast majority of structures and rules, many of which, such as word-order, may be common to all dialects of English, were of course too numerous and of too abstract a nature to be investigated by the codifiers. Codification, then, can only ever be partial: there remain large areas of choice available to the writer, particularly in syntax and lexis, and especially in the field of imaginative literature.

When we turn back to the Early Modern period we find that many of the processes of standardization had barely begun. In the course of the sixteenth century the selected variety had reached the stage of acceptance, at least among certain influential people, but its functional suitability in those domains previously occupied by Latin and French was still debated. It was not until the end of the period, for instance, that scholars would automatically choose English rather than Latin for learned discourse. Codification as we now know it was scarcely underway: as is well-known, Shakespeare wrote without the aid (or constraint) of grammar books, and the only dictionaries available to him were specialized glosses of 'Hard Words' borrowed from other languages. The spelling system, especially in handwritten documents of an ephemeral kind, strikes the modern mind as chaotic, but it is still the case that a degree of fixity was being introduced not by the conscious interventions of scholarly codifiers but by the practical constraints of the printing presses.

To what extent is it possible to speak of a SPOKEN standard existing at this time? Certainly there would have been a preponderance of south-east midland variants in such levels as morphology (*I am*, rather than south-western *I be*, or *I is* as in parts of the north). At the same time, however, we can trace the beginnings of an attempt to RECOMMEND certain spoken usages in preference to others. Paradoxically enough, this attempt seems to have occurred in relation to that least amenable level, pronunciation. In the course of the sixteenth-century we find a number of references to a 'natural' and 'true' pronunciation which is increasingly related to the 'learned' and 'literate' elements in society resident within what today we know as the Home Counties. One outcome of this was the emphasis on accent as a sign of cultivation (as opposed to rusticity, provincialism or vulgarism) – a process resulting in Britain today being perhaps the most pronunciation-conscious society in the world.

The creation of a particular pronunciation as a mark of social exclusiveness is a reminder that the whole standardization process itself is partly one of exclusion. A standardized language can occur only where boundaries have been drawn; and such boundary-drawing depends ultimately on the presence of power and authority within society. During the early modern period one such presence was the growing strength and ideology of the nation-state. As is well-known, the Tudor monarchs in particular were champions of political centralization, and Acts of Parliament passed in 1536 to curtail the use of both Welsh and Irish show that they knew the significance of language to this process. Seen from this political perspective, the standard variety is the one that represents the interests of the 'nation', and it must therefore engage in a struggle for dominance with other varieties and languages, constantly erecting the spectre of its opposite, the 'anarchy' of unlimited variation and of popular usage. From the viewpoint of the nation-state the liquidation of minority languages such as Irish, Cornish, and Welsh was just as important as the stigmatization of regional dialects of English.

This link between language and political centralization can be seen very clearly in the way that most histories of English have presented the course of linguistic change. In short, they tend to reflect the Tudor ideology. The early modern period in particular is seen as the era when England attained 'nationhood' – when the 'national community' was united by a standardized variety of the language. While the development of English up to about 1500 has been conceived by its chroniclers as the history of its dialects, its development since then has in effect been a celebration of standardization. The geographical dimension yields to a focus on the usage and idea of a small number of famous people representative only of a metropolitan elite – men like the Tudor courtier John Hart, Milton's schoolmaster Alexander Gill, and, of course, Dr Johnson. It is necessary therefore to acknowledge that just as the findings of contemporary sociolinguistics are to a large extent shaped by particular views of society, a certain view of history appears to have permeated English linguistic historiography. The statements of historians often have a triumphalist or nationalist ring when they deal with the early modern period: 'it was in language, as in many other respects, an age with the characteristics of youth – vigor, a willingness to venture and a disposition to attempt the untried', according to Baugh & Cable. For Partridge, English became 'a serviceable and resourceful instrument of the national mind'; and by about 1700 had achieved for Potter, in a chapter appropriately called 'Maturity', 'a certain balance or equilibrium [. . .] a very substantial achievement'. The same spirit is even exemplified in the actual titles of books, such as the *Triumph of the English Language* by R. F. Jones.

Such a view of history inevitably influences the presentation of linguistic change. This for the sociolinguist needs to be firmly located in a social and spatial context, as we have seen, but even allowing for the inevitable gaps in the evidence it is clear that historical treatments make too little of the possibility that they are dealing with the usage not of an entire nation but of certain groups within one area only, that of London. Certain changes in early modern English may perhaps be illuminated if we conceive of

London at this time as not totally dissimilar from the Belfasts and Glasgows of recent sociolinguistic inquiry – sites of intense linguistic stratification and change. Thus, the fact that sixteenth-century accounts of the pronunciation of words like *meat*, *mate* and *meet* do not agree need not surprise us, since they may reflect the different class-backgrounds of their authors. That of the phonetician John Hart, which shows that all three words were pronounced differently, may reflect his position as a court-herald, suggesting that he wrote for the benefit of the gentry; while that of Bullockar, which shows a merger of *meat* and *mate* (which, if it took place at all, has subsequently been reversed) may reflect his middle-class origins. If we bear in mind the sixteenth-century attitudes to pronunciation discussed earlier it would not be surprising if different pronunciations acquired the symbolism of particular social classes, and new pronunciations were adopted to maintain class-distinctions or to emulate one's social superiors.

Such an analysis suggests, or is dependent on, a view of the early modern period that finds not national unity but class-rivalry and even conflict. There is in fact some evidence to suggest that massive price inflation and rapid population increase at this time generated intense social friction that would have been magnified within London. One result of these was an expectation of social mobility among some sections of the population, something that contemporary models of social stratification could not accommodate. The official model was a status-hierarchy based on the ownership of land, where the chief concern was the identification of the 'gentleman' (a group constituting only 5% of the population). In an urban centre like London, however, the mercantile and professional groups acquired status by virtue of their occupations and income; to secure the status of the gentry, however, they needed to buy land, and were often resented because of this. Tensions of this kind may lie behind another linguistic change which is so well-known that historians of English have often tried to find explanations for it that relate in some sense to social structure. During the course of the sixteenth-century it seems that in London English at least the older second-person singular pronoun *thou* was being replaced by the form *you* (originally a plural). Since *thou* could be used non-reciprocally by a powerful person to a social inferior as a marker of higher status, it has been suggested by some linguistic historians that the spread of *you* was due to the rise of egalitarian sentiments (inspired, perhaps, by feelings of new-found national solidarity!). An explanation better fitted to the view of London society offered above would be that the 'power-coded' use of *thou* can prevail only in a society where status relations are felt to be static and transparent, and since in sixteenth-century London this was manifestly not the case, the habit of using mutual *you* arose among the middle class in public situations where their insecurity with respect to status would be clearly apparent.

III

From everything that has been said so far it should be clear that the standard neither is nor can ever be an entirely neutral variety of the English language. If we now return to the present we can still find that for many people standard English connotes formality, something which derives perhaps from its association with situations such as the law-court and the schoolroom where power is exercised. And for those whose customary usage is dialect (and those who claim to speak on behalf of them) the standard carries an inevitable connotation of social distance since it is associated with writing, a function denied to the dialects except in rather special circumstances (such as the local traditions of dialect-writing in areas like Yorkshire which reached their high watermark in the last century). I would like to conclude this chapter by discussing some of these points in relation to D. H. Lawrence, a writer who is particularly rewarding to examine from a sociolinguistic perspective.

Such a perspective is however very different to reconcile with the influential twentieth-century versions of the argument that 'literature' can be characterized by a particular kind, or use, of language. According to the Czech linguist Jan Mukařovský, 'literariness' is made possible by breaking the 'norm' of the language, something which he associates with the standard. The stronger the sense of the norm, the more possibilities there are for 'foregrounding' i.e. deviating from the norm by pushing into the foreground the properties of language itself, an operation that makes possible the creation of poetry (which, in a characteristic move, seems to stand for literature in general). Thus, poetry flourishes, it seems, the more the standard is naturalized – an argument difficult to apply to English at the time of Shakespeare!

First, sociolinguists would want to look very hard at the notion of the linguistic norm. WHOSE norm – where? and when? – is being postulated? In common with related constructs such as 'ordinary' or 'everyday' language that are necessary for such formalist theories, the norm tends not to be subjected to detailed linguistic analysis: its characteristics are assumed, rather than demonstrated. Secondly, the formalist assumption that literature is a 'given' category with intrinsic properties does not sit easily with the sociolinguists' insistence on establishing the WHERE, AMONGST WHOM, and WHEN: if literature, like language, is to be seen in its socio-historical context, it should accordingly be seen as an INSTITUTION in which certain kinds of writing are assigned value by a certain group of people. What norms, linguistic or otherwise, can be said to exist reside not in the language itself but in the RECOMMENDATIONS, explicit or otherwise, of that institution.

Essential to the discussion of norms are the expectations of readers. While these are subject to variation and change it has often been argued that the audience of the novel, for instance, has been a middle-class one; from this we might assume that certain expectations about LANGUAGE will be mobilized. A number of Lawrence's critics have accordingly referred to such expectations (with varying degrees of explicitness) when discussing the novelist's language. Of particular interest to the sociolinguist is the emphasis on Lawrence's social and regional background in attempts to explain the effects of his style. Lawrence's language is often felt to reflect the ordinary speech of the mining community. One (extreme) view, that of Christopher Gillie, is that Lawrence had 'the working man's incorrigible habit of using the language he needed to use, disregarding social and stylistic amenities . . . He wrote as he talked . . .' For Richard Hoggart, the opening of *Sons and Lovers* has a 'directness' missing from the cultivated and ironic discourse of Forster's *Passage to India*; in addition, it reminds him of the way stories were told during his own (working-class) childhood.

A sociolinguistic critique of these comments would go beyond making the familiar point that they are too impressionistic and lacking the necessary linguistic analysis. It is worth saying in addition that no-one can write as they speak, that no-one can use language entirely without social and stylistic amenities (unless they are monsters) and that there is now enough knowledge about the form of oral story-telling to refute Hoggart's claim. But there is one respect in which these impressions have a kind of validity, and this has to do with the use of non-standardisms in Lawrence's narrative style. For as we have seen, one 'norm' in the writing of prose fiction since the beginnings of the novel has been that it is done in standard English, so that we are able to say that vernacular usage would be 'foregrounded' if we were to meet it. But whereas many nineteenth-century writers would be likely to draw attention to such usages by glossing them, either in the text itself (as in the case of Hardy) or in a glossary at the end (Gaskell), supposedly in deference to their putative readership, Lawrence does not. Regional, occupational and working-class usages such as *eddish* (stubble), *butty* (a certain grade of collier), and *dinner-time* (denoting the mid-day rather than the evening meal) are embedded in the text as though they were common currency.

To address someone, even a stranger, as though they shared the same cultural knowledge and assumptions as yourself is actually a very common interactional strategy in speech. In recent years sociolinguistics has been greatly enriched by developments in the neighbouring fields of discourse analysis and pragmatics, and one particularly fruitful area is the study of politeness behaviour. One theory is that people are generally motivated by a desire to protect the 'face' both of themselves and of others. Sometimes the two desires may be in conflict, and different languages offer various formulae for accommodating this. It has been suggested that in general there are two strategies of politeness: one, called negative politeness, respects the personal 'territory' of the addressee, and accordingly uses the linguistic markers of hesitation, deference and indirectness: *Er, excuse me, I wonder if you could tell me the right time?* might be an example in English. In fact, the negative politeness model is what English-speaking people generally mean by politeness in general, but it is important to point out that this tends to be the middle-class pattern. Working-class usage, on the other hand, tends to favour the appeal to shared norms and common interests. Lawrence's own writing may accordingly be said to operate in a similar way, and this may help to explain the impressions of some of his critics.

There is however one aspect of Lawrence's fiction that could be said to foreground dialect and that is the representation of dialogue. The functions and symbolism of dialect are often mentioned in the narration, and the speech of certain characters (Morel in *Sons and Lovers*, Mellors in *Lady Chatterley's Lover*) is heavily marked for dialect (examples below). Such marking practices can cause problems for both readers and writers: that of unintelligibility for the reader, and of selection for the writer. In principle there is no limit to the ways in which spellings can be adapted to try to represent local usages, and the writer has to decide how far to start from scratch, as it were, and how far to use whatever conventions may have developed for the representation of different dialects (these, of course, have never been fixed). One outstanding feature of many of Lawrence's novels is that we find a continuum of marking practices where some characters (usually men) speak broad dialect, others standard English, and others who use a kind of general vernacular (characterized in part by such conventionalized forms as -*in*' for the verbal suffix -*ing*). In short, a sociolinguistic continuum is suggested which gives rise to several interesting possibilities of interpretation.

Readers often interpret represented dialogue according to various notions of realism, a dominant element in the criticism of fiction. Represented speech is especially suited to this perspective as it is an example of language being used to imitate language. In assessing it, however, people often involve different criteria of realism. Thus, the speech of a fictional character is often judged to be realistic if we feel that it is an 'accurate' reflection of the usage of the class or region to which he or she is supposed to belong. Or a conversation within a novel can 'ring true' if we feel that at a deeper level it mirrors the patterns of spoken discourse. Such perceptions may be illuminated by sociolinguistic knowledge. A recent study of represented child language in Dos Passos's *USA* shows that the dialogue is based not on actual child language (with its one or two-word utterances, known as holophrases) but on the altogether different variety called Baby-talk (the kind of language, attested in many cultures, that adults use to children). We are apt to project the latter on to the former because Baby-talk, being part of the adult repertoire, is closer to our consciousness.

In his depictions of different kinds of speech-behaviour Lawrence could be said to have anticipated many of the concerns of current sociolinguistics by half a century. Many of his novels and short stories clearly show a sensitivity to the social symbolism of different speech varieties and depict the kinds of vernacular cultures, in which dialect is associated with the male peer-group, that we have discussed earlier. In *The Rainbow*, for instance, it is the women who look towards 'the other, magic language' of the vicar; in *Sons and Lovers* it is Walter Morel, the dialect-speaking miner, who reviles his wife for trying to turn his son into a 'stool-harsed Jack' by steering him towards a white-collar job. Another pattern concerns the depiction of speech-events. In *Sons and Lovers*, for instance, there is a clear difference of function between dialect and standard. Morel's speech much of the time could be described as ludic – he loves to tell stories, to bicker, to boast, to engage in games of mock-combat. Thus:

He went straight to the sink where his wife was washing up.

'What, are thee there!' he said boisterously. 'Sluther off an' let me wesh mysen.'

'You may wait till I've finished,' said his wife.

'Oh, mun I? An' what if I shonna?'

This good-humoured threat amused Mrs Morel.

'Then you can go and wash yourself in the soft-water tub.'

'Ha! I can an' a', tha mucky little 'ussy.'

It is interesting to find that in the language of Morel's son Paul the functions of dialect have contracted to very specific speech-events involving very particular kinds of addressees: animals, and women with whom he is enjoying either a flirtatious or physical encounter. Such situationally determined shifting contrasts with the far more flamboyant and manipulative 'code-switching' in which Mellors, the gamekeeper in *Lady Chatterley's Lover*, indulges himself. In his relationship with the upper-class Connie, Mellors often uses dialect, which she does not understand, to distance himself from her, or to gain a temporary interactional advantage. Bidialectalism for him is a source of power; he is not averse to exploiting it for the purpose of dominating her. In one such instance, we are told that he lapses into an 'excess of vernacular'; the orthographic marking even suggests a kind of hyper-dialectalism:

'I mean as 'appen Ah can find anuther pleece as'll du for rearin th' pheasants. If yer want ter be 'ere, yo'll non want me messin' abaht a' th' time.'

She looked at him, getting his meaning through the fog of the dialect.

'Why don't you speak ordinary English?' she said coldly.

'Me! Ah thowt it *wor* ordinary.'

The last exchange, of course makes much the same point as I have done in this chapter. For Connie, 'ordinary' English is standard English, the only option of her class; Mellors, on the other hand, speaks here for the working class from which he is estranged. THEIR customary usage is dialect, except that in this case the word *ordinary* also has its pejorative connotations of 'commonness' and inferiority.

10

THE ENGLISH LANGUAGE OR THE ENGLISH LANGUAGES?

Tom McArthur

According to the best estimates, the world's population is nudging its way upward to the five-billion mark. If present trends continue, then by century's end around a quarter of that number will be regular users of the English language. Indeed, depending on what one understands by 'regular', 'user', 'English' and 'language', a quarter of the present world population may already be involved with English. IF this is so, then we are looking at a phenomenon that is unique in the history of the human race and its languages.

English is now such a widespread and varied language that it virtually defies discussion in terms of those theories and models of language which have been influential in our schools and colleges to date. Of course, it never was a simple, single phenomenon, but like most other languages it could in the past safely be treated as if it were. People could talk about Cherokees speaking Cherokee, the inhabitants of Japan using their own language Japanese, the Arabs employing Arabic, the French using French in France, and the English using and leading the way in English – one. society, one language, neat and tidy, even if allowances have had to be made for non-Arab Muslims using Arabic, for French being spoken in Belgium and Switzerland, and for English being the mother tongue to a whole family of nations. When Winston Churchill wrote *The History of the English-Speaking Peoples* – published between 1956 and 1958 – the language was widely perceived as still essentially an emanation from England, and the various peoples who used it were considered in the main as a diaspora from that 'Mother Country', however variegated their populations.

In a remarkably short time global circumstances have changed all that. Today English is not only the most egregiously successful language in the history of the world, but its very success has begun to demand a more sensitive description of how this has come to be than has been available until quite recently.

I

THE STATISTICS OF A WORLD LANGUAGE

At the beginning of the 1980s the statistics of 'World English' were staggering, but most of those interested in collecting them saw them as relatively straightforward. Such statistics were not, however, just the raw data of demography and censuses; they related to a theory or model of what English had been developing into throughout the preceding hundred years or more, and that model divides fairly handily into three parts or groupings.

The first of these groupings is the only one that many of us have traditionally recognized as legitimate: the just over 300 million inhabitants of what are often called the ENL nations, where the letters stand for 'English as a Native Language'. Next to these come another 300 million or so of people in the ESL nations, where the letters stand for 'English as a Second Language'. This second grouping does not have the language as a birthright, but its members have been educated largely or entirely in English, or need it for everyday occupational and other purposes, or both. Lastly, there come an estimated 100 million others, people neither born into nor raised with English around them, but who use it frequently as a foreign language – indeed, as their INTERNATIONAL language – in business, for leisure, or both. The bulk of these people first acquired English formally at school, and live in the EFL nations, where the letters stand for 'English as a Foreign Language'.

Simple arithmetic indicates that even if the third figure, for the EFL nations, is wildly wrong, by around 1980 the non-native users – one might almost be tempted to say 'consumers' – of the language had moved into the majority, a state of affairs which is unlikely to change in the foreseeable future, barring catastrophe. The native-born are, in a word, outnumbered, just as a time came long ago in the Roman Empire when the Romans were outnumbered as speakers of Latin. One analogy for this is what happens to a successful 'hard' currency; the time comes when there is more of it circulating outside the home economy than inside. This is the kind of analogy of which language purists are fond, because in such a situation the national currency is no longer under national control, and is in danger of being over-extended and therefore devalued. There are many people nowadays who argue that the English language is being devalued as a result of its phenomenal spread, or fear that it may be, but once again the question arises: What does one mean here by 'English language', and against what time or criterion of purity would one measure any such 'devaluation'?

The three groupings of the conventional model of modern English are easy enough to recognize as blocs of nations; they embrace one way or another every country on the face of the planet. The fact that the ENL, ESL and EFL groups are broadly recognizable, however, does not mean that they are easy to talk about, either in scholarly or in general terms. The three groupings represent official facts, but they are the outcome of such a mélange of geographical, historical, social, cultural, political and economic factors that they are not as stable as they might seem at first sight, and do not offer much of a basis on which anyone can erect hard statistical edifices.

The received model and its statistics are useful – at least initially – but remain simplistic; there is quite simply far more to English today than an easy division into one primary group of users by birthright and two other groups of users through acquisition. Their massed performances every day, in speech, print and writing around the globe, dwarf all of our past experience with any language and are a kaleidoscope of themes and variations, as are the attitudes of the users themselves. Even as they use English, they may vary in their feelings about it from enthusiasm to indifference, and from love through ambivalence to open hostility – and this is as true for the ENL as it is for the ESL and EFL nations.

The mother-tongue nations are, to start off with anyway, easy to recognize. Naming most of them as they come to mind (the inner eye running round the globe of the world) seems harmless enough, but trying to organize those names into a list is anything but easy. Only alphabetical order permits neutrality, an escape from the implicit pecking orders that emerge whenever some other criterion is used to create the list. ABC order may be decently antiseptic, but even it ultimately stirs hierarchical responses. Thus, in the order of the alphabet Barbados, Belize and Bermuda come near the top, while the United Kingdom and the United States come near the bottom, an arrangement that plays funny tricks with history, population size, ethnic tension, and economic clout.

If, however, the criterion adopted for making the ENL list were historical-cum-cultural, many people would place England at the top. But in present-day terms England is officially one of the four components of 'the United Kingdom of Great Britain and Northern Ireland', all of the components having a technical parity. In two of those components – Wales and Scotland – Celtic languages survive, languages whose roots go further back in the British Isles than the roots of English. If England were listed first and the concept 'United Kingdom' or 'Britain' set aside for the purpose of doing so, then Scotland, Wales and Northern Ireland would come next – in one order or another – but less as autonomous entities than as sociolinguistic satellites, representing the first diaspora of the English language throughout the home archipelago, before there occurred the second and vaster diaspora throughout the world. Once these were listed the United States would probably be next, as the first of the far-off growths to gain both political and linguistic autonomy. Others might then follow in a more or less tidy chronological order.

But there is more to modern life than history and culture. If the criterion were either population size or economic power the ordering would be rather different: here, the United States would come first by overwhelming right, with either England or the United Kingdom coming second. With around 230 million people the USA has by far the largest and most vigorous English-speaking population in the world, and it makes itself felt today much as England made itself felt in the 19th century. Until around the Second World War, the centre of gravity of the language was in the south-east of England, around Oxford, Cambridge and London. Nowadays, the center of gravity is closer to Ohio than Oxford, a state of affairs that many people in the home islands, especially members of the older generation, find hard to acknowledge or, if acknowledged, to bear. Their distress often finds an outlet in letters to the editors of UK periodicals, decrying the 'flood' of 'vulgar' Americanisms that pours across the Atlantic and endangers the language of Shakespeare and Milton.

Suppose, then, that we divide the hono(u)rs, allowing the United Kingdom a historical priority and the United States a numerical and economic priority. Either way, positions one and two on the list are taken care of, but this is not much help. Some Scots, mindful of their ancient literary heritage and the dialectal richness of THEIR English (often called 'Scots', sometimes called 'Lallans', and once known as 'Inglis'), might seek to open up the UK and place Scotland third, or in strict historical and cultural terms second. Some inhabitants of the two Irelands might wish the whole problem away, while others would shrug and say that their island and not the

United States was the first overseas territory in which English supplanted another language (and culture), and was indeed where many of the tactics of expansion were first tried out. They would then place themselves third, favouring history over both numbers and economics.

Inside both England and the United States arguments might spring up, pointing out that neither is a linguistic monolith, and that each has its own pecking order, where certain varieties are near the top and others near the bottom. While they were arguing (bringing in class, money, geography, race and many other issues), Canada and Australia could be considering the third place. Canada's population of 24 million might look better than Australia's 15 million, until one recalls the existence of the ESL province of Quebec (and other French-Canadian areas), the Canadian demographic total for 'anglophones' then falling to 17 million, in an officially bilingual federation.

In terms of both history and population, New Zealand might expect to come lowish on the list, but would it be above or below South Africa? The population of South Africa is some 30 million, but of that total only some two million are 'native' speakers of English, whereas New Zealand has three million. In both places, however, the very word 'native' poses problems, with racial undertones that are also important when we move to the varied and scattered territories in and near the Caribbean. There English is the only language (as in Jamaica) or the dominant language (as in Belize) or a minority language (as in Nicaragua). But in this area the very concept of 'English' becomes seriously unstable, because the majority of speakers in these lands and islands do not use the 'standard' language or even traditional 'dialects'; their speech forms are 'creoles', descended from 'pidgins', and although they are English in a broad sense are not necessarily English in a narrow sense as defined by many people who would not call themselves purists or racists. They would simply argue that a creole is English in such a NOVEL way, and is so unlikely to be intelligible to people outside its circle, that there is a serious functional sense in which it is not English at all.

And yet the official business and the educational processes in nations like Barbados, Bermuda, Jamaica and Trinidad go forward in an English that is internationally understood, and if these nations are not ENL then what are they? The millions who live there do not perceive themselves as speakers of some language distinct from English, but might yet prefer the ENL list to be alphabetic rather than historical, cultural, numerical or economic, because they would not find themselves relegated to the bottom in such a list.

This conundrum is a good point at which to move over to the ESL nations, because many such nations – like Cameroon, Ghana, Nigeria and Papua New Guinea – share with the Caribbean ENL nations varieties that are known widely as 'pidgins' or 'creoles'; indeed, if one thinks in terms of Gullah and the history of Black English Vernacular, they also share these varieties with the United States, and, in terms of a variety like London Jamaican, can also be said to share them, though on a small scale, with England. Large or small, the ESL countries were all in the not-far-distant past part of the British Empire (or, in the case of the Philippines and some other territories, part of the American equivalent of that Empire). In the process, each of them has been, as it were, veneered with English for administrative, commercial, educational, religious or other purposes. As colonial status changed to autonomy, this coating of English was turned, in most of them, into an official or quasi-official language, generally accompanied by a certain prestige and privilege.

The largest of the ESL nations is the Republic of India. With over 700 million inhabitants, it is the most populous of all the countries where English is a significant language. With upwards of 20 million regular users of the language it is, on the criterion of numbers, ahead of both Canada and Australia in the pecking order of World English. Since it is also a major publisher of periodicals and exporter of books in English, its position in that pecking order looks likely to grow stronger as we move towards the year 2000.

As will have become evident by now, the criterion by which a regular user of English achieves membership of the club in an ESL nation is quite different from the criterion in an ENL nation. Altogether, in such countries as India, Pakistan, Bangladesh, Sri Lanka, Burma, Nigeria, Ghana, Cameroon, Kenya, Uganda, Tanzania, Zambia, Zimbabwe, the Philippines, Singapore, Malaysia, Hong Kong and Papua New Guinea there are around 1.34 billion people. The principle by means of which 300 million of these people are classified as regular users of English at a significant social level is educational and occupational. These are literate people with a measurable competence linked with schooling, background and work. By and large they are the professional bureaucratic, mercantile, educational and other élites of the ESL nations, making up just under a quarter of the overall total. To be able to handle an internationally adequate variety of the language in a competent way is in most of these lands a token of status, ability and modernity; indeed, it has the official blessing of so many governments that more and more people in these nations are bound to seek control over English as their passport to better things. But, because of the very significance of English, we cannot suppose that the 300 million are ALL the users of English, in the way that the 300 million are assumed all to have been born into English in the ENL nations. These are the people on a continuum of use whose capacity is in some way certified; there are an unknown number of others – many millions – who use some sort of English quite frequently, but who have either insufficient certification or no viable credentials at all.

'I am struck', says David Crystal, while discussing the statistics of World English, 'by the remarkable amount of semi-fluent or "broken" English which is encountered in the Indian sub-continent, used by people with a limited educational background. The important point to appreciate is that this is broken *English*, not French, or Swahili, or anything else.' Are they not also, in some broader-than-usual sense, also club members, if not fully certified, then at least associate members of some kind? Crystal doubts that 'educated excellence' can be the only criterion here, and adds that 'some lower levels of competence might just as justifiably be proposed'.

That seems reasonable, especially as no educational criterion whatever is applied for the ENL nations, among which any bilinguals or multilinguals are also automatically assumed to be highly competent in English – which cannot be true for many millions, made up from a variety of such groups as Maoris in New Zealand, Ukrainians in Canada, Hispanics in the United States, immigrants of various kinds in the United Kingdom, and so forth.

'The usual response,' says Crystal, to the suggestion that a lower level of competence could be acceptable, is 'the thin end of the wedge' argument: 'If we allow in speakers with only 90% competence, why not 80%, or 50% or 5% . . . ? What about the many children, running about India at this moment, who have learned but a few words and phrases as part of their restricted language of begging? Can they be said to know English, in any sense? My point is, they do not beg with smatterings of Spanish, or Russian, or Chinese.'

Crystal's question has some intriguing implications in it. Many people would relegate the young Indian beggars to the uttermost limits of English, yet in accepting the statistics for the ENL nations would include new-born babies, uncertain three-year-olds, people with serious speech disabilities, the non-literate (for whatever reasons), and the immigrant non-native within the circle of 'native', if for no better reason than the difficulty of sifting them out. But the problem of sifting out, this conundrum of boundaries, invests the discussion of the statistics – and of the quality – of English not just in one community but in ALL communities, making the received statistics softer and softer as the discussion proceeds.

This is a suitable point at which to move on to the EFL nations; the issue of competence is as much a connecting point between ESL and EFL as the issue of the creoles ties ENL and ESL together. In a crude but serious sense the whole world is caught up in the acquisition of English – not every individual, of course, but sizeable groups in every corner of the globe. There are no precise figures for this unprecedented development, but from Finland to Paraguay, from the Soviet Union to Surinam, the trend is strong. In mainland China alone, out of a population around one billion, AT LEAST 100 million are said to be working on their English. In Portugal, out of a population of around nine million, 'a measured audience of 1.2 million' is known to have tuned in to the BBC television learning course *Follow Me* (an apt title if ever there was one). In both vast China and small Portugal the proportion of acknowledged individuals is similar – around 10% of the people (and an even larger proportion of the active adult population).

Now, some countries like Albania hardly teach English at all, while others like the Netherlands teach it to every child from the primary years onward, so that one wonders at what point such countries will shift from EFL to ESL status. Averaging out across the non-ENL, non-ESL world, however, the Chinese/Portuguese figures make a handy and conservative reference norm. If we take the present population of the world to be around 4.5 billion, and subtract the 1.75 billion of the ENL and ESL nations (as total approximate populations), we get 2.75 billion for the EFL nations. If we then apply the Chinese/Portuguese norm, we can say that in all likelihood some 275 million people in these nations are in the process of acquiring English – and are ranged out along a continuum of acquisition from the excellence of many of the 100 million first mooted to the halting efforts of beginners. For tidiness, make this 300 million, and then add it to the 300 million each of the ENL and ESL groups. The result is 900 million people. If we then take up the slack of all the 'broken' English speakers of the ESL nations, the number of people involved with English easily reaches the one-billion mark.

And that is more or less where one has to leave the statistics of

World English at present. There ARE no thoroughly reliable figures, but what figures there are suggest that, however judged, there must be around half a billion people on earth who are good communicators in English, and another half billion who, for various reasons, all legitimate, have a lower capacity or range but still function adequately in the language for many purposes. Beyond these lies a wholly unknown number who operate at the survival and smattering level, from people with a good reading knowledge but no skill in speech through tourists with just enough to get by to tour guides with a strictly limited range, small traders mixing several languages, and those beggars in the streets. They are legion too, but it would be utterly speculative to put a number on them.

A billion 'regular users', broadly defined, does however seem to be a fair estimate for the late 1980s, all operating in and on what Alan Maley has called 'the most chameleon of languages'.

II

PROBLEMS OF SUCCESS: THE LATIN ANALOGY

When Alan Maley made his reference to the chameleon quality of English, 'changing its colour to fit the background, wherever it has settled', he was not just discussing the characteristics of the language but also looking at its possible futures:

'One possible scenario for English as an international language is that it will succumb to the same fate as Latin did in the Middle Ages. That is, that the regional varieties will develop independently to the point where they become different languages rather than varieties of the same language.'

This is a reference to what is probably best called 'the Latin analogy'. In recent years this analogy has been brought into play with increasing frequency. Maley made his comment at the beginning of 1985. In a paper read to scholars attending a conference on English studies, organized to celebrate the 50th anniversary of the British Council and held about the time that Maley wrote his article, Randolph Quirk noted:

'Small wonder that there should have been in recent years fresh talk of the diaspora of English into several mutually incomprehensible languages. The fate of Latin after the fall of the Roman Empire presents us with such distinct languages today as French, Spanish, Romanian, and Italian. With the growth of national separatism in the English-speaking countries, linguistically endorsed not least by the active encouragement of the anti-standard ethos . . ., many foresee a similar fissiparous future for English. A year or so ago, much prominence was given to the belief expressed by R. W. Burchfield that in a century from now the languages of Britain and America would be as different as French is from Italian.'

Neither Quirk nor Maley endorses the Latin analogy as the most likely scenario for the future of English, but they concede its attractions. In his turn Burchfield discussed the separation of American and British as decently far-off – at least a hundred years away. In his preface to the fourth and final supplement to the *Oxford English Dictionary*, he acknowledges the striking diversity already exhibited by the language, noting that an *OED* editor no longer has the freedom or the right to fend off items of English that are not yet entrenched in (and canonized by) British acceptance: 'At a time when the English language seems to be breaking up into innumerable clearly distinguishable varieties, it seemed to me important to abandon Murray's insular policy and go out and find what was happening in the language elsewhere.' As a result, in noting this change from the first editor's policy, American reviewers of the fourth supplement commented that at last their variety of the language was being properly catalogued in the great book.

To the extent that this is so, and to the extent that other dictionaries are likely to follow Burchfield's lead, such books could very well serve as counterpoints to the prospect that varieties of English may become, in Quirk's phrase, 'mutually incomprehensible languages'. At the very least, significant elements of their disparate vocabularies would still be getting into prestigious wordbooks with worldwide markets. Be that as it may, however, the fact that modern English is not a monolith, and exists in 'innumerable clearly distinguishable varieties', has been obvious to many thoughtful travellers and readers for some time, and it must be a source of some gratification to them that at last the scholarly community has begun to provide reports and analyses of this fact. In the 1980s a surprising number of hefty volumes has been appearing describing – indeed, as one editor of one such volume has put it, 'celebrating' – the diversity of the present-day language. By 1986 the language had even earned itself a BBC TV series, accompanied by a glossy illustrated book, becoming in the process a topic for popular discussion on a par with wildlife, economics, famine, over-population, birth control, pollution and high technology.

Most of the books that have appeared have played safe in their titles: *English as a World Language, The English Language Today,*

English in the World, and so forth. At least two, however, have not, and have employed a rather startling bit of neologistic grammar that has caught on quite simply because of its appropriateness. These books are *New Englishes*, which looks largely at varieties of English in the ESL nations, and *Modern Englishes*, which deals in the main with pidgins and creoles.

'Englishes', a plural form for a word that until recently was never normally pluralized, has made impressive headway in recent years. As yet very few people talk about 'an English', when referring to just one of Burchfield's innumerable varieties, but the singular countable usage follows logically from the plural, and may yet catch on. The regular and increasing uses of expressions like 'American English', 'Indian English', 'Scottish English', 'British English' and even – though it had a slow start – 'English English' seems to have led inevitably to the plural 'Englishes'. Although as far as I know it has not yet been listed in a recent revision of a major dictionary, the term has been used by Robert Burchfield himself, where in HIS recent book, *The English Language*, he talks about features of 'the home variety' (that is, British English) which might or might not be 'shared by Englishes abroad'.

There is something inherently contagious and risqué, however, about a usage like 'Englishes', especially when combined with thoughts and fears concerning the break-up of a perceived monolith into fragments. It is only a short step from talking about 'the Englishes' to talking about 'the English languages', as for example in the following quotation from Robert McCrum, the script-writer for *The Story of English*, the BBC TV series mentioned above:

'Seven years ago I was reading V. S. Naipaul's *A Bend in the River*. Suddenly it struck me that there I was, in New York, reading a book about disappearing Africans by a Trinidadian of Indian extraction. I thought I would like to read something on the history of English languages but there was nothing. Everything concerned the history of English in England.'

McCrum's series and accompanying book certainly shift the emphasis. Indeed, they shift it so strongly that in a review by Catherine Bennett in *The Sunday Times* (London, 14th September 1986) the following virtual riposte appears:

'In the first episode alone, McCrum's urbane Canadian narrator, chosen because of, rather than in spite of, his transatlantic accent, takes us to California, Jamaica, Scotland, Italy, Japan, Sierra Leone, India, Singapore and, occasionally, England. Everywhere they are speaking English, and speaking it, it is continually implied, more imaginatively than we do.'

In such a prickly context, it is perhaps not surprising that one of the episode/ chapters of both TV series and book is entitled 'The Empire Strikes Back'.

The magazine that I edit, *English Today*, is part of the whole phenomenon not just of the burgeoning of English into the world's first truly universal language but also of the new industry of commenting on the phenomenon. Our subtitle is pointedly, 'the international review of the English language'. First appearing in late 1985, the magazine seeks to report on every possible aspect of English, but its title remains by and large conservative. Not so with a journal that used to be known as *World Language English* which in the same year metamorphosed into *World Englishes*, under the joint editorship of Braj B. Kachru and Larry E. Smith. Here the new title has an ideological impact, indicating that there are not just varieties but that these varieties have a high degree of autonomy. The logo-acronym *WE* also serves to indicate that there is a club of equals here, where the journal in its earlier incarnation tended to centre upon the standard language and the standards of language of south-eastern England. The previous editor was William Lee, an Englishman; the new editors are Kachru, an Indian from Kashmir, and Smith, an American domiciled in Hawaii. In a decade of great change in both English AND OUR PERCEPTION OF ENGLISH in the world, these two periodicals complement each other, the first emphasizing English as a unity, the second treating it as a plurality.

Braj Kachru, as a leading scholar of both international English and the Englishes of the Indian subcontinent, has taken up in his journal and elsewhere the issue of the democratization of attitudes to English everywhere in the globe, in the process questioning the received model of the ENL, ESL and EFL nations. He has not dissolved the trinity, but has re-named it, discussing first of all an 'inner circle' of those nations traditionally associated with the language, an 'outer circle' of those nations that are in effect in the process of NATIVIZING their forms of English, and lastly an 'expanding circle' of other nations which are in the process of adopting English in various ways for various purposes. This is a more dynamic model than the standard version, and allows for all manner of shadings and overlaps among the circles. Although 'inner' and 'outer' still suggest – inevitably – a historical priority and the attitudes that go with it, the metaphor of ripples in a pond suggests mobility and flux and implies that a new history is in the making.

In tandem with Kachru, Larry Smith is among the pioneers of a new approach to the teaching of English around the world, one that challenges traditional assumptions about learning English as a native language and the teaching of it as a second language (TESL) or a foreign language (TEFL). Smith talks about TEIL, the teaching of English as an international language, in a world where Burchfield's innumerable distinguishable varieties are constantly meeting each other, as people travel and seek to do business. The implications of the idea of TEIL are enormous, because they place a burden not just upon the ESL and EFL nations to do their best and learn English as well as they can, but also on the ENL peoples, who must compromise too, in the effort to understand and be understood. The processes of communication are not, as Smith and his colleagues see it, simply the assured and culturally secure native-users meeting the rest. Across the ENL countries of the inner circle adjustments and concessions have to be made too, as Cockneys from London have to make themselves understood by Newfoundlanders, while someone from Belfast has to accommodate to somebody from Jamaica or Texas. In the outer circles, Indians from Delhi and Madras have to be able to grasp each others' points in English, as well as do business with Japanese and Thais, and make sense to Australians and Turks. The circles constantly meet and mingle, in situations where few have permanent clearcut advantages, and all have to acclimatize. And this acclimatization is not only linguistic. It is cultural and philosophical as well; world travellers need to be ready not just for unfamiliar accents, grammar and vocabulary but also for special social assumptions, distinct forms of body language, and ultimately different mindsets as well.

On reflection, it is unrealistic to suppose that one language medium could ever neutralize the diversities of the world – and on further reflection it is clear that the spread of English to date has never succeeded in neutralizing the diversities – and attendant tensions – of the peoples of Kachru's INNER circle. English currently reflects the background and attitudes of all the groups who have ever used it: the class tensions inside England; the ethnic tensions among English, Scots, Welsh and Irish (which are far from being resolved); residual conflicts between Catholic and Protestant, Jew and Goy; the established rivalry between Britain and America; stresses between English and other languages, as for example with French in Canada and Spanish in the United States; race tensions between black and white in Africa, the Caribbean, the United States and the United Kingdom – and, at the end of the list but by no means insignificant, the built-in Eurocentric bias among the mainly white societies of the ENL nations, setting them apart from the other cultural blocs of Islam, Hinduism, Japan, and so forth.

As part of this complex interplay of social and historical factors, English possesses some rather curious and paradoxical features. It is, for example, at one and the same time the élite language of science and technology, education and modernity, and the populist language of rock music and reggae, sport and fashion. It is the primary vehicle of world finance and telecommunications, the register of airline pilots and those who keep the logs of the world's shipping – the most extensive and varied *koiné* the human race has ever known – and yet at the same time its varieties prompt as much loyal emotion as any other language: people from the north of England are as conscious of their 'dialect' as Danes are conscious of their particular Scandinavian tongue; the Scots are as aware of the special qualities of their English as the Catalans and Galicians are aware of the distinctness of their usage from Castilian; and Americans quite often call their language 'American', forgetting that it is 'English', while some English people might label it 'Americanese', refusing to accept that it IS in fact 'English'.

The Latin of the Empire may well have broken up in comparable ways, among the Lusitanians who created Portuguese and the Dacians who brought Rumanian into existence. French has sometimes been said to have arisen out of a Gallic creole of Latin, and standard Italian is still not a universal speech form in Italy, competing as it does with many strong dialects to which large numbers of people feel a greater loyalty. The Latin analogy is therefore attractive, especially when one considers the vastness of the numbers involved in using English.

There is, however, a flaw built into the Latin analogy, and one which is seldom discussed when the comparison is made between Latin in the so-called 'Dark Ages' and English today. That flaw relates to our very concept of what a language is, because the assumption is made – and left largely undiscussed – that there once was a single uniform spoken Latin used by large numbers of people that COULD then break up into other 'daughter' languages. Parallel to this, we must suppose too that there has been a single uniform spoken English used by large numbers of people that could also break up into further daughter languages. The evidence to support this monolithic view of both Latin and English is slight, as I hope to demonstrate. And if it is slight, then the idea that English 'is breaking up' or 'could break up' into mutually unintelligible languages may be founded on an illusion about both Latin and English.

III

A MODEL OF ENGLISH TO FIT THE FACTS

Over the decades there have been many works, often by scholars summing up a lifetime of observation, with titles like *A History of English* or simply *The English Language*. The tacit assumption behind each of them is that, throughout the history of certain communities living off the shores of North-Western Europe there has been a Germanic language of such conspicuous unity that one can call it 'English' while calling its comparable neighbours 'German', 'French', 'Welsh' and 'Gaelic'.

This is how we have all been brought up to label and think of the language systems in countries like England, Scotland, Wales, Ireland, Germany and France. It is a container model of language, whereby one puts a label on a mental box called 'French' and then puts all and only French inside that container, secure in the belief that it is possible to do such a thing. This is a legitimate process, not unlike creating the received statistics of World English; by and large it has served us well, but it is by no means sufficient as a model of such language systems. Inside the very books with such titles this becomes clear when we discover the scholars in question constantly amending the model by discussing continuums of dialect, deviations from standard forms, admixtures of other languages, the presence in other languages of elements of English, and so forth. Indeed, what emerges upon a closer examination of the conventional model for describing a language like English is various kinds of continuum models behind the container model, just as we have found all sorts of continuums in the present-day situation of the language from standard to dialect, standard to creole, highly competent and certified to less-than-competent and uncertified, and so forth.

Histories of English generally divide English into four successive forms: an Old English that transforms itself into a Middle English which then becomes first an Early Modern English and then a Modern English. Rough-and-ready dates are provided for the transition points from one to the other, and the processes of transition are tied in with various significant historical developments in the world, such as the Norman Conquest of England after 1066 which – in a period of remarkable linguistic turmoil – turned the language of *Beowulf* into the language of Chaucer's *Canterbury Tales*. The 'Old English' period of Beowulf is also often called the 'Anglo-Saxon' period, and generations of modern students of English have found themselves in university courses, equipped with little books like *Sweet's Anglo-Saxon Primer*, learning the first variety of 'English' in snippet fashion much as they had at school been learning packages of Classical Latin and possibly also Classical Greek. In such classes, it has always been hard to believe that *Of Iotum comon Cant-ware and Wiht-ware* was in any sense 'English'. The issue was left in a curious limbo; it both was and was not English. Such a system, however, is as far from modern English as Latin is from modern French, but no one has ever thought of referring to Classical Latin as 'Old French'. And yet it is Old French in much the same sense that Anglo-Saxon is Old English.

'Latin' in its day was also just as diverse as 'Anglo-Saxon'. The scholars who have commented on both languages always stress the dialect variety among both the Angles, Saxons and Jutes on one side and the communities of ancient Italy on the other. Unfortunately, the use of contrastive terms like 'language' (larger, containing) and 'dialect' (smaller, contained), each implying the same kind of rigid structuring, obscures the reality of flux and almost person-by-person variation. Since the few records left to us are in various ways standardized we are compelled to suppose that Cicero's Latin and Alfred's Anglo-Saxon were the 'true' forms of the language systems in question. It is so much more convenient to deal in monolithic models – even on a cautious AS IF principle – that we adopt them almost in spite of ourselves, and teach them to the next generation or to lay audiences because it seems to be the safe thing to do. This luxury may no longer be desirable or even possible.

Middle English is comparable to Old English. There was no strong centralizing influence on a vernacular like 'English' until after the invention of the printing press in the mid-15th century. Then, fascinated by their success in homogenizing the new printed word, language trendsetters used this norm to help them seek the kind of regularity and fixity that existed not in the spoken Latin of their time – which was so varied that it was widely considered 'degenerate' – but in the classical texts of ancient Rome itself. Having begun to work upon standard conventions of page layout, punctuation and orthography, they also began to look for a parallel consistency in the 'higher' spoken forms of languages like English, French and Italian, using for reference the only models they had – Latin grammatical rules and the religious, educational and philosophical tradition of the 'high' vocabulary of Latin. Together with the new printed texts and the norms of speech offered by certain royal courts and prestigious centres of learning, these aids worked over several centuries to produce – slowly and patchily – the 'standard' languages we talk about today. Like our 'standard' weights, measures and currencies, these draw their inspiration from the King's Standard, the flag that once rallied troops in battle.

By the time a certain measure of standardizing stability had emerged for the English language as used in England and Scotland – at the time when the crowns of the two nations were united in 1603 – the first ships were setting sail for North America with colonists who had no intention of returning. The language that was by then dominant throughout the off-shore islands of western Europe, the language of the Tudor and Stuart dynasties, the language of Shakespeare and the new 'authorized' Bible, was AT ITS LEVEL OF SHAKY STANDARDIZATION the 'same' language by the middle of the 17th century wherever it was spoken, whether in England, Scotland, Ireland, the North American colonies, the West Indies or anywhere else that its flag-bearers went. In the process it became normal for educated people to expect to understand each other in speech as well as on paper wherever they went, while it was also normal for 'dialect' speakers to have great difficulty when moved away from their home areas. A two-tier language became the norm, and has remained the norm ever since, whether in terms of dialects like Cockney and Brooklyn, creoles as in Sierra Leone or Jamaica, or varieties heavily influenced by other tongues, as in Quebec and Puerto Rico. The records, of course, have gone on being kept in the printed standard, by and large, as has the bulk of the literature or literatures called 'English', so that where Chaucer was often impossible and Shakespeare frequently hard to follow, from the late 17th century onward the records are almost entirely comprehensible to any educated reader today, regardless of spoken background.

Our historical model of English with its 'old', 'middle' and 'modern' is a masterpiece of retroactive legislation. The creator of Beowulf was entirely unaware that he was composing in 'old' anything, and Chaucer never suspected that his language was in the middle position between an 'old' and a 'modern'. Similarly, but in spatial rather than temporal terms, a child learning his or her home tongue in working-class Liverpoool, Brooklyn or Glasgow, in middle-class Tunbridge Wells or Morningside, in avant-garde Palo Alto or conservative Little Rock, in white homes in New Hampshire or black homes in Mississippi, in multilingual homes in New Delhi or New York, is entirely unaware that the form of English being imbibed is dialect, creole, standard, non-standard or sub-standard. Upon entering school, however, such distinctions may begin to impose themselves foggily on the consciousness of the child, as the educational process invites – persuades, coaxes, coerces or otherwise conditions – the child into focussing with greater or less success, with greater or less resistance, with greater or less peer pressure one way or the other, on the standard forms with their powerful heritage of print.

This heritage has contributed towards the unexamined conception of a language, and in particular the English language, as a monolith or, perhaps more frequently, as a normative citadel in terms of which its historically diverse and less literacy-based forms are perceived as 'deviant'. As an instance of the little-discussed power of this model, the 1,779-page Longman work, published in 1985 and entitled *A Comprehensive Grammar of the English Language* can be widely perceived as just that – whereas in point of fact it is the most comprehensive grammar ever made of the literacy-linked STANDARD language.

The Latin analogy tends to be invoked when we think of English as a monolith like the Latin monolith that never in fact existed. Like Latin, English was and is only a monolith insofar as broad diffuse language systems can be labelled contrastively, so that we know the limits of English in a rough-and-ready way by being able to say that it is not French, Arabic, Japanese or Sioux. When people fear the break-up at some imminent time of 'English' into various 'mutually unintelligible languages' they are not thinking of the totality of the English phenomenon throughout its history and geography. That totality has always had its mutually unintelligible forms, at least as distinct from each other as Danish from Swedish. What they are thinking about is the prized and print-related entity Standard English, which has also never had easily demarcated boundaries and has never been without a range of hotly discussed and disputed usage controversies.

There certainly is such a Standard English, and it is reasonable to say that there are stresses and strains operating upon it that are as powerful and diverse as ever they were – and made even more powerful and diverse by the sheer unprecedented numbers of people using or seeking to use that medium. For a long time now, however, even that 'Standard English' has not been monolithic, because since at least the 18th century, when the United States broke away from the British Empire, there have been alternative perceptions of the standard. Today there are in existence or in the process of developing a range of 'national standards' of English, each embedded in the continuum of usage in an England, a Scotland, a United States, a Canada, a Nigeria, and so on. Usage radiates out from them to all the various 'dialects', 'creoles', 'slangs', 'registers' and other forms that people require in their day-to-day lives. And in turn the various national standards and near-standards merge into a broad 'World Standard', which is of necessity somewhat flexible and accommodating.

The traditional container model of one English is useful when we compare 'English' with 'Spanish' or 'Arabic'. The more radical continuum model of various English languages that include, and centre on, World Standard English (with its varieties), is useful when we talk of American English as opposed to British, Canadian Standard (English) as opposed to Australian Standard or West African Standard, West African Pidgin as opposed to Jamaican Creole, Tok-Pisin in Papua New Guinea, Gullah, Black Vernacular, Quebec English, Cockney, Scouse, Brooklyn, and all the other 'innumerable varieties' within the circle. What seems likely is that we shall have to use both models side by side, entirely consciously – aware that we already live, and to some extent always have lived, in a world where there are both an English language and a range of English languages.

BIBLIOGRAPHY

1. *Language and Languages*

The scientific study of language – linguistics – begins, in a sense, in this century with F. de Saussure's *Cours de linguistique générale* (Paris, 1916) – translated into English by Wade Baskin as *Course in General Linguistics* (New York, 1959). In America the great names are those of Edward Sapir and Leonard Bloomfield, both of whom wrote a book entitled *Language* – E. Sapir, *Language: an Introduction to the Study of Speech* (New York, 1921 – reprinted in Harvest Books, 1955). L. Bloomfield, *Language* (New York, 1933, and London, 1935). The great Danish scholar Otto Jespersen wrote many books on language and on English, but these are in more traditional terms and deeply concerned with a historical approach. Two of the best known are *The Philosophy of Grammar* (London, 1924) and *Language: its Nature, Development and Origin* (London, 1922).

A number of general books on linguistics appeared in the fifties and sixties all in the American structuralist tradition, such as C. F. Hockett's *A Course in Modern Linguistics* (New York, 1958), H. A. Gleason's *An Introduction to Descriptive Linguistics* (New York, 1961), R. A. Hall's *Linguistics and your Language* (New York, 1960) and *Introductory Linguistics* (Philadelphia, 1964).

Since that time, however, linguistics has been greatly influenced, if not dominated, by the ideas of Noam Chomsky in what was originally known as 'TG' (Transformational-generative Grammar). Chomsky's earliest ideas were presented in *Syntactic Structures* (The Hague, 1957), but more recent works are much more difficult for the non-specialist. There are few explanatory books, but the best is that of Andrew Radford, *Transformational Syntax* (Cambridge, 1981). There have been very few general books too since that time. One is R. A. Robins, *General Linguistics: an introductory survey* (London, third edition, 1980); a work that is simpler and more limited in its scope is *Grammar* (Harmondsworth, second edition, 1984) by the author of this chapter, while a really basic introduction is *What is Linguistics?* (London, fourth edition, 1985) by David Crystal.

2. *Phonology: The Sounds of English*

The most comprehensive description of English (RP) at the segmental, phonemic/allophonic level is that by A. C. Gimson, *An Introduction to the Pronunciation of English* (London, third edition, 1980). A shorter treatment, and perhaps rather easier to read, is P. Roach, *English Phonetics and Phonology: a Practical Course* (Cambridge, 1983); it is accompanied by a Tutor's Book, and contains useful suggestions for further reading.

In the area of English intonation and related matters, the major work is D. Crystal, *Prosodic Systems and Intonation in English* (Cambridge, 1969). Two other books will be found easier going by the 'interested layman', but lack the comprehensiveness of Crystal's survey and represent in each case a particular approach to the subject – they should be read with this in mind; they are J. D. O'Connor and G. F. Arnold, *The Intonation of Colloquial English* (London, second edition, 1973) – the viewpoint here is similar to that of Part III of Gimson's *Introduction*, referred to above; and M. A. K. Halliday, *Intonation and Grammar in British English* (The Hague, 1967).

In recent years, a further approach has concentrated on placing intonation firmly in the context of 'discourse analysis' (and in the even wider one of 'pragmatics'). This is exemplifed in D. Brazil, M. Coulthard and C. Johns, *Discourse Intonation and Language Teaching* (London, 1980), in G. Brown, K. Currie and J. Kenworthy, *Questions of Intonation* (London, 1980), and in J. McH. Sinclair and D. Brazil, *Teacher Talk* (Oxford, 1982).

Alan Cruttenden's *Intonation* (Cambridge, 1986), though not concerned exclusively with English, can be read as a state-of-the-art exposition; it takes into account both discourse intonation and earlier approaches.

In addition to the above, all the introductory texts on linguistics (e.g. those listed in the bibliography to chapter 1 of this book) include sections on general phonetics. Further reading in this area should include J. D. O'Connor, *Phonetics* (Harmondsworth, 1973), or P. Ladefoged, *A Course in Phonetics* (New York, second edition, 1983). For general phonology, see L. Hyman, *Phonology: theory and Analysis* (New York, 1975), R. Lass, *Phonology: an Introduction to the Basic Concepts* (Cambridge, 1984) and S. R. Anderson, *Phonology in the Twentieth Century* (Chicago, 1985), though rather advanced discussions which cannot be read without a good preliminary understanding.

The above is of course a limited selection from the very large literature, but the reader will nonetheless quickly discover considerable variation in the terminology used – different terms for much the same phenomenon, or the same term used with rather different reference. This is particularly true as between British and American work, and particularly again in the field of 'prosodic' (or 'suprasegmental') features. While such variation is certainly unhelpful, and can be downright confusing at times, the persevering reader will also discover that often enough it merely conceals basic agreement, or at worst reflects alternative analyses which are equally valid as to 'how the language works'.

3. *Morphology: The Forms of English*

Treatments of morphology are to be found in the principal introductory works on grammar and on linguistics in general; these include D. J. Allerton, *Essentials of Grammatical Theory* (London, 1979), L. Bloomfield, *Language* (New York, 1935), and R. H. Robins, *General Linguistics: an Introductory Survey* (London, third edition, 1980).

A pioneering work on the principles and methods of morphological study in *Morphology* by E. A. Nida (Ann Arbor, second edition, 1949). A more recent discussion of the problems of (especially inflectional) morphology is P. H. Matthews, *Morphology* (Cambridge, 1974). A more specifically generative treatment is offered in M. Aronoff, *Word Formation in Generative Grammar* (Cambridge, Mass., 1976).

Amongst major works devoted specifically to the morphology of English, both *The Categories and Types of Present-Day English Word-Formation* (Munich, second edition, 1969) by H. Marchand, and Volume VI of *A Modern English Grammar* (London, 1946) by O. Jespersen, contain a wealth of detail. A more concise work is V. Adams, *An Introduction to Modern English Word-Formation* (London, 1973), and there is a neat summary of English word-formation in Appendix I of *A Comprehensive Grammar of the English Language* by R. Quirk, S. Greenbaum, G. Leech and J. Svartvik (London, 1985).

A blend of theory and practice is found in L. Bauer, *English Word Formation* (Cambridge, 1983).

4. *Syntax: The Structure of English*

Discussions of syntax figure prominently in all general introductions to linguistics. The best of these is still J. Lyons, *Introduction to Theoretical Linguistics* (Cambridge, 1968). An excellent introduction to the subfield of grammar for the general reader is provided in F. R. Palmer, *Grammar* (Harmondsworth, second edition, 1984). A very useful introductory textbook is E. K. Brown & J. E. Miller, *Syntax: A Linguistic Introduction to Sentence Structure* (London, 1980). The best introductory text to more recent developments in transformational syntax is A. Radford, *Transformational Syntax* (Cambridge, 1981). Outside the transformational approach, a most challenging and stimulating discussion of issues is to be found in P. H. Matthews, *Syntax* (Cambridge, 1981).

Descriptive studies of English are many and varied. A good general account, containing much detail and discussion, is R. Huddleston, *Introduction to the Grammar of English* (Cambridge, 1984). Shorter treatments may be found in G. Leech, M. Deuchar & R. Hoogenraad, *English Grammar for Today: a New Introduction* (Basingstoke, 1982), and N. Burton-Roberts, *Analysing Sentences: an Introduction to English Syntax* (London, 1986). The most comprehensive work is that of R. Quirk, S. Greenbaum, G. Leech and J. Svartvik, *A Comprehensive Grammar of the English Language* (London, 1985), superseding their earlier (and still useful) *A Grammar of Contemporary English* (London, 1972), from which a shorter version, R. Quirk and S. Greenbaum, *A University Grammar of English* (London, 1973), derives.

5. Lexis: The Vocabulary of English

The study of English vocabulary cannot be undertaken without the aid of a good dictionary. There are a number of excellent shorter dictionaries to choose from, such as H. C. Wyld, *The Universal English Dictionary of the English Language* (London, 1932); *The Shorter Oxford English Dictionary*, ed. C. T. Onions (third edition, revised with addenda, Oxford, 1956) – the fourth edition, ed. L. Burnett is expected shortly; G. N. Garmonsway, *The Penguin English Dictionary* (London, 1965); but the serious student is advised from the start to refer to what is probably the greatest dictionary ever produced for any language, *The Oxford English Dictionary*, being a corrected re-issue of *A New English Dictionary on Historical Principles*, ed. J. A. H. Murray, H. Bradley, W. A. Craigie and C. T. Onions (Oxford, 1933); *A Supplement to the Oxford English Dictionary*, ed. R. W. Burchfield (Oxford, 1986), has just been completed. A thesaurus of English is conveniently available in the Penguin edition of *Roget's Thesaurus* (London, 1953). *The Concise Oxford Dictionary of English Etymology*, ed. T. Hoad (Oxford, 1986), is valuable for the study of the origins of the English vocabulary. A useful historical study of loanwords is available in M. Serjeantson, *A History of Foreign Words in English* (London, 1935); A. J. Bliss, *A Dictionary of Foreign Words and Phrases in Current English* (London, 1966) provides a mass of contemporary material. The standard treatment of word-formation is H. Marchand, *The Categories and Types of Present-Day English Word-Formation* (second edition, Munich, 1969); a more accessible work on the same subject is provided by V. Adams, *Introduction to Modern English Word-Formation* (London, 1973). No full treatment of collocation in English is as yet available, but the subject is usefully discussed in A. McIntosh and M. A. K. Halliday, *Patterns of Language*, pp. 183–199: A. McIntosh, 'Patterns and ranges' (London, 1966); and in *In Memory of J. R. Firth*, ed. C. E. Bazell and others (London, 1966), by M. A. K. Halliday, 'Lexis as a linguistic level' and J. Sinclair, 'Beginning the study of lexis'. An invaluable study of sense-relations and the general problem of meaning is to be found in J. Lyons, *Introduction to Theoretical Linguistics*, pp. 400–481 (Cambridge, 1968), and, more recently, F. R. Palmer, *Semantics* (Cambridge, second edition, 1981).

6. *Style: The Varieties of English*

For further discussion and illustration of the approach outlined in this chapter, see D. Crystal and D. Davy, *Investigating English Style* (London, 1969). Other general works include N. E. Enkvist, *Linguistic Stylistics* (The Hague, 1973), R. Chapman, *Linguistics and Literature* (London, 1973), and A. Cluysenaar, *Aspects of Literary Stylistics* (New York, 1975). Detailed and systematic discussion of stylistic considerations in the study of poetry can be found in G. N. Leech, *A Linguistic Guide to English Poetry* (London, 1969), and W. Nowottny, *The Language Poets Use* (London, 1962). For the novel, see G. N. Leech and M. H. Short, *Style in Fiction* (London, 1981), W. Nash, *Designs in Prose* (London, 1980), and R. Fowler, *Linguistics and the Novel* (London, 1977). The style of many individual authors is analysed in several volumes of the *Language Library* (Oxford). A more traditional account of the study of style is J. Middleton Murray, *The Problem of Style* (London, first edition, 1922). Detailed study of a specific variety of English is in G. N. Leech, *English in Advertising: a linguistic study of advertising in Great Britain* (London, 1966). An illustration of stylistic detection work is A. Ellegård, *Who was Junius?* (Almqvist and Wiksell, 1962). A good bibliography of stylistics in relation to English is R. W. Bailey and D. M. Burton, *English Stylistics: A Bibliography* (Cambridge, Mass., 1968). Useful anthologies of articles are S. Chatman and S. R. Levin (eds.), *Essays on the Language of Literature* (Boston, 1967), D. C. Freeman (ed.) *Linguistics and Literary Style* (New York, 1970), and S. Chatman (ed.), *Literary Style: a Symposium* (London, 1971).

7. The Early History of English

Texts quoted

The Blickling Homilies, ed. R. Morris, Early English Text Society, vol. 73, 1880.
Twelfth Century Homilies, ed. A. O. Belfour, EETS, vol. 137, 1909.
An Old English Miscellany, ed. R. Morris, EETS, vol. 49, 1872.
Middle English Sermons, ed. W. O. Ross, EETS, vol. 209, 1940.

Further reading

C. Barker, *The Story of Language* (London, 1964).
A. C. Baugh and T. Cable, *A History of the English Language* (Englewood Cliffs, NJ, third edition, 1978).
N. F. Blake, *The English Language in Medieval Literature*, London, 1979.
W. F. Bolton, *A Living Language: The History and Structure of English* (New York, 1982).
R. Burchfield, *The English Language* (Oxford, 1985).
G. Cannon, *A History of the English Language* (New York, 1972).
J. W. Clark, *Early English* (London, 1957).
J. D. Gordon, *The English Language: An Historical Introduction* (New York, 1972).
J. N. Hook, *A History of the English Language* (New York, 1975).
C. Jones, *An Introduction to Middle English* (New York, 1972).
P. Lieberman, *The Biology and Evolution of Language* (Cambridge, Mass., 1984).
C. B. Martin and C. M. Rulon, *The English Language Yesterday and Today* (Boston, 1973).
J. C. McLaughlin, *Aspects of the History of English* (New York, 1970).
B. Mitchell and F. C. Robinson, *A Guide to Old English* (Oxford, revised edition, 1985).
L. M. Myers and R. L. Hoffman, *The Roots of English* second edition, (Boston, 1979).
A. C. Partridge, *A Companion to Old and Middle English Studies* (London, 1982).
T. Pyles and J. Algeo, *The Origins and Development of the English Language* (New York, third edition, 1982).

M. L. Samuels, *Linguistic Evolution, with Special Reference to English* (Cambridge, 1972).

B. M. H. Strang, *A History of English* (London, 1970).

J. M. Williams, *Origins of the English Language: A Social and Linguistic History* (New York, 1975).

8. *The Later History of English*

Good general histories of English are A. C. Baugh and T. Cable, *A History of the English Language* (London, third edition, 1978) and (more advanced) B. M. H. Strang, *A History of English* (London, 1970). General works on the history of the English vocabulary are J. A. Sheard, *The Words We Use* (London, 1954), and M. S. Serjeantson, *A History of Foreign Words in English* (London, 1953). A good account of methods of word-formation in the post-medieval period is given by V. Adams, *An Introduction to Modern English Word-Formation* (London, 1974). For an even more detailed treatment of the subject, see H. Marchand, *The Categories and Types of Present-Day English Word-Formation* (Munich, second edition, 1969).

The fullest historical treatment of Modern English is Otto Jespersen's massive work, *A Modern English Grammar on Historical Principles* (7 vols, Heidelberg I–IV, London V–VI, Copenhagen VII, 1909–49). More manageable, but still very detailed, is H. C. Wyld, *A History of Modern Colloquial English* (Oxford, third edition, 1936), which deals with the 15th to 18th centuries, and devotes most attention to phonology.

An account of the language between 1500 and 1700 is provided by C. Barber, Early Modern English (London, 1976). For 16th century attitudes to English, an indispensable work is R. F. Jones, *The Triumph of the English Language* (Stanford, California, 1953). E. A. Abbott, *A Shakespearian Grammar* (London, third edition, 1870) has an old-fashioned look, but is full of useful material. The phonology of Early Modern English is treated in detail by E. J. Dobson, *English Pronunciation 1500–1700* (2 vols, Oxford, 1968).

For good introductions to non-British varieties of English, see A. H. Marckwardt, *American English* (Oxford, 1958), and G. W. Turner, *The English Language in Australia and New Zealand* (London, 1966). For recent changes in British English, see C. L. Barber, *Linguistic Change in Present-Day English* (Edinburgh, 1964).

My account of the development of the dummy auxiliary *do* is based on A. Ellegård, *The Auxiliary Do: the Establishment and Regulation of its Use in English* (Stockholm, 1953); and my formulations on the auxiliaries in PresE owe much to W. F. Twaddell's little booklet *The English Verb Auxiliaries* (Providence, Rhode Island, 1960).

Essays about English are collected in W. F. Bolton, ed. *The English Language* (vol I, Cambridge, 1966).

9. The Social Contexts of English

Introductory books on the subject-matter of this chapter, aimed at the undergraduate student or the general reader, include the following: J. Chambers and P. Trudgill, *Dialectology* (Cambridge, 1980); J. Coates, *Women, Men and Language* (London, 1986); M. Coulthard, *An Introduction to Discourse Analysis* (London, second edition, 1985); V. K. Edwards, *The West Indian Language Issue in British Schools* (London, 1979); R. Fowler, *Linguistic Criticism* (Oxford, 1986); D. Leith, *A Social History of English* (London, 1983); J. Milroy and L. Milroy, *Authority in Language* (London, 1985); M. Montgomery, *An Introduction to Language and Society* (London, 1986); and P. Trudgill, *Sociolinguistics* (Harmondsworth, second edition, 1983). Key collections of articles for the more advanced reader include: S. Romaine (ed.), *Sociolinguistic Variation in Speech Communities* (London, 1982); P. Trudgill (ed.), *Sociolinguistic Patterns in British English* (London, 1978), especially the paper by J. and L. Milroy, 'Belfast: change and variation in an urban vernacular' and *Language in the British Isles* (Cambridge, 1984), especially the papers by V. K. Edwards, 'British Black English and education' and D. Sutcliffe, 'British Black English and West Indian creoles'. See also: P. Brown and S. Levinson, 'Universals in language usage: politeness phenomena', in E. Goody (ed.), *Questions and Politeness* (Cambridge, 1978); J. Cheshire, *Variation in an English Dialect* (Cambridge, 1982); R. Fowler, *Literature as Social Discourse* (London, 1981); G. Holderness, *D. H. Lawrence: History, Ideology, Fiction* (Dublin, 1982); W. Labov, *The Social Stratification of English in New York City* (Washington, 1966), *Sociolinguistic Patterns* (Philadelphia, 1972), and 'On the transformation of experience in narrative syntax', in *Language in the Inner City* (Philadelphia, 1972); B. McHale, 'Speaking as a child in the USA: a problem in the mimesis of speech', *Language and Style* 17, 1984; L. Milroy, *Language and Social Networks* (Oxford, 1980); and P. Trudgill, *The Social Differentiation of English in Norwich* (Cambridge, 1974).

10. *The English Language or the English Languages?*

The direct quotations in chapter 10 have the following sources: D. Crystal, 'How many millions? – the statistics of English today' and A. Maley, 'The most chameleon of languages: perceptions of English abroad', both in *English Today* no. 1, Cambridge University Press, January 1985; R. Quirk, 'The English language in a global context', in Quirk 'and Widdowson (below), 1985; Robert Burchfield, editorial preface, *A Supplement to the Oxford English Dictionary* (Oxford, 1986); Robert McCrum, quoted in Nicholas Shakespeare, 'English as she is being spoke', *The Times* (London), 13 September 1986.

The journal *World Englishes*, edited by B. B. Kachru and L. E. Smith, is published by Pergamon Press, Oxford.

Edited collections of papers on English as a world or major regional language include: R. W. Bailey and M. Görlach (eds.), *English as a World Language* (Ann Arbor, 1982/Cambridge, 1984); J. P. Pride (ed.), *New Englishes* (Rowley, Mass., 1982); C. A. Ferguson and S. Brice Heath (eds.), *Language in the USA* (Cambridge, 1981); P. Trudgill (ed.), *Language in the British Isles* (Cambridge, 1984); B. B. Kachru (ed.), *The Other Tongue: English Across Cultures* (Oxford, 1982); S. Greenbaum (ed.), *The English Language Today* (Oxford, 1985); and R. Quirk and H. Widdowson (eds.), *English in the World: Teaching and Learning the Language and Literatures* (Cambridge, 1985).

Related works include L. Todd, *Modern Englishes: Pidgins and Creoles* (Oxford, 1984); P. Trudgill and J. Hannah, *International English: a Guide to Varieties of Standard English* (London, 1982); P. Strevens, *Teaching English as an International Language* (Oxford, 1982); C. J. Brumfit, *English for International Communication* (Oxford, 1982); and L. E. Smith (ed.), *Readings in English as an International Language* (Oxford, 1983). The book accompanying the BBC TV series is R. McCrum, W. Cran and R. MacNeil, *The Story of English* (London, 1986).

Other works on the statistics of English around the world include J. A. Fishman, R. L. Cooper and A. W. Conrad (eds.), *The Spread of English: the Sociology of English as an Additional Language* (Rowley, Mass., 1977) and E. Gunnemark and D. Kenrick, *What Language do they Speak?* (Kinna, Sweden, second edition, 1985).

INDEX

The alphabetical arrangement of the index is letter-by-letter